S0-AEU-547

Louisiana Bicentennial Reprint Series

Louisiana Bicentennial Reprint Series

JOSEPH G. TREGLE, JR., General Editor

The History of Louisiana
translated from the French of M. Le Page du Pratz
JOSEPH G. TREGLE, JR., Editor

The Manhattaner in New Orleans:
Or, Phases of "Crescent City" Life
by A. Oakey Hall
HENRY A. KMEN, Editor

Norman's New Orleans and Environs
by Benjamin Moore Norman
MATTHEW J. SCHOTT, Editor

Charlevoix's Louisiana:
Selections from the History *and the* Journal
by Pierre F. X. de Charlevoix
CHARLES E. O'NEILL, Editor

The History of Loüisiana
by François Barbé-Marbois
E. WILSON LYON, Editor

THE HISTORY OF LOUISIANA

Barbé-Marbois during the Restoration,
portrait by Maurin.

THE
HISTORY OF
LOUISIANA

PARTICULARLY OF THE CESSION OF THAT COLONY

TO THE UNITED STATES OF AMERICA

FRANÇOIS BARBÉ-MARBOIS

Edited, with an Introduction, by
E. Wilson Lyon

Published for the
Louisiana American Revolution
Bicentennial Commission
by the
Louisiana State University Press
Baton Rouge and London

LIBRARY OF CONGRESS CATALOGING IN PUBLICATION DATA

Barbé-Marbois, François, Marquis de, 1745–1837.
  The history of Louisiana, particularly of the
cession of that colony to the United States of
America.

  (Louisiana Bicentennial reprint series)
  Translation of Histoire de la Louisiane.
  Reprint of the 1830 ed. published by Carey & Lea,
Philadelphia.
  Includes index.
  1. Louisiana—History—To 1803. 2. Louisiana
Purchase. 3. Paris, Treaty of, 1803.
I. Louisiana American Revolution Bicentennial
Commission. II. Title. III. Series.
F372.B2413   1977   976.3   77–5665
ISBN 0–8071–0186–9

1 : 29. 79

CONTENTS

FOREWORD

The Louisiana Purchase was the crowning accomplishment of Thomas Jefferson's public life. To the unparalleled definition he had already given to the substance and spirit of the democratic commitment, the Purchase provided for the addition of the great "laboratory" in which the validity of his vision might be demonstrated to a skeptical world. Ironically, it would in time put to rout the long-accepted doctrines of a major figure of that French Enlightenment so admired by the Virginian— Montesquieu, whose *Esprit des Lois* had dogmatically posited that republicanism was, by natural law, unable to survive in a nation of sprawling dimension and diverse population. Moreover, the Purchase came at a critical time in the life of the young American nation; already in 1803 settlement had reached the western extremity of the new state, and it was clear that the shaping force of the awareness of an almost limitless frontier was nearing exhaustion. The Purchase doubled the territorial extent of the United States and kept alive for generations to come the powerful American acceptance that the possibility of progress, change, and the betterment of all aspects of life was not an illusion but a treasurable reality.

In this sense, as well as others, the Purchase was largely a consummation of the American Revolution, and its his-

tory and particular significance are singularly appropriate concerns in the celebration of the nation's bicentennial. It is for this reason especially that the present
edition of François Barbé-Marbois' *History of Louisiana*
is so timely and so welcome. For none of the major protag-
onists who brought the Purchase to reality, except Barbé-
Marbois, has left us the kind of detailed and intimate account of its conception and realization that is to be found
in the *History of Louisiana*. Fortunately, he was ideally
suited to his task. Knowledgeable about America, privy
to Napoleon's aims and stratagems, insightful as to the
meaning of the great work in which he was engaged,
Barbé-Marbois has been too little known by the citizens
of the Republic he so admired.

If Barbé-Marbois is the ideal source to expand our
knowledge of one of the truly monumental events in American history, E. Wilson Lyon is most assuredly the ideal
editor to bring his work to the modern reader. President
emeritus of Pomona College, Dr. Lyon has long been
identified with the study of the role of Louisiana in French
diplomacy and has extended that interest into a full biography of Barbé-Marbois himself, testimony to the central
importance he assigns to the Frenchman's varied and
creative way of life. This new edition of the *History of
Louisiana* brings to us, in effect, the skill and wisdom of
two indispensable guides.

Joseph G. Tregle, Jr.

INTRODUCTION

François Barbé-Marbois (1745–1837) was a diplomat, administrator, and magistrate who achieved one of the longest public careers in the history of France. Except for intervals during the excesses of the French Revolution, he held positions of responsibility from his first appointment by Louis XV in 1768 until his retirement in 1834 in the reign of Louis Philippe.[1] In two periods Barbé-Marbois' duties concerned matters of greatest importance in the history of the United States. As a member of the French ministry to the thirteen colonies he assisted them in their struggle for independence. Twenty years after the success of the American Revolution Barbé-Marbois, then minister of the public treasury in France, conducted the sale of Louisiana to the United States. The *History of Louisiana*, which he published in 1829, gives the sole contemporary account of the motives that led Napoleon to

---

1. For the life of Barbé-Marbois see E. Wilson Lyon, *The Man Who Sold Louisiana: The Career of François Barbé-Marbois* (Norman: University of Oklahoma Press, 1942; second printing, 1974.) Biographical material for this introduction was drawn primarily from this book, which is based on research in the Archives du Ministère des Affaires Étrangères and the Archives Nationales in Paris, the archives of the department of Eure at Évreux, the archives of the city of Metz and the department of Moselle, the archives of the Historical Society of Pennsylvania and the American Philosophical Society in Philadelphia, the James Monroe Papers in the New York Public Library, the Jared Sparks Papers in the Harvard College Library, and the Papers of American Statesmen in the Manuscripts Division of the Library of Congress. In only a few cases did it seem necessary to include here footnote references to sources used in the biography.

cede that colony to the young republic. Since little has been written about Barbé-Marbois by either French or American historians, it is important to discuss his career while introducing his famous book.

I.

Barbé-Marbois was a member of the substantial middle class that contributed so effectively to the administration of France in the seventeenth and eighteenth centuries. Born at Metz, on February 1, 1745, he was the first son and third child of François Étienne Barbé, a prosperous merchant whose family had long been established in that city. The esteem in which M. Barbé was held locally was recognized by the monarchy; Louis XV appointed him director of the royal mint at Metz.

The education of young François was entrusted to the Jesuits, who imparted to him a love of the classics and a lifelong interest in literature. The youth was brought up in the expectation that he would enter business in Metz. However, when François was twenty his career took an entirely different direction. A wealthy woman from Paris, who spent some time in the Barbé home while successfully pursuing a lawsuit at Metz, was impressed with the young man's ability, and she persuaded his family to send him to Paris to study law. This was the decision that determined his career.

Young François settled, with his servant, in an apartment on the Place du Palais Royal. He soon found other interests, particularly literature, more absorbing than his legal studies. He cultivated men of letters and wrote

anonymously. When he found it difficult to obtain a position, his rich protectress decided the trouble lay with his
name, a very common one in France. "Take the title of
your land, the wooded pond (*Maré du bois*) at Woippy
where we went to gather forget-me-nots," she suggested.
"Call yourself Barbé de Marbois and you will make your
fortune." By this change the young man from Lorraine
passed from the bourgeoisie to the landed gentry.[2]

Opportunity came when Marquis de Castries, an influential member of the royal court, engaged Barbé de
Marbois as the tutor for his children. Castries was so
pleased with the young man that in 1768 he secured for
him a position in the foreign office. After a brief orienta-
tion in the department in Versailles, Marbois was assigned as secretary to the French legation at Ratisbon,
then the seat of the Diet of the Holy Roman Empire.
The French minister to the Diet, Count du Buat, was a
man of great learning with whom Marbois formed a warm
friendship. For nearly a decade Marbois filled positions
in the states of the Holy Roman Empire. When du Buat
was transferred to Saxony in the spring of 1771 Marbois
accompanied him as his secretary.

Marbois was one of the first Frenchmen to realize the
significance of the new German literature, which was still
largely ignored in France and Great Britain. From his
boyhood in Metz he had had a knowledge of the German

2. This was the first of the name changes that present difficulties in writing about
Barbé-Marbois. His name was changed more than was customary even in revolutionary France, being written in turn as Barbé, Barbé de Marbois, Barbé, Barbé-Marbois,
and the Marquis de Marbois. In this introduction, as in *The Man Who Sold Louisiana*,
the problem has been met by using in each period the name by which he was then
known.

language, and as a young diplomat he became proficient in reading contemporary German writings. Because his duties in the courts of the German states were not arduous, Marbois had time to pursue his literary interests. While in Dresden he translated Christopher Martin Wieland's *Diogenes of Sinope* into French and published the book in Dresden and in Paris in 1772.

Following Marbois' congenial and successful years in Saxony, Charles Gravier Vergennes, the foreign minister, assigned him to Bavaria in the summer of 1776. As *chargé d'affaires*, Marbois was to prepare the way for the new minister to Bavaria, the Chevalier de la Luzerne, a young Norman noble entering upon his first diplomatic mission. The minister and his secretary soon formed a close and lasting friendship. This was indeed fortunate, for their official service in Bavaria proved nearly disastrous for both men. Bavaria was caught in rivalry between Austria and Prussia over the succession to its throne;and the alliance between the Austrian and French royal families made the Bavarian succession question a matter of special interest at Versailles. In this situation Marbois unwisely championed Prussian policy, and Vergennes ordered Luzerne to give his secretary a severe reprimand. Although Luzerne had assured Vergennes that he was unable to find "even the appearance of an indiscretion on Marbois' part," he thought it wise to return to France in June, 1778, and talk personally with the foreign minister. Marbois' own sycophantic letter of appeal to Versailles was met with a stern command for him to leave Munich. He left for Paris on September 1, 1778, fearing that his diplomatic career had ended.

For a few months Marbois thought of returning to the
legal career for which he had studied before going to Germany. Offices were commonly sold under the *ancien
régime*, and he was able to purchase the seat of a retiring
councilor in the high court (*parlement*) of Metz for thirty
thousand livres (approximately $6,000). Marbois had
kept in close touch with his native city, where he had
been honored by election to the Academy of Metz in 1774,
and in 1778 there was every prospect that he would complete his career there as a respected jurist. But, unexpectedly, a new world and undreamed-of experiences
opened to him.

A French Diplomat in the American Revolution

While Marbois was en route to Bavaria, thirteen of
Great Britain's North American colonies had revolted and
declared their independence. France gave secret help almost immediately, but the French government refrained
from official support pending evidence that the revolu-
tionaries would be able to carry the struggle to a successful conclusion. The failure of General John Burgoyne's
campaign and the surrender of his army to the Americans
at Saratoga on October 17, 1777, provided this assurance.
On February 6, 1778, Louis XVI recognized the independence of the thirteen colonies and the plenipotentiaries of France and the United States signed a treaty of
amity and commerce, as well as a treaty of alliance. Foreign Minister Vergennes sent his private secretary, Con-
rad Alexandre Gérard, as first minister to the new republic. Unfortunately the failure of his health forced Gérard
to relinquish this important post in 1779.

It was a measure of Vergennes' confidence that he then turned to Luzerne as minister and to Marbois as first secretary of the French ministry in the United States. The two men accepted with alacrity and on June 17, 1779, sailed from Lorient aboard the frigate *Sensible*, which was accompanied by several other vessels. The adventure was particularly appealing to Marbois. Then thirty-four years old, unmarried, and without professional commitments in France, he was free to give himself to life in the New World. He would experience the America of which the *philosophes* wrote and dreamed, but which few had ever seen.[3]

The voyage on the *Sensible* gave Marbois and Luzerne a valuable introduction to the United States and some weeks to improve their knowledge of the English language, for aboard the ship were John Adams, returning from a two-year diplomatic mission to France and the Netherlands, and his twelve-year-old son, John Quincy. The elder Adams and Marbois spent much time together, and Adams reported to the Continental Congress that Marbois was 'a gentleman whose abilities, application, and disposition can not fail to make him useful in the momentous office he sustains."[4] Marbois was much impressed with the ability of John Quincy, who assisted the Frenchmen with their English, calling the lad a better teacher than his father and prophesying for him a brilliant

3. Eugene Parker Chase (ed.), *Our Revolutionary Forefathers* (New York: Duffield & Co., 1929). A translation, with an introduction, of Barbé-Marbois' memoirs of his years in the United States.
4. Francis Wharton (ed.), *The Revolutionary Correspondence of the United States* (6 vols.; Washington, D.C.: U.S. Government Printing Office, 1889), III, 277–78.

public career. Marbois, for his part, proved an apt pupil and by the time of the ship's arrival in Boston on August 3 he had made great progress in English. He would, of course, become fluent in this new language.

Their overland journey from Boston to Philadelphia gave Luzerne and Marbois an extensive acquaintance with much of the young republic. They visited Harvard College, Yale, and the College of New Jersey, now Princeton. En route west they met General Washington at Fishkill and sailed with him on the Hudson to his headquarters at West Point, where they remained for two days. Washington wrote Lafayette that he had "imbibed the most favorable impressions" of both Luzerne and Marbois.[5] In Philadelphia the minister and the secretary were welcomed by the ringing of bells and a cavalry escort of leading citizens.[6]

Two years of fighting would continue after the arrival of Luzerne and Marbois in Philadelphia, but the support of France gave assurance that the United States would win its independence. The representatives of Louis XVI thus enjoyed great official and social prestige. Luzerne soon acquired a commanding influence over Congress,[7] and he and Marbois were lionized by the society of Philadelphia. Marbois' command of English and his admiration of American institutions made him a great favorite. In March, 1780, both Luzerne and Marbois were honored

5. John C. Fitzpatrick (ed.), *The Writings of George Washington* (39 vols.; Washington, D.C.: U.S. Government Printing Office, 1931–44), XVI, 371.

6. J. Thomas Scharf and Thompson Westcott, *History of Philadelphia* (3 vols.; Philadelphia: L. H. Everts, 1884) I, 407.

7. Samuel Flagg Bemis, *The Diplomacy of the American Revolution* (New York: Appleton-Century, 1935), 189.

by election to the American Philosophical Society, in which both played active parts.

Marbois became a serious student of the thirteen states, both separately and as a group. Pursuing an interest in forestry, horticulture, and agriculture which would continue throughout his life, he collected seeds and sent them home to France. He built a botanical garden in Philadelphia for his own pleasure and planted there 250 varieties of trees and shrubs native to North America. Seeking information, he submitted twenty-three questions about Delaware to Thomas McKean, chief justice of Pennsylvania.[8] A similar request to Thomas Jefferson on Virginia brought him the material that Jefferson later published in his *Notes on Virginia*. Jefferson had been making notes on various aspects of his native state for a number of years, and he put these in logical order for Marbois' use.[9]

The triumph of French and American forces with the surrender of Cornwallis on October 17, 1781, signaled the end of the American Revolution as a military conflict. While awaiting a peace treaty the Americans and their French allies in North America could celebrate their victory. The winter of 1781–1782 was one of the most brilliant social seasons in the history of Philadelphia; a number of French officers and their families were in the city, as were French from the West Indies. Marbois had the

8. Marbois to McKean, February 10, 1781, in Historical Society of Pennsylvania Archives.

9. Albert Ellery Bergh (ed.), *The Writings of Thomas Jefferson* (20 vols.; Washington, D.C.: Thomas Jefferson Memorial Association, 1907), I, 90–91; "Letters of Jefferson to Marbois, 1781, 1783," *American Historical Review*, XII (1906–1907), 75–77.

pleasure of being a part of both French and American
circles.

With the prospect of peace Luzerne broadened Marbois' functions on September 28, 1781, by giving him the
additional duty of consul *ad interim* for Philadelphia.
This was a step toward the establishment of a consular
service for France in the United States. For Marbois this
interim appointment brought the pleasure of direct correspondence with Marquis de Castries, the patron of his
youth in Paris, who had become minister of the navy and
colonies and who, in this capacity, directed French consular offices in North America.

With the cessation of hostilities, the United States entered a critical period in which its government under the
Articles of Confederation was severely tested. For example, when a group of soldiers mutinied in Philadelphia on
June 21, 1783, because their pay was in arrears, Congress felt obliged to retire to Princeton. For the next two
years Congress held its sessions in other cities among the
middle states. The representatives of France of necessity
followed these sessions and thus Luzerne and Marbois
were in Annapolis when Congress met there in January
and February of 1784.

It was at Annapolis that Luzerne communicated the
plans of the French government for its consular service in
the United States. Marbois had been named consul general for the United States and under him were to be four
consuls and five vice-consuls. The program was approved
by Congress on February 11 and soon put into effect. To
Marbois thus belongs the distinction of organizing the

first regular consular service of any foreign government in the United States.

A period so critical for the government of the United States was an exceedingly happy one for Marbois person- ally. On June 17, 1784, he married Elizabeth Moore, the only daughter of William Moore (1735–1793), a wealthy Philadelphia merchant, who in 1781–1782 had been president of the executive council of the state of Pennsyl- vania. The bride was twenty years younger than the groom. Marbois had sought and received the approval of Vergen- nes before the engagement was announced. The promi- nence of the Moore family and Marbois' position made the wedding an event long to be remembered in Philadelphia. The bride, a Protestant, waived all reservations on reli- gion and a Catholic service was held in Luzerne's chapel. A Protestant service then followed in the Moore home.

Prominent Philadelphians and foreign diplomats ap- peared as witnesses for the two parties. Marbois was rep- resented by Luzerne; Van Berkel, minister of the Nether- lands; Thomas Mifflin, president of Congress; the French consul for Maryland and Virginia; and his own younger brother, Pierre-François Barbé, who had entered the French consular service in the United States. Appearing for the bride were John Dickinson, president of the exec- utive council of Pennsylvania; Charles Thomson, secretary of Congress; and her parents. The congratulations which showered on the couple included those of Mr. and Mrs. George Washington. "Though you have given many proofs of your predilection and attachment to this country," Washington wrote from Mount Vernon on June 20, 1784, "yet this last may be considered as not only a great and tender one, but as the most pleasing and lasting tie of affection. The accomplishments of the lady, and her connections, cannot fail to make it so." [10]

Luzerne had received an extended leave from his duties and he sailed for France three days after Marbois' wedding. On Luzerne's recommendation Vergennes appointed Marbois *chargé d'affaires*, and he remained the representative of France in the United States for the next fifteen months. One of his most interesting activities in this period was a journey in September, 1784, to the territory of the Oneida Indians in central New York, an area just being settled by the white man.

Congress was sending commissioners to negotiate a treaty with the Iroquois, and Marbois decided to accompany them. The presence of Lafayette, who was felt to have great influence with the Indians, gave unusual significance to the trip. Marbois took a sloop from New York to Albany, where he met Lafayette and James Madison, then a delegate from the Congress. The roads were so bad that the party soon gave up its carriages and proceeded on horseback. Marbois served as cook for the group. At Fort Schuyler they met Samuel Kirkland, missionary to the Oneidas since 1766, through whose efforts that tribe and the Tuscaroras had remained neutral during the Revolution. The representatives of the Oneidas and the Senecas met in reconciliation at Fort Schuyler, and the congressional commission secured a treaty which opened the

10. Jared Sparks (ed.), *Writings of George Washington* (12 vols.; Boston, 1839–40), IX, 50–51. Marbois had informed Washington of the forthcoming marriage on June 8. George Washington Papers, Library of Congress.

Mohawk Valley to peaceful settlement. Marbois said the meeting reminded him of the Diet at Ratisbon.[11]

Marbois returned from the Mohawk Valley to attend the Congress scheduled to meet in Trenton. He found the members so late in arriving that the opening session was delayed by more than a fortnight. "There is no Congress, no committee, no President, no minister of any department," he wrote Vergennes on November 20, 1784; "all affairs, especially the finances, are falling into confusion even worse than the past." Eventually a quorum assembled, and after several weeks in Trenton Congress moved to New York and continued to meet there until 1790. Before leaving Trenton, Congress appointed John Jay as secretary for foreign affairs, and he put order in his department and gave prompt attention to Marbois' communications.

In the spring of 1785 Marbois was much occupied with family affairs in Philadelphia. Following their marriage he and his wife had occupied Luzerne's house during his absence in France. There, on April 1, Madame Marbois gave birth to a daughter who was christened Marie Anne Sophie.

When the family was able to travel Marbois decided to follow Congress to New York. Soon after his arrival he organized the French merchants in New York into an assembly. As British troops had occupied the city until November 25, 1783, this was the first concerted attempt

11. François Barbé-Marbois, Extrait du Journal d'un Voyage Chez les Sauvages Oneidas, Tuscaroras, etc., in Archives des Affairs Étrangères, États-Unis, Vol. 28, ff. 204–38. This journal has been translated by Chase in *Our Revolutionary Forefathers*. This manuscript is the basis for Vicomte de Montbas, *Avec Lafayette Chez les Iroquois* (Paris, 1929).

to sponsor French commerce in New York. Marbois' reports from the new capital showed an able grasp of American affairs, including the misfortunes of the loyalists, the difficulties of Europeans in collecting sums due them by Americans, relations with the Indians, the opening and sale of western lands, and the growth of "Kentucke." He continued his travels as time permitted and toured much of Long Island.

However, Marbois' service in the United States was drawing to a close. At Castries' request, and with Vergennes' approval, Louis XVI on June 5, 1785, appointed Marbois the intendant of St. Domingue. This was the prime appointment in the French colonies and a logical promotion for Marbois, for he had advanced as far as a member of the bourgeoisie could progress in the diplomatic corps of the *ancien régime* in France. Major diplomatic posts were held invariably by members of the nobility, as Marbois had found in the Holy Roman Empire, Saxony, Bavaria, and the United States.

Intendant in St. Domingue

St. Domingue, the modern Haiti, was an outstanding example of the West Indian colonies so highly prized by European countries in the eighteenth century. Its exports of sugar and coffee created a rich planter class with great influence in French port cities and in the court at Versailles. Fifty thousand whites controlled a population of fifty thousand mulattoes and five hundred thousand Negro slaves. The colony was administered by a governor and an intendant appointed by the monarchy. The governor directed the general administration and commanded the armed forces, which in peacetime numbered around three thousand. The intendant, as in France, was concerned primarily with finance—the collection of taxes, provision for the military, and the upkeep of royal property. A number of areas were administered jointly by the governor and the intendant: religious affairs, inspection of the courts, agriculture, commerce, shipping, permission to free slaves, the care of rivers, handling of floodwater, the policing of harbors, and the building and care of roads.

Marbois and his family arrived in St. Domingue on October 22, 1785, and he spent the next four years on an extremely difficult mission to the colony. His predecessor had amassed a public debt of $1,400,000 and had allowed corruption to thrive. "A general spirit of graft reigns in St. Domingue," Castries wrote Marbois on his appointment. Marbois undertook to enforce the mercantilist policy of the government, to stop smuggling, and to strengthen the central administration in Port-au-Prince. At the same time he sought to advance horticulture and agriculture by importing seed, plants, and trees from other parts of the world. Progress was made in public works, particularly roads.

Marbois' rigorous administration and his strict enforcement of mercantile legislation aroused opposition within the colony, and attacks on him were published in Europe. Action early in 1789 by a newly appointed governor, setting aside long-established mercantile regulations, seemed to make Marbois' position impossible. When, however, Versailles supported Marbois and recalled the governor, the way appeared clear for Marbois to continue at his post. But forces greater than colonial squabbles soon ended his career in St. Domingue. The French Revolution had begun in France, and it would determine Marbois' career for a decade.

When Louis XVI in 1788 announced elections for the Estates General to meet for the first time since 1614, the planters and merchants in St. Domingue perceived an opportunity to redress their grievances over the mercantile restrictions and to overthrow the existing colonial administration. Although no provision had been made by the king for representation from the colonies, pressure for elections was so great in St. Domingue that the governor and the intendant allowed them to proceed. Some four thousand votes by the Third Estate were cast and thirteen deputies were chosen. Accepted in Versailles as members of the Estates General, these deputies vigorously attacked the colonial system and its officials.

The deputies from St. Domingue on June 29, 1789, unanimously requested "the immediate recall of the Intendant Marbois, justly abhorred by St. Domingue." Fortunately for Marbois he was in friendly hands, for Luzerne, with whom he had come to the United States, had become minister of the navy and colonies. There was, however, little that Versailles could do to protect a colonial official in the tumultuous summer of 1789, when revolution imperiled all institutions of the royal government. During his quarrels with the governor Marbois had requested and received a leave for the spring of 1790, and the royal council asked him to use it immediately. Luzerne wrote on August 10 that Louis XVI's regard for Marbois was unchanged but that "in the present circumstances it is difficult for him to sustain one of the persons by whom he had been best served." Luzerne feared for Marbois' safety and he asked the governor of St. Domingue to take special pains to protect him.

When the news of the fall of the Bastille and the abolition of privilege and most feudal dues in France reached St. Domingue, revolt swept the colony. The attack on the *ancien régime* centered on Marbois, who as intendant was considered its chief instrument. A group of young men from the northern part of the colony called for him "to be hanged and strangled until his death on a gallows," that "his body be burned, his ashes thrown to the wind, and his goods be confiscated for the use of the poor of the colony." Placards appeared urging the assassination of Marbois and the burning of his house. Luzerne's letter may well have saved Marbois and his family from a terrible fate.

The minister's letter arrived on October 19 and Marbois and his family sailed on the night of October 26, 1789. Their departure was advanced by a day when a deputation from the north marched on Port-au-Prince and had to be restrained by troops sent by the governor. Marbois thus described the dramatic departure: "Everything was ready by sundown, and at nine o'clock, taking leave of our friends, my family and I accompanied by the Governor went to the sea shore. The launches awaited us. Our children [a second daughter, Elizabeth Laura, had been born in 1788], astonished by the sobbing of their nurses, whom it was necessary to leave behind, by the sight of the sea, and by the novelty of this happening during their ordinary bed time, attracted everyone in hearing distance by their crying. A crowd soon collected. I embraced those who were friends. My wife and I, each taking a child in our arms, boarded the launch. We were soon in the open sea. United to all I held dearest in the world I had no feeling of bitterness, but was happy to be my own master again." Marbois and his family had embarked on the *Ariel*, a government vessel bound for Europe.

A Moderate in a Decade of Revolution

Marbois' friends in St. Domingue had urged him to go to Philadelphia and remain there with Madame Marbois' family until the turmoil subsided in France. He was drawn home, however, by the desire to face his detractors and the longing to be with his mother and family in Metz, whom he had not seen since he sailed for America in 1779. Leaving the *Ariel* at Cadiz, Marbois and his family proceeded to Paris, which had become the seat of the government. It was not until he neared the city that he sensed the intensity of the opposition to his administration in St. Domingue. He prepared a memoir which answered his critics and fortunately prevented any action against him. However, the opposition to him had been so serious that he remained in Paris until the end of April, 1790.

Sensing the egalitarian spirit of the French Revolution, Marbois in 1790 changed the way he wrote his name. "De Marbois" had become a handicap and a hazard to fortune.

"Barbé," to which he had been born, was more appropriate, and to this he returned.

As soon as he had secured himself from attacks on his administration in St. Domingue, Barbé took his family to Lorraine and began the life of a country gentleman on an estate he owned at Buchy, a village twelve miles from Metz. There on November 2, 1791, the family was saddened by the death of their younger daughter. His chateau, a three-story building dating from the early eighteenth century, dominated some thirty peasant cottages which surrounded the church. Except for a brief mission as minister to the Diet of the Holy Roman Empire early in 1792, Barbé devoted himself almost entirely to the management of his estate. He had great interest in the agricultural revolution emanating from England, and he made a study of leguminous crops, publishing in 1792 a book on clover, alfalfa, and sainfoin (a perennial forage herb) which received an award from the department authorities at Metz.[12]

Despite his quiet life Barbé could not avoid the dangers common to officials of the *ancien régime* from the fall of the monarchy and the violence of the Revolution. When Madame Barbé in August, 1792, planned to sail from Holland to Philadelphia for a visit with her family, she was prevented from leaving France and later denounced as an *émigré*. Having retained her American citizenship, she appealed to Gouverneur Morris, the American minister, who made representations in her behalf to

12. François Barbé-Marbois, *La Culture du Trèfle, de la Luzerne et du Sainfoin* (Metz, 1829).

the French government from March, 1793, to July, 1794. The best Morris could do was to assure Madame Barbé that she would not be in further danger "because the system of persecution will be less rigidly pursued than heretofore." On March 2, 1793, the same charge was brought against Barbé himself; he was arrested and imprisoned and seals were placed on all his goods and papers. Although he was released after two days and his name removed from the list of *émigrés* by the local committee in Metz, this was overlooked in Paris and the charge would plague him again five years later.

The frequent changes in Paris and their repercussions throughout the country left no peace of mind for men like Barbé. During the Terror he was placed under house confinement in Buchy by a decree ordering the arrest of all former intendants, even though the order applied only to intendants who had served within France and did not comprehend the colonies.

The fall of Robespierre in July, 1794, and the subsequent ending of the Terror brought moderates like Barbé again into public life. The representative of the national government in the departments of Moselle and Meurthe deposed the mayor of Metz and appointed Barbé in his stead. Although Barbé maintained his residence in Buchy, the family had spent considerable time in Metz and the appointment was not inappropriate. However, Barbé first set forth his views on the office in a pamphlet addressed to the citizens and awaited election by the council of the commune before accepting the office on February 25, 1795. Metz was a turbulent municipality, and there was constant conflict between moderates like Marbois and the radicals. However, Barbé felt secure enough in his post on September 28, 1795, to invite James Monroe, the new American minister, to visit him and his family at Metz. To his surprise, he received on October 14 a decree from the government in Paris removing him from office, alleging that the dismissal was at the request of a deputation from the department of Moselle. As both the commune of Metz and the department of Moselle issued resolutions of praise for Barbé the reason for his removal was unclear then and still remains so.

The rapid rise and fall of political figures was characteristic of the Revolution. Removed from local office in October, 1795, Barbé was elected that same month to a place in the national legislature. A new government, known as the Directory, had been drafted and Barbé became a member of the Council of Ancients, the upper house, whose 250 members were married or widowed men at least forty years of age and were expected to supply wisdom and restraint to the imagination of the younger men who constituted the lower house, known as the Five Hundred.

With his entry into national politics Barbé made a change in his name. The constitution of 1795 under which he had been elected was the work of conservative men of property and a departure from the extreme radicalism of 1793. The revival of "Marbois," therefore, would be safe, so former mayor Barbé became legislator Barbé-Marbois, the name under which he is best known in history. He thought that dangers from the Revolution had ended for him and his family.

Barbé-Marbois' activities in the Council of Ancients reveal a man of moderate opinions, inclined to censure but forget the immediate past, and loyal to republican institutions. He was one of an influential group whom the historian Louis Adolphe Thiers described as "not those extraordinary men who shine at the outset of revolutions, but men of solid merit, who succeed genius in the career of politics as in that of the arts."[13] Barbé-Marbois and his friends took great interest in the organization and operation of the legislature and exercised significant influence in the election of officers and the appointment of commissions. They respected the constitution, hoping to increase their power through succeeding elections.

Barbé-Marbois' interests and abilities were indicated in questions of finance, foreign relations, and education. "Representatives of the people," he wrote, "if you proceed with the restoration of our finances without being stopped by obstacles unworthy of your courage, you will leave an imperishable monument to our session." He desired a general European peace and rejoiced when the Treaty of Campo-Formio was concluded with Austria in 1797. The report on education which Barbé-Marbois submitted to the Ancients on March 20, 1796, was an analysis of the effect of the Revolution, which he felt had destroyed both the good and the bad in the nation's schools. He found the rural schools serving only half the number of children taught in 1789, but a somewhat better situation in the cities. Higher education, he said, was available only in Paris.

13. Louis Adolphe Thiers, *The History of the French Revolution* (5 vols.; London: Bentley and Son, 1881), IV, 346.

The moderate group to which Barbé-Marbois belonged maintained a steady attack on the executive, which under the constitution of 1795 was composed of five directors. Barbé-Marbois took an active part in these criticisms, insisting that the directors follow the letter of the constitution. He deplored the speed with which legislation was rushed through the Five Hundred and then presented to the Ancients under plea of emergency.

Barbé-Marbois and his associates made such headway that elections for one third of the members of both houses of the legislature held in the spring of 1797 brought an overwhelming victory for the moderates. Furthermore, when one of the directors retired, a friend of Barbé-Marbois was chosen as his successor. As another of the directors was sympathetic to their positions, Barbé-Marbois and his group represented a growing challenge to the Directory. In a long-established government the ensuing deadlock would have been wearied out until one group had a clear majority in both the legislature and the executive; but in faction-ridden revolutionary France such crises were resolved by resort to power. While Barbé-Marbois was telling the Ancients that "our constitution develops successively its useful and fertile roots and day by day the wisdom and blessings of that fundamental law become more evident," the majority of the directors were preparing to violate that fundamental law by suppressing their opponents. They were able to do this because the military had become hostile to the legislature.

Although there were rumors that the Directory was planning an attack on the two legislative bodies, Barbé-Marbois and his group were unprepared when the blow fell. In a swiftly executed *coup d'état* begun at 7:30 A.M. on September 4, 1797, troops surrounded the legislative halls and dissolved both bodies by force when they attempted to meet. Proclamations were posted charging a royalist plot. Finding themselves locked out of the legislative chamber, Barbé-Marbois and a group met at the home of the president of the Council of Ancients. There the assembled group was arrested and at 4:00 P.M. sent to prison, where they were closely guarded that night. Barbé-Marbois confidently expected his release the following day. But more than two and a half years would elapse before he was at liberty again.

A rump session of the Ancients and the Five Hundred annulled the elections of a number of their members and ordered the deportation of Directors Carnot and Barthélemy and the prominent opposition deputies, among them Barbé-Marbois. He was forced to leave Paris without seeing his wife, who was in Metz. When news of this arrest was rushed to her she followed the route of the deportees and caught up with them at Blois, where she was permitted only fifteen minutes with her husband. The prisoners were conveyed to the coast in iron cages and on September 25 eighteen were shipped to Guiana aboard the *Vaillante*. Political exiles of the French Revolution were the first unfortunates to be sent to that colony, which later became the symbol of the desolate imprisonment of dangerous criminals.

Barbé-Marbois' long exile in Guiana, from November 12, 1797, to January 23, 1800, was an outstanding illustration of the great resources of health and mind that made possible his long and remarkable career. The journal he kept, and later published, gives a vivid picture of his life in the wretched country to which he had been condemned.[14] A few days after the prisoners were landed at Cayenne, they were transferred up the coast to Sinnamari, a pestilential village of 110 in habitants. There Barbé-Marbois took lodgings in the humble home of a Madame Trion, furnishing his own bread and wine and paying eight hundred livres (approxi mately $160) a year.

Barbé-Marbois settled down at Sinnamari, to await his pardon or the fall of the Directory. He spent his time making wooden trinkets and furniture, gardening in the early morning and late afternoon, painting, and reading. He studied the Indians and visited a remote tribe in the interior. As French and American newspapers were denied the deportees, Barbé-Marbois was without news for six months. He finally secured some Dutch papers from neighboring Dutch Guiana and undertook to learn the language. "I would have learned Syrian in order to have news," he wrote in his journal. His years in St. Domingue had given him valuable preparation for living in a tropical climate. This was fortunate, indeed, because by September, 1798, eight of his fellow deportees had died of fever and Barbé-Marbois himself had been ill with it.

In France Madame Barbé-Marbois pled her husband's cause, petitioning the Directory to fix a place of exile for him in Europe and to allow him to live in Cayenne while his case was being considered. She joined the wives of two of the deportees in requesting that their husbands be transferred to the island of Oléron. Eventually Barbé-

14. François Barbé-Marbois, *Journal d'un déporté non jugé ou déportation en violation des lois décrétée le 18 fructidor* (2 vols.; Brussels: J. P. Meline, 1835).

Marbois was allowed to leave Sinnamari for Cayenne on August 1, 1799. When a new governor for Guiana arrived in Cayenne on January 6, 1800, he brought news that the Directory had fallen and passports, issued earlier by the Directory, for the deportees to be taken to Oléron, for which they sailed on January 23. However, when their ship arrived in Brest the deportees received the good news that they were to proceed to Paris.

Minister of Napoleon

Barbé-Marbois had returned in a period when he could be of great service to his country. The overthrow of the Directory, which General Napoleon Bonaparte had effected with a *coup d'état* on November 9–11, 1799, had been followed by a basic reorganization of the national government. A new constitution provided for a plural executive of three consuls, but concentrated power in the hands of the first consul, a position designed for Bonaparte. Recognizing the nation's desire for order and stability Bonaparte planned to consolidate the gains of the Revolution and to assuage its wounds. He sought to assure sound administration, stable finance, restoration of the church, and international peace. To assist him the first consul drew officials from all classes and political creeds, relying heavily on former members of the legislative councils of the Directory.

The election of Charles-François Lebrun as third consul opened the way for Barbé-Marbois to join the new administration. The two men had worked together closely in the Ancients, Barbé-Marbois describing Lebrun as "my friend for so many years, the confidant of all my political acts, the sharer of all my thoughts." Bonaparte received the news of Barbé-Marbois' return while at a ball and he immediately shared the good news with some of those present. He invited Barbé-Marbois to visit him at Malmaison and assessed his guest as they walked through the great park and talked at length. On July 24, 1800, Barbé-Marbois was named a member of the council of state, the body which advised the first consul on proposed legislation.

His background as an intendant qualified Barbé-Marbois for a position in finance. Napoleon soon sent him on a mission to restore the taxation system in several departments in the West. He rose rapidly in the esteem of the first consul, and on February 24, 1801, he was appointed director general of the public treasury, and officer in charge of disbursements. When the consuls effected a reorganization of the financial department on September 27, 1801, Barbé-Marbois was named to the new ministry of the public treasury, to which was entrusted the handling of expenditures and the national debt. Barbé-Marbois continued in this office for over four years, handling matters of great importance for France and a negotiation of transcendent importance to the United States. With these appointments under the consulate, Barbé-Marbois began an administrative career which, except for two brief interruptions, continued for thirty-four years. He was destined in 1803 to handle a transaction which determined the history of the United States and much of the course of the western world.

As Napoleon brought his administrative genius to the reorganization and stabilization of France, he also envisaged a restored and extended French colonial empire in North America. The Directory had followed such a policy and by a treaty in 1795 had acquired the Spanish colony embracing the eastern part of the island of Santo Domingo. The Directory failed, however, in its efforts to secure Louisiana. Napoleon vigorously pursued these negotiations and on October 1, 1800, Spain ceded Louisiana to France.[15] These newly acquired territories and the older French possessions in the West Indies could constitute an integrated colonial system, with Louisiana supplying grain, salted meat, and timber for the islands, which in turn would provide sugar and coffee for France.

While securing the retrocession of Louisiana, the consulate also sought to restore good relations with the United States. The Directory had produced a quasiwar with the young republic by maritime depredations and bungling diplomacy, which became famous as the XYZ affair. Napoleon took early steps to conclude these difficulties.[16] On September 30, 1800, French commissioners led by his brother, Joseph Bonaparte, and three American commissioners signed the Convention of 1800, which settled the outstanding differences between the two countries and also released the United States from its obligations under the treaty of alliance made with France in 1778.

15. On French policy regarding Louisiana see: E. Wilson Lyon, *Louisiana in French Diplomacy, 1759–1804*. (Norman: University of Oklahoma Press, 1934; new edition, 1974).

16. E. Wilson Lyon, "The Directory and the United States," *American Historical Review*, XLIII (1938), 514–32; and E. Wilson Lyon, "The Franco-American Convention of 1800," *Journal of Modern History*, XII (1940), 305–33.

The implementation of Napoleon's colonial policy required peace in Europe and the restoration of authority in the older French colonies in the West Indies, particularly in St. Domingue. The Treaty of Lunéville on February 9, 1801, ended the war with Austria, and the signing of the preliminaries of the Treaty of Amiens on October 1, 1801, ended hostilities with Great Britain.

The French colonies in the West Indies had been convulsed by the Revolution, and in St. Domingue the old colonial system had been totally destroyed. The slaves had risen against their masters and under Toussaint L'Ouverture had established a stable Negro state which desired self-government under French suzerainty. Napoleon decided, however, to reconquer St. Domingue by military force and placed his brother-in-law, General Charles-Victor-Emmanuel Leclerc, in command of an expedition of 20,000 troops which sailed from Brest on November 22, 1801, and arrived in St. Domingue at the end of January, 1802. Within three months the French troops were masters of the island and Toussaint had surrendered to Leclerc, trusting his word of honor that he would be well treated.

In France Napoleon proceeded with plans for the military and civil organization of Louisiana. The consuls decreed that there should be a military captain general at a salary of 70,000 francs and a prefect with a salary of 50,000 francs. Pierre-Clément de Laussat was appointed prefect and under him were to serve a chief justice, a sub-prefect for Upper Louisiana, an administrative commissioner, a director of estates, two surveyors, a paymaster general, two stewards, and a botanical gardener. The king of Spain had delayed in giving the royal order for the transfer of Louisiana, but this finally arrived in Paris on October 25, 1802. The way was thus clear for Laussat to depart; he sailed from La Rochelle on January 10, 1803, on board the *Surveillant* which, after touching at Santander in Spain and Cap Français in St. Domingue, came within sight of Balize on March 11. In Louisiana Laussat began a voluminous correspondence with Spanish officials looking to the arrival of the French military expedition and the transfer of the colony to France.[17] The expedition had been assembled at Helvoët Sluys in the Netherlands, under the command of General Claude Victor, and was expected to depart later in January, 1803. The vessels, however, were ice-bound in January and throughout February and destined never to sail for Louisiana.

In the spring of 1803 Napoleon faced the destruction of the bases upon which his North American colonial empire had been planned. The peace with Great Britain deteriorated, leading to a blockade of the Louisiana expedition by the British navy. The attempt to restore French authority in St. Domingue was a disastrous failure. Leclerc and most of his soldiers died from yellow fever, and the blacks recovered armed control of the colony. Facing the collapse of his plans in the West Indies and impending hostilities with Great Britain, Napoleon determined on a fundamental and dramatic change of policy.

17. On Laussat's service in Louisiana see: Robert D. Bush, "Colonial Administration in French Louisiana: The Napoleonic Episode, 1802–03," *Publications of the Louisiana Historical Society*, Series 2, Vol. II (1974), pp. 36–59.

The French government had handled its plans for Louisiana in great secrecy, and the government of the United States was late in learning of its intentions. The American commissioners who negotiated the Convention of 1800 were unaware that the retrocession of Louisiana was being concluded at that time. It was not until the spring of 1801 that rumors of the retrocession reached Washington. At first President Jefferson was untroubled. He wrote William C. C. Claiborne, governor of Mississippi Territory, on July 13, 1801, that "should France get possession of that country, it will be more to be lamented than remedied by us, as it will furnish ground for profound consideration on our part."[18] He continued in this mood even after Rufus King, the American minister in Great Britain, forwarded definitive news of the retrocession to Secretary of State James Madison, on November 20, 1801.

Robert R. Livingston, former chancellor of the state of New York who was appointed minister to France in 1801, was unable to secure any information on Louisiana from the French government. However, he found the repossession of Louisiana to be "a very favorite measure" in Paris. Barbé-Marbois told him "it was considered important to have an outlet for their turbulent spirits; yet would not explicitly acknowledge that the business had been concluded."[19] Talleyrand, again minister of foreign affairs, was more devious. When Livingston asked for assurance

18. P. L. Ford (ed.), *The Writings of Thomas Jefferson* (12 vols.; New York: G. P. Putnam's, 1892–99), VIII, 71.
19. Livingston to Madison, December 31, 1801, *Annals of Congress*, 7th Cong., 1st Sess., p. 1020.

that American rights on the Mississippi would be guaranteed, Talleyrand replied: "Do you doubt, sir, that the questions which concern the United States, the determination of which may affect their negotiations with France will be examined with equal interest and attention?"[20] Discussions were proceeding in this fashion when action by the Spaniards in New Orleans brought a crisis in Franco-American relations.

Under the Treaty of San Lorenzo, concluded on October 27, 1795, Spain granted the United States free navigation on the Mississippi and the privilege of depositing goods in New Orleans for reshipment in ocean-going vessels. The privilege of deposit was for three years, but Spain agreed to renew it or to allow similar use of another location on the Mississippi. On October 16, 1802, Juan Ventura Morales, the acting intendant of Louisiana, withdrew the deposit at New Orleans and did not provide an alternative location. Documents in the Archivo Histórico Nacional in Madrid show that the closing of the port was a Spanish measure taken in ordinary process of colonial administration, and without any consultation with France.[21] The port was closed in response to complaints of the intendants, alleging illegal conduct of Americans. However, it was generally believed in the United States in 1802 that the action had been taken at the request of France, and as a part of its future policy in Louisiana.

<hr/>

20. Livingston to Madison, October 28, 1802, *ibid.*, 1053–56.
21. E. Wilson Lyon, "The Closing of the Port of New Orleans," *American Historical Review*, XXXVII (1932), 280–86. See also Lyon, *Louisiana In French Diplomacy*, 167–76.

For the American government, the closing of New Orleans was a decisive factor in the negotiations regarding Louisiana. Such anger was aroused in Kentucky and Tennessee that the westerners were on the verge of taking matters into their own hands and marching on New Orleans. To calm the country and to gain time, Jefferson appointed James Monroe, former minister to France and former governor of Virginia, as minister plenipotentiary and extraordinary, and sent him to Paris on a special mission to assist Livingston. With his appointment rumors of war subsided, and the United States awaited the outcome of his mission.

The interest of the United States in Louisiana was more commercial than imperial, and the primary object of the American government was protecting free navigation on the Mississippi to the Gulf of Mexico. There was no thought of acquiring the entire colony. Livingston and Monroe were authorized to pay ten million dollars for New Orleans, the island on which it stood, and the Floridas, erroneously thought to have been ceded to France by Spain. By April 8, 1803, when Monroe arrived at Havre, Napoleon had made a momentous decision.

Dismayed by the losses in St. Domingue and foreseeing an early resumption of war with Great Britain, he decided that his purposes could best be served by selling Louisiana to the United States. The funds to be secured would help the French treasury, and the friendship of the United States would be an asset in the forthcoming war. So he called Barbé-Marbois to him, asked his advice, and then requested that he negotiate the sale of the entire colony with Livingston and Monroe. Within a month the transaction had been completed. Under a treaty and two conventions, all dated April 30, 1803, France transferred to the United States "the Colony or Province of Louisiana with the same extent it now has in the hands of Spain and that it had when France possessed it." The United States paid $11,250,000 to France and assumed the claims of United States citizens against France amounting to $3,750,000.

As minister of the public treasury, Barbé-Marbois handled the financial arrangements of the sale of Louisiana. The declaration of war by Great Britain on May 18, 1803, did not interfere with the financing of the transaction through London. The English houses of Hope and Baring bought the bonds issued by the government of the United States. Alexander Baring conferred with Barbé-Marbois in Paris on July 25 and then went to the United States to secure the bonds and bring them personally to Great Britain.

After 1803 Barbé-Marbois pursued a long and eventful public career in which he saw increasingly the tremendous consequences of the cession of Louisiana to the United States. His tenure as minister of the public treasury was ended in January, 1806, when Napoleon, who had become emperor in 1804, removed him in anger over a financial crisis in which Barbé-Marbois had made a serious mistake of judgment. But Napoleon prized Barbé-Marbois' financial abilities, and he recalled him to his service in September, 1807. Again Barbé-Marbois owed his appointment to his friend Lebrun, who had become archtreasurer of the empire. In this capacity Lebrun had organized the Cour des Comptes, and Barbé-Marbois was named its first president.

This new court had been instituted at the express wish of the emperor, who desired centralized oversight of all receipts and expenses that concerned public funds. The first president was given great authority, presiding over plenary sessions of the court and assigning work to the three divisions of the court. Barbé-Marbois was eminently suited to this position, and within five years he resolved the tangled accounts of the revolutionary period and brought the financial records of the country up to date. In the twenty-seven years he served as first president Barbé-Marbois established the Cour des Comptes as a permanent institution, making an invaluable contribution to the administration of France.

The Marquis de Marbois

Skillfully and successfully Barbé-Marbois adjusted himself to the changes in the national government during his long tenure at the Cour des Comptes. When Napoleon was defeated by the Allied Coalition in 1814, Barbé-Marbois supported the restoration of the Bourbons in the person of Louis XVIII, brother of Louis XVI. He was one of five members of the Napoleonic senate named to draw up the new constitution for France. The Charter of 1814, which emanated from their efforts, established a limited monarchy and a bicameral legislature, comprising a chamber of deputies elected for a five-year term by a highly restricted franchise, and a chamber of peers whose members were appointed by the king. Barbé-Marbois was named to the chamber of peers, where he took an active part. For a year he served as minister of justice, but in 1816 he returned to the Cour des Comptes, from which he had not resigned as president, and remained there for the next eighteen years. There his contemporaries "listened to him with the respect that Greece gave to old Nestor."[22]

Louis XVIII showed his further appreciation of Barbé-Marbois by advancing him in the peerage from the title of Count to that of Marquis, on May 2, 1818. He had been elected to the Institut de France, division of inscriptions and belles-lettres in 1816, and he was an active member of the councils of public education, hospitals, and prisons. Despite his duties at the Cour des Comptes Barbé-Marbois participated actively in the deliberations of the chamber of peers, where he served constantly on the committee for the budget. Members of the chamber were given leave to print their speeches as reports, and more than sixty such pamphlets were published by Barbé-Marbois between 1814 and 1830.[23]

The first president of the Cour des Comptes had no difficulty in adjusting to the reign of Charles X when that monarch succeeded Louis XVIII in 1824, nor to Louis Philippe, who became king when Charles X was deposed by the revolution of 1830. As the Marquis de Marbois he enjoyed the hard work at the Cour des Comptes and his associations in Paris. His home there was a meeting place

22. Eulogy by Count Siméon before the chamber of peers, January 17, 1838, Jérôme Mavidal and Jean-Baptiste Émile Laurent, *Archives Parlementaires*, CXV, 60.

23. They are all listed in the *Catalogue Générale des Livres Imprimés de la Bibliothèque Nationale*.

for distinguished American visitors to whom he rendered special courtesies.

The Marquis de Marbois also enjoyed the life of a landed noble in Normandy. After his return from Guiana he purchased the chateau of Noyers in the department of Eure for the price of 273,500 francs. This was the first of twenty purchases of real estate which he made in that department in the next nine years. By 1813 his investments of nearly 650,000 francs made him master of a large domain in Normandy. In addition, he retained his Lorraine property in Metz and Buchy. Revenues from his property and his salary at the Cour des Comptes combined to give him an income with which he could live the life of a paternalistic country gentleman. The chateau at Noyers was an ideal setting for such a role. Designed in the age of Louis XIV, its fountains and gardens were miniature reproductions of those at Versailles.

The marquis made generous donations to the commune of Noyers and to other Norman areas where he held property, most of these gifts remaining anonymous until after his death. He was especially interested in local schools, and in 1825 he rebuilt the schoolhouse at Noyers and endowed it with two acres of land. To Noyers he also made grants for the repair of roads, the maintenance of public washplaces, and the repair of roofs. One of his chief interests was the installation of noninflammable roofs in the countryside. He urged the peasants to replace thatched roofs with tile and for this purpose he contributed 77,000 francs between 1832 and 1835.

The interest in agriculture, which he had shown in the United States and had demonstrated on his Lorraine property at Buchy, had full range at Noyers, where he gave personal care to his estate. He was the first person in the region to have a threshing machine. An apple, *la Marboise*, was named for him. His farm was a model, his fields the best cultivated in the neighborhood, and unused acres were all forested.

The marquis' private life was in sad contrast to his public interests and prosperity. While he was in exile in Guiana, Madame Barbé-Marbois had suffered a nervous collapse that led to permanent insanity. She was placed in a house adjacent to the château at Noyers, and there she lived as a pathetic figure until her death on January 28, 1834. Her fate had been tragic since she and her husband fled St. Domingue in 1789. Never again did she see Philadelphia or any of the members of her immediate family.

II.

The interest in writing which he had shown as a student in Paris remained with Barbé-Marbois throughout his life. The experience he gained with his publications from the German states in the 1770s had been sharpened by the preparation of countless official reports from the great range of his official duties. When he was well established at the Cour des Comptes and order had been restored in French life, he began to write about major historical events in which he had participated. He wrote and published four substantial books from 1816 to 1835. Two of these came from his experiences in Guiana.[24]

The other two volumes concerned the history of the United States. The first dealt with the treason of Benedict Arnold in September, 1780. At that time Marbois had written an extended report on Arnold's conduct, which he forwarded to Versailles. Soon after the fall of Napoleon he reworked this report and published it as a book.[25]

The History of Louisiana

In the early 1820s the Marquis de Marbois determined to write a major book on the United States, one that would appraise its political and social institutions, and emphasize the cession of Louisiana in which his own role had been so important. Happily, we have unusual insights into the preparation, writing, and publication of this work. Marbois communicated his plan to James Monroe, then president of the United States, on August 18, 1822. Writing in French, he said:

> During more than forty years I have followed events in your country and the rapid progress of institutions that assure the welfare of society. You are developing the greatest and happiest experience which could be offered to the thoughts and efforts of wise men: the joining of public happiness and liberty. Among the memories that give me satisfaction I place first the advantage I had of working with you, sir, in the completion of a matter which I believe to be one of the most

24. François Barbé-Marbois, *De la Guyane de Son État Physique, de Son Agriculture, de Son Régime Intérieur, et du Projet de le Peupler avec les Laboureurs Européens* (Paris, 1822), and his *Journal d'un déporté non jugé ou déportation en violation des lois décrétée le 18 fructidor* (2 vols.; Brussels: J. P. Meline, 1835).

25. François Barbé-Marbois, *Complot d'Arnold et de Sir Henry Clinton contre les États-Unis d'Amérique et contre le Général Washington* (Paris: P. Didot, 1816).

useful and most honorable ever handled by negotiation. However it has become fashionable [in France] to criticize the cession of Louisiana. The circumstances which made it necessary are forgotten and people do not realize that it would have been taken from us if we had deferred the conclusion of the treaty by only a few months.

I believe, despite my great age, that I shall have the time to write this history and I would like to develop all the influence this event has had and the effect it will have on the destiny of your confederation and even of the world. But I lack many materials, and, thinking that Your Excellency will approve my design, I write with confidence of obtaining from you the despatch of the acts and documents relating to this event. Fortunately there is little that is secret in your government, since all that interests the public appears either in the journals of Congress or in papers presented to the members of Congress. I ask Your Excellency to send me the printed materials and also books that he believes will contribute to the improvement of what I propose to write on Louisiana.[26]

Although Monroe did not reply until February 10, 1824, he then sent two published volumes of *State Papers* through the new American minister to France, James Brown, who was leaving for his post in Paris. Brown would play a sympathetic and helpful role in the preparation of the book. He had met Marbois in 1818 and had found him extremely friendly to the United States. Furthermore, Marbois' book had a very special interest for Brown, who was a resident of Louisiana and had served as United States Senator from that state from 1819 to 1823.

26. James Monroe Papers, New York Public Library. This letter and other correspondence between Barbé-Marbois and Monroe in this collection were published in: E. Wilson Lyon, "Barbé-Marbois and His *Histoire de la Louisiane*: Correspondence with James Monroe," *Franco-American Review*, I (1937), 357–67.

Brown was greatly impressed with Marbois. "The vigor of intellect, and fine flow of spirits which Mr. Marbois possesses at his advanced age," he wrote Monroe on January 20, 1825, "is really extraordinary. He continues to take a very active part in public affairs and is highly respected for the probity of his character and the soundness of his judgment." [27] Two years later the American minister was equally astounded by Marbois' health, both of body and mind. "This extraordinary man," he reported to Monroe on June 28, 1827, "still preserves his intellects in their full vigor at eighty-two years and is unquestionably the most active intelligent and useful statesman in France. How strange it is, that amidst all the revolutions which have taken place in the last thirty-seven years, he has preserved his life, his intellects, his fortune and his reputation." [28] Brown was in position to encourage Marbois' book, and his high opinion of the author led him to give assistance in significant ways.

Marbois informed Monroe of his progress in 1824 and 1827, always writing in French. He wrote on May 22, 1824, that the materials Monroe had sent "contained data that corresponded perfectly" with the information he had assembled on the cession. "I desire not to write anything that does not conform to the exact truth." On June 6, 1827, Marbois informed Monroe, "I have written the history of our negotiation for the cession. The content has been much extended as I wrote, for I have connected to it a number of facts that the subject led me to discuss. You and Mr. Livingston have the honorable place which is

27. James A. Padgett (ed.), "Some Papers of James Brown of Louisiana to Presidents of the United States," *Louisiana Historical Quarterly*, XX (1937), 121.
28. *Ibid.*, 129

due you in this important affair. I still question whether I will publish the work or whether I should entrust this responsibility to those who will come after me. My doubt arises from the freedom with which I have spoken of the wisdom of your institutions and of the happiness which is the fruit of them."

Marbois' doubts on publication were resolved the following year by an American historian. Jared Sparks, then owner and editor of the *North American Review*, which he had published since 1824, went to Europe in 1828 to research and copy documents in the archives of England and France for *The Diplomatic History of the American Revolution*, which he had in process and would publish in twelve volumes in 1829 and 1830. Sparks was probably the first American to consult these archives,[29] and it was not easy to secure official permission to do so.

Sparks arrived in Paris on July 9, 1828, and soon called on the American minister for advice and assistance. Brown gave Sparks a letter of introduction to Marbois, whom he saw on July 15. The two men were immediately congenial. Sparks found Marbois "eighty-four years old, but erect in his person, and apparently with all his faculties as bright as at any period of his life. He talks English with considerable facility. He entered immediately into my concerns; said he took a lively interest in what relates to America, that he would write to the ministers."[30]

29. Samuel Eliot Morison, "Jared Sparks," *Dictionary of American Biography*, XVIII, 430–34.

30. Herbert B. Adams, *The Life and Writings of Jared Sparks* (2 vols.; New York: Houghton, Mifflin, 1893; reprinted, 1970) II, 89.

Sparks dined with Marbois at his home on July 19, and in the course of the evening Marbois told him of his book on Louisiana. "The marquis has in Manuscript a work on the United States, and particularly on the Louisiana Treaty," Sparks wrote in his diary. "He insisted on my taking it home and reading it. He wished me to peruse it, he said, with a critical eye, and to express to him freely my opinion. I could not decline this request, and promised to peruse his manuscript as soon as my leisure would permit, and to act the part of a critic with as much severity as he desired."[31] Sparks read the manuscript soon thereafter, and "a few slight alterations" were made at his suggestion.

Marbois' book was published early in 1829 and Sparks, who had remained in Paris busily working in the French archives, hailed it as "the best view of the government, institutions and recent history of the United States which had ever been published originally in Europe."[32] Sparks moved with a despatch that did much to give the book its significant place in American history.

He introduced the French edition to the United States with an early and extended review in the *North American Review*, unsigned but doubtless written by himself.[33] As soon as the book appeared in Paris he arranged with a Mr. Lawrence, who had been the American *chargé d'affaires* in London, to prepare an English translation. This edi-

31. *Ibid.*, 90–91, 98.
32. *Ibid.*, 118.
33. François Barbé-Marbois, *Histoire de la Louisiane et de la Cession de Cette Colonie par la France aux États-Unis de l'Amérique Septentrionale; Précédée d'un Discours sur la Constitution et le Gouvernement des États-Unis* (Paris: Firmin Didot, 1829). See also *North American Review*, XXVIII (April, 1829), 389–418.

tion, which is here reproduced in facsimile, was promptly
reviewed in the *North American Review*[34] and widely
noted in the United States.

The approbation of Sparks was a high tribute to Marbois'
History of Louisiana, for Sparks was at the beginning of
a career that inaugurated a new and more mature era in
American historiography. In 1838 he would be named to
the McLean Professorship of Ancient and Modern History
at Harvard, where he was the first professor of history,
other than ecclesiastical, in any university in the United
States. His interest in original documents and his success
in getting them published were illustrated by his interest
in Marbois' book, which was an example of the way he
"gave the American public a new conception of their history and provided a host of writers with material."[35]

The *History of Louisiana* illustrated the extraordinary
ability and intellectual vigor that both Brown and Sparks
had found in its eighty-four-year-old author. The book
was well organized, documented, lucid in style, and ex-
ceptionally interesting. The volume included a preface
and four approximately equal parts: an essay on the constitution and government of the United States, a history of
the French and Spanish regimes in Louisiana, an account
of the cession to the United States, and the story of the
final transfer of the colony. Though all four parts are well
done, the sections on American political institutions and

34. François Barbé-Marbois, *The History of Louisiana, Particularly of the Cession of That Colony to the United States of America; with an Introductory Essay on the
Constitution and Government of the United States*. Translated from the French by an
American Citizen. (Philadelphia: Carey & Lea, 1830). See also, *North American Review*, XXX (April, 1830), 551–56.
35. Morison, "Jared Sparks," DAB.

the cession of Louisiana have the greatest historic value.

One of Barbé-Marbois' purposes was to explain to his own countrymen the background and reasons for the sale of Louisiana. "The circumstances respecting the cession of Louisiana were not, at all, known in France, where even the treaties have not yet been authentically published," he stated in the preface of the volume. Accordingly, he documented his narrative with an appendix including the treaty of cession and the two conventions that implemented it, and fifteen additional documents, from both French and American sources, pertinent to the transaction or to the history of the colony.

Barbé-Marbois emphasized the significance of his subject: "The consequences of the cession of Louisiana will extend to the most distant posterity. It interests vast regions that will become by their civilization and power, the rivals of Europe before another century." To support this thesis he gave his fellow countrymen an analysis of the government of the United States, a comment on the progress of the republic, and a forecast of the nation's future. Barbé-Marbois wrote from half a century of knowledge and observance of the United States, extending from the Revolution to the beginning of the presidency of Andrew Jackson. No European had ever given such an accurate and sympathetic view of American institutions.

Barbé-Marbois' praise for the government of the United States and its evolution was unbounded. The American Revolution had shown "the virtues necessary to the foundation and preservation of states" and created a new government without a model in history. He lauded the openness of the American system: "The president, and the two houses of Congress, are without mysterious archives. They have no concealed and corrupting police, nor have they those secret reports so convenient for calumny." He commended the federal financial policy, which secured "an adequate revenue, arising principally from the duties paid on the importation of foreign merchandise, and from the sale of public lands that do not belong to the several states." Barbé-Marbois rejoiced in the high tone of American public finance. "No one would dare to propose to increase the public revenue by the establishment of a lottery or of gaming tables, or by any other means that would have the effect of enriching the state by corrupting the morals."

Barbé-Marbois praised both the federal structure and the state governments. To the United States "belonged the honour of having first presented a perfect model of the best federal constitution." The state constitutions all had "justice and equality for their foundation: what is just at Boston, is so at New Orleans." He saw much of the strength of American institutions in the emphasis upon individual freedom, and his book reflects the restrictions on liberty in Restoration France. He contrasted the nature of religious tolerance in the two countries, saying that in the United States "toleration is not as in Europe an arrogant indulgence of one sect toward another; it is a perfect equality among all."

The *History of Louisiana* portrays a new Europe, "a Europe truly free," rising in the vast domain of the United States. Barbé-Marbois predicted a population of "one hundred million inhabitants of the white race" by the end of the nineteenth century.

Despite his praise of its institutions Barbé-Marbois had one grave concern about the future of the United States. He was deeply worried by the existence of slavery, by its effect on society, and by its possible disruption of the federal union. He had seen the evils of slavery in St. Domingue, and he feared the consequences of the continuance of slavery in the United States. No part of his book showed greater foresight. Carefully, he pointed out the actual situation, saying that in 1827 there were in the southern states 1,800,000 slaves and 300,000 free blacks. He gave considerable attention to the efforts of the American Colonization Society, which had been organized in Virginia in 1817 and was still actively engaged in the transplantation of slaves to Africa and the development of a free black state in Liberia.

Rightly Barbé-Marbois saw slavery as imperiling the very existence of a united republic. "Slavery constitutes a perpetual cause of division," he noted. "The inhabitants of the north hold it in detestation, and those of the south wish in vain to deliver their country from it." The bitterness of the increasing sectional tension had been emphasized by the Missouri Compromise of 1820, and Barbé-Marbois sketched the issues in that momentous decision.

Barbé-Marbois was less prescient when discussing the future of the Indians in the United States. "We must predict with confidence," he stated, "that in less than two centuries, all these nations will disappear from the two Americas. History and geography will scarce preserve their names." He saw the policy, then emerging in the United States, of moving the Indian tribes to the west bank of the Mississippi as only an expedient. Ultimately, he expected Indian tribes and culture to be overwhelmed by the surrounding white civilization.

The reviewer of the English edition of his book found Barbé-Marbois' "knowledge of the principles and forms of our government, and of its practical operations, altogether unexampled in any other European writer. For this attention to our history and deep study into the effects of our political and social institutions, he claims the gratitude of every American, and above all for the pains he has taken in this work to diffuse in Europe accurate information concerning subjects which few on the other side of the water ever pretend to examine, and which none understands." Barbé-Marbois' study remains a valuable source for the history of the United States in the 1820s.

Barbé-Marbois' book was a forerunner of Alexis de Tocqueville's *De la Démocratie en Amérique*, which appeared in January, 1835. Interestingly, Jared Sparks had a part in both studies. He met the young de Tocqueville in Paris in 1828 and assisted him when he visited the United States from May, 1831, to February, 1832. Thus, within a decade France had studies of American institutions from both a venerable administrator and a young intellectual.

The Cession of Louisiana

The *History of Louisiana* constitutes source material of the greatest importance for American history. The heart of the book is Barbé-Marbois' account of the cession of

Louisiana, in which he was a participant. With great interest he relates the dramatic events that within a few weeks in the spring of 1803 determined the future of the United States and magnified its role in history.

Many forces converged in April, 1803, to resolve the future of the Mississippi Valley.[36] Napoleon, with his plan for St. Domingue destroyed, faced a renewal of war with Great Britain. The United States, much concerned by the closing of the port of New Orleans and rumors of French plans for Louisiana, awaited the outcome of the mission of James Monroe, whom President Jefferson had sent to assist Livingston. In Paris, Livingston continued unsuccessfully to elicit information from Talleyrand and, on his own authority, suggested a division of Louisiana between France and the United States. He proposed to Talleyrand that, in addition to New Orleans and adjacent territory east of the Mississippi, "France cede to the United States so much of Louisiana as lies above the mouth of the River Arkansas. By this, a barrier will be placed between the colony of France and Canada, from which she may otherwise be attacked with the greatest facility, and driven out before she can derive any aid from Europe. Let her retain the country lying on the west of the Mississippi and below the Arkansas River—a country capable of supporting fifteen millions of inhabitants."[37]

Barbé-Marbois is our primary authority for Napoleon's thinking regarding Louisiana and his decision regarding the colony. In a private conference in the Tuileries, Na-

36. On French policy regarding Louisiana, and its sale to the United States, see Lyon, *Louisiana in French Diplomacy*, 79–250.
37. *Annals of Congress*, 7th Cong., 1st Sess., pp. 1070–71.

poleon vented his indignation against Great Britain by
saying that "to emancipate nations from the commerical
tyranny of England, it is necessary to balance her influence by a maritime power that may one day become her
rival; that power is the United States. The English aspire
to dispose of all the riches of the world. I shall be useful to
the whole universe if I can prevent their ruling America
as they rule Asia." As the British had a naval force in the
West Indies and garrisons in Jamaica and the Windward
Islands, Napoleon concluded "that it was requisite to
change without delay his policy in relation to Santo Domingo, Louisiana, and the United States." [38] His primary
purpose was to keep Louisiana from "being turned to the
advantage of England."

Perhaps no matter of such importance has been handled with the despatch that Napoleon gave to the matter of
Louisiana. After the Easter service at St. Cloud on Sunday, April 10, Napoleon called for Barbé-Marbois and
Denis Decrès, minister of the navy and colonies. He related a conversation with Talleyrand regarding the selling
of Louisiana and asked their advice. Reviewing the de-
fenseless state of Louisiana and the weakness of French
forces before the British in North America, he told the
ministers that if there were still time he hoped to take
from the British "any idea they may have of ever possessing the colony." Napoleon said:

> I think of ceding it to the United States. I can scarcely say
> that I cede it to them, for it is not yet in our possession. If,
> however, I leave the least time to our enemies I shall

38. Barbé-Marbois, *History of Louisiana*, 262.

only transmit an empty title to those republicans whose friendship I seek. They only ask of me a town in Louisiana, but I already consider the colony as entirely lost, and it appears to me that in the hands of this growing power, it will be more useful to the policy and even to the commerce of France than if I should attempt to keep it.[39]

Decrès counseled retention of Louisiana but Barbé-Marbois urged its sale. "Nothing is more uncertain," he said, "than the future of European colonies in America. The exclusive right which the parent states exercise over these remote settlements becomes every day more and more precarious. The people feel humbled in being dependent on a small country in Europe, and will liberate themselves, as soon as they have a consciousness of their own strength."[40] "Even our merchants," he continued, "will soon acknowledge that Louisiana free, offers them more chances to profit than Louisiana subject to a monopoly."

The two ministers remained overnight at the palace of St. Cloud, and at daybreak Barbé-Marbois was summoned by Napoleon and asked to read the dispatches from London. "Irresolution and deliberation are no longer in season," Napoleon stated.

I renounce Louisiana. It is not only New Orleans that I will cede, it is the whole colony without any reservation. I know the price of what I abandon, and I have sufficiently proved the importance that I attach to this province, since my first diplomatic act with Spain had for its object the recovery of it. I renounce it with the greatest regret. To attempt obsti-

39. *Ibid.*, 264.
40. *Ibid.*, 266.

nately to retain it would be folly. I direct you to negotiate this affair with the envoys of the United States. Do not even await the arrival of Mr. Monroe: have an interview this very day with Mr. Livingston: but I require a great deal of money for this war, and I would like to commence it with new contributions.

Monroe arrived on April 12 and Livingston gave a dinner party that evening in honor of his arrival. While they were dining Barbé-Marbois was seen walking in Livingston's garden. He saw Livingston when the guests at the party were having coffee and asked that Livingston call on him any time before eleven that evening. Barbé-Marbois left without seeing Monroe, but Livingston informed Monroe of the purpose of the minister's visit.[41] As soon as Monroe had departed, Livingston went alone for the appointment with the minister of the public treasury. He was pleased to be able to begin the negotiations before Monroe's official presentation to the French government.

Barbé-Marbois' account is an invaluable record and interpretation of the negotiations that followed Napoleon's momentous decision. For Napoleon's minister, the association with Livingston and Monroe was a renewal of old acquaintances and a recalling of common experiences in the success of the American Revolution. "The plenipotentiaries having been long acquainted," Barbé-Marbois wrote, "were disposed to treat each other with mutual confidence. . . . They could not see each other again without recollecting that they had been previously associated in a design, conceived for the happiness of man-

41. Monroe to Lafayette, May 2, 1829, in the Pierpont Morgan Library, New York.

kind, approved by reason and crowned after great vicissitudes by a glorious success."

Although Livingston and Monroe were authorized only
to pay ten million dollars for New Orleans, the island on
which it stood, and the Floridas—still mistakenly thought
in Washington to have been ceded to France—the American ministers readily agreed to treat for the cession of
the entire colony. The price to be paid, the boundaries of
the colony, and the claims of American citizens against
France from the quasiwar with the Directory required
more time than the main question of the negotiations.

All matters were resolved at the end of April and the
beginning of May. The United States agreed to pay sixty
million francs for the colony and, in addition, to provide
twenty million francs to meet the claims of American citizens against France. The technicalities of the treaty were
settled by the three negotiators in a meeting at Barbé-
Marbois' home on May 1 and were approved the following
day by Napoleon. The treaty and the two conventions were
all signed with the date of April 30. Barbé-Marbois forwarded the final report on the negotiations to Talleyrand
on May 8, 1803.

We can be grateful that Barbé-Marbois had the desire
and the ability to write about his own role in the history
of France and the United States. As he lived until 1837,
sound in mind until the end, he enjoyed the reception of
his books in his own time. There can be no doubt that he
would be pleased and proud to know that his *History of
Louisiana* was selected for publication in facsimile by the
Louisiana American Revolution Bicentennial Commis-

sion. He would appreciate his introduction to a state and a nation, both stronger and more populous than even he envisaged in 1829.

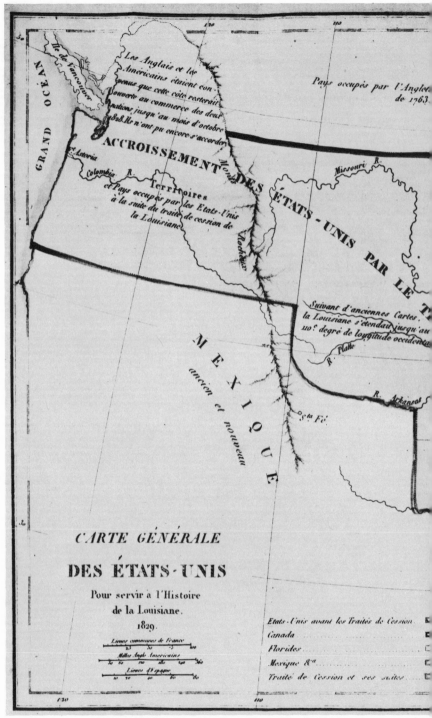

GRAND OCÉAN

Île de Vancouver

Les Anglais et les
Américains étaient con
venus que cette côte resterait
ouverte au commerce des deux
nations jusqu'au mois d'octobre
1828. Ils n'ont pu encore s'accorder

Pays occupés par l'Anglet
de 1763.

ACCROISSEMENT DES

ÉTATS - UNIS PAR LE T

Missouri R.

Colombia R.

Territoires
et Pays occupés par les États-Unis
à la suite du traité de cession de
la Louisiane

Suivant d'anciennes Cartes,
la Louisiane s'étendait jusqu'au
110.e degré de longitude occiden

R. Platte

R. Arkansas

MEXIQUE

ancien et nouveau

S.ta Fé

CARTE GÉNÉRALE

DES ÉTATS-UNIS

Pour servir à l'Histoire
de la Louisiane.
1829.

Lieues communes de France

Milles Anglo-Americains

Lieues d'Espagne

États-Unis avant les Traités de Cession

Canada

Florides

Mexique &.a

Traité de Cession et ses suites

The United States in 1829, showing the territory acquired by the
Louisiana Treaty of 1803, the Rush-Bagot Agreement with Great
Britain in 1818, and the Transcontinental Treaty with Spain in 1819.

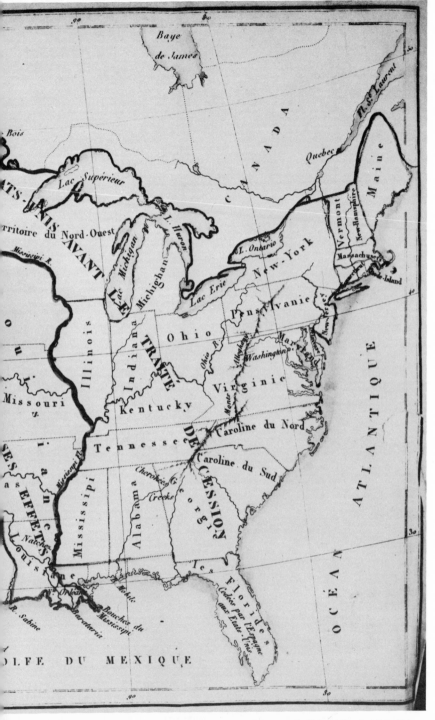

from the 1829 French edition of Barbé-Marbois' *Histoire de la Louisiane*.

THE

HISTORY OF LOUISIANA,

PARTICULARLY

OF THE CESSION OF THAT COLONY

TO THE

UNITED STATES OF AMERICA;

WITH

AN INTRODUCTORY ESSAY

ON THE

CONSTITUTION AND GOVERNMENT

OF THE

UNITED STATES.

BY BARBÉ MARBOIS,

PEER OF FRANCE, &c. &c. &c.

Translated from the French

BY AN AMERICAN CITIZEN.

PHILADELPHIA:

CAREY & LEA.

1830.

GRIGGS & DICKINSON, PRINTERS.

DEDICATION.

TO HIS ROYAL HIGHNESS, THE DAUPHIN.

SIR,

If you have read, with some interest, the book which I have the honour to dedicate to you, I owe it less to the facts that I have related than to the maxims of justice and virtue which you have remarked in it. A frequent witness of the benevolent actions that render your person so dear to us, I have been anxious to be permitted to publish my book under your happy auspices.

I beg your Royal Highness to accept the homage of my profound and respectful devotion.

BARBÉ MARBOIS.

CONTENTS.

TRANSLATOR'S NOTICE.

Most foreign books which have treated of the institutions of the United States have been compiled with such illiberal feelings, and are at the same time so very inaccurate, that when, a short time after my arrival in Paris last autumn, the following book was placed in my hands, I conceived that I could not employ a few weeks' leisure more usefully, nor in a manner more congenial with my former pursuits than by making it generally accessible to my fellow-citizens. I was in hopes that, while the circulation of the original in Europe dispelled many unfavourable prejudices respecting my native country, my humble labours might not be without some effect in attaching the people of America still more firmly to those institutions, on which an enlightened and distinguished foreigner had pronounced a high encomium.

The friendly spirit alluded to is not confined to the Introductory Essay, which particularly treats of the government, but will be found to pervade the whole of the subsequent History. Even while the political parties, into which the people of the United States were lately divided, were doing every thing in their power to induce the world to believe that on the election of a president were to depend the future destinies of that great and

prosperous nation; the author, estimating more favourably the nature of the American institutions, confidently stated that, "whatever might be the result of
this domestic contest, the wisdom of the constitution
was a guarantee as well for the moderation of the general as for the firmness of the magistrate."

But the History of Louisiana and of its cession possesses claims to attention, though of a different character.   It makes the citizen of the United States
acquainted with the origin of his country's title to a
territory, the importance of which, before the lapse of
many ages, will be scarcely inferior to that of all the
states of the original confederacy combined; and it un-
folds to the statesman a diplomatic transaction, little
noticed at the time, which must hereafter exercise the
greatest influence on the general balance of power
among the nations of Christendom.

In most of the important events to which he alludes,
the Marquis de Marbois had a direct participation, and
as few foreigners can be named, whose official relations
have been more beneficial to the United States than
those of this respected individual, a cursory notice of
his life may not be unacceptable to readers on the other
side of the Atlantic.   In French History he has long
held an important place.

Barbé Marbois was born at Metz in 1745.   He early entered the diplomatic service, and was appointed in
1769 secretary of the French legation to the diet of the
empire, which held its sittings at Ratisbon.   From
this post he was, two years afterwards, transferred in

the same character to Dresden, where, as well as in Bavaria, he for some time officiated as chargé d'affaires. On quitting the latter court he seems to have had the intention of entering on another career, and he was accordingly received as a counsellor of the parliament of Metz. But from his new pursuits he was soon withdrawn by the offer of employment in America, whose revolution then attracted universal attention.

The government of France, having determined openly to espouse the cause of the English colonies, concluded with them in 1778 treaties of amity and alliance, and of commerce. As efficient aid in men and money was promised by its ally to the new republic, the functions of the French legation to the congress were at that time far more important than in the ordinary cases of diplomatic representation. M. Gerard, the negotiator of the treaties, who was sent to the United States in 1778 as minister plenipotentiary, having returned home the following year, was succeeded by the Chevalier de la Luzerne. M. de Marbois with great readiness accepted the appointment of secretary of legation, with which place that of consul general was united, and it is well known that he was the principal agent in the important operations of the embassy. In April, 1784, M. de la Luzerne took leave of congress, and M. de Marbois was recognised as chargé d'affaires, in which situation he remained till his appointment in 1785 as intendant of St. Domingo, an office for which he possessed, in an eminent degree, the appropriate talents. While in the United States, he married a lady

B

of Philadelphia, by whom he had a daughter, now the
wife of the Duke of Plaisance, the son of Le Brun,
one of Bonaparte's colleagues in the consulate.

In 1790 Marbois returned to France, and was named
by Louis XVI. his minister to the Diet at Ratisbon,
but received instructions to proceed first on a special
mission to the Emperor Leopold. At this time, though
the king still remained an integral part of the constitution,
the revolution had made great progress. The princes
of the royal family and a large portion of the nobility
had actually exiled themselves, and were preparing to
attempt the recovery of their privileges by force of arms.
When M. de Marbois came back to Paris from Vienna,
he found that every thing indicated the near approach
of those bloody scenes which disgraced French liberty.
He asked permission to resign his place, which was
granted; the king and also the queen, at the same time,
graciously signifying that he should be preserved for
better times.

During the reign of terror which succeeded, M. de
Marbois's name having been placed on the list of emigrants, he was imprisoned, and recovered his liberty
only with the fall of Robespierre. Under the constitution of the directory he again engaged in public affairs. How far he was from upholding that old system,
the abuses of which time had rendered intolerable to
an enlightened nation, is sufficiently manifest from the
whole tenor of his writings. In the council of ancients, to which he was elected in 1795, he proved that
however much he might condemn the excesses of the

revolution, to which he was a stranger, his sentiments were those of a Frenchman. He paid a just tribute to the merit of the army of Italy, and of its illustrious chief, at the same time that he attacked, without success, the law which excluded from the public service nobles and the families of emigrants.

In 1797, when the contest took place between a majority of the directory and the legislature, M. de Marbois was president of the council of ancients, and had a great share in the nomination of M. Barthelemy as one of the directory. A powerful faction having prevailed by a revolutionary movement, Barthelemy and Carnot, two of the directory, as well as several members of both the legislative councils, were subjected to a species of ostracism. In this number M. de Marbois was included; he was transported, under circumstances of peculiar aggravation, to the pestilential regions of Sinnamari in Guiana. He remained there in exile till 1800, when he was recalled by the directory to the inhospitable island of Oleron, and soon after Bonaparte, becoming first consul, annulled the unjust sentence against him and his companions in misfortune.

On M. de Marbois's restoration to his country, he was made a counsellor of state and director of the public treasury. The latter office was changed in 1801 to that of minister of the public treasury, when he became a member of the cabinet. While in this situation, the negotiations with the United States for the cession of Louisiana, which gave rise to the present work, were confided to him as the plenipotentiary on the part of the French republic.

In 1805, he received from Napoleon several honorary distinctions; but being averse to a system, which substituted for the usual sources of revenue extraordinary contributions from all the neighbouring states, the consequences of which Marbois foresaw must ultimately be a general coalition of Europe against France, he resigned the ministry of the treasury in 1806, and retired to the country. He was, however, recalled to Paris, two years afterwards, to fill the office of first president of the court of accounts—the tribunal which has jurisdiction in all cases affecting the public receipts and expenditures.* In 1813, he was made a senator of the empire.

On the restoration of the Bourbons in 1814, the king created M. de Marbois a peer, and he was confirmed in the presidency of the court of accounts. Having been exiled by Napoleon, during the hundred days, he was on the return of Louis XVIII. named minister, secretary of state, and keeper of the seals; but he soon after resigned this office to resume his former place in the court of accounts, the duties of which, though now eighty-four years of age, he still performs with the greatest exactitude. He is also constant in his at-

---

* All the French courts are divided into chambers or sections, each of which has its own president. The first president is the magistrate who presides over the whole court when the several chambers meet together on important occasions. The public accounts are settled by judicial forms.

tendance in the house of peers, where he takes part in most of the important proceedings; and, at the opening of the present session, he was named on the commission to whom the king's speech was referred. In all institutions having for their object the melioration of the condition of his fellow-beings, M. de Marbois engages with deep interest, and, notwithstanding his numerous engagements, he has within a few days consented to be a member of a council formed for the suppression of mendicity.

The labours of M. de Marbois have not prevented his finding leisure for literary pursuits. Besides writing the Introduction to the Count de Goertz's Memoir on the Negotiations of 1778 for the Succession of Bavaria, he is the author of several works on Morals and Finance, and of some translations from German and English. He likewise published, in 1816, an account of Arnold's conspiracy, preceded by an essay on the United States, which is characterized by the same liberal spirit as the present Treatise. It was translated soon after its appearance by a distinguished American scholar.

Accurate as is the Marquis de Marbois in general, it is not improbable that the reader may find in the following work errors of detail that might have been corrected from public documents, had they fallen under the observation of the venerable writer. The instructions to the American plenipotentiaries, and their despatch, accompanying the Louisiana treaty, are published in the Appendix to the present edition. A few notes have also been inserted, but I have not felt myself at liberty, except in a single instance, to make any comments on the opinions which M. de Marbois has formed respecting either the political parties of the country or the prominent American statesmen, to whom he has occasionally alluded.

After these explanations, I will only farther observe that in submitting the History of Louisiana to my fellow-citizens in the United States, I pretend to no other merit, and wish to assume no other responsibility than that of a faithful

TRANSLATOR.

Paris, May, 1829.

PREFACE.

MANY facts worthy of being preserved pass into oblivion, from not being recorded by those who are best acquainted with them. A witness during my long career of various important public events, in some of which I took part, I always intended, as soon as I should have leisure, to write an account of those in which I was directly engaged. From year to year, I have had reason to think that this moment was drawing near; though, whether I deceive myself, or am still really able to attend to business and support the weight of years, I have not yet resolved on retirement. At the same time, I have not thought proper longer to delay writing the History, which I now publish, and this occupation has been to me a source of relaxation.

The treaty, by which Louisiana was, twenty-six years since, ceded to the United States, has lately given rise to regrets, which have appeared to me to merit the more attention from their being entertained in good faith. I have conceived that the history of that negotiation would dissipate some errors, and might throw light on the doubts which have been suggested respecting the policy of the measure.

France had, in 1802, just recovered Louisiana by treaty. But,.she had not yet taken possession, when a war broke out between her and England. Could we hope to retain that colony? Admitting that it might have been retained, and that it would, at a future day, become useful to the mother country, did it offer sufficient advantages to indemnify us for the expense of its settlement and defence? As an independent state, will it not make more rapid progress than if it were subjected to the laws of monopoly? Will not its constantly improving condition be more advantageous to our commerce than its possession and exclusive government would have been? Already, the doubts are, in part, removed.

I have put in order some materials, which I long since prepared for this narrative. The circumstances respecting the cession of Louisiana were not, at all, known in France, where even the treaties have never yet been authentically published; but it is in the great collection of the diplomatic transactions of the United States that the principal documents are to be found. It will, perhaps, be observed that the object of the negotiation was not to put an end to a war; that it was not accompanied by any remarkable incident, and that it was promptly terminated. It may then well excite surprise that it should furnish matter for a large volume, whilst so many other treaties, concluded after many communications and long conferences, only occupy a few pages in history. But most of these treaties have been so badly observed, and their influence has been so transitory, that they may be forgotten without much affecting the instruction or the interests of society. On the other hand, the consequences of the cession of Louisiana will extend to the most distant posterity. It interests vast regions that will become, by their civilization and power, the rivals of Europe before another century commences. It has crowned the important work to which Louis XVI., his armies, and the statesmen, who composed his council, gloriously contributed. The great advantages which the whole world has derived from that event have caused it to be forgotten that, at the time of the alliance of 1778, politics did not conform to the laws of morality.

This History is about to appear in the midst of the many good and bad books, which every season produces. But is there any one which entering, at this day, into a library, dares to look for a place there? They are all occupied. I know not what will be the fate of my book. If the great historians find in it some details worthy of being remembered, I beg them to believe that they are true. Two of their pages will be sufficient for the recitals of which I have made a volume. If some of the maxims have the happy effect of shedding a new lustre on public virtues, I shall rejoice that I have had an opportunity of writing them.

I have had my share in the calamities of our times. Literature and study, which, in tranquil circumstances, had contributed to my happiness, were my principal consolation in adversity. They have inspired in me

C

an attachment for liberty, regulated by wise laws.
They aided me to support with courage an unjust and
rigorous captivity. I may, perhaps, be permitted to
add, that in every situation of my life, whether prosperous or adverse, I have always believed it to be my
duty to render my labours useful to my country. May
those who read the recital on which I am entering, recognise in the sketch that I have traced of the institutions of the United States, my attachment for those of
France, and my firm persuasion that our happiness is
closely connected with the faithful observance of our
new laws.

INTRODUCTION.

ESSAY ON THE CONSTITUTION AND GOVERNMENT OF THE
UNITED STATES OF AMERICA.

INTRODUCTION.

THE origin of the greatest part of the nations of antiquity was attended with extraordinary occurrences. Their legislators proclaimed themselves the organs and confidants of gods and goddesses. They conversed with them, and the laws which they promulgated were dictated by a mysterious power.

No fable is connected with the primitive legislation of modern colonies. A benevolence truly divine was the Egeria of William Penn. If, from the history of the first period of the English settlements, we efface some acts of fanaticism, and of an intolerance always barbarous, often hypocritical, we shall find that the wisdom which presided at their infancy, never abandoned them during the most violent storms of their revolution.

These colonies, without violating their charters, inserted in their rising institutions a principle of liberty, which, from their very cradle, prepared the way for their future emancipation. Better constituted, freer and sooner peopled than the colonies of other nations,

3

if they had fewer motives for separating from their mother country, they were also better prepared for independence. Their settlement only dates back a century and a half; but their progress has been very rapid, and we will set out from their earliest epoch, in order to recall some circumstances connected with their origin, and present their principal results.

The discovery of America has had, during three hundred years, a great influence on the destinies of the old world. The independence of the United States will produce consequences still more important: it is, as it were, a second discovery. An irresistible impulse is given to all civilized countries. The liberty of the Spanish kingdoms in America has been probably advanced by it a century. This great event, which Columbus was far from foreseeing, is the most glorious result of his bold labours. Europe already participates in these happy changes. Some centuries will elapse before an end is put to despotism and slavery in Asia and Africa, but our posterity will witness even this other astonishing event.

It was not the wisdom and policy of the governments of Europe, but religious persecution and the vices of large towns, that peopled and cultivated America. These remote settlements offered to European rulers the means of freeing themselves from religious dissenters as well as from vagabonds, libertines, and convicts. The latter description of persons were sent, at first, in very small numbers, and it was only towards the middle of the last century that transportation for crimes was carried to a great extent. Sixty years ago, Franklin, in enumerating the grievances of the colonies, said to the English: " An act of parliament has authorized you to do us, by emptying the contents of your prisons into our cities, the greatest injury that can be inflicted on a people." This was the universal system of the maritime powers. It was without any design on the part of the statesmen of those days that the agricultural colonies have become the honour and happiness of the human race. It was the Catholics, the Puritans, the Huguenots, the Calvinists, and the Quakers who contributed most effectually to prevent the evils which would have resulted from the presence of criminals condemned to banishment. These sectaries brought to America frugal and austere habits, and they were all either well educated or conversant with some branch of industry.

But these unfortunate settlers were in many of the provinces, exposed to new persecutions. Some of them were cruelly treated, and the prevailing sects obliged the more feeble to seek elsewhere a new asylum. It may be observed that the colony of Maryland, which had been the refuge of the Catholics, was the most tolerant; it was successively peopled by dissenters, professing different tenets and escaping from the place of their first voluntary exile.

In the year 1662, Connecticut received from Charles II. a constitution which bound it but slightly to the mother country, and was framed with such wisdom, that the only change which it underwent at the Revolution, was the substitution of the name of state for that of king.

In 1818 this state gave itself a new constitution, the articles of which differ very little from those of its charter. The charter which Charles II. granted to Rhode Island, is dated at the same period with that of Connecticut. The people have found in it sufficient guarantees and have not been disposed to make in it the least alteration.

Locke, who was employed to prepare a charter for Carolina, did not succeed so well: he introduced in it seignors, barons, landgraves, cassiques, and palatines. This charter and all those which were drawn up by the counsellors of the crown underwent great changes to suit the views of the colonists. The governors could no where prevent the formation of those assemblies of delegates, which constitute the strongest as well as the most effectual restraint on abuses.

The colonists had, from the earliest times, frequent quarrels with their mother country, and projects of separation appeared long before the Declaration of Independence. This disposition will seem the less surprising, when it is remembered that the most numerous portion of the inhabitants of some of the provinces were not of English origin; and that all of them, from whatever nation they came, had fled from persecution, and preferred liberty among savages to oppression in a civilized country. The Dutch emigrants had brought into the colony of New York sobriety, industry, useful rules of economy, and an inclination for trade. A few

Swedes of upright character, and of religious and moral habits were spread over New Jersey and Delaware. A great part of Pennsylvania was settled by Germans and Irish. The revocation of the edict of Nantes peopled South Carolina with many industrious and rich French families: these unfortunate refugees had wished to settle in Louisiana, but were excluded by the intolerance and bigotry which then governed the councils of France. The historians of America render their sincere thanks for this persecution to the ministers of Louis XIV.

The planters and inhabitants of the English colonies, as free as the English themselves, and enjoying the same civil rights, were subjected to very severe restrictions on their trade and navigation, as well as on all kinds of manufactures, with which the mother country could supply them. The British government held it, also, as a maxim, not to suffer any settlements to be formed in the interior of the country or at a distance from the coast. The motives for this policy are explained in a Report, which was only made public at a very late period. "The territories of the West," says this document, "are fertile, the climate is temperate, planters would meet with but few obstacles in settling there; with little labour they would be able to satisfy their wants; they would have nothing to ask of England, and no returns to offer her." When the correspondence of some of the governors and other officers of the crown was published, it was found to evince the same intention of not favouring the industry of the co-

lonists, and the same fear that their independence might
be the result of a less exclusive system.

It cannot, however, be said that the English colonies
were tyrannically governed.   No colonies in the world
have enjoyed so many privileges; and if the general
government of the United States can exercise over
them an authority more extensive and less contested
than the kings of England ever possessed, it is because there is in the nature of the Federal Government a tendency to impose limits on itself.   The English governors only sought to extend their powers;—
congress attentively confines itself within its proper
sphere.

Every thing was ripe for a revolution; the duties on
tea and the stamp act were only a pretence.   The violent proceedings of the mother country taught the Americans that their liberty was in jeopardy.   The danger
aroused all those to whom this liberty was dear; and
when it is recollected with what ardour they sacrificed
their repose, their lives, and their fortunes, it must be
acknowledged that the fear of losing an inestimable
good could alone have inspired so much courage and
devotion.

They addressed themselves, at first, to their sovereign, not with their knees on the ground and quires
full of mournful complaints in their hands; but they
stated their grievances with calm and respectful firmness.   As its only reply, the British government attempted to punish them as mutineers and rebels.   They
then published that Declaration of Independence which

we now read, after a lapse of fifty years, without finding in it a single word to censure. The anniversary
of the day, on which it was published, is always celebrated with those fresh manifestations of joy which all,
without exception, feel at the bottom of their hearts.

Their undertaking, when it was announced, was seconded by the good wishes of all Europe, and, even in
the councils of Great Britain, a numerous party supported their efforts.

The cabinet of Versailles acknowledged their independence, in doing which it was perhaps as much drawn
along by the movement of public opinion as determined
by the deliberations that preceded the alliance. This
important resolution has since been censured, even by
some of those who had strenuously advised and demanded it. It is very true, that it hastened in Europe
the development of the principles of freedom, which
were then springing up on all sides, and were favoured
by princes themselves. But this unanimity was not of
long continuance: in France, even, where liberal opinions had been received with the most enthusiasm, a
few years sufficed to produce a violent explosion of an
opposite character.

The American insurrection had only to contend with
the armies sent from England: forces still more formidable suddenly threatened the rising liberty of France.
If reforms had become necessary, abuses consecrated
by ages were almost inseparable from the established
order of things. The reformers made some vain efforts
to proceed with prudence and deliberation; but, carried

away by the violence of parties, their acts soon bore the marks of injustice. Furious excesses justified the resistance of the clergy and nobility. This terrible struggle was followed by deplorable catastrophies. At this day, instead of acknowledging their true causes, some attribute to the American revolution the disasters and crimes of our own. They raise doubts respecting the wisdom of the ministers of Louis XVI.; and go so far as to assert that that prince, instead of succouring the Americans by his arms and the treasures of France, ought to have united the French troops to the Hanoverians and Hessians, in order to bring back the rebellious subjects to their allegiance. Perhaps the intervention of France in this great quarrel was not sufficiently justified either by imminent dangers or by those rules of justice which states should never violate. I even hardly dare to look for a justification of the part which was then taken in those maxims of precautionary policy, which it is so easy to bend to all circumstances. There is no doubt that Louis XVI., by allying himself with the United States, really advanced the emancipation of the English colonies. But, had France remained neutral, the independence of the United States would only have been retarded a few years. We may apply to modern colonies what has happened to all those of antiquity. Whatever may be the power of the parent state, its colonies are free as soon as they are sensible of their own strength. In vain would the mother country attempt to prolong their subjection by arresting their progress in every way, introducing dissension among the different classes of inhabitants, discouraging industry, and substituting constraint to affection, prejudices to reason. Such efforts would only serve to render these establishments burdensome rather than profitable, to engender the most profound hatred, to incline the people with more certainty to revolt, and to render an insurrection, by its being longer delayed, more terrible and destructive.

A glorious justification of the revolution, and of the assistance which France afforded to it, is to be found in the advantages that have resulted from it to society in general, and even to England. It depends on the Americans to justify it still further by the wisdom of their conduct.

Among the civil chiefs whom this people selected to govern them, after the declaration of their independence, among those to whom they confided the command of their armies, Arnold alone was misled by ambition and avarice; no other person in office took advantage of the public distresses to elevate himself or increase his fortune. The virtues necessary to the foundation and preservation of states, boldness in action, moderation in success, constancy in adversity, were exhibited without ostentation and without pomp. The rulers of that period also participated honourably in that species of fame which is acquired by arms, which is accompanied by the most dangers, and which the multitude, therefore, place above all others.

Washington is, in the eyes of his fellow citizens, more worthy of admiration—greater than was ever

Alexander or Cæsar, in the estimation of the Greeks and Romans. His natural moderation was such, that, after having vanquished the enemies of his country, he had not, like so many other men illustrious in arms, to combat his own ambition. He was delighted to lay aside the sword, in order to devote himself to the care of governing the republic, restored to peace. Desolation and ruins are the monuments of the lives of conquerors, and mark their course on earth. The happiness of mankind is the imperishable monument which must recall to future ages the name of Washington; and his glory, purer than theirs, surpasses in reality that of those pretended sons of the gods. The war once ended, it was especially to his civil virtues that the Americans were delighted to render homage.

They, at this day, prize one kind of glory above all others,—it is that which in peace is attached to sincere love of country, and which, without ambitious passions, and, with a sort of indifference for celebrity, exhibits itself in a modest desire to obtain the esteem of the people.

Several of their first magistrates, among whom are the two Adams* and Jefferson,† who have seen the republic flourish, are no more: they gave examples of private virtues, after having long exhibited those of a public nature. Madison and Monroe, who have re-

* Samuel Adams and John Adams.

† John Adams and Jefferson died on the 4th of July, 1826, the anniversary of the Declaration of Independence, which they signed fifty years before.

turned, without authority, without power, into the rank of private citizens, are there followed with as much veneration and affection as the king, who, on the throne, had best merited the love of his subjects, would obtain after his abdication. The magistrates, who succeed in their footsteps, have no other end in view than the good of the republic, and this good is made apparent by indications that never deceive; that is to say, by the public will,—by the opinion of all the citizens clearly and spontaneously expressed. Experience has taught them that the people, left to themselves, are the most capable of deciding on their true interests, and it is by pursuing the course which they point out that rulers are sure of obtaining general approbation and confidence.

I traced,* some years ago, a picture of the prosperity of this people; but they make such rapid advances, that the scene changes even whilst we are observing it, and in a few years it will be necessary to add new observations to those which can, at this time, be made.

They have already assumed a rank among the old nations of the world; but they have not, like them, to accomplish the immense task for which centuries do not always suffice,—the return from error to truth. We there see no relics of the usurpation of power, no old abuses seeking opportunities to resume their places, no oppressive laws of former ages, no ambitious leaders of sects abusing their authority over the consciences

---

* Preface to Arnold's Conspiracy, 1816.

of their followers, not the slightest trace of that feudal system, of which in Europe even the institutions of republics still bear the stamp, no rival classes disputing for rights, which belong as much to the one party as the other. The concurrence of the interests of the great number has smoothed all obstacles; it has protected the rising republic from those hateful acts, from those vindictive movements which, in the revolutions of other states, have successively disgraced the triumphs of the different parties.

The government of the United States has no model either in ancient or modern times. These new societies have not had, like all those of which history has transmitted any account, to encounter the difficulty of proceeding from experiment to experiment, from revolution to revolution, in order to discover the constitutions and systems of government best calculated to ensure their happiness. They consulted experience; they sought light in the writings of the many sages who have meditated on the means of rendering mankind happy. They did not despise the theories which prejudice and interest had so long ranked among chimeras. They conformed their institutions to those wise inspirations, and since their adoption no class of citizens, probably no one citizen, has desired any changes in the fundamental laws, though the forms have been ameliorated, when time has led to the discovery of defects.

It was in the midst of arms that these constitutions were framed, and even the presence of the enemy did not

permit the adjournment of this important work. We find
in them, however, all the marks of mature reflection.
The Americans examined, first, whether it would not be
advisable that the states should be divided into thirteen
communities, free from every federal tie and only united
by a perpetual alliance, which would in no respect alter
their several rights of independent sovereignty. Those
who would have preferred so complete a separation were
in a very small minority; they founded their argument
on the certainty of a great increase in the population,
and on the difficulty of retaining by a common tie and
subjecting to common laws, states separated by such
great distances. But this form of government would
have rendered the revolution impracticable, because
there would not have been any concert in the efforts
to resist England; and, though success might have encouraged some isolated efforts, dissensions would soon
have broken out among these numerous republics.
This proposition was easily put aside. The necessity
of a strict, indissoluble union, the want of a single central government were generally acknowledged. It was
left to time and other circumstances to make such regulations as might be expedient, when the extension of
territory should require the formation of other states.

A proposition was advanced, on which, however,
there was no discussion, but which we will mention,
because traces of it are to be found in some of the
writings of the period. It was proposed to have only
one single republic and one single supreme government, directing from north to south all the internal

and foreign affairs of this vast society. In adopting
this form of government, it would have been indispensable not only to renounce many articles of the different
charters, which had become, by long habit, dear to
the people, but also to place the authority in the hands
of an aristocracy or of a monarch. But an aristocracy, whether hereditary or elective, would have destroyed that equality which was the fundamental principle of the revolution. The Americans would have
had less aversion to monarchy, had not time effaced in
their hearts every trace, however slight, of that affection which renders all things easy to royal authority;
moreover, they were not disposed to admit the fiction,
which reserves to the prince the merit of all the good
that is done, and makes the ministers responsible for
all the evil that happens. Far from concluding from
this doctrine that the king is a being incapable of doing good or evil, they would have feared that a bad
prince would end by adopting the maxim himself.

The republican system of government was chosen
with great unanimity. All the authority of the confederated states was concentrated, during the war, in a
single assembly; which was the only form of government that could have suited them while engaged in a
revolution.

The common danger then commanded general obedience; and the power of the enemy silenced all the
jealousies, which that of congress inspired. It was
quite otherwise after the peace of 1783; ambitious
views openly appeared in several of the states. Some

of them would have wished to have had their army, their little navy, and their ambassadors. Prudent men were aware that if the federal knot were thus relaxed, the union would soon be dissolved, and the republic placed at the mercy of internal cabals and European intrigues; that the authority of the general government would be in danger and always insecure, if it continued to emanate from that of the several states, and that it would, on the other hand, be complete and entire if it had its source in the individual vote of every citizen of the confederation. This great change was accomplished not without difficulty, but the separate states have, at length, become accustomed to confine their attention almost exclusively to the affairs of their internal or municipal governments. They confide other matters to the wisdom of congress, where every state has some of its citizens.

The cession of Louisiana has given rise to several acts of this great body; the new states obey it in the same manner as the old ones; and to understand the facts, which we purpose narrating, requires a previous knowledge of the principal regulations of the constitution of the United States.

A convention, held at Philadelphia in 1787, proposed certain articles to the confederated states, "in order," as they said, "to form a more perfect union, establish justice, ensure domestic tranquillity, provide for the common defence, promote the general welfare, and secure the blessings of liberty to themselves and their posterity."

This constitution was adopted on the 17th of September, 1787. A congress composed of a senate and house of representatives exercises such legislative power, as was delegated to it by the constitution.

The representatives must have attained the age of twenty-five years, and have been seven years citizens; they must, also, be inhabitants of the states in which they are chosen. Their term of service is for two years. There can only be one representative for forty thousand free persons, calculating in this number of forty thousand, five slaves as three free men, or 66,000 blacks as 40,000 whites. This proportion may, however, be changed after a new census. By the constitution the number of representatives cannot exceed one for every thirty thousand inhabitants; but each state must have, at least, one representative.

Every state sends two senators. They are elected for six years; they must have attained the age of thirty years; have been citizens of the United States for nine years, and be inhabitants of the state which elects them. The senators are divided into classes, so that one-third go out every two years.

The house of representatives impeaches for state crimes. The senate tries them. The concurrence of two-thirds of the votes is required for a conviction, and the judgment only extends to disqualification to hold an office under the United States. But the convicted party may be, afterwards, prosecuted before the ordinary tribunals, sentenced and punished according to law.

Congress assembles at least once a year. A majority of each house constitutes a quorum to do business. Each house makes its own rules, punishes its own members for disorderly behaviour, and, with the concurrence of two-thirds, may expel a member.

The senators and representatives receive a compensation, which is paid out of the treasury of the United States.* They cannot be arrested during the session, nor in going to or returning from the place of meeting.

They cannot be questioned elsewhere for any speech or debate in either house.

No senator or representative can hold any office under the authority of the United States.

The bills passed in the two houses are presented to the president, and become laws when he has approved them. He can refuse his assent; but the bill acquires the force of a law, if two-thirds of each house insist on it after the president has returned it with his objections. This is likewise the case, if the president does not state his objections within ten days.

Congress has power to impose taxes, to contract loans, to regulate commerce with foreign nations, among the several states, and with the Indian tribes, to coin money and establish post offices, to constitute tribunals inferior to the Supreme Court, and punish piracy and offences against the law of nations, to de-

---

* Eight dollars a day, or forty-two francs for each senator and representative. The allowance for travelling expenses is regulated by the distance, and is eight dollars for every twenty miles.

clare war, and grant letters of marque and reprisal.
It is also authorized to raise and support armies and
navies; but no appropriation for the army can be made
for a longer term than two years. It may call out the
militia to execute the laws of the Union and repel in-
vasions.

No money can be drawn from the treasury, except
by virtue of a law, and statements of the receipts and
expenditures are made public.

The presidents of the United States never omit,
when they enter on their duties, to proclaim the principles which they purpose following. The forms of
expression may be different, but the essential part of
the declaration always consists in an engagement to
be equally just towards all, without distinction of religious or political principles. Peace, commerce, and
friendship with all nations, render useless, in their opinion, treaties of alliance, which they, moreover, consider at variance with true independence. They engage
to maintain the authority of the general government in
its constitutional vigour, as the best guarantee of tranquillity at home and peace abroad, and to support the
state governments in all their rights.

They recommend to the people to be attentive to
the privileges of the elective franchise, to be obedient
to the decisions of the majority, and to support the supremacy of the civil over the military authority. They
promise to carry on the administration with economy,
to preserve the public faith untouched, to encourage
agriculture and commerce, its principal agent; and,

finally, to watch attentively over the education of the citizens, the free exercise of religion, personal liberty, and the independence of the press.

The expectations which these speeches afford become a contract, which is faithfully observed. To infringe or elude it would be to destroy the very foundation of the government, which is good faith. Jefferson, on being raised to the presidency of the United States on the 4th of March, 1801, declared that in order to leave to his family the legacy of an honoured name, he must thenceforth occupy himself exclusively with the public business and with the promotion of his country's happiness. His presidency lasted eight years, and history teaches us how wisely and successfully he responded to the appeal which he had made to himself.

The president and vice-president of the United States are named for four years. They are elected in every state by special electors, who are neither senators nor representatives, and who do not hold any office of profit or trust under the authority of congress. No person, except a native citizen of the age of at least thirty-five years, or one who was a citizen on the 17th of September, 1787, can be named president. This magistrate is commander-in-chief of the army and navy of the United States, and of the militia, when they are called into the actual service of the Union. He grants reprieves or pardons for crimes and offences against the United States, except in cases of impeachment. He has power to make treaties, with the advice and consent of the senate, provided two-thirds of the members present concur. He names, by and with the advice and consent of the senate, ambassadors, public ministers, consuls, and judges of the Supreme Court. He fills up all the vacancies that may occur during the recess of the senate, by granting commissions which expire at the end of the next session.

The presidents of congress, under the old confederation, had the title of excellency. It is now only employed with reference to the governors of states. This emphatic appellation is all that remains in the United States of the forms of flattery, which European courtiers borrowed from the East, and which their masters eagerly adopted.

The president and vice-president, and all other civil officers of the United States may be removed from office on an impeachment for, and conviction of treason, and other high crimes and misdemeanors.

Every thing that is within the scope of the powers of congress is forbidden to the separate states. They cannot, without its consent, lay any duties on imports, nor keep in time of peace troops or vessels of war, nor make agreements or compacts with one another, or with foreign powers, nor engage in war, unless actually invaded or in such imminent danger as will not admit of delay.

The privilege of *habeas corpus* cannot be suspended, unless, when in case of rebellion or invasion, the public safety requires it.

There is at Washington a power, which has neither

guards nor palaces, nor treasures: it is neither surrounded by clerks nor overloaded with records. It has
for its arms only truth and wisdom. Its magnificence
consists in its justice and in the publicity of its acts.
This power is called the Supreme Court of the United
States. It exercises the judicial authority in all cases
affecting the general interests of the United States, in
their relations with one another and with foreign nations. The members of this tribunal can only be removed from office on account of bad conduct, and after a trial. Their permanent tenure is an additional
guarantee of their probity and of acquirements, which
are every year increased.

They have original jurisdiction, where ambassadors,
ministers, and consuls, or states are parties. In other
cases, which are generally those in which foreigners
are parties against states or citizens, their jurisdiction
is appellate. This court has other functions, that already alarm some friends of liberty. But what have
they to fear from a power whose justice constitutes its
whole strength, which can, it is true, reduce the other
powers to inaction by declaring that they are proceeding contrary to the constitution, but which would raise
the whole republic against it, if its decision was not
clearly correct?

The Americans, supposing that they might profit by
the warnings of history, have multiplied the barriers
against usurpation and the abuse of power. Their constitutions contain as many prohibitory as positive enact-
ments. But, experience has proved that these fears

are ill-founded. Their rulers are more anxious to restrain than to extend their authority.

The confederacy may admit new states, and it gua-
ranties to all of them a republican form of government.

The case of changes in the constitution becoming
indispensable has been foreseen. At the same time,
provision has been made, by prudent regulations, to
prevent their being attempted without mature deliberation. Amendments can only be made on the proposition of two-thirds of both houses of congress, or by
a convention, called on the application of two-thirds
of the states; and in neither case can they become articles of the constitution till they have been ratified by
the legislatures or conventions of three-fourths of the
several states.

Some amendments were, in fact, proposed by congress. The most important related to points, which
the convention had so generally acknowledged and
practised, that it had deemed it useless to mention
them. Congress judged otherwise, and limiting its
own power, proposed to insert in the constitution that
congress should make no law respecting an establishment of religion, or to prohibit the free exercise thereof, to abridge the freedom of speech or of the press,
the right of the people to assemble and to petition government, or their right to be secure in their persons,
houses, papers, and effects. These provisions were
adopted as parts of the constitution; but they were in
full force before their adoption.

It is necessary to consider all the relations of the Union with the particular governments of the different states, in order to understand how this people have united with the civil and political liberty of every citizen, the force and energy required in those crises, which even the wisest governments cannot always avoid. It will, then, likewise be seen how it has been possible to adapt the forms of a republican and democratical government to a country of great extent, and to unite successively to the same central authority new territories and new communities, which, without losing any of their liberty and independence, are added one after another to the Union, and increase its strength. These communities will extend the limits of the nation farther and farther; but it is not probable that the advantages, of which we have spoken, will then be preserved, without a separation of the states. Whatever may happen, we have no reason to fear that the principles of liberty will be at all changed in any of the separate confederacies which may be formed. These governments are established for the happiness of the people; the people themselves watch them; they cannot forget their glorious destination.

Such is, then, the first duty of the congress of the United States. The democratical element does not prevail there in the same degree as in the states separately considered; its authority is not very different from that which in limited monarchies belongs to the throne. It has only a very small army: its powers are, however, sufficient, because it does not abuse them, but only exercises them for the public advantage. It has, consequently, never experienced that resistance, to which absolute governments are exposed; and, although attempts have sometimes been made to introduce dissensions into this great body, although it has been obstinately predicted that the states will soon separate and make war upon one another, the spirit of the union has been more powerful than all the efforts made against it, and this union has never, perhaps, been seriously threatened except on one occasion, which was in 1815, when the Hartford Convention sent deputies to congress instructed to denounce the president. They have, indeed, since contracted the reciprocal engagement of never divulging the secret causes of this proceeding. The steps taken by this assembly cannot be approved, and yet it must be acknowledged that it was composed of estimable men, whom the people had chosen, and that their error was not attended with the melancholy results which had been apprehended.

Montesquieu supposed that free states were the most exposed to tumults and revolutions; but this great man was only acquainted with those nominal republics, in which the citizens are divided into classes possessing unequal rights, The tranquillity which reigns in the United States is founded on the perfect equality of the citizens. When the republic is at peace, all the parts which compose it are equally benefited, because there are no classes whom peace distresses and for whom public calamities are a means of power and influence.

If war takes place, it is carried on with a common ardour, since all equally feel the wrong and injury which occasioned it. There are twenty-four different states, but the American loves them all as his native land; and in whichever of them he happens to reside, he considers himself in his own country.

Conflicts have sometimes arisen between the authority of congress, the depositary of the federal power, and that of the separate states; but the states have more frequently been disposed to transfer to the general government a part of the power, which was reserved to them. The federal constitution emanates as directly from the citizens of each republic, separately considered, as its own particular constitution. It is this common origin of the powers of the confederation, which constitutes its strength. I shall hereafter mention the cause which may affect the good understanding between the states and congress. With this one exception, every thing moves on without difficulty, and while this submissiveness to the laws attests their wisdom, it assures us that men, associated in society, have made real progress in the career of happiness.

A remarkable proof of the good intelligence prevailing among the different parts of the Union, was not long ago afforded by the war of restrictions carried on between the United States and England. In such struggles victory belongs to the party which can longest support its own losses and embarrassments; and it was the perseverance of the Americans, that triumphed over the prohibitory system. They obeyed laws that were in opposition to all their habits, but these laws were enacted by congress. It was the United States that suggested to England the renunciation of her famous navigation act, and of that exclusive system, which she had so long maintained. Free commerce makes the law for enslaved commerce.

Of all the great powers, no one is in a situation more independent of the events and vicissitudes, which affect the repose of nations than the United States. Is a negotiation commenced? Their fundamental principle is equality in the stipulations. They have declared that they will only treat on this condition. The other party must conform to it or break off the conferences.

Skilled in navigation, and in all the sciences which constitute the pride of Europe, long initiated in all the operations of English commerce, freer now than even their former masters, they will soon become their equals, and England sees in them rivals, that will presently be more formidable to her than the maritime powers of Europe have ever been.* England, by her conduct towards the United States, first revealed to Europe the degree of power to which this new people had, in a very short time, arrived. She would not have willingly allowed the world to know how much she requires their friendship; but their forced participation in the

---

* The merchant tonnage of the United States, corresponding to the British registered tonnage, was, in 1827, 1,650,607 tons, while that of the United Kingdom, during the same year, is stated in the parliamentary returns to have been only 2,105,605 tons.—TRANSL.

profits of navigation and commerce seemed to her the presage of still greater losses. She believed, a few years ago, that there was yet time to arrest their progress. The haughty demeanour, threats, and seductions, which were in turn employed, only warned the United States to provide for their safety. War was declared almost simultaneously on both sides. But the English received from it a harsh lesson, and eagerly entered on negotiations for peace. A treaty, signed at Ghent in December, 1814, put an end to hostilities without destroying the germs of jealousy and enmity. Negotiations have been prolonged to this day. If the English bring forward a *sine qua non* proposition, the Americans immediately advance another. Reciprocity, their rule in commercial matters, is as simple as its forms are various. They have their discriminating tariffs, their countervailing duties, and their inflexible prohibitions. They have also an act of navigation, but different from the one which was so long regarded by England as the tutelary genius of her commerce. " We do not ask," they say, " that your ports should be open to us, we are far from requiring that you should change your laws, but leave us ours." England has at length learned that the military marine of the Americans is no longer an object of contempt, and that concessions must take the place of exactions. She no longer pretends to visit American ships, in order to take from them their own sailors; she has mitigated the rigour of her maritime code. The English West Indies cannot dispense with the productions of the United States; in vain have

the English, alleging the long possession of the colonial monopoly, wished to retain the profits of this navigation: in vain have they hoped that Canada would
provide for the wants of their islands. At length to
preserve, at least, in appearance, the prohibitory system, they established an entrepôt in the Bermudas.
The Americans, who had, at first, consented to this arrangement, again showed themselves inflexible, and
would not listen to any modification of the principle
of an entire reciprocity. Then, the colonists of the
islands, who bear all the inconvenience of the interruption of the intercourse, cried mercy; and, in 1822,
an act of the British parliament admitted these dreaded rivals to a direct trade from the United States to
the West Indies, and even to the English colonies of
North America. These concessions appeared to have
been made with regret, and had hardly gone into effect
when the president of the board of trade thus expressed
himself·in parliament:* "We wished to sustain with
the United States a contest of discriminating duties :
after persevering in it for several years we were obliged
to yield; but having entered into arrangements, founded on reciprocity, with the American government, we
could not refuse to extend this long neglected principle
to the European powers." In listening to these words,
one would have thought that the conciliation was complete; but, in the month of July, 1826, new orders in
council withdrew from the Americans the participa-

* May 10th. 1826.

tion which had been granted them in the colonial trade. Thus they refuse and grant, and retract again : the issue of the debate is always uncertain; and, if we believe men profoundly instructed in these matters, the interests of navigation, which England places above even those of commerce, are already endangered by the liberal system, to which the United States have since 1822 brought that power.*

Their vessels traverse all the seas of the globe, without any where undergoing those humiliations which English pride has so often attempted to impose on all flags and to which some have been obliged to submit. The United States have never supported such indignities. Their principle is that the flag assimilates a ship to the soil of the country to which it belongs, and renders it equally inviolable. The slightest insult would be immediately resented and revenged.

They respect the rights of other nations, and their rule is not to interfere in their affairs. The pretensions which they believe to be well founded they assert with firmness, and they will never maintain them feebly; for their strength increases even whilst the contest is kindling. Although disarmed, liberty puts them on an equality with the nations that continue under arms during the most profound peace.

Those treaties of alliance, those conventions for mutual succession, so common among the German princes, are scarcely known by name in the United

* March 19th, 1827. Parliamentary Debates.

States. They can only suit sovereign families, who set little value on the rights of the people, whom they often involve in quarrels of succession, which seldom result in the improvement of their condition.

If, during the recess of the legislature, difficult circumstances require a prompt decision, the president does not fail to take it, and he is sure of being approved, if he has done a necessary act.

There is more timidity even in absolute governments, where the ministers are only responsible to the throne. In critical circumstances, they seek to gain time, and proceed by expedients. The difficulty, in the meanwhile, grows worse: from being unwilling to submit to reason, they are obliged to yield to force; and they lose all, because they attempted to retain all.

The president, and the two houses of congress, are without mysterious archives. They have no concealed and corrupting police, nor have they those secret reports so convenient for calumny, so dear to the calumniators, so dangerous to the persons who are the object of them, and, oftentimes, even to those who employ them.

All the affairs of the republic are brought as soon as possible to the knowledge of the public, without any exaggeration of the favourable condition of some, or dissimulation respecting the bad state of others. And why should congress and the administration plot together to deceive the public, or to conceal from them untoward truths? They are themselves part of the public.

Measures which interest the state are never adopted till after the most mature deliberation. They are determined on in the presence of the citizens, and during their discussion, those whom they interest seldom fail to make known their opinion by publications, which the government never disregards. Publicity is only disagreeable to those who would wish to make their private interest prevail over that of the public. When the law is once promulgated, no one would dare either to prevent its going into effect, or to elude its operation.

The history of every day also cites to its bar the president and other rulers, and does not await their deaths before pronouncing judgment on them. Their acts are public, posterity already exists for them, and the powerful as well as the weak are disgraced or commended, while they are still alive.

The two houses profess the same political doctrines. There is no essential distinction in the character of the speeches delivered in them. Both are equally animated by a desire to render their country happy. More calmness and gravity are, however, observed in the deliberations of the senate, and more warmth and vivacity in those of the representatives. This difference does not exist without a cause. The functions of the members of the senate last for six years, and those of the representatives only two. The latter are therefore the most anxious to bring themselves into notice.

Congress, in its uniform course, ever consistent with itself, is not at different times under the control of dif-

ferent factions; but, in order to remain free from those
internal agitations, from which the most happy country is not always exempt, it constantly and sincerely
practices the maxim, that "the end of government is
the happiness of society."

There is henceforth no fear of the triumph of despotism over liberty: the old nations of Europe would
not have experienced this calamity, if, instead of simple traditions, subjected to human and variable passions, at the will of an ambitious chief and of an ignorant multitude, they had had constitutions written by
sages, and confided to the vigilance of all the citizens.

It is thus that the fundamental laws of the several
states of the Union are preserved. The sincerity and
clearness with which they are expressed, do not leave
any opportunity for sophistical interpretations, and the
introduction of obscure expressions, with a view of
hereafter arbitrarily explaining them, has been well
guarded against. If there are some differences in the
state constitutions, they are only to be found in the ex-
ternal forms of the government; they all have justice
and equality for their foundation: what is just at Boston, is so at New Orleans.

There is not a town or village, in which are not to
be found some men well instructed in the true interests
of their country: and if to the intelligence required in
those who engage in public affairs, they join the virtues of the citizens, they will infallibly be raised to the
first employments. Any man may be called to the
highest office. The great Washington had been a

surveyor; Franklin a printer's journeyman; Jefferson a planter. Magistrates chosen by those whom they are to govern, are easily obeyed. The infrequency of crimes and punishments is the proof as well as the consequence of the docility of the Americans to the restraint of the laws.

A long peace does not weary them. They do not fear that idleness will render their youth seditious; a war undertaken to employ them, to diminish their number, or on futile pretences, would seem to them sacrilegious, and would be impracticable. They have, at length, discovered the solution of the problem proposed so many centuries ago to the meditations of philosophers, and submitted to the experience of statesmen: "To render communities happy with the least restraint and at the smallest expense."

Congress disposes of an adequate revenue, arising principally from the duties paid on the importation of foreign merchandize, and from the sale of public lands that do not belong to the several states. It does not aim at raising the imposts as high as the patience of the contributors would bear; but the legislature ascertains where the comfort of families requires it to stop, and one of its fiscal principles is, that the less that is demanded from the people, the more will the improvement of their condition hereafter facilitate the augmentation of the impost.

No one would dare to propose to increase the public revenue by the establishment of a lottery or of gaming tables, or by any other means that would have the effect of enriching the state by corrupting the morals.

Smuggling could be very easily practised on coasts which are six or seven hundred leagues in extent, and are scarcely guarded, but every one knows that in the employment of the public revenue, there is neither profusion nor parsimony. All have an interest in preventing fraud, and it rarely occurs.

No useless pomp encircles the magistrates. Economy, so discredited and ridiculed in our courts and capitals, is held in honour at Washington, and even in those parts of the United States where large fortunes are not rare. Habits of simplicity are there more effectual than sumptuary laws would be. The senate and house of representatives have no guards but their door-keepers. The repugnance of the people for pomp and empty parade does not, however, prevent their being always disposed to incur expenses for objects that are truly useful to commerce, navigation, the safety of the confederation and of the different states, and sometimes even for such as conduce to public ornament.

Although they have no neighbour to fear, they have not neglected the military art. This science is taught at West Point, upon the Hudson, by officers of reputation. Some able engineers have been educated at this school.

The arsenals and magazines of the Union, and of the several states, are well supplied and carefully kept in order. Fortresses are in the course of construction.

From the year 1792 to 1812, the United States enjoyed a neutrality, which, though disturbed for a period, was the cause of the prosperity of their commercial marine, which, in its turn, has been the origin of their naval power.

The churches and other buildings destined for religious worship, those for the magistrates and legislative bodies, the court houses and prisons, are admirably adapted to their objects.

Manufactures, always prohibited to the dependent colonies of Europe, have made great progress in the United States. England, in spite of her jealous vigilance, has been robbed of those machines, by the aid of which she so long controlled the commerce of the world. Independent America has imitated and improved them. Her tariffs have for their principal object the protection which every rising branch of industry requires. The interests of the treasury are considered as only secondary. The decided advocates of protection to manufactures would even wish that the revenue should not be regarded at all in this matter.

The Americans consider public debts as one of the diseases of modern societies, and they are far from believing them a necessary evil. They have made large loans, but always with a view to an advantage proportionate to the magnitude of the burden which they were imposing on themselves; and these debts have been faithfully extinguished.

They know that loans are a slow poison, the sweetness of which has often deceived and seduced states-

men who were reputed wise. If the United States bor-
row, the reimbursement is always fixed at a definite
time, and the engagement is never eluded.

The Americans are constructing canals and roads
two or three hundred leagues in length, through territories still occupied by savages. Regions, whose waters flow to the north, will soon communicate with
those whose rivers have their courses to the south.
There will be a connected navigation from lake Michigan to the Illinois river, from lake Erie to the Wabash.
Steam boats will approximate the gulf of Mexico to
that of the St. Lawrence, and New Orleans with the
city of Quebec; both of which places were once under
the dominion of France, though the latter has become
English and the former now belongs to the United
States. The noble communications of this description,
so justly extolled in Europe, are not superior to these
new undertakings. Favourable to commerce and agriculture, they have another advantage which had never
been contemplated: they have, as it were, brought near
to one another men whom great distances separated.
It has not been possible to stifle all the sources of jealousy; but the confederation which had only laws for
its guarantee, is now cemented by private and common
interests, which are continually in contact, though
without clashing.

Such is, in its political economy, the conduct—such
are the maxims of a new republic—strong by its present greatness, and which increases so rapidly in resources, that its friendship is every year more to be de-

sired, its enmity more to be dreaded. It is no longer one of those nominal republics to which an equal rank with kings was refused, and whose ambassadors were admitted, as if by tolerance, after those of crowned heads. It would be vain to attempt to assign to it an inferior rank, to subject it to a different law of nations: as independent and sovereign as the monarchs on their thrones, this republic has on every occasion maintained an equality with them, and it will, undoubtedly, be sufficiently wise never to aspire to elevate itself above them.

Those whom representative governments annoy or incommode assert that they are the most costly of all political systems, and they find credulous or interested persons to repeat the opinion after them. It is true that employments may be multiplied and salaries augmented by the aid of this maxim, and those who propagate it have often their share in the profusion. But the example of the United States proves that it is false, and demonstrates that order and economy are the most certain means of avoiding public bankruptcies and preventing revolutions.

Among the circumstances that threaten Europe with the transfer of her pre-eminence to the new world, there is one which merits the particular attention of statesmen. The North American republics are disposed to make none but judicious expenditures. Europe, on the contrary, delights in extravagance, and most of her governments are only preserved by expedients.

It is, however, from England that the United States have received the first elements of representative government; but they have perfected it to a degree which cannot be attained in Europe, at least without great struggles. In America representation has its primary source in the suffrage of individuals, the right to exercise which is unattended by any embarrassing or difficult conditions. The possessor of a cabin and a few acres of land, participates by his vote equally with the proprietor of ten thousand acres, or the wealthiest merchant, in the formation of the legislative assembly of the state in which he resides.* Every thing which interests the community or its several classes is discussed in these assemblies, as well as in voluntary meetings, which, formed independently of the magistrates, and free from their inspection, proceed with as much regularity as those prescribed by law. Habit and a sort of routine there occupy the place of statutes, and without the least constraint the minority receive the law from the majority. It is by means of these private assemblies, that the knowledge of the true interests of the state is disseminated. It is thus that we find dispersed over the whole territory more

* At the late election for the American president (1828) nearly twelve hundred thousand votes, in a population of about twelve millions, were given either directly for the *electors*, whose duty it is to choose that officer, or for the members of the legislature, by whom, in two states, the presidential electors were named. In France, where the number of inhabitants is three times as great as in the United States, less than eighty thousand persons take part in the election of the chamber of deputies.—TRANSL.

than ten thousand persons, enlightened in the public interests and affairs, familiarized with the most important matters of legislation, conducting themselves in the assemblies of the smallest villages with gravity and decorum, and submissive to the orders of a president or moderator, who exercises, without effort, an authority in some sort absolute. It is either in the public assemblies or in these informal meetings, that those who are one day to govern the state are instructed in political eloquence. It was at them, rather than at the bar, that four lawyers, who became successively presidents, learned to discuss public affairs, less after the rules of oratory than according to those of wisdom and reason.

If, from the view of the general confederation, we pass to that of the constitutions of the individual states and of their relations with congress, we see, with admiration, these great bodies move harmoniously together, without any difficulties of a serious nature arising between the superior and subordinate governments.

The legislative, executive, and judicial authorities in the several states are invested with all the powers that have not been delegated to congress. Every state legislates in civil and criminal matters. During fifty years that this order of things has existed, it has been attended with none but happy results. As the confederation is enlarged, the power of congress, at the same time, increases. Some of the states have, of their own will, limited their extent and population, and aban-

doned vast territories, where other states are already
formed. The preamble to their act of cession was
thus expressed: " Whereas nothing under Divine Providence can more effectually contribute to the tranquillity and safety of the United States of America than a
federal alliance on such liberal principles, as will give
satisfaction to its respective members, we renounce our
claims, &c."

The wars which are excited among other nations of
the world by fanaticism, ambition, cupidity, and that
restlessness, which torments them and makes them
suppose that tranquil happiness cannot be the lot of
man, will never trouble the people of the United States:
not that all the individuals among them are free from
human passions; but the public councils are formed in
such a manner, that the decisions of government are
always dictated by the general interest. A country,
which will be larger than Europe, and which is composed of so many different states, enjoys a peace that
promises to be perpetual, and to fulfil the bright vision
of the good man.

The officers and magistrates are not named for life.
The duration of their functions depends on their conduct: their authority is defined by the laws with so
much precision that abuses are very rare, and can be
promptly repressed. A principle of representation,
which flows neither from hereditary rights nor from
any fictitious source, constitutes the force and energy
of the different magistracies: powerful in effecting good,

they are without strength to oppress, and for this reason disorders and tumults, when they occur, are never dangerous.

It has been for a long time held as a maxim, that temporary and elective magistracies are only adapted to states of limited extent and small population. The experience of the United States has proved that this is an error. If it sometimes happens that bad choices are made, the remedy is in re-election; and the experience of more than half a century has demonstrated that it is an efficient one. Thus, the example of the United States presents itself, whenever the object is to prove that liberty is in every respect beneficial and that it can never do harm. It likewise puts an end to the hopes of those whom this liberty alarms, and who can now no longer deny its benefits.

The judges, senators, and ministers are not, however, wiser or more intelligent in the United States than in many other countries. They have their weaknesses and their prejudices; but they ought to have them to a less degree than those who are raised to magistracies by accident, intrigue, or purchase. They have also an advantage which men elsewhere placed at the head of affairs do not possess: the laws and the publicity of their acts, submitted to the censure of all, render it a matter of necessity with them to be always just, always impartial; not to give employments, except to the most worthy, and never to sacrifice the good of the state to private passions and the interests of individuals. A sincere probity can alone ensure the public

8

confidence, which is ever ready to distinguish true merit from false. Impostors and hypocrites would soon be unmasked. Thus even, though accident should raise to an important post a man inclined to be bad, he would be obliged to govern like those who were naturally virtuous, or he would not be able to retain his office.

These wise institutions are protected for the future against the ravages of time: free presses preserve them, and are a more effectual defence than the towers of the Louvre or of London. Under this guarantee, more powerful than was ever the authority of the tribunes, we may be assured that the benefits of social order will be durable. A moderate republic will never become an absolute democracy, and we may add, in reference to other countries, that, with the liberty of the press, a royal government can never degenerate into despotism.

It is objected, however, that these presses may, at least, endanger the peace of families, and injure individuals in their private interests. It is but too true that they have often served the cause of calumny; but this is an evil, which even the most severe prohibitions have never prevented; and the remedy for the injury which they can do is, under the system of liberty, effectual as well as prompt.

The shafts of calumny, so justly compared to poisoned weapons, resemble them likewise in this respect; the most ferocious savages scarcely dare to discharge them lest they should be turned against themselves.

Different from most things, the liberty of the press is improved and strengthened by time, and becoming every day more useful, it likewise becomes more innocent.

That it was not so during the early periods of the American revolution, we readily admit; but the enemy was then present. Royalty had warm partisans, and the presses on both sides were actuated with an equal violence. Jefferson himself was for a moment alarmed by it. At this time an animated contest is going on; and it is possible that a good citizen may be injured through the too great warmth of the conflict. But the blows soon become harmless, and without taking the trouble to justify himself, he may, by maintaining silence, leave to a pure life and irreproachable conduct the care of his defence. There is no example in the United States of a journal open to irreligious essays, to the recital of licentious anecdotes, or to offensive personalities having been long supported. The disgust of the readers administers justice with more promptitude and with more certainty than even the tribunals; so much do this people love decorous truth, and so ready are they to distinguish it from falsehood. Among them nothing is so rare as prosecutions for libel before the courts.

There is then nothing which the liberty of the press cannot improve; and the Americans would think that their government had lost its reason, if they saw in their budget an appropriation destined to the corruption and recompense of the journalists. To pay fo-

reign newspapers to publish articles carefully prepared
for them, would seem at once culpable prodigality and
a useless act of folly. I will, however, admit that this
liberty is not without danger for all kinds of ministers.
Cardinal Wolsey said to Fisher, "If we do not put
down the press, it will put us down." Fisher replied,
" Let us do our duty as good and wise ministers, and
not fear any thing from the malice of the press. If
we would interrogate ourselves, we would find how
greatly we are indebted to the freedom of the press;
when it notices not only our past faults, but also
warns us of those to which we are exposed. I am
accustomed to receive advice from the press. It is
a torch which sometimes hurts my eyes; but, were it
extinguished, I should think that a bandage covered
them."

The diplomatic correspondence is printed by order
of congress, as soon as it can be published with propriety. The cases are rare in which it is kept from the
knowledge of the citizens. The newspapers, by their
eagerness to gratify curiosity, often anticipate the most
diligent couriers. They sometimes give as much information as secret and ciphered despatches. These
frank communications are a great innovation in the relations which foreign powers entertain with one another; and those who preside in the cabinets of Europe
have not yet been able to accustom themselves to read
in the gazettes of Washington, the conferences which
they have had with the American envoys. One would
think that they are afraid of showing to what an easy

science the art of good government is reduced. The despot Wolsey then had just motives for dreading free presses. It is only ministers, who are truly worthy of the name of statesmen, that can, with a tranquil eye, contemplate their action and brave their power.

The right of public petition, the recourse of oppressed weakness to a wise and efficient protection, is rarely exercised. It exists, it is not a vain formality, it is adequate to restrain unjust magistrates, and this means of defence is rarely employed, because it may always be resorted to.

These republics which, fifty years since, still bore the names of colonies, provinces, and plantations, have already founded several new republics. They gradually extend themselves; cities and towns rise up in all directions, without being menaced by any citadels or castles that overlook them from the neighbouring heights. Uncultivated districts, which were scarcely inhabited by a few Indian families when Washington and the two Jumonville met and fought there in 1754, have been changed into rich fields, and are now as well peopled as many countries of Europe.

All the difficulties which a community experiences at the moment of its formation, disappear before equal, just, and free laws. The rapid progress of these settlements is without precedent. Families associate together, at their own instigation, and without any superior sanction, to go and occupy the uninhabited lands that are situated even beyond the territory of the states of the Union. These self-created societies name their own magistrates, their officers of justice and police, put themselves in a state of defence against the Indians, and make their own regulations, to which they render an exemplary obedience. One of these associations, composed of three hundred families, took possession of a district lying on the borders of the Red River; the new society had not to encounter the weakness of infancy; it possessed from the beginning the vigour of mature age, and, a few years after its establishment, it became part of one of the new states.

It may be remarked, in reading the acts which have emanated from congress during a period of thirty years, that they have seldom for their object the old states of the Union. The names of some of them do not occur a single time. Firmly established on imperishable foundations, they have only occasion for local laws, and even these are not numerous. Their constitutions being formed, and their fundamental principles well consolidated, the protection of congress is no longer necessary to the old states. On the other hand, it is constantly occupied with those new communities, which have been founded to the east and west of the Mississippi, since the general peace of 1783. At first districts, then territories, and at length admitted to the rank of states, they enjoy all the rights of the old members of the confederacy. Until they have attained their strength, it is necessary that congress should guide them, instruct them and defend them from their own errors; and, as its authority is only exercised for their advantage, it rarely encounters any obstacles. From whence, indeed, could resistance arise? These new communities are not like ancient or modern colonies formed by a superabundant population, of which the mother country wished to relieve herself, by sending it beyond the seas to people desert or savage countries. The new states that are formed exist by themselves and for themselves, without being subjected to the state from which the emigration proceeded, and without alarming it by their complaints and their insurrections. The system called colonization is at an end. It would be vain to attempt new enterprises of this sort. No people are either sufficiently rich or sufficiently powerful at sea to imitate what the English have done in New Holland, and the settlements which other nations would form there would only have with Europe the relations of commerce and navigation, not those of political subjection. To attempt at this day to found dependent colonies, is to waste, without advantage, human life and public treasure. Year after year, however, these attempts are prolonged, and the fear of admitting that we have been deceived might have prolonged them indefinitely, if the United States had not declared that they could not hereafter approve such attempts in America.

France, England, and Spain have all of them in turn, through jealousy, prevented the rival nation from founding new colonies. War was near breaking out in 1770, on account of the Falkland Islands, and more recently on the subject of Nootka Sound. It was tacitly agreed that these countries should remain desert. The Americans, more just and more powerful in these regions, wish that they should be peopled, and they proclaim, at the same time, with a sort of authority, and perhaps with too much haughtiness, that they will not henceforth suffer any European colony to be established in the new world. Thus another Europe, a Europe truly free, rises up in this vast continent; and, before the end of a century, the United States will count one hundred millions of inhabitants of the white race. Whether they remain united in one single confederacy or separate into several, the forms of government which they have adopted do not leave any opportunity for ambitious aggrandizement, and the wisdom of their laws will preserve among them a friendly understanding. If Europe must lose her pre-eminence, she can never lose the many treasures of science and intelligence which centuries have accumulated. It depends on the people and on their rulers to retain advantages which will not be inferior to those of any people of the world. They will be retained, if, instead of repelling the advantages of a just liberty, we only avoid its extravagance and licentiousness; to effect which, education wisely and universally diffused throughout the nation is the most certain means.

There is not one of the American constitutions which does not contain provisions relative to education and the advancement of science. Commissioners, chosen by the inhabitants, superintend the education of youth. They with pleasure see them instructed by a master, who has a wife and children, and who teaches them by his example to become one day good heads of families. They have avoided, with great care, confiding them exclusively to military men, to lawyers, or to priests. They believe that to form useful citizens, it is proper that a young man should enter into society without factitious inclinations, without prejudices, and free to choose the profession to which his taste and natural capacity incline him.

Their legal code was originally drawn from that of England. They have not yet entirely removed the confusion with which huge commentaries have embarrassed the distribution of justice in the mother country. They are, however, engaged in this reform, and even now their laws no where offer any traces of feudality. The rights of confiscation, of primogeniture, the disabilities on the inheritance of aliens exist no more. There are no longer advantages accorded to men to the prejudice of women in the distribution of family estates.

The law once promulgated, the tribunals have not to fear either the influence of the legislative or executive power. Oral evidence, which the laws of other countries only admit with a great deal of caution, is very much used in the United States. It is not observed that any abuses result from it, and this respect for the declaration of a witness, who has taken an oath to tell the truth, is a homage rendered to the national probity.

The general constitution and those of all the states prohibit with great care the granting of any titles of nobility. There are, in fact, in the United States, no institutions which distinguish certain hereditary classes, and yet it would not be rigorously true to say that they do not acknowledge high descent. There are in the country several families, settled there at a remote period, who are known by their hereditary merits. It is never in vain that citizens have recourse to the counsels and assistance of these patricians. Their virtues are revered, and a homage is paid without difficulty to a nobility, which consists in services rendered to individuals and to the republic. The names are important, so long as the children preserve the high qualities of their fathers. It is on this condition that all the good which their race has done is carried to their account. If they forget the duties which their eminent standing imposes on them, they fall lower than those who had never been thus distinguished; and other citizens, the names of whose ancestors are unknown, become equal in reputation to the most illustrious men of their time.* Such is nobility in America, and it has in it nothing that offends the principles of equality. This exception is the work of those, who, in abolishing the nobility of birth, have preserved that of virtue.

At the opening of a session of the legislature in one of the recently formed states, the governor addressed the following words to a numerous auditory:†

---

* Nam genus et proavos et quæ non fecimus ipsi
  Vix ea nostra voco!   OVID. Metam. lib. xiii.

† Our author is mistaken as to the source from whence the extract in the text is derived. It is taken from a speech delivered by Judge Story, in the Massachusetts convention of 1820.—TRANSL.

"In our country the highest man is not *above* the people; the humblest is not *below* the people. If the the rich may be said to have additional protection, they have not additional power. Nor does wealth here form a permanent distinction of families. Those who are wealthy to-day pass to the tomb, and their children divide their estates. Thus property is divided quite as fast as it accumulates. No family can, without its own exertions, stand erect for a long time under our statutes of descents and distributions, the only true and legitimate agrarian law. It silently and quietly dissolves the mass heaped up by the toil and diligence of a long life of enterprise and industry. Property is continually changing like the waves of the sea. One wave rises and is soon swallowed up in the vast abyss, and seen no more. Another rises, and, having reached its destined limits, falls gently away, and is succeeded by yet another, which, in its turn, breaks and dies away silently on the shore. The richest man among us may be brought down to the humblest level; and the child, with scarcely clothes to cover his nakedness, may rise to the highest office in our government."

The development of all these advantages is no censure on those old governments, which, formed many centuries since upon other plans, can only be improved slowly and after mature deliberation. We cannot, indeed, but be astonished at the progress which these last mentioned states have made in spite of the many obstacles that they have had to encounter. At the same time, let us not hesitate to acknowledge that if the

Americans have profited by the learning and wisdom
of Europe, the people of the old world will, in their
turn, receive like benefits from America. Her example
and recent facts have taught us that liberty does not
diminish the vigour and energy necessary for the execution of important enterprises. If it does not enervate
republican governments, there is no reason to fear
that it will become a principle of weakness in limited
monarchies. Already, in spite of resistance on all
sides, the laws are improved, and wise monarchs have
acknowledged that the throne can only be solidly established by uniting the interests of the prince and the
people: placed on any other foundation, it may be
continually shaken by internal agitations and attacks
from abroad.

The constituent assembly of France made some
progress towards great improvements, when, forty
years since, in obedience to the almost uniform instructions of the people, it reformed our legislation. It
had intended to consolidate the throne in a country
where the royal government had very deep roots. But,
although its work was in part destroyed, the spirit of
it is preserved, and no effort will prevent France from
again becoming, what indeed she now already is, a monarchy limited by a national representation.

The Christian tenets are acknowledged throughout
the whole extent of the United States. Whatever may
be the modifications which distinguish the different
sects, most of them are discreet and conform to the
wise laws which the first author of our religion taught

to man. Divided on articles of faith, they agree in the principles of morality. Some of them, however, profess extravagant maxims, which would be dangerous, if a real toleration did not soon consign them to contempt and oblivion. The government only interferes to hinder doctrinal points from invading the domain of civil or political legislation, and to keep the priests from meddling in matters foreign to religious worship. It is not less attentive to prevent every establishment of an ecclesiastical jurisdiction; and all matters which belong to that jurisdiction, in England, are cognizable in America by the ordinary tribunals.

Several of the state constitutions, in interdicting public functions to priests, could not comprehend in the exclusion their eligibility as members of the two houses of congress. A few clergymen of different tenets are to be seen in them, and, in 1823, the territory of Michigan named, as its delegate, a catholic priest. These nominations are productive of no inconvenience, because the representatives are citizens before they are priests.

But the exclusion of ecclesiastics from office is more important in the United States than elsewhere, inasmuch as there are not in their villages, as in most of those of Europe, local bailiffs and lords of manors, who, by the authority which belongs to their rank and situations, balance that of the priests. Without the provision in question, ministers of religion, armed with the power which they possess over the consciences of their parishioners, might induce them to regulate their opinions and public acts according to the interests of the prevailing sect.

A few remarks respecting the catholics will show the happy effects of a general toleration. The catholics, while the country was under the English government, were subjected to a great many restraints in the exercise of their religion. Even after the peace, and as late as 1790, there was only one mission for the whole United States. At this day there are ten bishops under a metropolitan. The catholic societies of females have been greatly multiplied. Among those of the men, the establishments of the Jesuits are the most remarkable. In 1806, a brief of the pope permitted them to preach, teach, and administer the sacraments. The progress which this society soon made would have been deemed dangerous in any other country, and congress well knew how formidable its ambition and intrigues had rendered it in Europe; but it did not suppose, it could ever become so in a country where fanaticism can never stifle liberty of conscience; and it apprehended no danger from forming a college of Jesuits at Georgetown into a university, with power to confer degrees in all the faculties. A timidity, the cause of which is understood, has prevented this enterprising society from resuming its true name; but congress would not have opposed any obstacle to it. It only sees in its members the propagators of a morality useful to the community and to the instruction of youth. Every one knows that they blindly obey a foreign authority to which they are secretly subjected. This occasions no alarm, for full confidence is reposed in the goodness of the constitutions: nor will there ever be any reason to repent of this policy, since the press is free and can never be enslaved by the Jesuits.

It is said, that in the city of New York alone, where there were only three hundred catholics twenty years since, there are now twenty thousand. The increase is principally to be ascribed to the emigration from Ireland and Germany.

There is not in America a single statesman who is not persuaded that social order can only be maintained by the aid of religion, and it is to the establishment of a dominant sect that opposition is alone made. Where all kinds of Christian worship are mutually tolerated, there is no longer but one religion.

What an advantage for legislators, who lay the foundations of a community, not to have to contend against the errors and licentiousness of paganism, the intolerant theocracy of the Hebrews, or the fanaticism and ignorance of the Mussulmans! Jefferson and Franklin found Christianity established in the United States. Of all the systems of religion that have been proposed to the human understanding, no one is more conformable to the rules of sound morality, no one better calculated to render man happy, and of this the sages of America have borne honourable testimony.

The catholic, the quaker, the methodist, the unitarian, and the English episcopalian are all equal before the law. Toleration is not as in Europe an arrogant indulgence of one sect towards another; it is a perfect equality among all. Religious quarrels, without the interference of government, are always innocent. To appease the combatants, it is sufficient to let them alone.

The acknowledgment of one God, creator and benefactor, is the characteristic which distinguishes the civilized and educated from the savage and ignorant man. Many Indian tribes have hardly a vague idea of the Deity, or of the immortality of the soul. All of them are in a truly wretched state.

On the other hand; men, who enjoy social advantages, acknowledge that it is to Providence that they are indebted for them. The state of New York modified its constitution in 1821, and the new act commences by a homage rendered in these terms to the Deity: " We, the people of the state of New York, acknowledging with gratitude the grace and beneficence of God, in permitting us to make choice of our form of government, do establish this constitution."

Thus we see that the Americans, after the example of kings, found the power of the state on divine right; this they do with great propriety; for to make men happy is an obligation imposed on rulers, which should be placed in the first rank among eternal truths, and it is to Providence that they must be indebted for the ability to perform this duty.

An article of this constitution proclaims liberty of conscience, and the one which follows is expressed in these words : " Whereas the ministers of the gospel are, by their profession, dedicated to the service of

God and the care of souls, and ought not to be diverted from the great duty of their functions; therefore no
minister of the gospel or priest of any denomination
whatsoever, shall, at any time hereafter, be eligible to
or capable of holding any civil or military office within this state."

The Americans have not to dread those conquerors
who, in Europe, have arrested and destroyed the advances of civilization. In this situation a people will
never retrograde; it will always advance, in spite as
well of the ambitious as of the intolerant, and henceforth nothing in the world can deprive the United
States of the honour of having first presented a perfect model of the best federal constitution.

At the period of the cession of Louisiana, at the west,
only the mouths of the rivers tributary to the Mississippi were explored. Twenty-five years have scarcely elapsed, and the United States already form, on the
coasts of the Northern Ocean, commercial establishments, which are the germs of states that will be
founded there before the end of the century. They
have given Columbus's name to one of the principal
rivers of those regions,* thus restoring to this great
man the honours unjustly decreed to Americus Vespu-
cius. Congress has not announced the design of hereafter extending the confederacy to the Pacific Ocean;
but its intention of securing to these territories a republican government cannot be doubted. This system

* A ship from Boston, called Columbus, first entered this river
in 1791.

is about to embrace, by a general impulse, the whole
of the new world; and it may be predicted that the several states, which we see rise up in the south, will
make the constitutions of the United States their mo-
dels.

Already strong by the irresistible power of numbers,
the new republics of the southern continent advance
in the career of independence, which they have conquered. They have their own principle of legitimacy,
which is the will of all. They have just proclaimed
that " nations exist by the decrees of a universal and
Divine Providence, and that rulers only derive their
power from the will and consent of the people." They
may be divided among themselves on questions of political expediency; but in the midst even of the tumults incident to new states, not a sigh of regret towards their powerless and decrepit parent-country
ever escapes them.

Even the Indian population is but thinly scattered
over the immense space which extends from the great
river to the Western Ocean; and the Americans find
few obstacles in pushing on their settlements over regions, which, in spite of the richness of the soil, have
been long useless to man. Whatever may be our respect for the ancient rights of property, it is difficult
to admit those of a single family to ten square leagues,
where ten thousand persons could be supported in
abundance.

The Indians maintain that liberty, with the obligation of labouring and obeying the laws, would be real

slavery. Europe has wished to civilize them in her way, by giving them her laws and her learning: the efforts of three centuries have not tended to meliorate their condition; while the advances made, three or four centuries before the discovery of America, towards the introduction of social order in Peru and Mexico, prove that, left to themselves, reason would have probably conducted the aborigines, by other roads, farther than our example has carried them.

The neighbourhood of these tribes and the view of the profound misery which harasses them make us appreciate still more the advantages of good laws. On one side, we see society in all its vigour, splendour, and beauty; on the other, a state of weakness, the inevitable consequence of the absence of knowledge and social order. The aborigines, witnesses of the benefits of civilization, have profited little by it to meliorate their own situation. Our example has not yet taught them that the division of lands among families is the first condition of the social state, that the smallest proprietor loves the field which he has cultivated, and that this attachment to the soil is the surest guarantee of the repose of society. The savage has no property except in his bow, his canoe, and a few ornaments, with which he delights to decorate himself in battle or on holidays. Less free than is supposed, he is dependent for his daily wants, and is unacquainted with the most ready means of supplying them. In the civilized state, science and experience teach these means to man, and his well-being

advances with his knowledge. It is for a contrary reason, that error and ignorance are so favourable to
despotism. The Indians do not, however, live wholly
without restraint: travellers have found none of them
in that primitive state, which we have called the state
of nature, and in which even the ties of families do not
exist. Their liberty is not the right of doing whatever
they wish: they have customs which occupy the place
of laws, and which, though they are ferocious and sanguinary, serve to moderate their excesses. A savage
came one day to Sinnamari and said to Simapo, his
chief, " Aricapoto has killed my brother; I have killed
him, and his son likewise." I heard Simapo reply,
" You have done well." " I am going also," continued the Indian, " to kill the brother of Aricapoto."
Simapo forbade him, and the injured man stopped his
vengeance.

Reason has banished from our codes what was for
a long time called public vengeance. The civil authorities no longer punish except to restrain the guilty and
to deter, by example, others from the commission of
crime. But, among savage tribes, vengeance is pursued by families, and the public power sometimes in-
terposes its aid. If the murderer takes refuge among
a neighbouring and friendly nation, it is obliged to deliver him up; or, should it refuse and protect him, the
refusal almost always becomes a cause of war.

The aborigines are not ignorant of the horror, with
which the custom of eating prisoners of war inspires
us, and I have never been able to obtain any precise

information from those whom I have questioned on this subject. But the vagueness of their replies, or their silence, has led me to believe that our exhortations have not put an end to the practice. It is more common among the northern than the southern tribes.

From the earliest period, of which we have any account, the savages of North America have been formed into distinct tribes; every one of which constitutes a small nation. These tribes, whom a common interest should have united against the Europeans, are distinguished to the west of the Mississippi by four languages, which bear no common resemblance. Each language is again divided into dialects, which are so different that it may be concluded that the separation into small tribes dates back several centuries. They, nevertheless, resemble one another in their customs, and above all by the profound ignorance, in which they obstinately continue.

These independent societies are seldom at peace; and in their wars it often happens that the most powerful, after having conquered the weaker tribe, either incorporates it with itself or exterminates it.

Some savages have pacific dispositions towards the whites. Indemnified at a small expense for the lands which they abandon, tolerated on their own territory, they observe the new-comers without interrupting their progress. The community which is forming is like a spectacle presented to their curiosity; they conceive neither jealousy nor alarms respecting it, and, for trifling indemnities, religiously observe the peace of which

the calumet is the symbol. A subsidy, though annual, is only in their eyes the price of the land which
they abandon. If they received it as the condition of a
peace, they would consider their tributaries interested
in breaking the treaty.

Others have warlike dispositions and are not so easily subdued. Those who are still scattered along the
borders of the Mississippi and of the numerous streams,
from which that river receives its waters, might arm
twenty thousand warriors, but they are in no condition
to unite their forces: they fear the Americans, who are
so superior to them in numbers and skill. They were the
auxiliaries of the English in the war of independence,
and in that of 1812. They continue since the peace
to trouble their neighbours, less indeed by constant
hostilities than by frequent surprises on their extreme
frontiers. If they attack with fury, it is not so much to
avenge the loss of their territory, as through hatred of
civilization. They are irritated at the progress of social
order, as soon as they fear that it is intended to subject
them to it: they detest its advantages, because they
cannot reconcile them with a liberty which cannot en-
dure control. Rather than subject themselves to the
restraints inseparable from the civilized state, they fly to
a distance, abandoning their native soil and the abode
of their fathers. But whether they remove or whether
they remain, when war is once terminated by a treaty,
they lay down their arms and only resume them for the
chase. To go during peace to visit their chief or their
friends, with the bow or the tomahawk in the hand,

would appear to them as unreasonable as to march to battle without arms.

There are with them only two principal employments—those of hunters and warriors. Some, it is true, have become shepherds: it is thus that a more regular society begins to be formed; wherever there are masters, there are servants. The chief, then, has new wants, he wishes to be better fed than on bread and milk, to be better clothed than his servants, and a simple sheep-skin will not satisfy him. It is, at this first step, that the civilization of many of the Indian tribes stops.

The aborigines have more readily adopted our vices than our virtues, and the whites afford them, indeed, more opportunities to imitate bad than good examples. Those who trade with them are seldom capable of giving them lessons of morality and good conduct. It is thus that these Indians, familiarized with some of our usages without our morals, have become the most depraved and the most miserable of men. Those, who are for the first time known by the whites, exhibit more hospitality and frankness. A very few of the tribes have begun to cultivate land, and to exercise the rudest mechanical arts. But it has been in vain attempted to teach them our religion and its mysteries. They listen to the missionaries without interest, and without assenting to their doctrine or refusing their belief. What has been narrated by the authors of " The Jesuit's Letters," what the English and other missionaries have published, has not been confirmed by the testimony of any traveller. A child six years old, educated among us, is better acquainted with the Christian religion than an Indian who has been instructed in it for ten years. The whole of the Old and New Testaments has been translated into the language of the most numerous of these nations.. Two editions of the work have been printed in England; but not one Indian even knowing how to read could understand this book, in which there is scarcely a word in ten that belongs to his language. It is a useless labour, dictated by ignorance, or perhaps undertaken to deceive persons indiscreetly zealous for the conversion of the savages.

The missionaries, whom zeal still carries into these regions, are soon convinced that they have given too much credit to the narratives of those who have preceded them.

An imposter, who represented himself as a missionary, was hospitably received by the tribe of Osages. He pretended to have the gift of exorcism, and taught the people in what this power consisted. Several demoniacs presented themselves, and were delivered. Many sick then came from neighbouring tribes, with whom he had the same success; but these men, proud of their supernatural cure, became turbulent, and quarrelled with one another and with the other families. The sachem or chief of the Osages considered it prudent to send away the pretended exorcist, and, as soon as he was gone, there were no more men possessed with devils.

We may predict with confidence, that, in less than

two centuries, all these nations will disappear from the two Americas. History and geography will scarce preserve their names: if a few feeble fragments of their races should still remain, they will be confounded with the whites, and there will not be seen on the same soil two rival people, one subject and conquered, the other prolonging the right of war, and perpetuating in peace the power of victory.*

The Americans hold it as a maxim of their public law respecting the Indians that it is advisable, with a view to their own happiness, to remove them to the right bank of the Mississippi; that their existence, as separate and independent tribes in the bosom of the confederacy, is incompatible with the civilized state. The Cherokees and Creeks first resisted this policy, by which it was intended to drive them from Georgia, and they have not been enticed away either by pecuniary grants or offers of a more extended territory in the western regions. The negotiation is, however, still going on.

"An attempt to remove them by force," (said Mr. Monroe, in a message to congress of the 30th of March, 1824,) "would in my opinion be unjust. In the future measures to be adopted in regard to the Indians within our limits, the United States have duties to perform and a character to sustain to which they ought not to

* Travellers have given statements of the population of all the Indian tribes, that inhabit the regions to which the United States will extend in advancing towards the great ocean. Their researches fix the number of souls at 534,656. These calculations are necessarily very uncertain.

11

be indifferent. My impression is equally strong, that it would promote essentially the security and happiness of the tribes within our limits, if they could be prevailed to retire west and north of our states and territories. Surrounded as they are, and pressed as they will be on every side by the white population, it will be difficult, if not impossible for them, with their kind of government, to sustain order among them."

The cession of Louisiana will facilitate to the Americans of European descent the execution of the greatest designs. They have already made, in a very few years, more progress towards happiness and civilization than Asia has made for many centuries. This they have done, because they have founded the social state upon its true basis; because they have been the first to find out that the face of the world is changed by the great discoveries of modern times—the mariner's compass,—the art of printing, and the liberty of the press,—the abolition of the slave trade,—steam navigation and the many other conquests of science and wisdom, whose utility can no longer be called in question.

A steam boat can ascend from the mouth of the Mississippi to the junction of the Yellow Stone with the Missouri, a distance of eight hundred leagues. Mines of coal, the indispensable auxiliary of this navigation, are found near the banks of the rivers, and beds of this combustible are almost on the surface of the earth.

The territory washed by the great river and its tributary streams is in general fertile, and is in extent three or four times the size of France.

The governments of Greece and Rome, which were called republican, were very different from these new republics. Did they wish to form a confederation among themselves? Nothing was more difficult, inasmuch as they had not the same institutions, and frequently not even the same customs. There is not only more rapid and frequent intercourse between Boston, Charleston, and New Orleans, than ever existed between Corinth and Athens, or between Rome and Syracuse, but their respective views are much more easily made to accord.

Newspapers constitute a power unknown to antiquity: they put questions and give answers, they have millions of readers, and the orators of Rome and Greece from the height of a tribune could only address five or six thousand auditors. A journal is read calmly, and families peruse it during the leisure hours of the morning. There is no reason to fear from the reading of newspapers the sudden and unexpected tumults, which an impetuous tribune could excite in the public square. The ancient republics were almost always concentrated in cities; the American republic, of homogenous elements and uniform laws, exists in villages as well as in large cities, and extends over an immense continent. Its progress will not be limited even by the shores of the vast regions discovered by Columbus. This great man believed that he could go to India by moving round the globe to the west. His design is about to be accomplished. A navigable breach through the isthmus which joins the two Americas will one day be-opened to approximate Europe and Asia, and future ages will admire this triumph of science over nature.

Panama, or rather some other neighbouring city, will unite the deputies of thirty republics, or, to speak more correctly, of a great part of the globe. This council will confine its deliberations to the interests of America, as that of the Amphictyons did to those of Greece. But, without taking any active part in the events of Europe, the imperial and royal cabinets must expect that its example will have an influence there.

It is in the boundless regions of America that the human race may henceforth freely multiply. There, for many centuries, want will not throw impediments in the way of the conjugal union, nor will parents have to fear that the earth will refuse the means of support to those to whom they may impart existence.

Who can contemplate, without vivid emotions, this spectacle of the happiness of the present generation, the certain pledge of the prosperity of numberless generations that will follow? At these magnificent prospects, the heart beats with joy in the breasts of those who were permitted to see the dawn of those bright days, and who are assured that so many happy presages will be accomplished. I had that good fortune.

I have readily yielded to the pleasure of rapidly sketching the picture of this new people, but I will not venture to assert that they are secure from all contingencies. Their union now constitutes their strength, and yet there are between the northern and southern states, principles of division which in many cases embarrass the most prudent statesmen. The northern states were founded by the puritans, those of the south by the cavaliers or royalists. A century and a half has not effaced the traces of this difference of origin: an hereditary antipathy will one day perhaps be the cause of a separation that will not be effected without a great shock. The arts and navigation are honoured in the north-eastern states, the southern are principally devoted to agriculture. Hence the sources of rivalry between the north and the south. Slavery is abolished in the north, at the south it is the principal means of cultivating the soil. Attempts are also now making to employ the slaves as mechanics and in manufactures.

The government of the United States holds, as an incontestable maxim, that public morality, like that of individuals, is founded on doing what is right, not what is expedient. This rule is not, however, applied to all classes of men without distinction. The blacks are an exception. Liberty only exists without restriction, and for all creatures endowed with reason, in seven or eight of the north-eastern states. In the other states, the enjoyments of the citizens and free inhabitants are the price of the oppression of a numerous class, and slavery is the condition of almost two millions of blacks. If this is in the southern states a means of riches, it is there, at the same time, a more horrible scourge than slavery ever was in Europe. Without repeating what has been re-echoed by so many voices, during fifty years, respecting the injustice and barbarity of slavery, I will point out the obstacles which, until the present time, have prevented the effectual cure of this great calamity, and the dangers to which the masters themselves are exposed, whether they either maintain slavery or abolish it.

It is acknowledged that to perpetuate it is to support in the bosom of every family enemies, who are but too well aware that the time of their manumission is arrived. They are impatient at the sight of three hundred thousand freemen of their own race, who, in the United States alone, were slaves like themselves. Irritated from seeing themselves in a state so different from that of their fellow-blacks, they sometimes engage in secret plots, and at other times assemble in large numbers prepared for revolt. The mere sound of the whip, the slightest punishment, makes a whole plantation foam with rage. Domestic plots and attempts of open force, alike to be dreaded, are motives for the masters to draw tighter the bonds of slavery. Humanity and justice, however, call for that manumission, which was formerly so useful in Europe. But it would have, in America, consequences which the emancipation of the serfs never produced. They, as well as their masters, were of the white race. No natural mark distinguished the free born man from the manumitted slave; the amalgamation was easy, and emancipation having put an end to all political distinctions, the others were soon effaced.

In America distinctions, humiliating to the emancipated slaves, still separate them from the white race. They have in many states neither the right of voting at elections, nor of giving evidence in courts of justice, except in trials among themselves. Excluded from public employments, and deprived of the opportunity of connecting themselves in marriage with the whites, they are only half citizens. They are every where held as a degraded race, and this opinion universally diffused, necessarily debases and corrupts them. Continual objects of the contempt of the whites, they in the end lose their self-esteem; elevated sentiments and the ambition of rising above this abject condition, are rare qualities among them. If some superior characters distinguish themselves, they are soon pushed back into the crowd: it may even happen that the advantages which they have received from nature, useless as virtues, are converted into vicious inclinations, which render them enemies of society.

In 1827, there were in the southern parts of the United States about 1,800,000 slaves, and at least 300,000 free blacks. The number of slaves was to that of free whites in the proportion of one to two in some states, and of one to three in others. The comparison of these numbers, and the difference of colours render it sufficiently manifest that a general manumission could not take place except to the injury of the whites, and with imminent danger to them. On the other hand, reason revolts at the idea of a mixed race, and of the degradation which would necessarily result from the amalgamation. To keep the two classes distinct, and let them equally enjoy the benefits of liberty, is to resolve on a civil war. Difficulties present

themselves on all sides. Means of rendering their increase less rapid have been sought in vain. The importation of negroes ceased in 1808, and since then the
white population has augmented faster than the black;
but, at the south, the climate is favourable to the increase of the people of African descent. Humanity
has, we are assured, rendered their treatment more
mild in most of the plantations. But it is still slavery.

Emancipation has become general in the northern
states, without being favourable to the increase of the
blacks. They enjoy there all the rights of citizenship;
but their number is so small, as to be scarcely remarked. This is the case from the states of Maine
and New Hampshire to those of Pennsylvania and
Delaware. But in Maryland and the other southern
states the number continually grows larger, and it has
doubled in ten years in many families of slaves. It
diminishes, on the contrary, after manumission, and
the white population increases. Slavery in all its rigours exists in these states; some have even thought
proper to prohibit emancipation. In other states, individuals have liberated all their slaves. Washington is cited among those who first set this example;
but it is acknowledged that this generous resolution
had its inconveniences, and the manumitted slaves, as
I have just said, only enjoy a part of the civil rights.
Their admission to the legislative assembly would lead
sooner or later to the emancipation of all. The existence of one of the two classes would be jeoparded; for nature, by distinguishing by an indelible

mark the blacks from the whites, has rendered a sincere reconciliation impossible, and there would always be reason to dread the extermination of the weaker party. In the meantime, imperfect liberty by the side of complete liberty is, for the people of colour, slavery itself. Alarmed by so many dangers, some statesmen have attempted, since 1815, to form on the western coast of Africa a colony of free blacks born in America, and thus restore to this part of the world the inhabitants whom America formerly received from thence. For this purpose, expenditures have been liberally incurred. But the result has disappointed the hopes that were, at first, entertained. The blacks themselves regard this exile as the climax of their misery. Whether it arises from affection for the country which rejects them, or from fear of finding slavery in Africa, there were scarcely four hundred persons in this colony in 1826; the founders, however, begin to flatter themselves that their perseverance will triumph over all obstacles, and they have been encouraged by the last reports which have been made to them of the condition of Liberia.

In 1823, Boyer, the chief of the republic of Hayti, also invited these affranchised blacks. Offers of hospitality, and the certainty of obtaining grants of lands seemed calculated to attract them. About three thousand were induced by the prospect thus held out to them; but they were idlers, without means, who expected to live in St. Domingo, wholly without labour. The government of Hayti was soon tired of these useless and exacting guests. President Boyer was obliged to withdraw the advantages which he had announced, and the republic gained by sending them back, at its own expense, to the United States, from whence they had come. Finally, it has been proposed to assign to the free blacks a territory in America, situated to the west of the Rocky Mountains, and at a great distance from the whites. This project has met with the strongest opposition, and has not even been put to the trial. The entire race detests the whites, who have so long oppressed them. Such neighbours would, at a future day, be more to be dreaded than the savages. The proximity of the republic of Hayti inspires the United States with just and lively alarms, and they refuse to acknowledge the independence of the Haytians, because they are of the same colour with their slaves. When the designs of nature have been violated for many centuries, the best intentions every where meet with difficulties.

The abolition of the slave trade has palliated these evils; but they are always very great ones, and while the whites are themselves suffering inconveniences from the faults of their forefathers, the slave remains without consolation. Another distressing consideration is, that slavery constitutes a perpetual cause of division. The inhabitants of the north hold it in detestation, and those of the south wish in vain to deliver their country from it.

This irritation was manifested in an alarming manner, when the time arrived for admitting into the Union the territory of Missouri, which, with those on the right bank of the Mississippi, formed a part of ancient Louisiana. The inhabitants seriously reckoned among the rights of man, that of possessing slaves. The opponents of slavery reproachfully asked them in reply; "Do you, who enjoy all the inestimable advantages of liberty, while slavery still afflicts the neighbouring states, do you wish to introduce it in a new state? These regions, which have never seen slaves, will receive from you an institution that has become the horror of the world, and is the most abominable one that has ever dishonoured society."

The Missourians answered, "That their want of slaves was manifest, and that necessity made the law, that congress ought not to interfere in the formation of a state constitution, except with respect to its republican character." They added, that, "if it was intended to oppose obstacles to their happiness, they would be able to do themselves justice."

The general constitution of the United States has excepted such questions from the number of those on which it belongs to congress to pronounce. It discusses, but does not decide them.

Some ambitious men would have seen, without regret, these discontents produce two independent confederations;—one to the north, the other to the south. They believed it possible to introduce in the northern section a government conformable to that of England. They would have been resigned to even have had, instead of hereditary chiefs, only presidents for life. The south would have preserved its laws.*

If the separation had taken place, it would not have overturned the most beautiful monument of liberty that mankind has ever erected; but the strength which union necessarily gives to growing states would have been lost, and England would probably have seen, without regret, a division in the bosom of the only maritime power that she has reason to dread.

After three years' discussion, the menace of this separation made the partisans of slavery triumph. It was authorized in Missouri, on condition that the slaves introduced there should come from the other states of the Union.

Other causes will weaken for a still longer time the advantages offered to Europeans in this part of the new world. If no property attaches them to the soil of Europe, or, if tired of exhausting their strength in the cultivation of a few acres of land, they go to America in quest of extensive plantations, the clearing of the

* On matters of opinion, where he has differed from the author, the translator has not in general deemed it within his province to offer any comment. He cannot, however, be accessory to the publication of this book in America, without alluding to the mistake, that is entertained abroad respecting the views of those who took part in the Missouri controversy. Without referring to the merits of the question, it may be confidently asserted that no member of either house of congress, during its discussion, looked to the separation of the Union as a consequence of the vote that he was about to give. In both the parties to which that dispute gave rise, were to be seen men of the purest patriotism and most elevated views, who honestly differed on a point of public policy.—TRANSL.

land will require on their part indefatigable courage. The more fertile the land is, the more reason is there to fear its unhealthfulness. Those dreadful maladies, from which Europe is not even at this day exempt, produce fatal and rapid ravages in countries where new clearings expose to frequent changes of temperature and great humidity. Fevers, as dangerous as the plague, have within a few years appeared in those regions. Friends, even neighbours, cannot easily visit one another. It is sometimes necessary to renounce for a long season that social intercourse, which in our poorest villages renders the greatest misery supportable. To the tediousness of solitude are joined the rigours of winter. Rains and drought endanger the existence of the newly arrived planter. He has settled in the neighbourhood of a river, the shores of which he has seen enriched with green meadows. Twenty years of peaceable possession have successively encouraged him to enlarge his estate. But a scorching summer comes on; melted snows descend in torrents from the tops of the mountains; the brooks suddenly swell the rivers; the waters rise in a few hours to fifteen or eighteen feet above their natural bed; one day destroys the labours of long years; flocks, barns, and dwelling houses are all carried off by the flood, and the planter is not always able even to save himself and family.

Other emigrants begin to settle, without having provided necessaries to support them after a bad harvest. One description of insects destroys their crops, while others, more to be dreaded, attach themselves by swarms to the labourer engaged in clearing the new land, and by their many acute stings occasion torments unknown in Europe. The lands near the Missouri are sometimes torn up by frightful earthquakes. When the swellings of this river unite with those of the Mississippi, they destroy the embankments which nature or art has formed along their shores: the inundation enters through vast breaches, and extending thirty leagues from the river, kills the cattle and lays waste the cultivated fields.

Of all the inconveniences to which a family commencing a settlement is subject, the neighbourhood of the savages is most to be dreaded. Some are ferocious, and disposed to acts of treachery even in the midst of peace, and carry on war for the most futile causes. Some tribes preserve the horrible custom of eating their prisoners. The settlers are obliged, after the fatigues of the day, to keep guard against sudden attacks during the night, and they sometimes watch in vain. The Indians look out for the moment when the head of the family is absent, in order to cut the throats of his wife and children: they carry off or disperse the cattle, and set fire to the barns and crops. It has been vainly attempted to meliorate their customs by education. Ignorance is dear to them, and from Algiers to the hut of an Osage, ignorance has for its companions barbarism and all the vices.

We see in our sacred books man already civilized and religious from the very origin of the world. The brutishness of the savages obliges us to assign them, if not a more ancient, at least an unknown origin. It is with such tribes that we should commence the history of the human species. It appears to be still nearer its cradle among the hordes of Australasia than with the inhabitants of the banks of the Missouri. The difference, however, only consists in the degrees of ignorance and ferocity.

Every thing authorizes us to predict the end of these calamities, and the great events which are now passing in America, call the views of statesmen to an approaching melioration. This immense country is no longer dependent on Europe. From the Atlantic to the Pacific Ocean, rapid changes bear glorious testimony to the progress of the new world. Numerous republics daily make new advances, and it is thus that the guarantees of happiness in the civilized world increase. Let us, then, prepare for the most important changes. Let the hope of retaining the people in slavery by the aid of ignorance be abandoned. Let us submit, without regret, to a happy necessity, and let us acknowledge that limited and constitutional monarchies, far from having to dread liberty, will find in it their firmest support, and a bulwark against licentiousness and revolts.

I will explain, before concluding this essay, how the United States have been able to make so great progress in so short a time.

From the year 1787, the period when the constitution received its last form, those who presided over the public affairs directed all their attention to the means of securing the benefits of the new system for every class of citizens. The diminution of the fiscal charges appeared to them the necessary consequence of the return of peace. The long agitations of their revolution had ceased, and the resolution of faithfully paying the public debt tranquillized all minds. They were careful in all their negotiations not to contract any engagement that could oblige them to take part in European quarrels. But Europe came to seek them, and they could not remain isolated. It was in 1793 that those beautiful maxims of neutrality were proclaimed, the sincerity and advantage of which an experience of thirty-five years attests. Some, however, professed their admiration for the principles of our revolution, though they entirely condemned the acts which dishonoured it: others appeared as the open partisans of England. Congress was obliged to declare war rather against the directory than the people of France. Napoleon had hardly seized the helm, when he acknowledged the great impolicy of this war. He made peace in 1800, but the Americans only signed it on condition of preserving the principle of neutrality. This system secured, during five or six years, to their merchant-marine the commerce of the richest portions of the globe. England and France, however, soon irritated at their success and jealous of their great prosperity, attacked, both at the same time, navigators enriched by the quarrels of Europe. The American government, in the midst even of its harassing difficulties, effectually persevered in its maxims, and it was then that it was indebted to its navigation and commerce for the ascendency, which it acquired in all the affairs of America, as well as for its influence in those of the world at large.

The Americans consider taxes imposed on the introduction of foreign productions less burdensome, because they pay them only indirectly. Mr. Jefferson acquired great popularity by substituting them for direct taxes, real and personal. The war of 1812 obliged Mr. Madison, who succeeded him, to have recourse anew to internal taxation; but this people would consider themselves no longer free, if the weight of the imposts should become disproportionate to their ability. The opposition, which was then only the English party, again manifested great activity, when the return of peace in Europe put an end to this source of excitement. A new president of the United States, Mr. Monroe, found himself, in his turn, in a situation to lighten the internal taxes: he returned to import duties: his popularity equalled, and perhaps surpassed, that of his predecessors. It was under his peaceable government that the prosperity which now astonishes the world was seen to assume new channels. Agriculture, manufactures, and navigation animate all the parts of these numerous republics. The violence and animosities of the parties are appeased. Both have, by different means, equally served the state, and to the almost hostile dispositions which heretofore distinguished each of them has succeeded an emulation, which, by increasing the fortunes

13

of individuals, contributes to the general prosperity. The great riches acquired by commerce are applied to vast undertakings.

The population increases at a rate which surpasses all conjectures. The citizens enjoy an entire liberty of conscience, and no where are more families to be seen sincerely religious. Political equality is perfect among them, but it does not exclude the consideration and respect that are the attendants on personal services and merit.

To what are such glorious advantages to be attributed? To the goodness of the laws and the wisdom of the government.

We have seen Bonaparte overturn and build up thrones at his pleasure. If these sports of his prodigious power had for their object the debasement of royalty, he was greatly deceived. It is true that he has irretrievably destroyed that great mystery of power, which gave to monarchs a supernatural and almost divine existence. It is well known at this day that they are men like ourselves; but nothing can take from them a proud prerogative, a privilege, the loss of which would carry with it their destruction. I mean the obligation of being just, virtuous, and good, under the penalty of being deemed incapable of reigning; and it is thus that the maxim, so often false, " that kings can do no wrong," has become true.

In writing this essay it has several times occurred to me, that my remarks might be regarded in the light of allegories imagined by timid moralists to moderate the severity of their counsels. Such has not been my intention. How is it possible to assimilate the condition of America with that of Europe? How can we pretend to treat in the same manner a country where boundless and fertile territories will present themselves for more than a thousand years to the activity and wants of man and our Europe, where five families out of six are wholly destitute? I have wished, I say it frankly, I have wished that it should be admitted that there are no great distinctions between the principles of monarchies and those of republics.

The sovereign, whether called king, magistrate or people, can henceforth only govern by the aid of respect for political liberty. There cannot be mischievous magistrates in the United States, and it appears to me that there can no longer be mischievous kings in Europe. The love of nations for good kings is formed as naturally as that of children for their parents. The citizens of a republic have not the same kind of affection for their magistrates; but they have confidence in their wisdom, and they are attached to a constitution of which they every day experience the benefits. It depends on the princes, who now reign over the nations of Europe, to unite all these advantages. They will then taste the highest felicity which can be the lot of man on earth, that of making numerous generations happy. Educated in the maxims of wisdom and virtue, and firmly resolved always to practise them, they will soon inspire their courtiers with the love of them. The people in turn will be eager to follow the example of the prince. Morality will resume its empire. Expenditures for luxury and public festivals will cease to be held in honour. Whatever is extravagant in the different modes of government, separately considered, will be moderated by skilfully combining them, and all voices will unite to proclaim the excellence of monarchical government.

THE

HISTORY OF LOUISIANA.

PART I.

LOUISIANA UNDER THE SOVEREIGNTY OF FRANCE AND SPAIN.—
THE RELATIONS OF THE COLONY WITH SAINT DOMINGO.

THE

HISTORY OF LOUISIANA.

PART THE FIRST.

LOUISIANA UNDER THE SOVEREIGNTY OF FRANCE AND SPAIN.—
THE RELATIONS OF THE COLONY WITH SAINT DOMINGO.

THE history on which we are about to enter will not extend to the indigenous tribes, who, before its occupation by Europeans, inhabited the country now known by the name of Upper and Lower Louisiana. Researches, made with the greatest care, have not removed the obscurity in which their origin is still enveloped. Their traditions are contradictory. In the absence of authentic documents, analogies are sought between their respective languages and those of other people in different parts of the globe. So few have, however, been discovered, that are not either contested or accidental, that no inference can be drawn from this source. Many rude monuments afford certain indications of the existence, at a former period, of nations more populous and less ignorant than those which were found there by our ancestors. But even these more ancient aborigines had made very inconsiderable

progress in civilization; it is, indeed, doubtful whether
after having advanced some steps, they did not retrograde or become the conquest of a race still more barbarous.

About a century and a half has elapsed since a
French colony, under the name of Louisiana, was
founded on the Mississippi.   This settlement languished till within a recent period, and if the treaties
by which Napoleon ceded it to the United States offer
matter for a particular narrative, it is because the consequences of that measure are already of the greatest
importance to those states, to all America, and even to
Europe.

The sea-coasts, islands, and mouths of rivers have
long been the first spots noticed by those who have
gone in search of new regions.   The countries of
which we shall treat were discovered by exploring the
interior, at a distance of more than three hundred
leagues from the mouth of the great river which traverses them.

In 1672, the French, who had been settled a century
in Canada,* learned from the Indians that there were,
in the neighbourhood of the great lakes, the sources
of a river which flowed towards the south, crossing
magnificent forests: they called it Namesi-si-pou, that
is to say, the river of fishes.   They added that those

* The coasts of Canada were discovered by the French in 1504.
Cartier sailed up the St. Lawrence in 1534, and took possession of
the country in the name of His Most Christian Majesty.   Quebec
was founded by M. de Champlain in 1604.—TRANSL.

vast regions had never been visited by the white nation. One hundred and eighty years had elapsed since Columbus discovered America, and yet the course of this river was so little known, that many placed its mouth in the Vermilion Sea, between Mexico and California. Some intelligent travellers set out in 1673 from Quebec to explore this country; they descended the Mississippi to the mouth of the river of the Arkansas, which is to the right of the great river, and empties into it in about the 33d degree of latitude. The accounts which they gave, on their return, to Count Frontenac, governor of Canada, did not permit him to doubt the importance of the discovery. La Salle, his successor, was authorized to examine the country himself.

In 1679, proceeding from the north towards the south, he advanced as far as the river of the Illinois, which he called Seignelai, a title that it did not long retain. The name of Colbert, given to the Mississippi, was likewise soon forgotten. La Salle was accompanied by Hennepin, a Franciscan monk, a man of considerable acquirements, and inured to the hardships inseparable from travelling in unexplored regions. This person was subsequently intrusted with the charge of an expedition that went to the north, following the upper branch of the Mississippi; he published an account of his travels. Other similar works also appeared, all of which attracted general observation. These narratives contained no exaggerated statements, and Louis XIV. was led by them to entertain views in accordance

14

with the principles of the colonial system, which then
began to be adopted by all the maritime powers. A
more considerable expedition was determined on; and,
in 1682, La Salle descended the Mississippi with sixty
men. He stopped in the country of the Chickasaws,
where he built fort Purd'homme, after which he pursued
his journey and reached the great gulf. Delighted
with the beauty of the countries which he had seen,
he gave them the name of Louisiana. On his return
to France, he proposed to the government to unite to
Canada the discovery which he had just made, and
thus secure to France the sovereignty of the territories in the interior, situated between the northern sea
and the Gulf of Mexico, into which the Mississippi
falls. This vast and magnificent project was favourably received by Louis XIV. It was even at that time
perceived that the colony, which was about being
founded, might effectually contribute to the advancement of St. Domingo. La Barre, governor of Canada, was ordered "to keep up a regular correspondence
with the governor of the French islands in the gulf,
as these colonies might derive very great benefit from
a reciprocal trade in their staple productions." In
1684, it was supposed that advantage might be taken
of the truce, which had then just been signed between
France and Spain. La Salle set sail from La Rochelle
with two hundred and eighty persons, one hundred of
whom were soldiers, and with every thing necessary
for a new settlement. But, deceived in his reckoning,
he passed the mouths of the Mississippi without being

aware of it, and landed on the 18th of February, 1685, one hundred and twenty leagues beyond them in the bay of St. Bernard. He took possession of the country, built forts, placed garrisons in them, and the post of St. Louis acquired some importance. This brave officer was assassinated a year afterwards by some of the men employed in the expedition, who feared the severity which their culpable conduct had deserved. Other detachments, under the authority of the king of France, then reconnoitred these countries in different directions, and a few feeble colonies were established. War was declared between France and Spain in 1689, and interrupted these attempts till 1698, when peace was restored. During this interval, the planters, deprived of aid from the mother country, had made no progress.

In 1699, D'Ibberville, a brave and intelligent adventurer, was sent to the Mississippi to establish a new colony there and be its governor.* The country, of which possession was taken in the name of France, extended from the mouth of the Mobile, which crosses Florida, to the bay of St. Bernard. The occupation was hardly contested by the Spaniards, and the relations of amity and common interest which were esta-

* It is mentioned in a Memoir of the Count de Vergennes, laid before Louis XVI. during the war of the American revolution, that in September, 1699, the English, conducted by some French deserters, came in a vessel of twelve guns to explore the mouths of the Mississippi, but were compelled to retire by the Chevalier de Bienville, (the brother of D'Ibberville,) who commanded a post which was then already established on that river.—TRANSL.

blished at the beginning of the eighteenth century between the two kingdoms, put an end to any claims on
the part of the court of Madrid.   There was, however, no settlement of boundaries, and it appears, that,
on the one side, the Spaniards were afraid that, if they
were accurately described, they would have to consent
to some concessions; and, on the other, the French
were unwilling to limit, by precise terms, their possible
extension of territory.

At the same time, the English colonies, founded
twenty or thirty years before, were beginning to prosper.   Their charters granted to them the countries
which extend, between fixed parallels of latitude, from
the Atlantic to the Pacific Ocean.   These colonists
did not, however, advance their settlements beyond the
Alleghany mountains.   This chain and a few rivers
were the first boundaries between the French colonies
and those of England, which, having attained their independence, are at this day known as a powerful and
happy nation, under the name of the United States.
At the origin of their settlements, the planters, who
had come from England, finding fertile lands on the
sea-coast, or at a short distance from it, were in no
hurry to advance towards the mountains.   No one
then foresaw that these colonies, flourishing as a consequence of their good laws, would be the first to effect their independence; that their caravans would one
day extend beyond the Mississippi, and penetrate by
discoveries and settlements in the interior to the western coast, where it is washed by the Northern Ocean.

The laws given to the colony of Louisiana seemed to be intended to perpetuate its dependence, by checking the rapidity of its progress. The care of peopling this new and almost uninhabited country, instead of being placed under the charge of the superior departments of the government, was principally confided to the agents of the Paris police. Louis XIV., however, by letters patent of the 14th of September, 1712, granted to Crozat, a rich financier, the exclusive trade of the colony for twelve years. The names of the Mississippi, the Illinois, the Wabash, and the Missouri were suppressed in these letters. It was attempted to replace them by those of St. Louis, St. Stephen, and St. Jerome; but these designations, imagined by the authors of the letters patent, are no longer remembered. Those to which the Indians were accustomed have been preserved. It was not then known that the countries traversed by these rivers are several times as extensive as France; and the government had only a very vague notion of what it was granting. It made a present of the colony to Crozat, or rather it relieved itself of a burden. The limits of Louisiana were not afterwards much better defined; but agreeably to the practice, which certain maritime powers had made a principle of the law of nations, the effect of the occupation of the mouths of the rivers and streams extended to their sources.

Crozat showed that he was more of a statesman than the ministers. His plans were wisely conceived, and, so far as depended on him, he sent to the new colony only robust and industrious people, and some poor families, recommended by their good morals, who were indeed the only settlers that succeeded. Being, however, soon tired of his privilege, and of the great advances which the first settlements required, he renounced the grant. He gave it up in 1717, and the regent transferred the colony to the company of the west.* Louisiana did not rise under this new government from the state of languor in which it had remained since its discovery. But the exaggerations and falsehoods of a few travellers ascribed to it riches in mines of gold and silver superior to those of Mexico and Peru.

The deplorable state of the French finances led the people, and even the ministers, into these illusions, and they indulged them with an ardour which was soon communicated to other countries.

A foreigner of an eccentric mind, though a skilful calculator, had engaged the regent in operations the most disastrous possible to the finances of a state. John Law, after having persuaded credulous people that paper money might advantageously take the place of specie, drew from this false principle the most extravagant consequences. They were adopted by ignorance and cupidity, and perhaps by Law himself, for he was frank and high-minded, even in his errors.

There were, however, some men who were not deceived, and many members of the parliament of Paris opposed to these illusions the lessons of experience.

* The letters patent are dated August, 1717.

Their prudence was without effect. John Law succeeded in persuading the public that the value of his stock was guarantied by the inexhaustible riches that were concealed in the mines near the Mississippi. These chimeras, called by the name of system, do not differ much from the schemes that are brought forward in the present age, under the name of credit. Some have asserted that so many unjust operations, so many violations of the most solemn engagements, were the result of a deeply meditated design, and that the regent had only consented to it in order to free the state from a debt whose weight had become insupportable. We cannot adopt this explanation. It is more probable, that, after having entered on a pernicious course, this prince and his council were led from error to error, to palliate one evil by another still greater, and to deceive the public by deceiving themselves. Had they acted according to a premeditated plan, their artifice would have been even more disgraceful than the open injustice of the French directory, when in 1797 it reduced the public debt to one-third of its amount. Whatever may be the fact, the name of Mississippi was soon associated with that of bankruptcy, and it is only after the lapse of a century that the real prosperity of the country has effaced the infamy connected with its name.

We will not recall the consequences of John Law's system; it is sufficient to say, that, in order to give it an apparent consistency, he kept up the relations of the company with Louisiana. He had acquired for himself an estate of four leagues square, situated on the Arkansas, in the neighbourhood of the Mississippi. Its soil was remarkably fertile, and he had obtained permission from the regent to erect it into a dutchy.[*] He brought together about two thousand French and Germans, and embarked all the articles necessary to found a large settlement. But the year 1720 was the last of his ephemeral greatness. His projects in France having failed, the colonial enterprise experienced great embarrassments, and Dupratz calculates, "that the grant occasioned the loss to L'Orient of more than a thousand persons before the embarkation." The vessels which carried the remainder of the emigrants only set sail from the French ports in 1721, a year after the disgrace of this minister; and when he himself could give no attention to this wreck of his fortune. The grant was transferred to the company. The emigrants were landed at Biloxi, at Mobile, as well as on the banks of the Mississippi. Thus dispersed and deprived of the care of the person who had sent them to the country, most of them became victims to the rigour of the climate. It was easy to conceal from the public the calamities without number to which these Frenchmen were subjected. The communications with the metropolis were rare, and the only correspondence that was carried on was conducted with secrecy. Europe had not then any of those periodical writings, which,

---

[*] Dupratz's History of Louisiana, vol. i. page 170. Lower Canada is still subjected to the feudal system, and the barons and seignors are very much attached to their privileges and titles.

as they are often independent and honest in spite of all the shackles that are attempted to be imposed on them, ultimately give, by proclaiming the truth, information to governments as well as to the people.

Enlightened and prudent men formed, however, a sound judgment on the state of things in Louisiana. Father Charlevoix, a Jesuit, travelled through it in 1720, 1721, and 1722. The extreme discretion of the society of which he was a member did not permit him to tell every thing; but he is honest in what he says, especially in his relation of what he saw. When at the end of his contemptuous observations upon the pretended metallic riches of Louisiana, he speaks of the real riches which agriculture must one day develope there, when he predicts the degree of splendour to which the hamlet of New Orleans will rise, though it then had no other place but a tent for the celebration of the festivals and ceremonies of religion,* we cannot but admire his penetration and the solidity of his judgment.

" The mournful wrecks," says he, " of the settlement on M. Law's grant, of which the company has become the proprietor, are still to be seen opposite the village of the Kappas.† It is there that the six thousand Germans raised in the Palatinate ought to have been sent, and it is very unfortunate that they did not go there. There is not in all Louisiana a district better adapted to every kind of grain and the pasturage of cattle." It was at-

---

* New Orleans was founded in 1717.—Transl.

† Attakapas, almost opposite New Orleans, on the right bank of the Mississippi. Dupratz and Charlevoix do not agree as to the situation of this grant.

15

tempted to manage at Paris or Versailles plantations which could only prosper under the eyes of a proprietor, who was in a condition to make great advances. "The people who are sent there," Charlevoix further remarks, "are miserable wretches driven from France for real or supposed crimes, or bad conduct, or persons who have enlisted in the troops or enrolled themselves as emigrants, in order to avoid the pursuits of their creditors. Both classes regard the country as a place of exile. Every thing there disheartens them: nothing interests them in the progress of a colony of which they are only members in spite of themselves, and they are very little concerned with the advantages which it may procure to the state; the greater part are not even capable of appreciating them."

"Others have only found misery in a country for which they have incurred enormous expenses; and they attribute to it, without reflection, those evils which should be solely imputed to the incapacity or negligence of the persons to whom its settlement was intrusted." Then, alluding to the system, he adds: "You are not ignorant of the reasons which led to its being reported that Louisiana possessed in its bosom great treasures, and that its occupation brought us into the neighbourhood of the famous mines of St. Barbe, and of others still richer; from which we flattered ourselves with the prospect of easily driving away the present possessors.

The letters of this Jesuit were addressed to the Duchess de Lesdiguieres; and were kept very secret. If

they had then been published, the colony would infallibly have had a different destiny. but this correspondence only appeared twenty-five years afterwards.

Dupratz, author of a History of Louisiana, ingenu-
ously states, "that all the letters which were sent to
France were intercepted. We consulted together on
the means of forwarding them to their destination; we
discovered it, and availed ourselves of it."*

" The writers of history are obliged," he farther observes, " to treat with equal caution the dead and the
living; and, so delicate a matter is it to give utterance
to the truth, that the pen often falls from the hands of
those who are most disposed to be accurate."

A few colonists, however, returned to France; they re-
counted the misfortunes from which they had escaped,
and some truths began to make their way to the public. But, instead of taking advantage of this information, to found an agricultural settlement, the practice
still continued of transporting to Louisiana such vagabonds and prostitutes as could be removed. No measure was adopted for giving order to this collection of
drones; and if the instructions prepared at Versailles
ever reached the colony, they remained unexecuted.

A company for the Indies was created in 1723. The
Duke of Orleans was declared its governor. Its privileges embraced Asia, Africa, and America. In the deliberations of this association, composed of great no-
blemen and merchants, India, China, the factories of

* History of Louisiana, vol. i. page 166, 168, 169; printed in
1758, with the Royal approbation.

Senegal and Barbary, the West Indies and Canada were, in turn, brought into view. Louisiana holds a principal place in these discussions. Public utility, as much as the greatness and glory of the monarch, had, under Louis XIV., led to the favourable reception of the first proposals for the foundation a powerful colony. But nothing in the execution had answered to this intention; the new company was conducted with even less ability than those which had preceded it. We in vain seek in its acts the marks of the great colonial design formed by the government. We find at almost every page of the numerous registers which contain the deliberations of the association, tariffs of the prices fixed on tobacco, coffee, and all the other productions that were subjected to the monopoly. We also meet with speeches made in the general assembly, setting forth the flourishing state of the affairs of the company, which almost always terminate by proposing loans, to be guarantied by a sinking fund. But the sinking fund was deceptive: the debts accumulated to such an extent that the interest could not be paid, even by mortgaging the capital. Statements of accounts, bankruptcies, law-suits, and a multitude of documents prove that the operations, ruinous in a commercial point of view, were only profitable to a small number of the partners.

Nothing useful or good could in fact result from such a government. A single circumstance, selected from a mass, will enable every one to judge how far these abuses were carried.

The governor and the intendant of Louisiana were from the nature of their functions, in a manner interposed between the company and the inhabitants, to moderate their reciprocal pretensions and prevent oppression. But these magistrates were named by the members of the association. We read in its proceedings *that to attach the governor and the intendant to the interests of the company, there shall be assigned to them an annual gratuity and an allowance on the exports of the staple commodities to France.* The consequences of this system were most injurious to Louisiana, without enriching the stockholders.

A statement, prepared in 1726, made them creditors of the colony for the sum of 3,174,000 livres. This debt was not disputed by the colonists, but there was no means of constraining them to pay it. The public mind became exasperated, and the discontent manifested itself in revolts against the company. The superior council took part in them, and supported the cause of the inhabitants. Its acts were, however, reversed or rejected, and the members removed from office and recalled to France, which only increased the resistance of the colonists.

Eight or nine hundred soldiers were distributed in different garrisons; but they were not even adequate to subject the colonists to the police regulations in a country of such vast extent.

Another calamity,—misunderstanding with the native tribes,—afflicted the French wherever they settled. The friendly dispositions which the Indians had previ-

ously exhibited, changed in consequence of the bad
treatment that they experienced from the agents of
the company, who had quitted France, seduced by the
hope of obtaining the fortunes which Law had offered
to their cupidity. Instead of the metallic treasures
which the earth refused them, they traded in furs with
the Indians; and as they had been at first obtained at
a cheap rate, they wanted to have them at the same
price when they became scarce. It was, indeed, to the
French hunters themselves that this scarcity was to be
attributed. The Indians had always a sort of regard
for the innocent communities of beavers and otters.
They respected the peaceable families of these animals, whose habits deserve to be studied. Our hunters, on the contrary, appeared to take pleasure in destroying their retreats, and in penetrating even to the
subterraneous recess where the industrious tribe assembles after finishing the common labour.

In the trade with the natives, the French being
the stronger and more cunning party, first gave the
law; but injustice on the one side was followed by
resistance on the other. The French posts and garrisons were separated by great distances and could not
afford one another mutual aid. Petty wars broke out
in all directions, and lasted from eight to ten years.
Sieges and conspiracies have furnished to travellers
and historians materials for narratives, which would at
this time be without interest or utility. It is only necessary to remark, that in these quarrels the civilized
race was always unjust, which rendered in some sort

excusable the acts of cruelty that the natives committed. The war carried on against the Natchez, one of
those to which we refer, was attended with dreadful
consequences. This nation, peaceable before our arrival, was considered less cruel than the others. Irritated by the violent conduct of a French commander,
it had recourse to horrible reprisals. The governor of
the colony, conceived that the insurrection required
that a great example should be made; and the tribe
was exterminated with the exception of a few families
who escaped the general massacre, and were received
and protected by the neighbouring tribes. From time
immemorial, the Natchez had been governed by a family of chiefs whom they believed to be children of
the Sun. General Perrier, the commanding officer,
had them all carried away and transported to Cape
Français. The most important member of this dynas-
ty died there, a few months after his arrival. The
other *Suns* were maintained by the company for the
moderate sum of 1,888 livres 7 sous. The company
applied to M. Maurepas to defray this expense.* On
the 22d of April, 1731, the minister wrote to the directors, as follows: "I am not aware that there is any
other course to adopt in this matter, than to order the
survivors of these two Indian families to be sold or
sent back to Louisiana."

The registers of the company contain the following
resolution. "It was resolved to order the sale of the

* Registers of the Company of the Indies, deposited in the archives of the Court of Accounts. Appendix, No. 4.

survivors of the said two families of Natchez Indians."
At the very time that this order was given, the company was pretending to the glory of civilizing a people
whose chiefs were sold as slaves.

A few feeble detachments of French soldiers had
been sufficient to reduce these tribes, who had not yet
learned to use our weapons. They made war on them
in a great many places, and with pretty constant success. But these petty victories weakened the French
themselves. The chimeras of the system appeared no
longer, even to its greatest dupes, any thing but an audacious falsehood.* Louisiana had become rather a
burden than an advantage to the company. In 1731
it gave up its privileges to the king, who declared the
trade free to all his subjects. The company no longer
exists. To know what it cost the state during its continuance and since its dissolution, requires the produc-
tion of the registers of the time. In 1786, 5,250,000
livres were paid to its cashier by the treasury, to meet
expenditures for which there were no receipts; and this
payment was not the last.

It was in the Illinois country that a covetous ignorance
had placed those mines of silver and gold, which the
speculators said were richer and more abundant than
those of Mexico. Many families, dupes of an error

---

* On the 11th of August, 1728, the company surrendered to
the king all its rights against John and William Law. This proceeding was founded on a judgment in its favour for twenty millions, the value of which had only been furnished in part. The
king accepted the surrender the 3d of September following.

that was almost general, had transferred their fortunes there. They found, instead of treasures concealed in the bowels of the earth, a soil of almost inexhaustible fertility, one of the mildest climates in the world, several navigable rivers, all of which might have been decorated with the title of *beautiful river*, which was given to the Ohio. The colonists, recovered from their illusions, turned their attention to agriculture: this small part of New France from that time made considerable progress. Honest and industrious agriculturists, merchants in easy circumstances settled there; and such is the power of labour and property that the colony began, between 1732 and 1740, to assume a little more importance. It was at this time that the French government wished to realize the great plan, formed sixty years before, of uniting Canada and Louisiana, in the hope that this union would shut out from the English colonies all access to the regions of the west. Although no one was then at all acquainted with the countries which extend from the Mississippi to the Western Seas, their future importance was fore- seen.

The memoirs written on this subject have been preserved: their authors sagaciously prognosticate the high destinies of the two colonies thus united. They meet objections, and combat them all with one exception: no one of them foresees that these provinces, as they increase in population, and as a consequence even of their prosperity, must aspire to and finally attain independence. They notice the discontent with which

16

the plan of the union of Canada and Louisiana must inspire England; but nothing foretells to them that the provinces of English America will rise up and free themselves from the dominion of their mother country, and that the colonies conquered from France will one day be the only ones that Great Britain will retain on that continent.

When knowledge is once diffused, its progress can no longer be arrested; every thing contrary to nature and reason has become impossible. But, in the middle of the last century, the most penetrating minds, the most attentive statesmen were still far from foreseeing the independence of the English provinces.

After the peace of 1748, the French ministry took a deep interest in the settlement of Louisiana, and held out encouragements to all who wished to establish themselves there; but, at the same time, it greatly neglected the measures necessary to the success of such a design. The plantations should have been kept close together, and only gradually extended. But the colonists, on their arrival in these savage regions, thought themselves released from all restraint. The greater part of them did not even care about obtaining for their titles the sanction of a grant; it was not easy to restrain them from settling wherever their hopes or fancy conducted them. The Indians, however, were beginning to recover from the hatred with which the French had momentarily inspired them. The missionaries exerted themselves to make them Christians, and laboured with an admirable zeal to render them more humane. The governors did not allow fire-arms and strong liquors to be given in exchange for furs. They distributed to them cattle and instruments of tillage. It is true that those benevolent cares did not produce the desired effect; but the natives were grateful for them, and the French were then able to scatter themselves among them, without apprehension: they shared their idleness and their misery. They oftentimes married Indian women, and were then of right incorporated into the tribe. But the Indian families preserved with pride the foreign names of their new chiefs, which are still to be recognised, though altered by local idioms.

The chase, the amusement of civilized man, is the principal business of savages. The French, having become equally capable of fatigue with the Indians, were always ready to accompany them, and to second them in all circumstances; they therefore scarcely ever experienced the treachery so commonly employed towards the English, who attempted to form isolated settlements. But, besides the inconvenience arising from this dispersion, there was another obstacle to the progress of the French colony; the officers from Europe had, for the most part, only false notions with respect to colonial government. They were named through favour, and the most important places were oftentimes only filled by dependants, who accepted them in hopes of making or re-establishing their fortunes.

The expenses resulting from want of order had no limits: in no condition to provide for them, the heads of the government had recourse to paper money, the desperate resource of financiers without capacity. The following remaks on this subject are from a despatch of M. Rouillé, minister of marine.

"The disorder, which has for some time prevailed in the finances and trade of Louisiana, principally arises from pouring into the province treasury orders and other kinds of paper money; all of which soon fell into discredit, and occasioned a depreciation of the currency, which has been the more injurious to the colony and its trade, as the prices of all things, and particularly of manual labour, have increased in proportion to the fall in the treasury notes."

It was on the 30th of November, 1744, that this minister thus expressed himself with regard to the chimerical systems of credit, which have never been more in vogue than in our time.

This internal difficulty originated in the bad legislation of the French colonies, while those of England prospered by the aid of wise institutions. France was always less powerful on the continent of America, and she was there successively stripped by England of her principal settlements. These losses are not foreign to the circumstances attending the cession of Louisiana, and we will point them out, commencing with the earliest.

The French were beginning to settle in Carolina, when the English, by a better conceived enterprise, took possession of it. It remained theirs without treaty, without cession, and by the simple fact of occupancy.

The treaty of Utrecht inflicted in 1713 a still severer blow on the French power in the new world. Hudson Bay was by that treaty restored to England, and Acadia, as well as Newfoundland, was ceded to her, in full sovereignty. Acadia, which subsequently received the name of Nova Scotia, was inhabited by an excellent race of Frenchmen. The circumstances which reduced them to the most wretched state are not generally known: we will relate them, not for the purpose of nourishing national animosities, but in order that the indignation, which these persecutions must inspire, may prevent the return of acts of injustice, as much opposed to humanity as to the law of nations.

The Acadians, always attached to the country of their origin, even after it had been obliged to abandon them, had obtained permission never to be compelled to bear arms against it. Religious, docile, and loyal, they persevered in retaining the language, manners, and habits of France: they had succeeded in causing themselves to be regarded as neutral, which is the name that was at length given to them.

When the seven years' war broke out, those unfortunate people, forgotten by their native land, still bore with pain their subjection to a foreign government. They allowed it to be too plainly seen that their wishes were always favourable to the country of their origin.

The English, resolved to put an end to the influence of France in the affairs of America, took umbrage at some indications of this affection of the Acadians, and fearing that they might be induced to afford aid to the French in Canada, they determined not only to banish them from Acadia, but to disperse them so as to prevent, for the future, all concert of such a nature.

The fate intended for them was with great care kept secret. On a sudden, they were collected by districts under pretence of the harvest. They were hardly assembled, when it was notified to them that they were prisoners; that their lands, cattle, and all their moveables were confiscated. They were only allowed to carry away their silver and the trifling effects, which they could put on board of the vessels. Their estates were laid waste, so that they might retain neither the hope nor desire of returning to them. In one single district two hundred and fifty-five dwellings, two hundred and seventy-six barns, eleven mills, and one church were destroyed. A few families took refuge in the woods, but they were pursued with fire and sword: some young persons were killed in their flight by sentinels, and the other fugitives were obliged to deliver themselves up. These unfortunate people were distributed in the English colonies, where they were humanely and charitably received. At Philadelphia, Benezet, descended from a French family banished at the revocation of the edict of Nantes, treated them like brothers. Twenty-five years after this event, we have seen this individual, who was a model of all the charitable virtues, guide the Acadians like a father of a family, and they really regarded themselves as his children. The cares of this excellent man preserved them; but he could not put an end to the misery and dejection into which this barbarous act had plunged them. They still continued, even after so many years, to regret France and the colony which they were never again to see.*

Louis XV., touched by their fidelity, proposed, through his ministers, to the English government to send some vessels to the different provinces and plantations to bring them back to France. Mr. Grenville, the English minister, hastened to reply: "Our navigation act forbids it,—France cannot send vessels to our colonies."†

Some of these exiles fled to Louisiana. Several of them settled in French Guyana; and the French who were banished to Sinnamari in 1798 found there an Acadian family, that received them with these hospitable words:—" Welcome," said Madame Trion to one of them; "our fathers were banished like you, they taught us to alleviate misfortunes: welcome, we feel pleasure in offering you consolation and an asylum in our cabins."

It is also proper to mention the other mitigations that attended so great a calamity. Some Acadians and Canadians had taken the part of the United States during the war of the revolution. Congress, warned by sad notoriety of the misery which these refugees and those who had formerly been banished from their country experienced, because they remembered that

* Minot. Continuation of the History of Massachusetts. Ch. 10. Entick. General History of the Seven Years' War.

† Letter of December, 1768, from Jasper Mauduit, agent of Massachusetts at London.—Massachusetts Historical Collection.

their fathers had been Frenchmen, attempted to form settlements of them. Having become rich in land by the acquisition of Louisiana, it made them free grants. It was in this country, formerly French, that after so many vicissitudes they again met like a family.* Other Acadians had preceded them there. They have given the name of Acadia to a district of Louisiana, where they have settled. It is bounded by the parish of Ibberville and lake Maurepas. The Mississippi washes its shores, and its inhabitants have the people of New Orleans for neighbours. Thus surrounded, they consider themselves in France, their posterity will lose the remembrance of the misfortunes which a jealous and suspicious policy made them experience, and will for ever bless the beneficence and humanity of congress.

France, when she abandoned Acadia in 1713, preserved Canada and Cape Breton, likewise called Isle Royal. This island was of great importance on account of its excellent harbours, and of its neighbourhood to the fisheries of Newfoundland, the principal school for seamen. England had conquered it during the war, which the peace of Aix-la-Chapelle terminated in 1748. Reciprocal restitutions were stipulated

* This statement respecting the proceedings of congress is incorrect. The settlement of the Acadians in Louisiana was formed soon after the melancholy transactions which are related by the author, and in consequence of a grant of land from the Spanish government. The United States have, however, in conformity with the resolutions of the old congress, from time to time, passed laws, making grants of land to the Canadians and Nova Scotians, who became refugees on account of the American revolution.—TRANSL.

by this treaty, and among others Cape Breton was given up to France. Its lands are fertile. The harbour of Louisbourg is one of the largest and safest in the world; and the sea never freezes there. This island was not long to remain ours. England had determined to leave to the French in those latitudes only the rocks of St. Peter and Miquelon. Commerce is friendly to peace, but the merchants of London, in despite of this maxim, were the most violent in exciting to war. They considered that they had a flourishing navy on their side, while the fleet of their neighbours was entirely ruined. Too certain of their maritime superiority, they continually called the attention of the parliament and the ministry to their interests in the continental colonies of America. Without troubling themselves about the reciprocal rights of other nations, and without examining if the respective limits were traced between the territories of the two powers, they alleged in their petitions the injury that the Canadian hunters occasioned them, and the loss which they would experience, if they were deprived of the fine furs of the beavers and otters.

To these causes for a war, in which so much blood was to flow, were added a general clamour which proceeded from the thirteen colonies. Franklin, as skilful in politics as he was zealous for the improvement of natural science, was the principal organ of the complaints of the English colonists. Franklin, whom Paris saw twenty-five years afterwards employed in exciting the opinion of France and of all Europe against

17

England, was, in 1754, the promoter of the expedition against our remaining possessions in the northern part of the new world. "No tranquillity," said he, "no tranquillity can be expected for our thirteen colonies, so long as the French are masters of Canada." Neither this ardent republican, nor any statesman then foresaw that after this conquest, the provinces would have too much repose to remain long in a dependent state; and that twenty years later, freed from all anxiety respecting the Canadian frontier, they might, with more hope of success, undertake to throw off the yoke of the mother country.

The jealousy which the English had of the increasing power of France in India, confirmed their determination for war. Negotiations were still proceeding in Europe; or rather England, by a feigned negotiation, was endeavouring to prolong the security of the cabinet of Versailles. From the month of May, 1754, hostilities had begun on the Ohio. In June, 1755, the British ministers sent in their justificatory memoirs; and, at the same period, almost on the same day, a squadron of thirteen English vessels meeting on the banks of Newfoundland two French vessels of the line, approached them with pacific demonstrations, and took possession of them.

Canada and the neighbouring countries became the theatre, on which during five years the two powers displayed all the resources of courage and skill. To see the fury with which two rival nations disputed, not only for the inhabited country, but even for totally barren spots, one would have thought that they attached more interest to those territories than to their European provinces. The French had for a long time the advantage in this violent struggle, to which the capacity of Montcalm contributed as much as his valour; but the issue depended upon maritime superiority. A part only of the destined succours in men and money arrived at Quebec. After deeds of high valour and a battle in which the two chiefs, Montcalm and Wolf, found a glorious death, the English completed the conquest of Canada. This vast province, peopled by French, its forts constructed with so much expense, two cities that were already flourishing, were all lost to France; because in spite of incredible efforts to balance the English on the ocean, in spite of the bravery and skill of the French mariners, her naval armaments were never as numerous, or as soon ready for sea as those of the English.

While France was still in possession of Canada, she neglected nothing to carry back its limits. She advanced upon land designated in general terms in the English charters. She opposed to those charters the edicts and letters patents of our kings. These documents and the memoirs produced on both sides could not spread a great deal of light upon these discussions: for the frontiers of the belligerents did not meet; they were separated by territory, which the Indians still possessed. The peace of 1763 terminated this great dispute. England retained her conquests, and thenceforward regulated according to her own will the frontiers

of Nova Scotia. Turning to her advantage in the negotiation every thing that France had alleged in order
to establish the limits of Canada to the south, she
made her cede all the territory, which had depended on
her, to the left bank of the Mississippi. New Orleans
was excepted, and it was stipulated that a line drawn
through the middle of the great river should separate
the part of Louisiana left to France from the possessions of England. English ambition seemed at first
satisfied with this great increase of power in America.
But a few years gave it quite another development.
The peace of 1763 only extended the cession to the
countries which we had possessed. It is, however, in
consequence of that treaty that England has since taken
possession of an immense territory to the north and
west, which extends even to the Northern Ocean, and
to the coasts opposite Asiatic Russia.

So many losses and a humiliating peace distressed
the French nation. The ministry accused and prosecuted its own agents on their return to Europe. The
court of the *Châtelet* for their collusions and vexations
banished them, and condemned them to restore twelve
millions.

At the sad remembrance of the loss of these provinces, of so much bloodshed, of works executed at
such great expense, of debts contracted after peace to
discharge the expenses of a useless defence, we may
ask ourselves to what point of prosperity would France
have risen if all these many efforts had been employed
within the kingdom, and in improvements for the

benefit of our agriculture, manufactures, and commerce?*

The bad system of government under which Louisiana long suffered, was attended with the consequences which were to be expected from it; the sovereignty of one of the finest countries in the world, a country which might have become another France, was of no use to the parent state, but was even a charge to her. After the experience of several years, the government, wearied with a possession which its faults and ignorance had made burdensome, felt disposed at the peace of 1763 to abandon it; and probably it only intended to make, by ceding it to the Spaniards, an arrangement which by diminishing its expenses would relieve the finances of the kingdom.

In 1761, a family compact was concluded between France and Spain.† From the title given to this treaty one might have supposed that there was only a question of a contract, by which the mutual interests of the different branches of the house of Bourbon were

* Appendix, No. 5.

† Fifty years afterwards, the cabinet of St. James took advantage of a favourable opportunity to agree with the court of Madrid that this treaty should never be put in force. Some persons have asserted that England, instead of being alarmed by it, should have desired its renewal, by which means we might have been involved in all the difficulties incident to a badly governed state, without enjoying, after the loss of America, any compensation for a useless burden. These questions are too complicated not to offer ground for different opinions. But we are persuaded that Spain, even after her irreparable losses, is a fine and powerful monarchy, and that this union would sooner or later have contributed to strengthen the repose of Europe.

regulated without regard to considerations truly national. But the principal stipulations were not less favourable to the one people than to the other. For, as
long as Spain was a maritime power and possessed the
sovereignty of her fine kingdoms in America, the union
was equally beneficial to the two nations, and it is
on account of the advantages which they both found
in it that it has been called a family compact. According to the 18th article of this compact one of the
powers is obliged, by means of the conquests acquired
during a war, to indemnify the other for the losses
which it has sustained from it.

Havannah had fallen into the power of the English a
few months before the peace, and this conquest would
have secured to them the possession of the whole island
of Cuba, an island of which a less incapable government
would have made a flourishing kingdom. Such as it was,
it would have been a loss to the Spaniards which nothing
could repair. England consented to restore it, on condition that the countries which Spain claimed east of the
Mississippi should be ceded to her in exchange. Florida was comprised in this cession, and the English derived from the treaty the advantage of rounding their
possessions. They had already the ocean for the eastern boundary, the Mississippi for the western, and the
gulf of St. Lawrence to the north. At the south, the
possession of the Floridas secured them a great superiority in the gulf of Mexico. The cabinet of London
even supposed that these fine regions, thus united under a single master, would not only be safe from all at-

tacks, but that they would sooner or later guaranty to England the greatest influence over all America.

France, on her side, had experienced greater losses than her ally. The court of Madrid, however, asserted that the abandonment of territory which it was making put Spain in a situation to claim the execution of the 18th article of the family compact. The French ministry received, in this case, the law from the Spanish cabinet, and justified itself to the nation by considerations derived from the disastrous events of the war. "Canada," it said, "had been conquered by England, and French valour had succumbed on the land, because insufficient naval forces had badly seconded it. The same fate threatened Louisiana, and France therefore abandoned what it could no longer preserve."

All the events of the war on the sea had proved that without an equality of maritime means, the colonial system was more ruinous than advantageous, and that to be obstinately bent, while inferior in strength, on the preservation of this colony, was to throw away, without the shadow of utility, the resources of the state in men and money, and to give to England a new pledge of dependence.

At that time, Forbonnais, a man of a great deal of experience, wrote as follows: "Would it not be more prudent to direct our attention to our internal resources? Our property at home would not be at the mercy of a hostile and jealous nation. The markets of Europe are open to us. Her interest will make her unite with us against the common rival. This commerce is less precarious than that of America and Asia."

Louisiana was abandoned to Spain by a private treaty signed on the same day with the public one. This agreement was kept secret by the two cabinets for a year. It was only on the 21st of April, 1764, that the governor, D'Abadie, received orders from Louis XV. to acquaint the colony with it. This magistrate was profoundly distressed with the duty which he was instructed to fulfil, and the grief which it occasioned was the cause of his death. The Louisianians rendered an honourable homage to his memory. The following eulogy on him is from a manuscript chronicle of the colony:—

"M. D'Abadie has died universally regretted, and yet he never made the least effort to gain partisans. A disinterested ruler, just towards all, he was inflexibly firm in causing the laws to be respected. He conciliated the interests of the trade of the mother country with those of the colony: he held a firm hand in the execution of the judgments which condemned debtors to pay their creditors, so that he easily induced a diminution to be made on the interest of commercial advances. He severely repressed the excesses of masters towards their slaves: the Indians were also protected against every kind of oppression. He, by his example, caused religion and morality to be honoured. It was thus that, without making any effort to please the colonists, he has left a memory which will always be dear to them."

The government of colonies is absolute, and their history has almost always consisted of the acts of those who have administered them.

Aubri, the successor of M. D'Abadie, announced the cession. At the news of it, the consternation was general throughout the province. The colonists had a great aversion to the Spanish government, and they publicly manifested it. The administration remained in the hands of the French even in 1768. The court of Madrid then sent, as Captain-General, Don Antonio D'Ulloa. He was a discreet man, but his instructions obliged him to re-establish the prohibitory system. He attempted it without success. He could not openly exercise all his authority. The colonists at first debated whether they would not emigrate to the right bank of the river. They renounced this project, and sent deputies to Versailles to obtain permission to remain French. Louis XV. declared to them that the cession was irrevocable.

The Spanish general, O'Reilly, replaced Don Antonio D'Ulloa. He brought to New Orleans three thousand men, which he supposed to be a sufficient number to put an end to resistance. The colonists attempted to prevent their landing, which was only effected through the intervention of the French magistrates. O'Reilly, an enemy of conciliatory measures, a warrior of reputation in his profession, thought that a colony might be governed even more despotically than a conquered country. The barbarian indulged in acts of violence and ferocity, which he mistook for prudence

18

and firmness. He seemed not to know that subjects do not renounce, at the will of treaties, an ancient allegiance to which they have been long accustomed; that it is allowable for friends and relatives to regret those from whom they are separating, and that the indications of their grief ought to be viewed with indulgence. Scaffolds were erected at New Orleans. Six colonists paid by their heads for the courage with which they had manifested their attachment to France.* The court of Madrid secretly disapproved of these acts of outrage; but, fearing to endanger the authority of its governors, it abstained from condemning O'Reilly, and even from disowning him by an authentic act.

The colony, though immediately after this revolution less flourishing than ever, was subsequently better governed. Don Carondelet, an enlightened governor, was aware that the admission of foreign settlers of every creed was one of the most certain means of promoting the prosperity of the province.

Gayoso de Lémos, who succeeded him, reformed some great abuses which had been introduced in the granting of lands. These favours had been lavished with so little prudence, that individuals had obtained tracts of ten thousand acres. The regulations of this governor would have left nothing to desire, had they not been tainted with a violent spirit of religious intolerance and proselytism.

* M. de la Fresnière, attorney general of the colony, Messrs. De Noian, Caresse, Villeret, Marquiz, Millet, all of them officers, were shot by order of O'Reilly.

Aversion for Spain was gradually effaced; but affection did not take its place, and nothing but indifference could be hoped for from a colonial population of so mixed a character. The greatest part were the descendants of the first French settlers of the colony, together with whom were a few Spaniards and English. Subsequently to the termination of the war of independence, many families from the United States were likewise to be found there, as well as (though at a still later period,) some French, who had escaped, almost by a miracle, from the disorders to which a horrible revolution at St. Domingo gave rise. Elements so incongruous could not produce that public spirit, that attachment which is felt for one's native soil. All that could be expected from so many different interests was that they should consent to be governed, and they were the more easily managed, as Spain bore all the expense of the colonial government from funds sent from Mexico, while the imposts were very light, and the contraband commerce with the United States was neither attentively watched nor severely punished.

But, under its new system, the colony was of very little use to the mother country. The facility of communicating with different nations had made other interests than those of Spain predominate, and these foreign interests were every day acquiring new strength.

It was whilst Louisiana was experiencing these vicissitudes, that the great change which placed the English colonies in the rank of the most important states of the world was prepared and consummated.

The first circumstances of this revolution have no immediate relation to Louisiana.   But the alliance of France with the new republics had the greatest influence on the fate of its former province.   Therefore, a succinct mention of the negotiation, which was succeeded by the treaties of alliance and commerce of 1778, will not be foreign to this history.*

It has been asserted in some of the memoirs of the present day, that as the government of France was not able to defend itself against the general resentment which the peace of 1763 had created in the nation, the Duke of Choiseul sent to America emissaries empowered to sound the views of the most important

---

* The Count de Vergennes, in the memoir already referred to, and which seems to have been prepared before the treaty of alliance of 1778, attempts to establish the claims of France to a large portion of North America on the ground of prior discovery and first occupancy.   He gives, under the head of "practicable means to reconcile the pretensions of the English and French as to the limits of their North American possessions," a *projet* of a treaty, by which England was to cede to France all the conquests made by the former power during the war ending in 1763, and especially renounce all claims to Canada, and to every portion of ancient Louisiana, the Spanish part of which was also to be receded to France.

It is hardly necessary to add that it was in consequence of the events, then occurring in the British colonies, that France expected to regain her lost provinces.   By the sixth article, however, of the first treaty, concluded between His Most Christian Majesty and the United States, the French king renounced all claim to the Bermudas and to the North American colonies, which had been previously, or were by the treaty of 1763, acknowledged to belong to the British crown.   By the preceding article it was stipulated that the British possessions in North America, or the Bermudas, if subdued, should be confederated with or be dependent on the United States.—TRANSL.

individuals in that country; and to foment, in concert with them, the germs of an insurrection. Whatever mystery may attend intrigues of this description, it is impossible that such a secret should be always kept, and too many people must have been made acquainted with it, to allow of its not being sooner or later revealed. We have had direct relations with the principal citizens of that country: memoirs in great numbers have informed us of every thing which preceded the revolution, and we sincerely declare that we have no where been able to discover the least indication of these practices, which are undoubtedly opposed to sound policy, and still more so to the reciprocal obligations of nations. It is only known that, a few years after the peace of 1763, the Baron de Kalb was authorized to visit the English colonies, and that he in fact spent some months in them. But, on his return to France, he was coldly received by the minister, and his mission was unattended by any result. It was several years after this time that a connexion began to be formed, and if the cabinet of Versailles did not at first aim at exciting the thirteen provinces to revolt, it was not an indifferent spectator of the dissensions which arose between the mother country and her colonies. Towards the end of 1775, it listened to the overtures of the agents of the American congress. Vergennes, Turgot, and the other members of the king's council, persuaded themselves that their temporizing and mysterious measures, the execution of which was confided to obscure or unknown agents, might still be kept secret; and that, without hostilities, without jeoparding their neutrality, it was allowable to supply the insurgents with money, provisions, and even arms.

According to the statements of the agents of congress, the French ministers only saw in an open course of conduct, and in a declaration of war, the danger of reconciling the mother country and the colonies, whom they called a couple of friends at variance.

Beaumarchais, a man celebrated by his intrigues and great talents, served as the medium for the first communications, and the American agents in Paris confidentially acquainted with them a committee, to whom congress had judged it necessary to refer exclusively the secret of the negotiation.

The envoys at Paris, in conformity with the pressing injunctions of Count Vergennes, required that the committee should not give congress any knowledge of this delicate intercourse. Two only of the members of the committee, Dr. Franklin and Robert Morris, who was afterwards at the head of the finances of the United Sates, were at Philadelphia when the messenger arrived. They learned that, in the autumn of 1776, a shipment of arms and munitions to the value of 5,000,000 livres tournois would be made to St. Eustatius, Martinique, and Cape Français, where the Americans were to receive them: that three millions of livres were put at the disposal of the American commissioners, through a banking house, under the form of a loan.*   It was

* Secret Journals of the Acts and Proceedings of the Old Congress.

in this way that men, distinguished for their discretion, and who had had a long experience of the law of nations, conceived that they might aid a people engaged in an insurrection, and at the same time avoid the calamities of a war. But the injunction of secrecy sufficiently proved that the French ministry did not regard its proceedings as altogether safe from the censure of a wise and just policy.

The attention of the English government was directed towards the conduct of France in this violent crisis. Its suspicions were about breaking out in reproaches of perfidy, when information was received in Europe that, on the 16th of October, 1777, the English general, Burgoyne, and all his army had been made prisoners at Saratoga, in the state of New York. The Americans, from that time equal, and perhaps superior to their enemy, seemed no longer rebels, and the French government renounced the undignified mystery, in which it had supposed that it might envelope itself.

We will here relate a circumstance calculated to give an idea of the cautious character of Count Vergennes. The war for the Spanish succession, at the beginning of the last century, and the one which ended in 1762, had made him acquainted with the danger that France must incur in fighting by sea and land at the same time, and had convinced him that in the event of such a double contest the advantage must be on the side of her rivals. Europe was tranquil in 1776; but the Elector Maximilian was the last prince of a house which had reigned in Bavaria for several centuries. It was feared that, to the prejudice of another branch of his family, the Austrians, who have often in reserve documents applicable to the most unexpected occurrences, might intend, at his death, to take possession of a country which would be a most convenient acquisition for them. A war in Germany was then to be dreaded; and, before exposing himself to a rupture with England, Vergennes wished to know if there was any reason to fear the early death of the elector. Marbois, the king's chargé d'affaires at Munich, answered that there was no ground for expecting that this prince would meet a premature death, unless from the small pox.* The minister of Louis XVI. thought that so slight a chance of war was not sufficient to prevent the execution of designs of a much higher order. There was no delay in concluding the treaties of alliance between France and the United States, which were signed on the 6th of February, 1778.

It is easier for us to point out the wise principles on which they are drawn up, than it would be to justify the conduct of France towards England. We had access, fifty years since, to the archives of France as well as to those of congress. The originals of the documents relative to these treaties, before and after their conclusion, were in our hands. They are, as far as respects the United States, the monuments of an

* Appendix, No. 6.

elevated policy. France was never more magnanimous; she treated with a state in its very cradle, resigned to submit to unequal conditions; but they were all disinterested, and as equal as the respective situations of the contracting parties permitted. The mysteries and secrets of those times are already the property of history, and the narratives of them may be esteemed among the most important of their kind that belong to the last century. We would here express our wish that they may occupy the attention of a writer conversant with high matters of state policy, and that he would make us acquainted with the history of the treaty of alliance of 1778.

It is certain that, in signing it, no one thought either of Louisiana, which had become Spanish, or of the many other important colonies, that had passed from the sovereignty of France under that of England. The principle of reciprocity, so wise, especially when a treaty is made with weak states, was alone consulted; and it dictated conditions, which the most powerful as well as the most feeble had an interest in respecting.

France had successively lost, during the last century, all her continental colonies. She scarcely retained a shadow of power in India, where for so long a time the French and English companies had kept one another reciprocally in check.

At the same period, a writer, who was also a statesman, made this prediction: "If France should, one day, be deprived of her insular, as she is now of her continental colonies, we shall see her prosper by her own means as much as those states who retain all theirs, and she will probably even surpass them in happiness and tranquillity."

France, which had been dear to the Louisianians, so long as they had been the object of her protection and solicitude, was effaced in a manner from their memory, after she had transferred them to another power, without any mark of regret.

A melancholy event, that happened at New Orleans in 1778, afforded the French colony of St. Domingo an opportunity of proving that the old attachment was not entirely extinguished. In consequence of a great fire, the finest quarters of the city were reduced to ashes. The Marquis de Carondelet, the Spanish governor, immediately informed the officers at the head of the administration of St. Domingo of this misfortune, and requested them to communicate it to the French merchants, and urge the sending of assistance. The following answer was given to M. de Carondelet's letter:—

" On receiving the news of the conflagration, which has laid waste your capital, we did not deem it proper to confine ourselves to asking aid from our merchants. The state of the timber yards and storehouses of our colony, as well as the condition of its finances, permits us to do for you more promptly all that you desire. A frigate is about to sail. It carries to you every thing that is most immediately necessary for the rebuilding of your houses. Merchant-ships will soon follow. We would have assisted, in the same manner, any other colony suffering under so great a misfortune; but we feel double satisfaction in relieving our former countrymen.

" Vincent and de Marbois."

It was, in a great measure, owing to this aid that the losses occasioned by the fire were promptly repaired. But the colony, always enslaved by the prohibitory system, continued to languish, instead of advancing in a degree proportionate to its extent and natural advantages.

The cabinet of Madrid seemed firmly persuaded that, as the allegiance and submission of its subjects in the two worlds had lasted for centuries, it would never experience any alteration. It is, however, possible that it saw the magnitude of the danger; but that it feared, by showing a desire to prevent the disaster, to expose itself to the reproach of having created it, and therefore preferred following the beaten track, and leaving the matter to time and fortune.

The great change which is now attaining its consummation in the condition of the former kingdoms of Spain in America, authorizes me to make here a few observations on the frequent warnings which the court of Madrid received respecting the approaching crisis, and the little regard it paid to them. These remarks also affect Louisiana.

In the latter years of the reign of Louis XIV., and on occasion of the Spanish succession, the question was considered of admitting all commercial nations to trade with the colonies of that monarchy. But most of those, who pretend to a knowledge of the future, are exposed to errors, and their false prophecies prevent attention being paid even to the opinions of the wisest statesmen. M. Mesnager, whose name is to be found in all the proceedings at the peace of Utrecht, belonged to the latter class. From the beginning of the last century, he regarded the admission of the commercial states to all the ports of Spanish America, as a means of removing one of the principal obstacles to peace. " It would be advantageous," he said, " even to the interests of that monarchy, to secure to all the nations of Europe the commerce of the new world." This proposition was worthy of one of the greatest politicians of Europe. M. de Torcy, who has transmitted it to us, adds, " The king relished the project."* But there was at Madrid a royal and supreme council of the Indies, and this council knew no prosperity for a state without colonies subjected to a rigorously exclusive monopoly. It rejected the proposition. The time, however, arrived for declaring that the old rules were abandoned for new maxims, but it was then too late.

The Count D'Aranda, a man to whose enlightened views Europe has rendered a just homage, foresaw, a few years after the alliance of France with the United States, the consequences of that event on the destiny of the trans-atlantic kingdoms of Spain. Fully admitting that the independence of the thirteen colonies had

* 1707. Negotiations for the succession of Spain, by M. Colbert de Torcy, vol. i. page 181, 182.

been inevitable, he was soon alarmed at their aggrandizement. He proposed, in 1789, to the king his master, to divide Spanish America into three great states; each of which should be governed by one of the *infants*, with the title of king. They would have been bound to pay a considerable subsidy to the mother country, and she would only have retained her dominion over the islands of Cuba and Porto Rico. This great design was thwarted by the royal council, whose importance it would have destroyed. It would have been a tardy concession, and we will not inquire whether the thrones, which the Count D'Aranda proposed to erect, could have been long maintained in the neighbourhood of a people raised by independence to the height of prosperity.

From 1778, a royal ordinance had allowed a trade between the colonies and the principal ports and places of the mother country. The success of this experiment surpassed every one's expectations, and yet the eyes of the Spanish ministers were not opened. Intercourse with the colonies was more rigorously than ever forbidden to foreigners. The severity had degenerated into an absolute despotism, when, in 1785, internal commotions announced dispositions tending to a general insurrection of the aborigines, and even of the colonists.

It was about this time that Miranda, a young, enterprising, and bustling creole from Carracas, arrived at Philadelphia. He had there several interviews with the writer of this history, to whom he made the fol-

lowing remarks: "Our American kingdoms will soon
experience a revolution similar to the one which you
have witnessed here. A wise and prudent government
might moderate its violence or delay its effects. But
such warnings only offend ministers. They have a
great aversion for all wisdom except their own, and
they always make those advisers, who are too well informed for them, feel their anger. I have told them
that the rising of the Mexican Indians in 1778 was a
warning of the highest importance. I have spoken of
admitting foreigners into all our colonies. From the
manner in which this proposal was received, I have
thought it prudent to fly, as if I had been guilty of a
crime." The chargé d'affaires of France transmitted
to the Count de Vergennes an account of this conversation.*

Miranda has since been conspicuous in the troubles
of Europe, and in the civil wars of America. He
finished his stormy career in a melancholy manner in
1816.

The Count Moustier, a discreet observer, filled in
1788, the office of minister of France in the United
States. He gave similar information. His counsels
tended to produce great changes in the government of
the Spanish colonies. Their execution required as
much courage as ability. But the court of Madrid, regarded as perpetual institutions, whose wisdom seemed
attested by the experience of three centuries. The

* Archives of the Department of Foreign Affairs.

statesmen of that period were far from thinking that, before thirty years should elapse, Europe would cease to have America as an appendage.

Spain thought that circumstances only required from her an easy sacrifice. She consented in 1788 to cede the free navigation of the Mississippi to the states, founded on the left bank of that river. But she so little understood the spirit of those republicans, that she had no hesitation in proposing, as a condition of this grant, that it should only take effect, in case they determined to form an empire distinct from that of the Atlantic states.*

This overture, in which the intention of destroying the federal union so indiscreetly appeared, was not even taken into consideration.

What is still more surprising than this proposition is, that Count de Vergennes, who had advised and negotiated the alliance with the United States, afterwards feared the effects of their example, and allowed a presentiment of future calamities to escape him. This minister to whom the affairs of Europe were so familiar, had not at that time foreseen, that this treaty would hasten the emancipation of the rest of the new world, and that the monopoly to which the islands in the gulf were subjected, could not long be maintained near a powerful republic, interested in rendering the commerce of the whole world independent and free. Always imbued with old notions, he was beginning to

* Marshall's Life of General Washington, 5th vol. page 152.

fear the preponderance of the United States, when death terminated his useful labours.

The Count Montmorin, the successor of Vergennes, thought that it was possible to prevent the independence of the rest of America, and that it was his duty to do so. The following lines are from the instructions transmitted to the French envoy in the United States: "It is not advisable for France to give America all the stability of which she is susceptible. She will acquire a degree of power which she will be too well disposed to abuse." Strange words to follow the alliance concluded in 1778. This epoch was still recent; the French ministers, seconded by the wishes not only of France but of all Europe, had, by effectual and sincere efforts, contributed to the independence of the thirteen states; and ten years afterwards, the view of their own success amazed them, and inspired them with alarms that came too late. Instead of following the inevitable developments of this revolution, and conforming their conduct to it, they had conceived the idea of checking its course. They imagined that a few lines of instructions, given by the cabinet of Versailles to an envoy of the king, would arrest the progress and change the views of many millions of families settled in fertile and boundless territories, and enjoying all the advantages of independence.

Montmorin was alarmed at the progress of the thirteen states of the American Union. But, if his judgment respecting them was erroneous, all the other cabinets, that had then become hostile to this revolution, were equally blinded. Such were the dispositions of Europe towards America, when troubles that had been long foreseen began to agitate France. Germs of insurrection had likewise been scattered, and were fermenting in all parts of the new world. Events which occurred in 1793 pointed out the influence that Louisiana would one day have in the affairs of that continent, and from that time the lot of this great province might have been predicted.

The revolution, that had taken place in France, had put an immense power in the hands of men without experience in public affairs, and incapable of making a good use of their authority. They had too little intelligence to conceive that a state can prosper without colonies. They sent to the United States a new minister plenipotentiary, who was particularly instructed to sound the dispositions of the Louisianians with respect to the French republic; to omit no means of taking advantage of them, if circumstances should appear to him favourable; and to direct, in a special manner, his attention to the designs of the Americans on the Mississippi.

This minister was Genet, a young man whom an excellent education had prepared at an early age for public affairs; though he was by his restless, turbulent, and bold character, as well as by his views as a politician, entirely on a level with the statesmen who had chosen him. It was then seen to what errors the sentiment of liberty may conduct even those who taste its true benefits. The Americans, separating the liberty

20

which France had just assumed to herself from every thing violent and criminal that she had connected with it, received young Genet as the messenger of humanity restored to its rights. He arrived at Charleston in April, 1793. The envoy of a rising republic, he was received with demonstrations of joy that he might well have regarded as universal. Intoxicated by a welcome of which there had been no example, except at the epoch of the alliance between France and the United States, he did not wait, before announcing his character, to be recognised by the government; but, as soon as he landed, he engaged in transactions that were justly considered by those who were not blinded by their passions as a real violation of the law of nations. Too soon invested with a character which requires great maturity of intellect, he authorized the fitting out of privateers, instituted consular courts of admiralty, and considered himself entitled to confer on the French consuls the power of pronouncing the condemnation of prizes taken from the English, and ordering their sale. The instructions which he had received from the committees of the convention breathed the hatred that they bore to Washington, who was, they dared to say, entirely devoted to England. After Genet was recognised by the American government as minister of the French republic, he redoubled his boldness, and set no limits to the rights which he claimed in his official character. At fifteen hundred leagues from France he thought himself as powerful as if he had been sent, supported by a French army, to the court of an insignificant European prince. The federal government behaved with firmness and dignity, and effectually resisted his attempts; but the young minister renewed them without cessation, and as his official notes and memoirs, swelled with citations from publicists and learned men, made no impression on the cabinet, he scattered them every where, and exerted himself to produce an excitement in the public mind. He had secret or avowed adherents in several of the states, and even in congress. Inflated by their support, and having become truly formidable, he carried his audacity and imprudence so far as to accuse Washington himself, who was then president of the United States, of violating the constitution. He even allowed the menace to escape him, " of appealing from the president to the people, of carrying his accusation before congress, and of including in it all the aristocratic partisans of England, and monarchical government."

Soon apprized of the state of things there, by the reports of his correspondents, and of the adventurers who had advanced to the Mississippi, he believed, with much reason, that if he could make a sudden attack on Florida and Louisiana, he would find, not only among the inhabitants of the western territories, but even at New Orleans, a numerous party prepared to second him. He was assured that all Louisiana desired to return under the dominion of France, and he seriously set about making the conquest of it: he prepared a co-operation of naval forces, which were to rendezvous upon the coast of Florida. The principal body of land troops was to embark in Kentucky, and descending the Ohio and Mississippi, to invade unexpectedly New Orleans. He had regulated in advance the pay of the troops, their rations, the distribution of the booty, and even the division of the lands among the soldiers, with the portion reserved to the French republic. Finally, he abused the privileges of legations so far as to raise bodies of troops in the two states of South Carolina and Georgia, and he received in them French and Americans, without distinction. Though restrained for a moment in his extravagances by the moderation and firmness of the government, he soon recommenced his attacks by exhausting all the declamations which the conventional doctrines could furnish, and thus resumed his ascendancy over the multitude.

The federal government was informed of the favourable reception which the proposition of invading New Orleans met with in several of the states. These hostile preparations gave it the more uneasiness, as it was then carrying on, with the court of Madrid, a negotiation relative to the navigation of the Mississippi. Washington promptly addressed instructions to the governor of Kentucky, with a view of moderating this excitement. He informed him that four Frenchmen, bearers of commissions from M. Genet, were openly travelling through that state preparing an expedition against Louisiana. That minister himself, he added, was to be the commander-in-chief. The inhabitants of Kentucky were but too well disposed to second him. They resolved, in their private assemblies, to lay before congress their claim for the most entire liberty of navigating the Mississippi, and recommended to their representatives to employ decent but imperative terms, and such as suit the language of a people speaking to their servants. The governor replied to the despatches of the secretary of state, that " he had neither the power nor intention of preventing the people from asserting rights necessary to their existence; and, as to those who had planned the expedition, he doubted whether there was any legal authority to restrain or punish them, at least before they have actually accomplished it." From the exaggerated consequences to which the first magistrate of Kentucky carried the abstract rights of man, we may judge of the greatness of the crisis.

Washington, personally insulted by the diplomatic proceedings of Genet, considered the public tranquillity in danger. To appeal from the president to the people, was to summon the people to sedition. Five or six months after the arrival of this plenipotentiary, who had become, as it were, the chief of a faction, the American ministers informed the French government " that the proceedings of its envoy in no respect corresponded with the dispositions that animated the French republic; that, on the contrary, he was exerting himself to embroil the United States in war without, and to spread discord and anarchy at home, and they demanded his recall as necessary to the maintenance of a good understanding."

The answer to this demand was delayed by the distance. Genet continued his bold practices, and the
government was about to suspend his diplomatic functions and deprive him of the privileges attached to his
official character, when it received the news of his recall. His successor arrived soon after, and through
this new plenipotentiary the United States were informed that the French government entirely disapproved the conduct of Genet. This young man, who
seemed destined by his talents and acquirements to fill
honourably his public career, fell into a sort of obscurity, in consequence of his having been prematurely
called to perform duties that require experience and
prudence even more than learning. His active mind
was subsequently directed to the useful arts, and without doubt his efforts in those matters have been attended with more fortunate results than his political
proceedings. But the seditious and violent impulse to
insurrection which he had given to the people of the
west had been so well received, that it lasted after he
had ceased to be its principal mover. The inhabitants
of Kentucky, deprived of the hope of conquering Louisiana, presented petitions, in which, reducing their
demand to the free navigation of the Mississippi, they
accused the administration of the United States of in-
attention to the public interests, threatened it with a
dismemberment of the Union, and declared that "by
the law of nature, the navigation of the Mississippi belonged to them; that they wished to have it, that they

would have it, and that if the government neglected to secure it to them, it would be guilty of a crime towards them and their posterity."

The senate and house of representatives did not notice the violent language, and the disregard of the rules of rational liberty, with which these representations were drawn up, but they took into consideration the state of a numerous agricultural population, without manufactures, which, spread on the banks of the Mississippi and its tributaries, could only exist and extend itself by commerce, by the sale of the products of the earth, and by a free navigation of that river. The two houses declared that " the right of the United States to this navigation was incontestable, and that the necessary measures should be taken to secure its enjoyment."

After the recall of Genet, a small force which was to have co-operated in the projected invasion, landed on the coast of Florida. It was said to be only the advanced guard of a more considerable body. On the arrival of these feeble auxiliaries, a few French and Americans assembled in Georgia. But these volunteers, being deprived of their chief, dispersed; the French passed over to the Indian territory to await new orders. They were there in a most destitute condition, and many of them became victims of the Indians.

A few deserters from the army of the United States had joined these bands of adventurers. They saw with regret the rich booty, at which they had aimed, escape

them. These tumults were not entirely calmed till towards the middle of 1794; but other troubles broke
out, and were felt even in Pennsylvania. These disturbances affected the popularity of the great Washington, and troubled the peace of his last years. By
prudent and vigorous measures, however, he succeeded in appeasing the clamours of the factions, but it was
easy to see that the navigation of the Mississippi and
the possession of what remained of Eastern Louisiana
would always be an object of ambition to the new states
of the Union. This truth did not reach the politicians
of the French convention. The committee of public
safety thought that it might try other means of restoring
to France the province which she had not been able
to recover through the attempts of Genet.

During the negotiations of Basle, in 1795, this committee gave instructions to M. Barthelemy, the ambassador of the republic, " to demand the restoration of
Louisiana and the cession of the Spanish part of St.
Domingo, or that France should retain the province of
Guipuscoa, and particularly Fontarabia and St. Sebas-
tian, which had been conquered by her arms."

Louis XIV. had also entertained the design of uniting
the province of Guipuscoa to France, and at the time
of the treaty of partition of the 11th of October, 1698,
for the Spanish succession, it had formed a part of the
Dauphin's portion.*

The lands of the Spanish part of St. Domingo are

* Colbert de Torci. Negotiations for the succession of Spain.

not inferior in quality to those of the French: they are better watered and much more extensive. But cultivation had made the French colony twenty times more valuable than the Spanish. The convention, glancing at these advantages, had imagined that to acquire territory was to ensure productions. We believe that such success could only have been attained after a long course of years, and that it depended on conditions which it was not in the power of France to fulfil. The present state of St. Domingo renders useless the examination of these questions.

Barthelemy opened the negotiations on the three propositions contained in his instructions. Spain thought at that time that it was for her interest to retain Louisiana, and, though St. Domingo was the oldest of her settlements in America, though its civil and ecclesiastical jurisdiction extended over the islands of Cuba, Porto Rico, and other possessions, it decided to cede it.

The directory succeeded, at this period, to the national convention. Principally attentive to the affairs of Europe, it learned with a sort of indifference the sacrifice to which Spain consented, as well in order to preserve peace as on account of the disordered state of her finances, and the absolute impossibility of making a resistance proportionate to the dangers to which she was exposed.

England, on the other hand, according to the rules of her ordinary policy, and conformably to maxims, the

soundness of which was guarantied by experience, directed her attention to all the islands, and to every
part of the American continent.　An incident, the particulars of which deserve to be reported, sufficiently
showed that she would never be indifferent to the fate
of Louisiana.

Spain, by the treaty of October, 1795, had ceded to
the United States her possessions on the left bank of
the Mississippi, only reserving the Floridas.　But afterwards, being closely allied with France, and foreseeing
an approaching rupture between that republic and the
United States, into which she was afraid of being drawn,
she had regretted the sacrifice.　She refused, under all
sorts of pretences, to proceed to the demarcation of
the new boundaries, and to the evacuation of the ceded
territories.　The Spanish governor retained the post of
Natchez, which, according to him, was the only defence
of Louisiana against the English troops assembled at
Quebec, and against the Indians whom the government
of Canada was arming and disarming at pleasure.　The
Americans of Kentucky and Tennessee did not appear
to him to be less objects of dread.　In fact, the inhabitants of the ceded territories, the greater part of
American or English origin, murmured at seeing their
new government show so little anxiety to enter on the
possession.　They manifested great impatience to pass
from the arbitrary sway of the Spaniards under the free
government of the United States, and excited the savages to keep themselves prepared for war.

It was under these circumstances, that the audacious project of a man, important by his rank and official station in the United States, was discovered.

Mr. Blount, governor of the territory of Tennessee and commissioner of the United States among the Indian tribes, had acquired, during a long residence in those districts, an intimate knowledge of the country and its inhabitants, and enjoyed a great influence there. Subsequently named a member of the senate, when the territory was admitted into the Union as a state, he filled that office in 1797, the last year of the presidency of Washington. Blount was not worthy of the confidence of which his fellow-citizens had given him a proof by sending him to congress. His affairs were very much deranged, and he conceived the idea of retrieving them by a signal service which he proposed to render to England, at that time engaged in a war with Spain. He formed the plan of invading Louisiana, by means of forces sent from Canada. According to this scheme, the English troops, secretly embarked on the lakes in the autumn of 1797, would have landed at the southern extremity of Michigan, from whence the Illinois river is not far distant. The invading army, descending this river to its junction with the Mississippi, was to find the inhabitants every where prepared to second it. It would have crossed in arms, it is true, a part of the country belonging to the United States; but this violation of their territory had not seemed to Blount a circumstance of great importance. The troops, when they arrived at the great river, would have found there provisions in abundance, and boats in sufficient number, sent from the Ohio, by the inhabitants of Kentucky. A rapid navigation was to carry them in a few days to New Orleans. This place had only a feeble Spanish garrison, in no condition to offer resistance. The capital once occupied, all the country was in the power of the English, and the Floridas would have been subjected with the same facility.

Blount first disclosed his plan to Mr. Liston, the English envoy to the United States. This minister, a prudent observer of the usages of diplomacy, without either welcoming or repelling confidence, let the senator understand that he must address himself directly to the British cabinet, which this intriguer accordingly did. Obliged to deliver his plans and memoirs to an intermediate agent, he betrayed himself by the care which he took to recommend great secrecy, and by the mystery with which he accompanied all his proceedings. His memoirs, having been put on board of the vessel in which his messenger was to embark, fell into the hands of the captain, who considered it his duty to transmit them to the president of the United States, who was then Mr. John Adams, the successor of Washington in that station. The president communicated them to congress, by whom they were published. The envoy, Mr. Liston, gave formal assurances of being a stranger to the plot, and the American ministers publicly declared, "that it was not probable that the English had any knowledge of it." The offence committed by Blount was not provided for by law. A committee of the house of representatives proposed to prosecute him for the crime of high treason; he was not, however, tried, but the senate expelled him by a vote, not of two-thirds only, as the constitution requires, but unanimously. We are aware of only one other case of expulsion from the senate. In the house of representatives not a single one has occurred, from 1787, when the constitution of the United States was adopted, to the present day.

This enterprise, though abortive, was a warning for Spain. Her means of defence in America were by no means proportionate to the vast extent of the dominions which she possessed there, and the policy of England was no mystery.

The Louisianians supposed their country for ever a stranger to the movements of Europe, when the events of the French revolution, and the troubles in the West Indies recalled it to the attention of the ephemeral authorities that then governed the new republic. From the committee of public safety, the authority had passed to a directory, still more incapable of managing the affairs of a great state. The maritime war between France and Great Britain had lasted for eight or nine years. The United States were about to be drawn into it by a party friendly to England, in spite of all their efforts to preserve a neutrality from whence they derived immense advantages. But France and England were exerting themselves with equal ardour to break it for their own benefit, and they each calculated that, by obtaining the assistance of these neutral states, its own commerce would come in for a share of the profits that they were then enjoying. The directory, through its imprudence, rendered a rupture inevitable. It had pursued a course opposed to that long-sighted policy, which, without imposing on the United States unequal and onerous conditions, had dictated the treaties of 1778. These treaties, congress, in consequence of the most offensive provocations, declared in 1798 to be broken and rescinded.

As France and the United States were separated by great distances, the land-armies could not reach one another, and there were only a few naval engagements. Hostilities of the most unjust and vile kind that war authorizes were not, however, on that account less frequent;—these consisted of attacks of privateers on disarmed merchant vessels, incapable of defending themselves, and the owners of which, in the regular course of their own business, are constantly employed in forming innocent and peaceable connexions among all the countries of the world. Louisiana had rather gained than lost by this state of things so favourable to contraband trade, and the Spanish governors themselves willingly lent their aid to the blows which were continually inflicted on the prohibitory system. Its rigour was also moderated in the other Spanish colonies, and such great advantages resulted from it, that the cabinet of Madrid shut its eyes to the consequences that this relaxation might have on the maxims of its ancient policy.

At the peace of 1763, Spain had recovered the Havannah, a conquest made by England, only by abandoning to her the Floridas in exchange. This acquisition was then important for the English, because it covered Georgia and the other continental colonies which were still subject to them. Spain had again made herself mistress of the Floridas during the war of American independence; and England, to whom their possession had formerly appeared so advantageous, found them almost a burden after the thirteen colonies had ceased to belong to her. They would have been a subject of misunderstanding between the United States and the British government. England, therefore, abandoned them to Spain at the peace of 1783. But by thus enlarging its territory, this power became exposed to be attacked upon an immense extent of sea coast. It also began to take umbrage at the rapid increase of the confederated states. On no side did it see the means of safety, when an unexpected event entirely changed the aspect of affairs.

The directory of the French republic, in the midst of the innumerable difficulties which its ignorance had accumulated, after having involved the country in war with the United States, had entirely lost sight of the colonies, which France still retained. This incapable and base government was, almost without resistance, stripped of its authority by a general, who, to great military talents, united most of those qualities which constitute the statesman. To this day he is incontestably the first among the illustrious men of the world;

it may be doubted whether posterity will assign him a place among the great men.

Bonaparte, in assuming the supreme conduct of affairs, found those of politics and war in extreme confusion. This condition of the country did not surprise him, and he thought that he was adequate to every thing. It was, indeed, from the midst of this chaos that he originated and brought to a happy conclusion the most important negotiations. Still young, and already celebrated by more victories than the most famous captains have achieved in a long career, he aspired to another kind of glory, when he saw himself at the head of the government. He then only considered peace as a means of carrying to the greatest height the commerce, navigation, and manufactures of France, and his passion for war seemed for a time to be put to rest. The English, on their part, masters of the commerce of the world, would have wished to retain it without rivals. As to other matters, the two nations were well disposed to a sincere reconciliation. Equally distinguished by almost incredible progress in the sciences and arts, pursuing with the same zeal every thing which can embellish and meliorate society, it appeared that nothing farther was required from the governments than to abstain from thwarting these good dispositions. The first overtures of peace made by France were, however, immediately repelled at London, where the phantom alone of a French republic, active and powerful, still inspired dread. But as the cabinet of Madrid, encouraged even by its ignorance, was necessarily more inclined to negotiate, Bonaparte considered the occasion a favourable one for realizing the project in which the directory had failed.

The cession that France made of Louisiana to Spain in 1763, had been considered in all our maritime and commercial cities as impolitic and injurious to the interests of our navigation, as well as to the French West Indies, and it was very generally wished that an opportunity might occur of recovering that colony.

One of the first cares of Bonaparte was to renew with the court of Madrid a negotiation on that subject. He was then far from thinking that contributions forcibly imposed on Europe could take the place of those immense tributes, which she voluntarily pays to the manufactures and navigation of commercial nations.

The possession of Louisiana seemed to him particularly favourable to the project that he had formed of giving to France a preponderance in America. He connected with his views another design, which he subsequently attempted to realize—a league of all the maritime powers against the pretensions of England— and he hoped in this way to put an end to the dominion which she had arrogantly assumed over the sea. "France," said he, "cannot reconcile herself to this inert existence, this stationary tranquillity, with which Germany and Italy are contented. The English reply with disdain to my offers of peace; they have protected the black rebels of St. Domingo, even so far as to liberate them and give them arms. Very well,—I will make of St. Domingo a vast camp, and I will have there an army always ready to carry war into their own colonies."

Reflection soon made him abandon these chimerical plans; and, skilfully profiting by the great ascendancy which the victory of Marengo and the fortunate events by which it was succeeded gave him, he opened a negotiation at Madrid, and easily persuaded the Prince of Peace, the all powerful minister of the catholic king, that Louisiana, by being restored to France, would be a bulwark for Mexico, and a security for the tranquillity of the gulf.

On the 1st of October, 1800, a treaty was concluded at St. Ildephonso, the third article of which is in these terms: " His Catholic Majesty promises and engages to retrocede to the French republic, six months after the full and entire execution of the above conditions and stipulations relative to His Royal Highness, the Duke of Parma, the colony or province of Louisiana, with the same extent that it now has in the hands of Spain, and that it had when France possessed it, and such as it ought to be after the treaties subsequently entered into between Spain and other states." The treaty of Madrid of the 21st of March, 1801, renews these dispositions; and the first article contains a detailed account of the conditions on which the cession was made. The motive specially assigned was, "that the reigning Duke of Parma, as a compensation for that duchy and its dependencies, as well as of the cession which the king of Spain made of Louisiana, should be put in possession of Tuscany, under the name of the kingdom of Etruria." These stipulations, which could not then be executed, became subsequently the ground of many complaints on the part of the Spaniards, and Louisiana continued for some time longer under their dominion.

Spain, by uniting Louisiana in 1763 to her vast American states, was not actuated by any intention of extending her navigation or augmenting her treasures. She still followed the ancient policy of those barbarous nations, who only think their frontiers secure when vast deserts separate them from powerful nations. The neighbourhood of France seemed to her less to be dreaded than that of the United States.

The English and Americans go in quest of vacant countries in order to settle in them; and it is by a numerous population that they provide for the defence of the frontiers of their colonies. But the French were the friends and allies of the Spaniards, and their contact was not dangerous; since, notwithstanding continued efforts during a century and a half, they had never been able to make a single continental colony prosper.

Spain, in consenting to the retrocession, inserted a condition, that she should have the preference, in case France, in her turn, should be disposed again to cede Louisiana. We shall see, in the sequel, the embarrassments which resulted from this stipulation.

Whilst these things were passing in Europe, the internal and foreign policy of the United States underwent a great change, which had so much influence on the fate of Louisiana, that it is necessary that the principal circumstances connected with it should be known.

From the time of Washington's presidency, two systems of government had divided the opinions of the most distinguished American statesmen. One party, extravagant champions of democracy, wished to restrain the powers of the superior government and strengthen the authority of each of the thirteen states, by giving to the state governments whatever power could be taken from the general confederacy. This party, which was called republican or democratic, reckoned in its ranks the most able men. The other party had Washington for its head, and it could not have had a more virtuous leader nor one more deserving of confidence. This great man retired after a presidency of eight years. His successor was Mr. John Adams, a statesman who entertaining probably too high an opinion of his own great superiority, had succeeded in impressing many other persons with the same sentiments respecting him. But, when he reached the presidency of the United States, he did not entirely justify either his own confidence in himself or that of the party which had advanced him so high. He professed great admiration for the British government; it has even been asserted that he would have seen, without alarm, the presidency of the United States held for life by the same individual. He did not dissemble his aversion for the French nation and the little esteem that he entertained for their government. The American people were, however, far from sharing his opinions. A sort of instinct, the fervour of which was not yet relaxed, drew them towards the doctrines and principles which the French revolution had adopted.

It was this difference of opinion between the people and their rulers that ruined the party of Mr. Adams. The federalists, who had abused their power to remove the republicans altogether from the management of affairs, after having had the control of the government for a few years, lost their influence in most of the states of the Union, and their efforts could not effect the re-election of Mr. John Adams for a second presidential term.

Mr. Jefferson, the most distinguished citizen in the republican party, succeeded him, and the aspect of things immediately changed.

Mr. Adams, yielding to the general opinion, had, probably contrary to his own wishes, commenced negotiations with the directory. They acquired more consistency when Bonaparte took the reins of government. This negotiation and that of Madrid were terminated at the same time. The convention with the United States was signed at Paris on the 30th of September, 1800, and, on the next day, October 1st, the treaty with Spain was concluded at St. Ildephonso.

The war with England still continued. The cession of Louisiana by Spain to France, stipulated by the treaty of St. Ildephonso, was not yet made public, and Bonaparte was careful not to divulge it by taking possession of the province.

A maritime peace was an essential preliminary to the undisturbed enjoyment of this acquisition by France; but, in treating of peace with England, it would have been embarrassing to have asked the consent of that power, or even its tacit acknowledgment; the negotiation would have been fettered by it, and perhaps broken off. It cannot be doubted that Louisiana might have been attacked by the English and easily conquered, had they been informed during the war that it had again become a French colony. Under such circumstances, secrecy was the most prudent advice that could be offered to the newly formed cabinet of the Tuileries.

England had in fact found herself obliged to listen to new propositions of peace. All the powers were eager to negotiate with Bonaparte, and treaties of peace rapidly succeeded one another. After having had numerous allies, Great Britain was on the eve of being left alone. A negotiation was then commenced at London. All the difficulties were soon removed, and preliminaries were signed on the 1st of October, 1801, a year after the treaty of St. Ildephonso.

The first consul then regarded the termination of the war as the surest means of confirming his authority. Those who closely observed his conduct and heard his remarks, would have thought that he was animated by really pacific intentions, if his conditions of definitive peace had not been at the same time directly opposed to the maxims of the power with which he had just signed the preliminaries. He desired an entire re-

ciprocity and equal tariffs in matters of commerce.
He reminded the people of Europe that the new maritime code, of which England pretended to dictate the
articles, was only an abuse of force, and that all the
other powers ought to unite to prevent its being acted
on. He raised their courage by his own example,
and he hoped to be able to revive the league, honourably formed under Louis XVI., for the free navigation
of neutrals, and which was so unfortunately dissolved
before it had acquired consistency. Disposed to make
a sincere peace, he was not the less persuaded of the
necessity of using against England the means by which
that power sustains its supremacy over the seas. In
the state of depression to which all the nations whom
navigation formerly enriched were fallen, he was convinced that, in case of new aggressions, they must
agree to shut the ports of the continent to English vessels. It was in this view, as yet scarcely developed,
that he required that the treaty should secure a free
navigation to all flags; that the naval forces of the maritime powers should at the peace be reduced to what
might be necessary for the protection of the coasts
and adjacent districts. He wished that their employment, when not at war, should be confined to putting
an end to piracy, to cultivating naval science with
more advantage than merchant navigators are capable
of doing; and, finally, to affording to commerce such
assistance as may be necessary in difficult circumstances.

There was an interval of six months between the

conclusion of the preliminaries and the peace of
Amiens, which was signed on the 27th of March,
1802.   The slowness with which the business proceeded disappointed the public impatience at London,
where open murmurs were already heard.   However,
these six months had been sufficient to produce a great
change in the political state of the world.

A man of an elevated genius, of a decided and determined character, too young to have reflected on the
rights of other nations, and on the danger of wound-
ing their independence, was continually hurried on, to
omit nothing which could increase his own glory and
render the nation, whose destinies he had undertaken
to direct, powerful and formidable.

The first acts of his government, after the treaty,
augured favourably, however, for the duration of peace.
The general amnesty to the emigrants was, as it were,
a first pledge of his sincerity.*   Numerous classes of
banished Frenchmen, who were flying from place to
place, suffering all the ills of poverty, were, in spite of
menacing and barbarous laws, recalled by degrees to
their common country.   The restoration of the altars
was felt as a general want, and this work was entered
on without intolerance or fanaticism.   Wise laws were
promulgated, and treaties of peace concluded with different powers.   In this same year, 1802, the finances
of France were in a more flourishing state than at
any previous or subsequent period.

* April 20th, 1802.

This prosperity was not owing to those foreign tributes which afterwards gave to the treasury a transient opulence, the source of hatred and reprisals. There was no longer a war establishment: far from fearing new taxes, there was an expectation that old ones would be lightened, and the continuance of peace was calculated on as the necessary condition of the re-establishment of order.

France found in peace all the advantages to which she had long aspired; she obtained for her northern provinces a frontier conformable to the great divisions traced by nature, and which had been, for centuries, the object of her ambition; for her commerce and navigation she had the most justly founded expectations, that the possession of Louisiana and the subjection of St. Domingo, enlarged by the whole part that had belonged to Spain, would enable her to resume her rank among the maritime powers and commercial states.

The republic, in these new circumstances, and under a wise and pacific government, might, without giving umbrage to its neighbours, have attained to a sufficiently high degree of prosperity. The earnest desire for peace, which had been entertained in England during the latter part of the war, had caused the preliminary articles to be received there with that joy and enthusiasm which indicate the assent of the people.

But these feelings of good-will were not of long continuance. It was early perceived that the genius

of Bonaparte, so vigilant, so well calculated to conceive and to act in war, would not be long resigned to
the repose of peace.   His activity was soon directed
towards foreign commerce, and ardently bent on the
navigation and colonies, which before the revolution
secured to France advantages that peace had not enabled her to recover.   Then, this ambition, though altogether legitimate, awakened in the English government those distrusts and fears from which ministers,
who are really responsible, can never be free.

It was in the interval between the signing of the preliminaries and the definitive treaty of peace, that the
first consul caused himself to be recognised as president of the Italian republic.   The English ministry did
not, however, think it requisite on that account to
break off the negotiations, and it even abstained from
making any observations on so extraordinary a proceeding.

Bonaparte had been named, in 1799, first consul for
ten years.   On the 8th of May, 1802, a decree of the
senate added ten years to the first term.   Three months
afterwards, he was named for life, with the privilege of
designating his successor.   Europe was astonished at
these innovations, when other decrees of the senate
spread still more lively alarms.   These acts, of a description altogether new to the public law of Europe,
successively united to France different countries, without any other motive than that of convenience; and
the first consul even disdained to enter on an explanation of these bold measures.   It was from the parlia-

ment of England that his pride received the first lesson.

Opinions can be openly expressed in those assemblies with a publicity, which, if it is sometimes indiscreet, has the inestimable advantage of keeping rulers constantly on their guard against their own faults; of making them acquainted with the wishes and opinions of the people; of informing them of every thing that relates to the good of the country, and of enlightening them on its real interests. The truth, thus made public, benefits every one, and oftentimes even the censures by which the ministers appear the most offended, are those from which they expect to derive in secret the greatest advantage. This was the case at the conjuncture to which we refer.

The sessions of parliament for 1802 and 1803, were distinguished at their commencement by the ability of those who attacked and defended the terms of the peace,* and, at a later period, by the agreement of all parties in a desire to recommence the war. We will only refer to the discussions which relate to Louisiana, and to the interests of France and England in America.

The address of the house of commons in May, 1802, on occasion of the definitive treaty, contained these remarkable words: "We rely on his majesty's paternal wisdom for resisting every fresh encroachment, (of whatever nature,) which shall be attempted on the

* Signed on the 27th of March, 1802.

maritime, commercial, or colonial rights of the British empire."

There was nothing, however, in the first debates that announced an approaching rupture. Some distinguished statesmen approved of the peace. They considered it bad policy to keep a rival nation in a state of inferiority, and without the power of unfolding the means of prosperity for which it is indebted to its genius, or which it derives from nature; and they were of opinion that no reconciliation is sincere, if there is not a reciprocal advantage in it, and that it is thus that generosity benefits even those who practise it. "Let us allow," said they, "let us allow the French to have at heart the glory and happiness of their country, as we desire the glory and happiness of our own. France has only obtained by the peace advantages suitable to her situation; they will be the surest guarantees of her tranquillity and moderation abroad, and the pledge of the contentment and repose of the people at home."

About this period the plan of reconquering St. Domingo was more fully known; it powerfully contributed to awaken the jealousy, with which our prosperity has so often inspired England. "This expedition," said a member in addressing the house of commons, "is formidable, and surpasses any heretofore seen in the American Archipelago. It seems to menace Touissaint-Louverture, but we shall probably see the French turn the black regiments of that chief towards the conquest of Jamaica." The chancellor of the exchequer, but too clearly foreseeing the future, replied; " This expedition should be for us a source of tranquillity rather than alarm; for the usurpation of authority by the blacks is an event truly to be dreaded, and one which puts in jeopardy the security and repose of our West India colonies."

Several articles of the treaty gave rise to more animated discussions; and the ministers, whose work the last peace was, were defended by their own friends with so little warmth, that from that time an imputation, too grave to be lightly entertained, gained ground. Many members of parliament condemned the facility with which Lord Cornwallis, a distinguished warrior, but inexperienced in negotiations, had acquiesced at Amiens, in several demands of France; it was, they said, a proof that it was only intended to gain time.

These traducers of the peace were not so numerous, but they were more clamorous than its advocates; they wished to establish it as a point of national law, that no change of sovereignty, no accession of territory could take place in Europe or America, without the acquiescence of England.

Thirty years before, whilst Great Britain was extending its sovereignty over the finest parts of Asia, without any other state's thinking of demanding an account of her conquests, we had seen her jealousy carried so far as to wish to make war on France and Spain, in order to prevent the latter power from occupying a few desert islands in the neighbourhood of the straits of Magellan.

The opposition blamed Lord Cornwallis for not having expressly inserted the usual clause, by which all previous treaties are maintained and confirmed, so far as they are not at variance with the last. " This omission was," they said, " an indirect ratification given to the abandonment made by Spain to France, agreeably to the treaty of Basle, of half of the island of St. Domingo. The silence of the treaty of Amiens, is, as it were, a confirmation of the union of Belgium with France, a union very dangerous to England, as the shores of that province are opposite the Thames, that is to say, of London itself. In a word, not to revive the former treaties, particularly those of Utrecht and Fontainebleau, is to put in question the rights of England to Nova Scotia, Canada and Cape Breton." Thus the English claimed the stipulations agreed on at Utrecht, while they, a few years afterwards, considered as abrogated the articles of the same treaty which had consecrated the rights of neutrality. The clamours on the subject of the cession of Louisiana to France were still more ardent. " It wounded essentially," it was said, "the interests of England. The ports which France was about to have at its disposition would afford facilities for her naval dépôts, and multiply the dangers of the English colonies, in case of war. Canada, which was adjacent to northern Louisiana, would be soon exposed to the attacks of the French. They would acquire over the United States an ascendency, which would, sooner or later, draw that republic into an alliance against the naval greatness of England, and the superi-

ority of her flag. New Orleans was the key of Mexico: the two Americas ought to be alarmed at a change,
which above all threatened the Spanish kingdoms of
that great continent; and the cabinet of Madrid could
only have consented to the treaty in obedience to force.
If it had been known by the two houses of parliament,
when the preliminaries were communicated to them,
they would have paused before they approved them.
But the ministers were acquainted with it before signing the definitive treaty, and they were inexcusable for
not having considered it an obstacle to making peace."

Lord Hawkesbury conceived that he ought to give
explanations, and his answer deserves to be reported.
"To judge of the value of Louisiana in the hands of
the French," said he, "let us recollect that they have
heretofore possessed it for a long period, without being
able to render it prosperous; though they, at the very
same time, derived great advantages from their insular
colonies. As to the United States, this transfer does
not expose them to any danger. I have too high an
idea of their power and resources, to entertain any
fears for them on account of their new neighbours.
Were it, however, otherwise, their alarms could but
lead them to unite more closely with us."

This minister also uttered these other words, so extraordinary in the mouth of a statesman: "We only
wished to make an experimental peace." Lord
Hawkesbury thus expressed himself, immediately after
the signature of a treaty, all the articles of which both
parties had promised to execute with sincerity and

good faith. Such words sometimes escape from a speaker, who, in his desire to please, forgets that they will be echoed elsewhere than in the chamber which he is addressing. However, the explosion of public discontent in England did not long permit the first consul to deceive himself. He could from thenceforth judge of the effect which would be produced by a knowledge of the design that he entertained of securing to France commercial advantages in America, and of creating for her great maritime interests.

The treaties of peace, which he dictated as a consequence of his victories, left him alone formidable in Europe, and it depended on him to execute them at his pleasure, whilst he could prescribe a mute obedience to the other powers: this unnatural situation could only last so long as they were in no condition to change it. But Napoleon, who did not then foresee the near return of war, but was, on the contrary, drawn by his disposition to the adoption of prompt and decisive measures, thought that he ought to proceed without delay to the execution of the plan that he had formed. It consisted in first subjecting the revolted colony, by sending there such considerable forces that he might be justified in regarding success as infallible. After the reduction of the rebels, a part of the army was to be conveyed to Louisiana.

The events, of which St. Domingo was then the bloody theatre, are closely connected with the history of the treaty of cession. We shall therefore anticipate the course of the principal narrative, and state summa-

rily the issue of the expedition, which had for its object the re-establishment of the French sovereignty in
that island.

At the end of the last century, and after the frightful
catastrophes that resulted from a manumission impru-
dently proclaimed, order had begun to be re-established
in that fine colony. But ambition soon after induced
a black man and a mulatto to take up arms, and the
rivalry of these two men kindled anew a civil war,
which the mother country had not excited, but which
she probably witnessed without dissatisfaction.

The two factions and their chiefs were equally ardent in the profession of attachment to France, and
it was difficult to refuse credence to their declarations; for they had both equally contributed to the expulsion of the English. But the character of their
fidelity was affected by the difference of their casts.
Rigaud, a free born mulatto, had wished, while he restored the colony to France, to maintain slavery, and
to keep for his party the plantations conquered from
the whites, who had emigrated or been allies of our
enemies. He united with a remarkable capacity the
advantage of an excellent education. He had become
chief of all the people of colour, who were born free
or had been manumitted before the revolution. These
men, for the most part owners of blacks, refused to
obey the laws of the convention, which, by proclaiming the abolition of slavery, only left them land without value, for they did not conceive the possibility of
its being cultivated in any other manner than by slaves.

Liberty, moreover, appeared to them to be less precious, since the multitude were admitted to enjoy it in the same manner with themselves. This chief commanded, in the south of the island, an army composed of about six thousand mulattoes and blacks, and a few whites. This band was very much attached to him; but a feeling of hatred, which was sometimes open and declared, and at others secret and dissembled, divided the mulattoes and blacks, even though they followed, whilst under his orders, the same standard.

Touissaint-Louverture, a black, and formerly a slave, commanded at the Cape and in all the northern and central parts of the colony. He had recalled the former proprietors who had emigrated, had protected them and restored their lands, with the exception of a few plantations that had been seized on by his friends and himself. But he had only exhibited this generosity in tranquil times. He acted very differently in war, and being persuaded that it was necessary to carry it on without mercy, when the sword is once drawn, he pushed his success without giving his adversaries any intermission, and if he met with a reverse, he revenged it by fire and plunder. His enemies accused him of hypocrisy and dissimulation. He was, they said, coldly cruel, and the extermination of the whites formed part of his plan for rendering the colony independent. His partisans made him a hero and a statesman.

Touissaint may be more impartially judged from a view of his life. Obliged in his infancy to obey as a slave, unexpected events suddenly made him the equal of the whites, and he filled his new place without embarrassment or arrogance. He entirely forgot what he had suffered in his first condition, and was generous even towards many of whom he had reason to complain. His activity and strength were prodigious, and he moved with extraordinary rapidity from one extremity of the colony to the other, according as circumstances required his presence. Vigilant, sober, and abstemious, he quitted the table and gave up every relaxation the moment that business demanded his attention. An upright judge, without learning or education, an able general from the very day that he ceased to be a private soldier, he was dear to his army, and the negroes obeyed with a sort of pride a man of colour, whom they considered the superior, or the equal, at least, of the most distinguished white man.

He was aware that a community, without labour or industry, soon falls into a state of barbarism, and he had revived agriculture by regulations which had been attended with the most happy results. The privileged productions, the precious aliment of a flourishing commerce, had become as abundant as formerly; but their destination was much changed. The plantations were sequestered, and the greatest part of the revenue was paid into the colonial treasury, instead of being sent to France. Touissaint and his government thereby disposed of immense riches, which gave rise to the opinion that he possessed a hidden treasure. There is no sufficient authority for this conjecture, though we are far from rejecting it. He exacted labour, not

in order to accumulate treasures, but to fulfil one of
the conditions of the social state. "I know how," he
frequently said, " to unite liberty and labour." To this
end all his proceedings were directed, but as soon as
he perceived that its attainment was questionable, he
became, though he was not without elevation of soul,
suspicious and implacable. He saw flow, without pity,
the blood of every one who was convicted of having
put in danger that liberty which was so dear to him,
on his own account, as well as on that of all the people of his colour, and he no longer treated of business
with the candour and good faith that smooth all difficulties. According to him, it was the safety of the blacks,
his own safety that obliged him to oppose cunning to
perfidy; and the secret intelligence which he kept up
with the emissaries of the government of Jamaica was
rendered necessary by the condition of St. Domingo, at
the period that he was acknowledged as its master.

His army was composed, in 1800, of about twelve
thousand blacks. War between men who are distinguished from one another by the colour of the skin is always terrible, because they at last believe themselves to
be of two different species; thus when a black man and
a mulatto met, each saw in the other an enemy. The
slightest hostilities had then an exterminating character
scarcely known among savages. Treason and secret
violence destroyed in this colony more human beings
than battles. Rigaud, too weak against adversaries
infinitely superior in number, had thought proper to
abandon an unequal contest, and had fled to France.

'Touissaint made a constitution for the colony; he sent it to the first consul, who was very much dissatisfied with it, and declared that it should never be put in force.

Such was the state of affairs, when Bonaparte, on the faith of the preliminaries of London, and on the point of concluding the definitive peace, conceived the design of sending to the colony a fleet and army under the command of General Leclerc, his brother-in-law. Eighteen thousand troops were, at first, embarked on board of thirty ships of the line, for he was afraid to give, by freighting transport vessels, too much publicity to an expedition which he wished to keep secret. It was, however, well known at St. Domingo, as the English did not neglect to apprize the mulattoes and blacks of it.

Suspicions and jealousies are the ordinary relations of cabinets with one another, and at the very moment that they are making mutual professions of entire confidence, they fear not only probable perfidies, but even all such as are possible. Although the first consul had only been a short time at the head of affairs, foreign statesmen conceived that they were acquainted with his character, and they did not rely enough upon his political probity to have their impressions of his real intentions removed by a simple declaration.

Re-enforcements were, from time to time, sent both to the fleet and army. There was among the French officers an extraordinary emulation to be of this expedition. Accustomed to glory, the attendant on great

successes, they had foreseen none of the dangers,
which are incurred by all who are exposed to the sun
or even the night air in tropical regions.   It was considered a high favour to belong to the expedition, and
the number of generals and officers, compared with
that of soldiers, far surpassed the ordinary proportions.
A part of these forces was composed of Spaniards
and Germans; some Poles were also among them.
These legions, which had been drawn from their country to contribute to the great events that changed the
face of Europe, had become embarrassing to France
in her new state of peace.   The idea occurred of
sending them to St. Domingo.   Thus these soldiers,
many of whom were scarcely manumitted from servitude, were destined to restore to the bonds of slavery,
Africans, with whom they had no ground of quarrel.
The French troops landed on the 3d of February,
1802.   On the arrival of these forces, the black general, Christophe, set fire to Cape Français, and this
beautiful city was partially consumed.   The blacks
adopted it as their law to lay waste their own country,
and to burn down the houses, in order to deprive the
enemy of resources.   This rage, and these conflagrations but too well announced the disasters which en-
sued.   From the beginning, the success of the Europeans, who gained several battles from the blacks, was
balanced by the losses that they sustained from the
climate.   There was no longer any question of rebellion, but the hostilities had assumed the character of a
war between two independent nations.

A great change had followed the abolition of slavery. During a century and a half, an habitual terror had kept the blacks in the most abject subjection to their masters. They had then such an idea of the superiority of the whites, that, in the thickest and most solitary forest, the sight of a white man would have been sufficient to inspire twenty blacks with dread. This almost supernatural power, which had vanished at the proclamation of liberty, had been suddenly renewed, on the arrival of a numerous army of white troops, and, for some time, it only required a mere patrol to put to flight a battalion of blacks. Some, however, resisted with success, and then almost every engagement became a battle. These whites, so long dreaded as beings of a superior species, were but ordinary enemies, when the negroes discovered that it was so easy to make them prisoners, or put them to death. They daily recovered their courage, and soon had as their rallying words, wherever the French were found in small numbers; "Let us kill our oppressors." The mulattoes and free negroes practised atrocious vengeance on the whites; they were in their turn thrown by hundreds into the ocean, and the sight of their carcasses, washed back on the shores, drove this unfortunate race to horrible reprisals. Where they could not massacre, they set fire to the house.

Leclerc committed still greater faults in his political conduct than as general of the army. It is doubtful, however, whether these faults should be imputed to him alone. Government had wished to direct every

thing from Paris. His public instructions ordered him to
make use of the influence of those who were free before the revolution, in order to bring back all the newly
manumitted population to an intermediate state, which
it was wished to assimilate to the condition of serfs.
He had also been authorized to hold out the expectation, that the estates would be soon restored to the
former possessors. This he announced, and his public acts, which at first conformed with his declarations,
did not entirely satisfy any party.

But another design, of which the first consul had
confided to him the secret, was to convert the estates
of the emigrants into military grants, and to indemnify,
by these usurped riches, the generals and other officers
to whom the peace of Amiens had closed in Europe
the career of glory and fortune. There is reason to
believe, that many of them would not have wished to
profit by this spoliation, which it would, moreover,
have been difficult to carry into effect. The negroes,
although they had been brought back to labour by
Touissaint and his officers, would have resisted new
masters, who would only have had over them the right
of conquest. The right of property, resulting from
purchase, was consecrated by the practice of so many
centuries, that the slave himself deemed it entitled to
respect. The first consul had been advised, but not
convinced, that if there was any means of re-establishing discipline, and even slavery, it was only to be effected by recalling to their former plantations the mas-

ters, to whom the blacks had for so long a time belonged. At the sight of them, habit, fear, affection, that consciousness of degradation, which in an abject state debases a man in his own eyes, would have rendered obedience comparatively easy.

Leclerc commenced the execution of the unjust plan of making a distribution of lands to officers of the army. He was obliged to renounce it almost immediately, inasmuch as he had only a short and precarious possession of the different parts of the colony. He had recourse to other expedients; but, instead of making concessions with sincerity, deceptive promises were profusely given. Sometimes there was a show of moderation, at others of severity, but never either frankness or firmness.

The first consul had been advised, that, if Rigaud returned to St. Domingo, his presence would occasion an open schism between the blacks and mulattoes, which, according to the vulgar maxim, would advance the authority of the French government. He was, therefore, sent to serve under the general-in-chief; but, when he left France, the change that had occurred in the views of Leclerc and his counsellors towards the mulattoes was not known. The French general had at first apparently shown a disposition to employ the aid of this cast, but the mulattoes soon became objects of suspicion and jealousy to his habitual associates. Rigaud, who was welcomed on his return by all the people of his colour with transports of joy, inspired the white population with great dread. Touissaint was also

25

alarmed by the presence of his old enemy, and Rigaud was re-embarked for France, by order of General Leclerc. The other mulattoes soon perceived, that, after they had been employed against the blacks, they would be sacrificed in their turn. Wearied by frequent accusations, and by the constant watch that was kept over their conduct, they became so many secret enemies. Touissaint-Louverture maintained a defensive position, which differed little from actual hostilities. He seemed for a moment disposed to submit to retirement, but he soon found that a person, once all-powerful in arms, and supreme chief of the government, cannot safely return to obscurity. The parties sought him, and he again engaged in intrigues, which were not long kept secret. Leclerc, after some hesitation, conceived that he ought to open a secret negotiation with him, for the war and climate had already destroyed eight thousand Europeans.

Great caution was at first employed in treating with Touissaint. Trusting to friendly expressions, which were communicated to him through his children, he by degrees approached the general-in-chief.

Still treating as an equal with the French generals, he consented to lay down his arms on the following conditions: "The sovereign dominion of the island to be restored to France; the soil, buildings, and other immovable property, to the old proprietors; liberty to the slaves, who are to labour for wages." These propositions, the sincerity of which appeared doubtful, were rejected with disdain; and, after having sent back to France the chief of the mulattoes, the design was entertained of depriving the blacks of a still more formidable leader.

Violence and stratagems, which it has been in vain attempted to justify, placed Touissaint in the power of Leclerc. This general made him embark for France. The blacks foresaw but too well the fate that was reserved for their idol, who was thus removed from their affections and their cause. But the whites began to regain their courage. They might have believed, during a few months, that the colony was restored to its obedience to the French republic. Commerce was carried on with confidence; many of the proprietors returned to their plantations. The blacks seeing themselves without any guide appeared confounded; but this manifest violation of plighted faith had spread among them a secret indignation and the desire of vengeance. The confidence of the mulattoes had been destroyed by sending away Rigaud; the resentment of the blacks was excited when Touissaint was stolen from their affection. These feelings were soon openly manifested, and the rising was general, because it was the work of reflection: the perfidious then experienced the effects of their own treachery, as all their proclamations passed for gross falsehoods, and not a black remained faithful to the French.

The fleet and army at their departure from Europe had been furnished with abundant supplies for six months: those who had advised the expedition had not failed, in order to remove all objections, to say that it was sufficient to provide the first supplies, that so rich a colony offered immense resources, and that the war would support itself. But great difficulty was soon experienced in combining vast operations in a country destitute of most things necessary for a European army. The commanding general had supposed that, as he was the near connexion of the first consul, he might, on his arrival at the place of destination, render all interests subordinate to the success of his expedition. In such circumstances, a general, removed for some thousand leagues from any authority superior to his own, pushes to extreme consequences the principle, " I must support my army." What had happened forty years before in Canada and India was here repeated; the colony was made acquainted with requisitions against which all France had risen in arms, forced loans, and every thing that could irritate it against its pretended liberators. The embarrassments were not diminished by this abuse of authority, and in the distress which the army experienced, the chiefs, while they took possession of every thing that could be useful to them, adopted the plan of making payments in bills of exchange drawn on the treasury of France. Destined at first to satisfy real wants, they were soon used to reward friends and appease the discontented. Those who had been plundered, under pretence of requisitions, found afterwards the means of settling amicably the price of their effects and the rate of compensation for their losses; and as the sums, thus stipulated to be paid, occasioned no other trouble than that of manufacturing drafts, they were given with such profusion, that they were presented in a short time, at the French treasury, to the amount of more than sixty millions. The French also sent to the United States to ask assistance and credit, but all these resources were insufficient; for when a design miscarries, the disorder is unbounded.

Other chiefs rose up in the place of Touissaint-Louverture. Dessalines, who assumed the command of the black army, was very inferior to him in capacity. He was, however, endowed with a vigorous and persevering character. Naturally sanguinary, he had by terror and executions acquired a great authority over the blacks. His army was every day increased by those who abandoned the labour of the plantations. The month of August, so fatal to Europeans, had arrived, and the French army was constantly weakened by irreparable losses. The crews of most of the merchant vessels were reduced to a fourth of their complements. Debauchery, strong drinks, and unhealthy food likewise contributed to destroy the army; and an epidemic, more murderous than the sword of the negroes, carried its horrible ravages into the French camp.

The general-in-chief, attacked nine months after his arrival with a mortal malady, began to reproach himself for the faults which his inexperience and interested counsels had led him to commit. He died on the 2d of November, 1802, as much in consequence of chagrin as of the unhealthfulness of the climate.

Rochambeau assumed the command after Leclerc's death. Considerable re-enforcements were sent, and he at first obtained some advantages. But after a year of alternate successes and reverses, he was obliged to shut himself up at the Cape with the wreck of his army. Besieged by the negroes on the land side, blocked in on that of the sea by an English squadron, he had recourse to some desperate measures to prolong his resistance. He imposed contributions on the inhabitants, which could only be levied by violent acts. A merchant, who had probably exhausted all his means, declared that he could not pay the sum at which he was assessed. The general caused him to be shot, while even the blacks viewed the execution with horror. He capitulated on the 18th of November, 1803, with Dessalines for the evacuation of the town, and, on the 29th, with the English for the surrender of the ships of war and merchant vessels. Six or seven thousand whites, who were received on board the English fleet, considered themselves fortunate in having thus got away from the fury of the rebels.

These voluntary exiles fled to Louisiana, the United States, Cuba and Jamaica. Some of them, who were in an entirely destitute state, awaited in those countries better circumstances, which never arrived. Others had opportunely sent a few slaves before them; they carried with them their activity and experience, and the countries of their adoption were enriched by the dispersion of these planters, and the ruin of the richest

agricultural and commercial settlement that the world
has ever seen.

Dessalines had caused himself to be named general-
in-chief of the army. Many white inhabitants, impru-
dently confiding in his solemn promises,* had remained
in the colony. On the 1st of January, 1804, about a
month after the evacuation and departure of the
French, he made a declaration of independence. He
continued to hold a language calculated to encourage
the white proprietors. But soon using as a pretext the
information, either real or fictitious, that the whites
were preparing to rise up against him, his fears, and
still more his natural ferocity, carried him to horrible
excesses. He repeated that, if ever the French should
be re-established in their plantations, they would be
forced, for their own preservation, to strengthen the
irons of slavery; that there was no middle state for
the blacks between liberty and the most horrible servitude, and that the safety of the colony depended on
the entire extermination of the whites. From all sides
dreadful words were re-echoed, announcing a general
massacre. "Let us avenge ourselves of these tigers
who thirst after our blood. The Almighty commands
us to shed theirs. If a single individual among us
feels the least pity, let him fly, he is unworthy of
breathing the pure air of august and triumphant liberty."

He went through the colony from north to south,
marking his passage by the massacre of all the whites

* Dessalines' Proclamation of the 25th of November, 1803.

that could be discovered. They were collected by hundreds, and when they were thus assembled he took pleasure in seeing them shot or cut down by the sword. These executions commenced at Cayes, in February, 1804, and were continued from town to town till they reached the Cape, where Dessalines redoubled his cruel excesses. The massacre lasted there from the end of April to the 14th of May. Neither age nor sex was spared; and violations of the person often preceded the murder. The whole number of victims was two thousand four hundred and twenty.

I have brought together in a few words the principal circumstances of the disasters of St. Domingo. The loss and ruin of this magnificent possession have caused to the commercial affairs of France injuries, which active internal industry alone can repair. But another direction must be given to trade, and this will be effected by a transfer of business, which the new condition of the former Spanish possessions in America renders easy. Without considering these reverses irreparable, except with reference to the general plan which the first consul had formed, it is sufficient to say that Louisiana had been destined to supply the other colony with provisions, cattle, and wood; and as St. Domingo was lost to France, the importance of Louisiana was also diminished: but these disasters were not yet known to Bonaparte. He expected to make use of the one colony to preserve the other, and he was particularly fond of occupying himself with his new acquisition.

It was agreeable to him to suppose that, notwithstanding their long separation, the Louisianians had
preserved their affection for their mother country, and
that they would be happy to resume their French character. Recollecting the regrets manifested at the time
of the cession to Spain, thirty-five years before, he persuaded himself that the re-establishment of the French
authority would be a matter of general rejoicing. He
had been led into this error by reading letters written
from New Orleans by some of the St. Domingo colonists who had escaped there. The cession revived all
their hopes; for the two colonies being in the neighbourhood of one another, the one which was tranquil
might facilitate the subjection of the blacks in the other,
afford succour, and above all furnish subsistence to the
army sent to conquer it, and at that time hopes of success were not abandoned.

But if these colonists, stripped of their wealth, had
an interest in drawing the inhabitants of Louisiana
into their cause, the Louisianians had contrary interests. They had reason to fear for themselves the calamities which had been, for many years, ruining the
other colonies of France. St. Domingo was the most
agitated and unfortunate of all. The colonists repeated with horror, at New Orleans, these words which
the first consul had caused to be proclaimed, in his
name, in the revolted colony, and which were there
addressed to all classes. "Inhabitants of St. Domingo, whatever may be your colour or your origin, you
are all free, all equal in the eyes of God and the re-

public." General Leclerc, on his arrival in the colony, had said; "I promise liberty to all the inhabitants."

It is true that, a few months afterwards, these promises had been retracted by a law of an entirely contrary nature, which re-established slavery, and authorized the slave trade as it existed before 1789.

Nothing is more calculated to destroy confidence than these changes in the will of rulers, and the holding out of expectations which are given or withdrawn according to the circumstances and interests of the moment. The intercourse is prompt and easy between Cape Français and New Orleans, and few weeks passed without information being received in the latter place of some new disaster that had occurred in St. Domingo.

The whites themselves till the land in some parts of Louisiana, but the great plantations, and especially the sugar estates are cultivated by black slaves. Even the drivers are chosen from among this class, and the slavery of the blacks is deemed a necessary condition of the riches of the whites. Some of the refugee colonists had brought a part of their negroes to Louisiana, and were therefore secretly far from desiring another removal or participating in the views of those who had lost every thing. They easily made the Louisianians acquainted with the danger that they would incur, in case the French republic, as the supreme legislative power, should one day proclaim manumission and freedom in their colony.

They foretold, what was subsequently verified in St. Domingo, an appropriation of the land in large and small portions to all the blacks who had borne arms, from the generals down to the private soldiers, and to all the civil agents; the men to whom liberty was new avenging themselves with fury of their former abject state; the rights of property disregarded; the negro, the usurper and master of the soil which he had fertilized by the sweat of his brow, but living on little, placing the supreme good in repose, and having no regard for the enjoyments of luxury or the profits of a laborious commerce. It was then said, that "the free Africans in America would do still less labour than the slave in Africa." From all these disasters the Louisianians expected to be preserved if the sovereignty of the catholic king was not transferred to the French republic.

We must add to these just causes of uneasiness, the revolution which had been operating on the mind for thirty years, and which had penetrated even to the least enlightened classes. It was no longer thought that princes had the right, except in consequence of a disastrous war, to dispose of their provinces according to their own will, to mortgage or hypothecate them, to exchange them or transfer the sovereignty to others without the consent of the people; and maxims, which had been long received as part of the public law, had thus lost their authority.

Scruples of this kind did not even occur to the first consul, impatient to establish the French government in Louisiana.

He at first selected for the chief command in the colony a distinguished personage,—General Bernadotte,*—of whose ambition and activity he entertained fears. This important employment would have removed him from Europe in an honourable manner, and the first consul expected marks of satisfaction from the general. Bernadotte, whose character for firmness and boldness without rashness is well known, thought that he ought, before accepting this mission, to prepare the means of securing his success. He made it a condition of his departure, that he should carry with him, besides three thousand soldiers, an equal number of cultivators of the soil, and that he should, moreover, be provided with every thing that was necessary in a remote place, where he might be prevented, for an indefinite period, from communicating with France. Bonaparte replied to these proposals; "I would not do as much for one of my brothers:" and he named General Victor governor, and appointed at the same time the prefect and chief judge.

Always uneasy, however, at the presence of Bernadotte, he determined, at the beginning of 1803, to send him to the United States in the character of minister plenipotentiary of France. This was a kind of exile, and, to diminish its bitterness, he was given to understand, that it was in contemplation to cede to those states a part of Louisiana, and that he would be employed in the negotiation. Personal advantages were

* The present king of Sweden.—Transl.

held out to him as the price of the success that he might obtain.

Bernadotte accepted the mission. He repaired to Rochelle, and the frigate in which he was to embark was about putting to sea, when he learned that a rupture between France and England was on the eve of breaking out. He immediately returned to Paris without waiting for leave, and firmly declared that he would not engage in any civil employment so long as the war lasted. He did not even see the first consul, who had evinced a great deal of dissatisfaction at a return, which he had not authorized. Some time elapsed before common friends could reconcile them.

General Victor, the captain general, Laussat, the prefect, and Aymé, the chief judge, had been appointed. A consular decree of the 11th of September, 1802, had regulated their functions. Victor was preparing to set sail from Helvoetsluys with the garrison intended for New Orleans, and the other troops that were to be sent to the colony. He had so little idea of a change of destination, that he was purchasing and putting on board of the vessel in which he was to embark the presents that he intended for the Indians. Hostilities between England and France commenced about this time, and the general's departure did not take place.

M. Laussat had received his instructions, and the order for his departure on the very day that the dissatisfaction that was manifested in the English parliament was known at Paris. He set sail on the 12th of January, 1803.

He was cordially welcomed at New Orleans by the Spanish government, and immediately announced by a proclamation, the expected arrival of his two colleagues; but General Victor was alone authorized to receive the colony from the hands of the Spanish officers. This formality necessarily preceded all others, and as he did not come, the colonial prefect was without duties or authority. He, however, published several laws of the republic that were calculated to give confidence to the colonists and particularly the one of the 20th of May, 1802, for the maintenance of slavery and the slave trade, as they existed before 1789. A few public officers who accompanied him, were likewise without any active duties, and a sum of one hundred and eleven thousand Spanish dollars, delivered to him on his departure, remained unemployed.

The events, of which he was informed on landing, were not calculated to make him augur great success from his mission. A ship that arrived from Cape Français, almost at the same time with him, brought the news of the reverses and disasters of every kind which had succeeded the death of the general-in-chief. A serious difference had also just arisen between the United States and the government of Louisiana, the particulars of which will be hereafter mentioned.

M. Laussat not having as yet any character that authorized him to take part in the administration, the powers of the government remained in the hands of Don Manuel de Salcedo, and of the Marquis of Casa Calvo. In a proclamation, in which they took the title of commissioners of the king for the cession of the province to the French republic, they announced the change of sovereignty and gave the inhabitants assurances respecting the preservation of their rights and of their property in the lands that had been granted to them, and farther promised, that the titles to grants that had been confirmed, and even to those that were not confirmed, should be respected.

These officers of the former government, in concert with the one who had just arrived, applied themselves in good faith to inspire the inhabitants with sentiments favourable to their new masters. But those, who were in any condition to foresee the future, did not think that the situation of the population would be meliorated by the cession, or that France could derive any real advantages from it. Even the merchants, eager as they always are to welcome flattering expectations, did not promise themselves any benefit from this change.

There was, therefore, no open indication of those marks of satisfaction, which the return of the French would, at other times, have produced. An eye-witness, speaking of the sentiments which were manifested on occasion of the arrival and reception of M. Laussat, expressed himself in these terms:—

" Every one will be astonished to learn, that a people of French descent have received without emotion and without any apparent interest a French magistrate, who comes to us, accompanied by his young and beautiful family, and preceded by the public esteem. Nothing has been able to diminish the alarms which his mission causes. His proclamations have been heard by some with sadness, and by the greater part of the inhabitants with the same indifference as the beat of the drum is listened to, when it announces the escape of a slave or a sale at auction."*

How much gratitude, on the other hand, would have been shown to the first consul, if instead of prohibitory laws, his envoy had proclaimed freedom of trade, and declared that France renounced for ever the system which has been pursued for the settlement of colonies in modern times. It would have been a measure of enlightened policy to have solemnly admitted that their prosperity continually advances with a free system, and that their relations with the parent states become useful in proportion as their commerce is extended without restraint. For exclusive privileges and monopoly, the best quality of merchandise, and the most moderate profits should have been substituted; in a word, according to the example of the ancients, the colony ought only to have been retained by the ties which favours create, by the recollection of a common origin and the affection which lasts a long while, when the parent state and her offspring have the same habits and language, and interests that are easily reconciled.

* Appendix, No. 7.

If such a plan could have been adopted, instead of the practices that have prevailed for two centuries, it would have silenced England, calmed the disquiet of the western states of the American Union, and France would have found inestimable advantages in the return to the ancient principles on which colonies were founded.

At the same time Louisiana would have efficaciously contributed to the prosperity of the insular colonies; and if those fine settlements could have been preserved, this province, united to the Floridas, would have built up the navy of France and revived its navigation. But the principles of free trade were very far from being followed in relation to Louisiana. The Spanish intendant had, a short time before, re-established there the prohibitory system in all its rigour, and his conduct had caused great excitement in the very bosom of congress.

Twenty-five years had scarcely elapsed since the United States had assumed a place among nations, and their population was already increasing with astonishing rapidity, especially in the territories situated to the west of the Alleghany mountains. The federal government had not interfered, except to give to those new communities a direction conformable to the spirit of the general association, and in a little time the superintending care of a wise government had contributed more to all kinds of improvement than the European states had effected in the colonies subject to them during three centuries. The best lands were every

27

where offered to the choice of settlers, and the indigenous inhabitants yielded them up without much resistance. They only lived by the chase, and as the
game quitted the places that were inhabited, and
stripped of their forests by the new clearings, they
were obliged, with the deer, to fall back on more remote wildernesses.

Whilst in Europe the occupation of a single village
may give rise to a war, the Americans laid, without
any apprehensions, in their recently explored territories,
the foundation of ten new states, any one of which
is equal in extent to a quarter of France. Nothing
arrests these peaceable conquests. If the natives
require an acknowledgment of their rights, if they
even make a serious resistance, a few bales of goods,
some presents of little consequence, or a moderate
annuity most frequently suffice to quiet them. Far
from there being any difficulty in finding, in the United
States, lands suitable to the enlargement of the territory, its very extent already alarms the inhabitants
of the old states, who are interested in checking the
emigrations which take place to the new ones. It
is in fact very certain that the increase of the territories of the confederacy is one cause of the weakness
of the older portions. The augmentation of their
population, however great it may be, does not compensate for the continual emigrations. This draining
will not abate till the banks of the rivers which flow
from the west of the mountains to the Mississippi are
occupied and cultivated. It is there, that by an inde-

fatigable activity, the face of the soil is constantly changed. Even the emigrants who have commenced settlements soon find themselves straitened for room in a country, which was a few years before a wilderness. The heads of families prefer to all other enjoyments, that of giving to every child fertile lands with a virgin soil. Many sell the farms which they themselves have cleared, in order to settle at a greater distance. There is a continual flowing in one direction without any return. The lands, the most remote from the country already settled, are the cheapest. Some of excellent quality are to be had for less than two dollars an acre; and the farther the colonists advance in the interior, the more can they enlarge the inheritance of their posterity. But a condition indispensable to the success of all these emigrations was, that the rich and abundant crops of the west should have access through the mouths of the Mississippi to all the markets of the world. The Americans had already, for more than twenty years, asserted, as an incontestable right, the free navigation of that river to the sea; and neither Spain, nor subsequently France, had been inclined to this concession, so contrary to the exclusive system. At that time sufficiently powerful to refuse and effectually sustain their refusal, they did not suppose that the moment could ever arrive when their new neighbours would be in a condition to give them the law. For this, however, every thing was preparing, without the governors that were sent from Europe paying the least attention to the progress of the Americans, and the change was already effected when they remarked its consequences.

At the close of the year 1802, congress was informed of the cession which Spain had made to France of Louisiana; and, almost at the same time, it learned that this last power was preparing to take possession. The news of this change of sovereignty excited lively alarms in all the western settlements. It was feared, and congress partook of the apprehension, that the neighbourhood of the French would not be so pacific as that of the Spaniards.

The Spaniards, nevertheless, considered themselves masters of the province, so long as the formalities of the cession to France were not fulfilled. The severe regulations, which in the other Spanish colonies maintained the monopoly of the mother country and protected its exclusive commerce, had not been observed in Louisiana. This wise relaxation suddenly ceased. Those absurd systems, which by means of prohibitions more or less rigorous, keep the finances and commerce of two neighbouring states in a situation resembling war, and which sometimes bring about real hostilities, were all at once put in full force in this colony. Don Juan Ventura Moralès, the intendant, said, with ignorant confidence, that "colonies were only useful under the prohibitory system, and that if produce, received *in transitu*, was not subjected to import and export duties, the indulgence would have all the bad effects of authorized smuggling."

A treaty, concluded on the 27th of October, 1795,

with Spain, had granted to the United States "the right to deposite their merchandise and effects at New Orleans for the space of three years, and at the end of that time the privilege was either to be continued or an equivalent establishment assigned on another part of the banks of the Mississippi."

The intendant, after the expiration of this term of three years, had not interrupted the operation of the grant, and it had been prolonged by a kind of tacit agreement. But, in 1802, he suddenly imagined that an indulgence introduced during the war should cease with the peace.

M. Moralès, contrary to the opinion even of the Spanish governor, who looked upon every suspension of the entrepôt, without an equivalent, as an infraction of the treaty, put an end to the enjoyment of a privilege which he was afraid to see perpetuated by a sort of proscription. He declared, by a proclamation of the 16th of October, that the right of deposite no longer existed.

This measure spread great consternation among the American planters in the western territories. Congress was beset from all quarters with complaints and statements of grievances. The excitement redoubled as soon as the petitioners heard the news of the cession to France, and, according to the generally received opinion, the suspension had only taken place in consequence of the demand of that power.* Louisiana, by the

* Memoir of Mr. Monroe, page 7.

terms of the treaty, "was to be delivered up in its present state."* This present state was, they said, the exclusion of the Americans from the port of New Orleans. They drew from this circumstance the inference that the intendant had not acted without orders; that the return to the prohibitory system had been concerted between the two powers, and that it was in order to ensure its execution that France was sending an army.

A census of the new states, east of the Mississippi, made their population amount to nearly 800,000 souls. The old states sent there by land the merchandise necessary for these new colonies. The numerous fine rivers which flow from the north-east, empty into the Mississippi to the west; and this river, with the gulf of Mexico, served to export the productions of the new settlements, and especially their abundant harvests of every description of grain. The trade, which was carried on from the continent through the gulf, was the only means that the planters of the new western states had to pay for what they received from the other states of the American Union. No rivers of Europe are more frequented than the Mississippi and its tributaries. To impose obstacles on this navigation was to stifle these new communities, and to condemn vast regions to the barrenness, which, after so many centuries, had just been replaced by an admirable fertility. The prohibition affected this prosperity, and the agricultural

* The Decree of the king of Spain of the 30th of July, 1802.

productions suddenly lost half their value as well at New Orleans as at Natchez, the place from whence they were forwarded. Already the cry of alarm was heard, not only in the states of Ohio, Tennessee, and Kentucky, and in the territories of Indiana and Mississippi, but even in all the old states, whose limits extend beyond the western mountains, and it was repeated by the numerous emigrants who flocked from all quarters to share in the magnificent inheritance so long neglected by the savage tribes. The new settlers compared the feeble and unarmed population of Louisiana with their own numbers. Proud of the superiority of their strength, they found in it the basis of an incontestable right. They longed for a rupture, when they might occupy New Orleans. " The Mississippi is ours," they said, "by the law of nature; it belongs to us by our numbers, and by the labour which we have bestowed on those spots which, before our arrival, were desert and barren. Our innumerable rivers swell it, and flow with it into the gulf sea. Its mouth is the only issue which nature has given to our waters, and we wish to use it for our vessels. No power in the world shall deprive us of this right. We do not prevent the Spanish and French from ascending the river to our towns and villages. We wish in our turn to descend it without any interruption to its mouth, to ascend it again and exercise our privilege of trading on it and navigating it at our pleasure. If our most entire liberty in this matter is disputed, nothing shall prevent our taking pos-

session of the capital; and when we are once masters
of it, we shall know how to maintain ourselves there.
If congress refuses us effectual protection, if it for-
sakes us, we will adopt the measures which our safety
requires, even if they endanger the peace of the Union
and our connexion with the other states. No protection, no allegiance!"

These maxims are not, in all respects, those of the
publicists; but such proceedings, and the roughness of
the language were to be expected from men, still surrounded by the vestiges of a primitive state, where
every individual thinks that he has a right to whatever
he considers necessary for his preservation and well-
being.

The country of the Natchez had passed under the
dominion of the United States. Mr. Daniel Clarke, a
rich proprietor, and a man of activity and cleverness,
who had his plantation there, had neglected no means
of exciting discontent. At the first news of the retrocession to the French, he had gone in haste to Paris, and
had sought by different means to produce a misunderstanding between the French general, for whom the
command was intended, and the colonial prefect. On
his return to Louisiana he found the disposition of the
public favourable to his designs.

In the uncertainty which then existed as to the part
that would be adopted, either by France or Spain, respecting the right of deposite at New Orleans, the Americans of the west favourably received Mr. Clarke's
proposal to establishing at Natchez the entrepôt that

had been refused them by the Spaniards. This port is situated on the eastern bank of the Mississippi, in the territory of the United States, forty leagues above New Orleans, and the climate was said to be more agreeable than at the latter place. Much stress was laid on the advantages of a situation that was more protected from the insults and attacks of a maritime power. But the two towns being equally exposed to the epidemical diseases, with which these countries are afflicted as soon as the lands begin to be cleared, the project failed.

There was much excitement likewise in congress, of which the parties endeavoured to take advantage. Mr. Jefferson was president, and in order to maintain the flourishing condition of the confederacy, this magistrate made every exertion to prevent, by all possible means, the disturbances that might result from these occurrences. They, nevertheless, appeared to him so grave, that though he allayed the fears of the governments of Kentucky, and the other western states and territories, as to the consequence of the measures adopted by the Spanish intendant, he brought the subject to the knowledge of the house of representatives, by a message of the 22d of December, 1802, in which he added, " that he was aware of the obligation to maintain in all cases the rights of the nation, and to employ for that purpose those just and honourable means which belong to the character of the United States."

To this message and another one that was transmitted to them shortly afterwards, the house of representatives replied, that "relying, with perfect confidence, on the vigilance and wisdom of the executive,
they will wait the issue of such measures as that department of the government shall have pursued for asserting the rights of the United States—holding it to
be their duty, at the same time, to express their unal-
terable determination to maintain the boundaries and
the rights of navigation and commerce through the
river Mississippi, as established by existing treaties."

It was at first not known whether France would not
attempt to assign new frontiers to her province and revive old titles, in opposition to treaties and the interests of the United States.   Every thing appears suspicious to a people, when they have once conceived
distrust.   They recollected the expeditions of the
French governors to the frontiers of Canada.   The
armaments, which the first consul was preparing at
Flushing, were, they said, intended to usurp the territories of the Union, and re-establish the ancient limits
of Louisiana.

The proclamation of the Spanish intendant, executed with rigour, only served to make more apparent
truths, which were not even suspected by him, namely,
that exclusive privileges are useless barriers against
local and natural necessities, and that no opposition
could move the Americans on these two principal
points—the free navigation of the Mississippi, and the

privilege of exporting their productions and importing their merchandise through that great river.

The prohibition soon became very injurious even to the inhabitants of New Orleans. Flour and other supplies were no longer brought there. The fear of famine obliged the intendant to permit their importation and exportation, at first, indeed, on conditions almost as onerous as the prohibition itself, though he was afterwards obliged to connive at the total disregard of his own regulations.*

But this indulgence might be precarious, and the Americans wished to exercise rights that were free from all dispute. In vain had a letter been published from Mr. Livingston, the minister in Paris, containing assurances that the treaties with the United States would be strictly executed. These explanations had not been sufficient to tranquillize the public mind, and delays were no longer in season.

It is necessary to take advantage of the favourable months, in order to navigate the Mississippi. At other periods of the year, stationary or floating masses of ice are not less to be dreaded than the rocks or sand banks that are hid under the water. Trees of a prodigious size, which the river carries along with it when the thaw is accompanied by inundations, often obstruct its channel. It is again made navigable by labour, and the obstructions cease on the return of spring. The month of May was approaching, and

* Proclamation of the 5th of February, 1803.

at that period the Mississippi and the minor rivers, swollen by the melting of the snow, are every year covered with boats, men, and agricultural productions. But the usual course of trade was interrupted, and the inhabitants considered themselves devoted to certain ruin, unless it was averted by vigorous arrangements. The excitement was so great that some officers of the American army proposed plans both for offensive and defensive operations. They were urged on by a party, which had been as ardent for war as its opponents were zealous for the maintenance of peace.*

The treaty, by which the independence of the thirteen colonies was acknowledged by England, had been on the part of that government an act of great wisdom. There were, however, in the two countries, some persons so badly informed respecting public opinion, that they believed it possible to bring back those provinces, not indeed under the sceptre of the king of England, but under an influence which would procure for the mother country all the political advantages of sovereignty. Their intrigues had encouraged the forming of the party, denominated federal, whose conduct and proceedings were for a long time directed by the principle of attachment to England, and enmity to France.

The principal leaders had influence only in four or five states of the north, and it was supposed that their secret object was to separate them from the Union.

* Mr. Monroe's Memoir, page 7.

" The interests of the northern states cannot," they said, " be reconciled with those of the southern and western states." And, in fact, the climate, productions, navigation, and the existence of slavery had introduced very different habits in the various sections of the United States. But there is no country of so great an extent where such differences are not found, and they do not prevent all the parts of the confederacy from being united by a common bond. Many federalists had really the public good for their object, and the purity of their intentions cannot be doubted, when we know that Washington had given them his support. But it was also suspected, and with too much foundation, that some ambitious men had been introduced among them, who, under the guise of zeal for liberty, only aspired to power. A treaty had been signed at London by Mr. Jay, the American plenipotentiary, which contained clauses favourable to England, prejudicial to the United States, and was not ratified without difficulty.

The governor of Canada secretly excited the federalists, and it must be admitted that England might have effectually profited by a separation, which, by placing five states under her protection, would have created two factions in the bosom of her rival, and rendered the cabinet of London the arbiter of their differences.

The party known under the name of republican, was more independent of all European intrigues, and, though it was not devoted either to England or France, it saw less danger in preferring the friendship of this latter power, in which it found a surer guarantee of the commercial and maritime independence of the confederacy.

The practices of the ambitious could not be long concealed, and they lost all their influence as soon as their true designs were known. It was even in the northern states that they experienced the strongest opposition, and at the moment that we are writing a great change is accomplished. Animosities and feelings of hatred have been, by degrees, dissipated. Harmony is now the soul of this great confederacy. From New Hampshire to Louisiana the prevailing principle is, that a good understanding between the different parts of the Union ought to be maintained, even at the price of some sacrifices, as the basis of the public tranquillity, and of the prosperity of each individual state.

Party names are almost always an artifice of those who wish to have among the same people, in the same nation, two hostile nations, and it is in this way that enmities are perpetuated. The names of federalists and republicans are now no longer in use. The title of opposition is, however, still given to a party, which is really composed of observers, who, far from being opposed to the government, confine themselves to cautioning it against falling into errors. During a period of forty years congress has made a great and honourable experiment: it has constantly observed the fundamental laws, to which it owes its existence, and it has scarcely ever been found in direct opposition to the opinion of the people. What had long been only a matter of hope and theory has become a truth confirmed by fact; namely, that the confederacy has within itself the principle of its own strength and permanency, and that nations are the only sure guarantees of their own repose and happiness.

THE

HISTORY OF LOUISIANA.

PART II.

CESSION·OF LOUISIANA BY FRANCE TO THE UNITED STATES.

29

HISTORY OF LOUISIANA.

PART THE SECOND.

CESSION OF LOUISIANA BY FRANCE TO THE UNITED STATES.

WHILST even in congress a very active faction was secretly endeavouring to induce a declaration of war by the United States against France, the rulers of the confederacy sincerely desired to maintain a good understanding. On its side the consular government appeared to wish to pursue towards this republic an opposite course of conduct from that of the directory. War between France and England seemed inevitable, and the American cabinet easily perceived that, in case it should break out, the first consul would be under the necessity of putting off the occupation of Louisiana. On the 15th of December, 1802, Mr. Jefferson thus addressed congress: " The cession of the Spanish province of Louisiana to France, which took place in the course of the late war, will, if carried into effect, make a change in the aspect of our foreign relations." The circumstance in question presented, in fact, to the United States a chance, which might never again occur, of commencing negotiations for an amicable ces-

sion of territories which it was extremely desirable
that they should possess. " Besides," said the friends
of peace, " we are not prepared for war. Ten years
of peace are necessary to make us respectable and
powerful, we shall then be in a situation to face every
danger." It was determined that an envoy extraordinary should be sent to Europe to treat with the first
consul, and if no satisfactory arrangement was to be
made with him, to enter into communications with the
courts of London and Madrid. The choice of Mr.
Jefferson fell on Mr. Monroe, ex-governor of Virginia,
a man zealous for the interests of his country, who enjoyed great popularity in the western states, was very
influential in the republican party, and was already advantageously known in France, where he had resided,
as envoy, in the time of the directory. In 1786, Mr.
Monroe, then a member of congress, had written a
memoir to prove the right of the western country to
the navigation of the Mississippi. The president confided to his friend the most important transaction of
his administration, and he regarded him as the negotiator best calculated by his experience to ensure its
success.

Mr. Livingston, the minister of the United States at
Paris, had warmly pursued this affair for many months.
He had sent to the minister of foreign affairs a note in
which his arguments were supported by intimations that
were almost menacing. He did not confine himself to
demanding the cession of New Orleans; he also proposed that France should cede the vast territories that

are to the north of the river of the Arkansas and on the right bank of the Mississippi.* But his overtures remained unnoticed, the suspicions that he had long entertained, that new Orleans could only be obtained by force of arms, became with him in some sort matters of certainty, and his official and private correspondence urged the adoption of extreme measures. We have seen that Mr. Jefferson did not participate in these hostile dispositions.†

* Appendix, No. 8.

† The course of President Jefferson at this crisis was very decided. Notwithstanding the charge of partiality to France, usually imputed to him, it will be seen by the instructions from the secretary of state to Messrs. Livingston and Monroe, dated April 18, 1803, and published in 1826, that war with the first consul was regarded by the administration at Washington as probable. In case the free navigation of the Mississippi or the right of deposite at New Orleans was denied to the United States, the American ministers were directed to consult with England, with the view of making common cause with her against France. See Appendix, No. 18.

Mr. Jefferson also wrote to Mr. Livingston, as follows:— "The day that France takes possession of New Orleans, fixes the sentence which is to restrain her for ever within her low water mark. It seals the union of two nations, who, in conjunction, can maintain exclusive possession of the Ocean. From that moment we must marry ourselves to the British fleet and nation. We must turn all our attention to a maritime force, for which our resources place us on very high ground, and, having formed and connected together a power which may render re-enforcement of her settlements here impossible to France, make the first cannon which shall be fired in Europe the signal for tearing up any settlement she may have made, and for holding the two continents of America in sequestration for the common purposes of the united British and American nations. This is not a state of things we seek or desire. It is one which this measure, if adopted by France, forces on us as necessarily, as any other cause, by the laws of nature, brings on its necessary effect."—TRANSL.

The confidential letters, by which he informed Mr. Monroe of his nomination, form a proper prelude to the negotiation, and are calculated to make us acquainted with the views and foresight of this statesman. They deserve to be preserved.

"*Washington, Jan.* 10, 1803.

"Governor Monroe:—

"Dear Sir—I have but a moment to inform you, that the fever into which the western mind is thrown by the affair at New Orleans, stimulated by the mercantile and generally the federal interest, threatens to overbear our peace. In this situation, we are obliged to call on you for a temporary sacrifice of yourself, to prevent this greatest of evils in the present prosperous tide of our affairs. I shall to-morrow nominate you to the senate, for an extraordinary mission to France, and the circumstances are such as to render it impossible to decline; because the whole public hope will be rested on you. I wish you to be either in Richmond or Albemarle till you receive another letter from me, which will be within two days hence, if the senate decide immediately; or later, according to the time they take to decide. In the meantime, pray work night and day, to arrange your affairs for a temporary absence— perhaps for a long one. Accept affectionate salutations.

Thomas Jefferson."

The senate sanctioned the nomination; and on the 13th of January the president wrote to his friend the following letter:—

" *Washington, Jan.* 13, 1803.

" DEAR SIR—

"I dropped you a line on the 10th, informing you of a nomination I had made of you to the senate, and yesterday I enclosed you their approbation, not having then time to write.   The agitation of the public mind on occasion of the late suspension of our right of deposite at New Orleans is extreme.   This in the western country is natural, and grounded on operative motives.   Remonstrances, memorials, &c. are now circulating through the whole of that country, and signing by the body of the people.   The measures which we have been pursuing, being invisible, do not satisfy their minds; something sensible, therefore, has become necessary, and indeed our object of purchasing New Orleans and the Floridas, is a measure likely to assume so many shapes, that no instructions could be squared to fit them.   It was essential, then, to send a minister extraordinary to be joined with the ordinary one, with discretionary power, first however, well impressed with all our views, and therefore qualified to meet and modify to these every form of proposition which could come from the other party.   This could be done only in frequent and full oral communication.   Having determined on this, there could not be two opinions as to the person.   You possessed the unlimited confidence of the administration and of the western people, and were you to refuse to go, no other man can be found who does this.   All eyes are now fixed on you; and were you to decline, the chagrin would be great, and would shake under your feet the high ground on which you stand with the public. Indeed I know nothing which would produce such a shock; for on the event of this mission depends the future destinies of this republic. If we cannot, by a purchase of the country, ensure to ourselves a course of perpetual peace and friendship with all nations, then, as war cannot be far distant, it behooves us immediately to be preparing for that course, without, however, hastening it; and it may be necessary, (on your failure on the continent,) to cross the channel. We shall get entangled in European politics, and figuring more, be much less happy and prosperous. This can only be prevented by a successful issue to your present mission. I am sensible, after the measures you have taken for getting into a different line of business, that it will be a great sacrifice on your part, and presents, from the season and other circumstances, serious difficulties. But some men are born for the public. Nature, by fitting them for the service of the human race on a broad scale, has stamped them with the evidences of her destination and their duty."

It is apparent that New Orleans and the Floridas were still the only objects of consideration. However, it was natural to ask of the French republic, the new sovereign of the country, at the moment that the possession of Louisiana was passing from Spain to France, redress for a grievance of which the intendant, Morales, seemed the only author. but of which nothing announced the definitive termination. Mr. Monroe was, therefore, instructed to state that a solemn treaty with Spain had not prevented a simple depositary of the royal authority from ordering, at his own suggestion, a suspension of commerce that was necessarily prejudicial to both parties; that it was dangerous and contrary to all rules of prudence that colonial officers, at a distance of two thousand leagues from their sovereign, should have the power to jeopard, by arbitrary and capricious measures, the peace and good understanding which their governments were desirous of maintaining; that the surest way of preventing every source of dispute would be the cession of the city of New Orleans, situated on the eastern bank of the Mississippi, and that this measure would tend to benefit Western Louisiana, now the property of France, as well as more effectually secure its possession to that power. The directory no longer existed, but it had made the disorders of the French finances too well known for a foreign state to expect to treat in any other way than with ready money. Mr. Monroe was authorized to offer the price of this cession, which had been fixed by the American government at two millions of dollars.

Until then the Americans had only asked that the course of the Mississippi should be divided by a line that would put New Orleans within the territory of the United States, which they declared to be the sole means of securing to them the free navigation of the river. Projects for the cession of the entire colony were at

that time neither popular nor the subjects of much discussion. It was, indeed, natural to fear that if the sovereignty of the United States should be extended on
the right bank of the Mississippi, the unity of interests, so necessary to the strength of a community,
would not only be relaxed, but that it might be entirely destroyed by the continual emigrations from east to
west. If the future consequences of the increase of
this new population were regarded, it could not be
hoped, without contradicting history and experience,
to embrace within the federal union regions so remote,
nor expected that congress, whatever might be its
place of meeting, could long govern the countries on
the right bank of the Mississippi. It was, on the contrary, indisputable that these acquisitions becoming
powerful, in their turn, would detach themselves from
the old states whenever their interest should require it.

These observations had reference to a remote futu-
rity. But a present object, which affected a great
number of the merchants and ship owners of the
United States, was to form part of the negotiation intrusted to Mr. Monroe. We refer to the injuries ascribed to the directory, the government that had immediately preceded that of the first consul, the repa-
ration of which the envoy was instructed to demand.

It is necessary to go back a few years in order to
understand the object of this important part of the negotiation. The interests of commerce, colonial settlements, and navigation have effected great changes
in the reciprocal relations of the nations of Europe.

The independence of the United States has rendered them still more complicated. But such changes are not often remarked by statesmen themselves, till they have committed great faults by persevering in old errors.

The directory, led astray by false notions of the situation of the French colonies, had not remarked that their existence depended upon the preservation of a good understanding with the United States. Instead of re-establishing friendly relations with the American Union, it had, after more than once putting it in jeopardy, finally broken the alliance which had been the precious fruit of the policy of the councils of Louis XVI. Mutual discontent had not yet resulted in direct hostilities; but even in peace captures were made by privateers bearing the French flag, which became the subject of great complaints on the part of the United States. It was likewise, at this period, that the first disasters of the French colonies led to the emigration of many families, who from great opulence had fallen into deep distress. Numbers of them took refuge in the United States. Never was hospitality more nobly exercised than under these circumstances; never were more sincere and effectual consolations offered to misfortunes by a grateful people. This generosity towards refugees, the objects of the persecutions of the directory, was not regarded by its members as a motive for reconciliation with the American republic. They had inherited the animosities of the convention, and the West Indian possessions were the victims of them. These colonies, prosperous in time of peace, are exposed to all sorts of calamities as soon as war breaks out. Their intercourse is interrupted; a parent state, weak at sea, can neither supply them with provisions nor export their produce, and is most frequently incapable of defending them. If they resort to neutrals, this relaxation of the prohibitory system habituates the colony to privileges, which make them look on the return of peace with indifference. The directory, in order to maintain their prohibitory laws, had permitted the local authorities to provide for the preservation of the colonies by arming privateers, and these agents encouraged them to fall indiscriminately on all flags. They carried their disregard of the rules of justice and the laws of nations so far as to condemn, as lawful prizes, ships that had entered the ports with subsistence and provisions intended for the inhabitants of the islands that they governed. Victor Hugues, one of these colonial rulers, openly professed and put in practice the maxim, that—" In time of want all kinds of provisions are good prize." The American government, before commencing hostilities with France, wished to exhaust all pacific measures. It had sent three ministers to the directory towards the end of 1797.* On their arrival at Paris they were circumvented by all sorts of intrigues. Their correspondence is a monument of the base manner in which the French government at that time managed their political affairs. " The most disgraceful cupidity," they wrote to their

* Messrs. C. C. Pinckney, Marshall, and Gerry.—TRANSL.

constituents, "was openly manifested at Paris." The
American commissioners were told that "their government paid money to obtain peace with the Algerines
and with the Indians; and that it was doing no more
to pay France for peace."

This negotiation lasted for six or seven months: it
was broken off when it was found impossible to continue it on such erroneous principles.

Congress, without declaring war, had announced
through the president, (John Adams,) on the 28th of
May, 1798, that, "whereas armed vessels, sailing under authority or pretence of authority from the republic of France, have committed depredations on the
commerce of the United States in violation of the law
of nations and treaties; it should be lawful for American armed vessels to retake any ship so captured, as
well as to seize and bring into port such armed vessels as had committed depredations on vessels belonging to citizens of the United States."

The animosity was still increasing in 1799; when
congress, renouncing vain attempts at moderation, resolved that all intercourse with France should be suspended; that the treaties had ceased to be obligatory;
and that the capture of French vessels was permitted.

From the beginning of the consular government a
wise policy had put a stop to all reprisals: a convention
had been signed on the 30th of September, 1800;* but
according to a stipulation, without which the reconci-

* The American plenipotentiaries were Messrs. Ellsworth, Davie. and Murray.—Transl.

liation would have been impossible, indemnities were to be paid for all prizes unlawfully made. Ministers had been subsequently interchanged, and the envoy of the United States had calculated on prompt satisfaction. The commu:. :ations which he addressed to his government authorized this hope; but the expectations were not realized, and in fact the finances of France had scarcely begun to emerge from the chaos in which the bad government of the directory had°plunged them.

This part of the convention of 1800 therefore remained unexecuted; and this contempt of the most ordinary rules of justice carried the general irritation in the United States to its greatest height. The president and his cabinet, compromitted by their moderation, were beginning to make their reproaches heard, and talked of doing themselves the justice that was refused them. The American minister at Paris had received orders to make this discontent known, and his notes were drawn up with a firmness to which Bonaparte was not accustomed. If one of the continental powers of Europe had dared to employ similar language, the invasion of its territory would have been the consequence. Congress, separated by the Atlantic Ocean, could without danger assume a menacing attitude; and the first consul was cautious how he exhibited a resentment, which would have only manifested his own weakness. But as the notes of Mr. Livingston, the American minister, remained unanswered, the injured merchants and ship owners lost their patience, and murmured against their government. The enemies of France in the United States, attentive to this general discontent, hoped to avail themselves of it, in order to force the Union into an alliance with England.

These matters were discussing with warmth, when news from the west greatly increased the public excitement.* Not only had the Spanish intendant put his proclamation in force, but new orders forbade all communication between the Louisianians and Americans. In the number of the colonies, formed in the western part of the United States, was one, not yet admitted into the Union, situated on the left bank of that river, and denominated, not without reason, the territory of Mississippi. It was the nearest to New Orleans, and openly expressed more animated complaints when it deemed moderation useless. " We saw," said these planters, in a memorial to congress of the 5th of January, 1803, " our trade flourishing, our property rising rapidly in value, and we felicitated ourselves in being the free and happy citizens of an independent republic. Reposing in national faith for a continued observance of *stipulated* privileges, we had indulged the sanguine expectation that this state of prosperity would not have been so soon interrupted. A recent order by the government of Louisiana has considerably increased the embarrassment upon our trade, and breathes a spirit of still greater enmity to the United States. Conscious of the wisdom, justice, and energy of the general government, we tender to our country out lives and fortunes in support of such measures as

* Appendix, No. 9, 10.

congress may deem necessary to vindicate the honour and protect the interest of the United States."

This petition led to a proposal which the federal party had secretly prepared. About the middle of February, 1803, Mr. Ross, a senator from Pennsylvania, offered a resolution, in a public sitting of the house to which he belonged, to take possession of New Orleans by force. "Let us not await," said he, "the arrival of the French, but since a solemn treaty is violated, let us not hesitate to occupy places that ought to belong to us. The people of the west are quite ready, and there would be excessive simplicity in supposing that the city will be yielded to us spontaneously, or even by virtue of a treaty with the first consul."

On his pronouncing these words, another senator, seeing the danger of a public discussion, required that the galleries and tribunes should be cleared and the doors closed. The proposition was opposed by those who, with Mr. Ross, wished to inflame the public mind. But as the rule of the senate provided that the demand of a single member should be sufficient to exclude strangers, the sitting became secret. Mr. Ross continued thus: "We must no longer await the uncertain results of diplomatic correspondence, Louisiana ought to belong to the United States, the people of the west are impatient to do themselves justice; and if the French are allowed time to arrive, the Americans, in those parts of the Union, will refuse to pay taxes to a government too feeble to protect them. Never will there be so favourable an occasion to annex to the federal union a country without which half of our states could not exist; it is easy to seize on it, as France is on the eve of going to war with England; the English on their part will neglect nothing to gain the friendship of the United States; the advances which they make to obtain our alliance prove that they value it at a high price, and consider it indispensable to the success of the new measures that they are forced to adopt. It is time to teach the world that the balance of America is in our hands, that we are as dominant in this part of the globe as other nations are in Europe, that we fear none of them, that our period of youth is over, and that we are entering on the age of manhood and are prepared to make use of our strength." He concluded his remarks by proposing to place five millions of dollars at the disposition of the president, and to raise fifty thousand men to take possession of Louisiana by force.

The house of representatives, on its part, took up the question, and its deliberations were likewise secret. When the doors were again opened, it was announced that the president had been requested by the house to correspond with the governors of the different states, to urge them to organize their militia and put it on the footing established by law.

The senate continued its deliberations. After two sessions, with closed doors, it was decided that Mr. Ross' motion should be publicly discussed.

Gouverneur Morris, who was in France, as the envoy of the United States, at the beginning of the revolution, was a member of this assembly. He had not awaited this public occasion to say, "that the arrival of the French should be anticipated, that the acts of the intendant were not revoked, that the decree of the king of Spain announced no modification, that the French troops were already at sea, that the inhabitants of the menaced territories were losing patience, and that it was time to come to an open rupture."

This senator was considered one of the most distintinguished writers of the party denominated English. This English policy will be discovered in most of the circumstances which we are now about to narrate. From the beginning of the revolution of the United States, Mr. Morris had been recommended to the public suffrages by his easy and elegant elocution, and by his talents, but still more by his boldness and self-confidence. Such qualities give to their possessors in times of violent excitement a sort of importance, though men of this character are rarely fit to manage public affairs; and Gouverneur Morris soon saw the end of the consideration which he had enjoyed. He fell in a great measure into obscurity, as soon as the cloudy times passed by.

Mr. Livingston, the American minister at Paris, was persuaded that the United States would never possess New Orleans by treaty, and that it ought to be taken by force. His intercourse with the French ministry confirmed him in this impression,* and it is probable that the opinions of Mr. Ross and Gouverneur Morris

* Mr. Monroe's Memoir, page 10.

were derived from the correspondence of this envoy; but the wise Jefferson persisted in his hopes, and temporized in order to avoid adopting any false measures in the midst of so much uncertainty. Placing great reliance on Mr. Monroe's mission, he took the utmost care to prevent any violent proceedings in the neighbourhood of the Mississippi.

But this envoy had not yet quitted America; the uncertainties of navigation, and the distance did not authorize the hope of a prompt issue from so many difficulties. England, on her side, was making seductive proposals, and her friends, in order to induce their reception, might take advantage of the five or six months which must elapse before the result of the negotiation intrusted to this plenipotentiary could be learned at Washington.

It was known, on the 20th of February, 1803, and before Mr. Monroe sailed for Europe, that the commander of the squadron, on board of which the division of troops intended for Louisiana was embarked, had received orders to postpone his departure. This news, which was very agreeable to the friends of peace, momentarily disconcerted the partisans of war or extreme measures. But soon resuming courage, they had recourse to publications and different artifices by which it would be so easy to excite troubles, if the free presses that are employed for doing mischief, were not a still surer instrument of correcting it, even when they have not been able to prevent it.

The discontented party had recourse to a stratagem that did not long succeed.

An article was published in a Kentucky newspaper, in which the eastern states were accused of sacrificing to their own views the interests of the western states, and the latter were advised to separate from the Union and contract an alliance with the French republic.

The author of the piece, who was an inhabitant of Kentucky, bore a French name. A general outcry obliged him to keep concealed. His effigy and his writings were burned by the people to show the horror with which counsels tending to the division of the country inspired them. At the opening of the federal court, the grand jury, who alone could take cognisance of the matter, indicted the editor. The Americans have never supposed that there ought to be a distinction made between political and other crimes, and that special tribunals should be established to try them. They know that if such a weapon was in the hands of a party, every accused person of the other party would, when arraigned, have to encounter the fatal prepossession of his judges.

The flight of this libeller put an end to the prosecution; but it was fully established that every faction that attempted to fortify itself by the support of either England or France, would draw on it the animadversion of all good citizens.

Congress adjourned on the 3d of March, 1803, after having received from the different legislatures proofs of their entire confidence in its wisdom, and the promise of seconding it by all those measures of vigour that circumstances might render necessary.

M. Pichon, the chargé d'affaires of France, considered this crisis so important, that he took it upon himself to write to the Spanish governor of Louisiana to conjure him to prevent hostilities by revoking the prohibitory ordinances, of which the intendant was the sole author.

The public mind was a little calmed by the assurances given by the Marquis Casa Yrujo, the minister of Spain, in a note of March 10th, 1803, in which he officially declared that the intendant had acted without authority, and that, in conformity with the treaty, a place of deposite instead of New Orleans would be assigned.

Mr. Monroe sailed from New York on the 8th of March, 1803, but as the object of his mission was still kept secret, the public apprehension was not quieted.

President Jefferson, feeling full confidence in the measures on which he had decided, did not think proper to reply to those who charged him with pusillanimity.* The first consul, informed of the purport of Mr. Monroe's public instructions, supposed that the president had also left it to the plenipotentiary's prudence to enter, if necessary, into more extended stipulations, in relation to the projected acquisition. The possibility of a war between France and England,

* Appendix, No. 11.

which this statesman foresaw at the distance of a thousand leagues from Europe, had suggested to Mr. Jefferson the measures which he had just adopted.

The history of the negotiation renders necessary some details respecting the difference which arose between the cabinets of the Tuileries and London in the early part of 1803. Europe was enjoying a momentary respite after the many revolutions she had undergone. She then witnessed the recommencement of the most violent crisis that ever perhaps affected her repose, and which continued to agitate her during ten years. The events that I am now going to relate are the forerunners of every thing connected with the cession of Louisiana.

The Grenville party, as the English termed it, was composed of men of great capacity. They were earnestly intent on the increase of the royal prerogative, which was already strengthened by the persevering policy of Mr. Pitt: they reckoned this statesman in their ranks, although he affected independence, confining himself to manifesting that hatred for France which he had inherited from his father.

Mr. Fox was the soul of an opposition which seemed less ambitious than zealous for the public good. He was a worthy rival of William Pitt, and would have triumphed over his adversary, if his private conduct had been more in accordance with the uprightness of his political principles.

The ministry, as it ordinarily happens, maintained a position between the parties. It had, at its head, Mr.

Addington* and Lord Hawkesbury, since known under the name of Lord Liverpool. Doubts have been raised as to the sincerity of their intentions when they concluded the peace of Amiens; but we believe that Mr. Addington really desired that it might be durable. It has been said that the chief consul placed from the beginning little reliance on its continuance, and that he only regarded the peace as a truce. He pursued without any intermission his designs in Upper Italy, and united to France under equivocal denominations those countries which had been so long disputed between her and Austria. When these changes, and those which he was effecting in Holland and Switzerland, had given him a great preponderance in the affairs of Europe, he felt that in order to confirm this new order of things and exercise this vast supremacy, he in his turn required the maintenance of peace. But he desired it on condition of being in some sort the universal dictator, and he was so much the more averse to every concession, as the revocation of one single act of his power would have been followed by his rival's requiring the revocation of all the others.

Like all conquerors, this great captain had placed his happiness and glory in transporting from one country to another bodies of youthful warriors; in putting masses of population in motion, and in astonishing the world by the promptitude and success with which he executed the vastest and most complicated designs. But there was at this time reason to think

* Subsequently created Viscount Sidmouth.—TRANSL.

that the convulsions of empires had less attraction for
him; he spoke of them with a sort of disdain, and appeared to direct the prodigious activity of his genius
to works which in peace embellish society and secure
tranquil enjoyments to nations.

To give to France better civil laws, to plan a reform
of the codes, to re-establish order in the finances, to
revive commerce and industry, were the objects to
which, assisted by able counsellors, he consecrated his
time, prolonging his labours even to midnight. If, with
these generous sentiments, he had thought that liberty,
under good laws, was the most noble present that he
could make to men, the age in which we live would
have been called by his name. Withdrawn, for a short
time, from the designs of a continental war, he conceived that his republic could not be flourishing without a commercial marine, sustained and protected by
great naval forces. He often repeated the following
maxims: "Without the liberty of the sea, there is no
happiness for the world. But, to obtain this liberty, it
is requisite that the continental powers should impress
the English with serious alarm for their commerce. Instead of opposing to their maritime forces inefficient
fleets, instead of constructing vessels of war, which
will sooner or later increase the English navy, they
should, on the first appearance of hostilities, arm privateers, which, issuing from all the ports of the continent of Europe in pursuit of merchant ships, would be
protected by their number, and even by their dispersion. The English cannot have recourse to reprisals,

for they have taken possession of almost every branch of commerce. If they leave us a few colonies, it is for the purpose of exhausting us in vain expenses for their preservation, and to make us, in spite of ourselves, disposed to peace through the fear of losing them. Finally," he added, "the liberty of the seas must be odious to the English, because it would confine them to their natural share in the general prosperity."

That the possession of colonies is a dangerous burden to a nation, to whom the ocean is closed as soon as a maritime war commences, was then but imperfectly perceived, though twenty-five years later it became an admitted truth.

The two powers were still at peace, when, in the middle of January, 1803, the news of the death of General Leclerc was received; and the chief consul, persisting notwithstanding that event in his first views, had with reluctance abated his exertions for the speedy departure of the new forces which he purposed sending to America.

These armaments had only St. Domingo and Louisiana for their object; but nothing was farther from the habitual policy of Napoleon than half measures and timid efforts. There never had been an example, while the powers of Europe were at peace, of sending such considerable forces into remote countries. The anxiety of the English for their colonies in the gulf of Mexico might be easily justified, and their ambassadors and ministers were excusable for not putting entire confidence in the protestations of the first consul

32

on that subject. We believe that they were sincere; but France, once great, strong, and powerful in those seas, who could answer for the future and guaranty Jamaica and the other British West India islands? By what means could the French be prevented from getting possession of all the trade of the Spanish dominions in America? Moderation rarely continues with a great increase of power.

After the peace of 1802, Egypt and the Cape of Good Hope were evacuated by the English; but they continued to occupy the island of Malta. The first consul demanded that it should also be evacuated in conformity with the last treaty. He farther asked that certain editors of newspapers who abused him should be expelled from England, by virtue of the alien law; and, finally, he complained of plots that were formed against him even in London, and under the direction of men who held high offices.

The English government increased his resentment by causing the courts of justice to interpose in these complaints. Bonaparte was also offended with the leniency of the punishment adjudged against the authors of the libels.

The parliament had been opened on the 23d of November, 1802, and from that time it had been expected, as well in consequence of the king's speech, as of the debates to which it gave rise, that the opposition would make every effort to render war inevitable.

"The last treaty of peace," Lord Grenville said, "was ratified in May, and the incorporation of Piedmont

took place in the month of June following. Parma
and Placentia have had the same fate, and Louisiana
has been extorted from Spain by treaty." " Our natural and inveterate enemy," said Mr. Canning, " unre-
mittedly pursues his designs against our commerce and
navigation. The hostile intentions of France towards
this country can no longer be questioned."

Both sides were far from being amicably disposed,
and the grounds of dispute were only increased by several public proceedings. The first consul, on the 8th
of February, 1803, laid before the *Corps Législatif* a
statement of the affairs of the republic, in which he
bitterly complained of a party in England that had
sworn implacable hatred to France, as well as of the
refusal of the cabinet of London for the last eleven
months to execute the treaty of Amiens. In this paper was the following phrase: " Five hundred thousand
men must and shall be ready to defend and avenge the
republic."

The English government appeared firmly determined
not to retrograde one step, and it manifested this resolution in the most public manner. On the 8th of
March the king of England sent a message to the two
houses of parliament, in which he gave intimations of
an approaching rupture. It stated " that His Majesty
thought it necessary to acquaint them, that, as very
considerable military preparations were carrying on in
the ports of France and Holland, he had judged it expedient, though these preparations were avowedly directed to colonial service, to adopt additional mea-

sures of precaution for the security of his dominions; and that he relied with perfect confidence on their public spirit and liberality to enable His Majesty to adopt such measures as circumstances might appear to require for supporting the honour of his crown and the essential interests of his people."

Two days afterwards the two houses received a message to the following effect: "That in consequence of the formidable military preparations carrying on in the ports of France and Holland, pending the discussion of an important negotiation between His Majesty's government and that of France, His Majesty had thought it necessary to exercise the power vested in him by acts of parliament for calling out and embodying forthwith the militia of these kingdoms."

This first cry of alarm, on the part of the ministry, was regarded in France as the precursor of approaching hostilities. The governments of the two countries, however, looked on the war with a sort of dread, which became proportionably greater as its certainty increased. The first consul himself, although resolved not to yield on any point, regretted that, after having advanced so far, he could not get out of the difficulty with honour. But, according to his usual practice, he soon pretended that this rupture was a fortunate occurrence, and that had it happened two or three years later, the vigour of his armies might have been weakened by repose.

The two messages of the king of England had been followed by a vote for ten thousand seamen. The rage of the first consul was at its height. The minister of foreign affairs received orders to throw off all disguise with the English ambassador, and the following explanation only served to show that an open rupture was near breaking out:

"All the world knows," said M. Talleyrand to Lord Whitworth, "that the naval expedition which we were preparing at Helvoetsluys was intended for America, and that it was on the eve of sailing. The embarcation of our troops and the departure of our fleet have, however, been countermanded in consequence of the messages of the king of England."

This readiness to stop the sailing of an armament, commenced at great expense, did not at all accord with the character of the first consul; but, in fact, he yielded nothing. Before he was acquainted with the message of the 8th of March, 1803, he had looked on war as inevitable; he had therefore, without hesitation, renounced the intention of sending troops to America, being well aware that the fleet would have been captured during the voyage and carried into England. Thus, what M. Talleyrand promised accorded with the new plan which had just been decided on.

After making this easy concession, the French minister added: "We have wished to give proofs of our anxious desire to calm the uneasiness of the British government, and we hope that it will give us in its turn a satisfactory answer respecting its preparations. If our expectations are deceived, it will be necessary that the first consul should send twenty thousand men to Holland; a natural consequence of this movement will be the forming of a camp on the frontiers of Hanover; there will be another one at Calais. Even the most ordinary prudence will require that the French army should be put on a war footing, and that preparations should be made for placing France in a situation to act either offensively or defensively. The first consul was on the eve of withdrawing the troops from Switzerland; but he now is necessarily obliged to keep them there, as well as to send new forces to Italy. Reflect, my lord, on this state of things: if it is not one of war, it is very near it." There was also some conversation on the occupation of Tarentum, a post as important as Malta for a new invasion of Egypt.

After this conference, the first consul sent Duroc to Berlin, Colbert to Petersburg, and persons in whom he had the greatest confidence to other courts to acquaint them with the measures which the message of the 8th of March had rendered necessary.

A private and almost domestic incident was then very much commented on, and we will now relate it on account of the importance of the circumstances with which it was connected.

Bonaparte had not obliged himself, like other princes little initiated in the mysteries of their own policy, to treat with ambassadors and envoys exclusively through a minister. He conversed with them tête-à-tête, and even in public, and frequently availed himself too freely of his privilege of speaking in the name of a powerful nation. Only a few days had elapsed since the date of the two messages of the king of England. The respective ambassadors of the two countries were not on that account less assiduous in their attendance at audiences and formal receptions. At Paris, these assemblies, which were held at the Tuileries, were frequented by a great many persons, and the foreign ministers mixed with the crowd of courtiers. One evening the first consul was seen entering in a thoughtful, pensive mood surrounded by his usual retinue. He shortened the circuit which he commonly made in the reception room, and approaching the English ambassador, said to him in a loud voice: " You are then determined on war?" " No," replied Lord Whitworth, " we are too well acquainted with the advantages of peace." To these measured words, the first consul, without being restrained by the presence of so many attentive and inquisitive personages, replied with warmth; " We have made war on one another for fifteen years; the storm thickens at London, and appears to menace us. Against whom do you take precautions? Wherefore your armaments? Is it that you desire another fifteen years' war? I do not arm. My good faith is manifest. Full of confidence in a treaty, the ink of which is hardly dry, I have not listened to any malevolent rumour, but have banished that mistrust which would make peace as detestable as war. I have not a single ship of the line armed in my ports; I have shown no hostile intentions. The contrary supposition is an egregious calumny. I am taken unawares, and glory in it. If the English are the first to draw the sword, I will be the last to sheathe it. If we must cover solemn treaties with black crape, if those who have signed the peace desire war, they must answer for it before God and man."

It was by these haughty menaces rather than by good arguments,—by this harsh and immethodical eloquence,—that Napoleon meant to establish his claims, or make his enemies fear measures that he had not yet entirely decided on.

But the English could defend their conduct by similar arguments, and they were not more just in their proceedings. Both sides had, however, in fact disarmed, and both sides also pretended to act by way of reprisals.

The excitement was confined, at Paris, to the palace and the hotels of the ministers. At London, it had been manifested in parliament and among the people. The ministers were drawn on farther than they had anticipated; the message of the 8th of March had rendered the opposition triumphant, and it flattered the national vanity by offering the hope of immediately restoring England to the first rank which she had lost.

The conquests of Bonaparte had substituted to diplomatic forms and discussions, hasty decisions adopted, as it were, on the field of battle. England, so long accustomed to interfere in all matters, was now in the habit of learning, all of a sudden and without being previously consulted, that a province or vast country had changed its master and its constitution. She exclaimed against the overthrow of the European system,

as well as against the acquisitions made by France
of the Spanish part of St. Domingo and of Louisiana;
and whilst she was complaining, the accession of other
territories disturbed still more the former condition of
Europe.

The English ministry had long refused to state
clearly its complaints. At length, on the 16th of
March, Lord Hawkesbury sent a note respecting them
to the English ambassador at Paris, with orders to
communicate it. It was in these terms: " The treaty
of Amiens, like every other antecedent treaty or convention, was negotiated with reference to the actual
state of possession of the different parties, and to the
treaties or *public engagements* by which they were bound
at the time of its conclusion; and if that state of possession and of engagements is so materially altered
by the act of either of the parties as to affect the nature of the compact itself, the other party has a right,
according to the law of nations, to interfere for the
purpose of obtaining satisfaction or compensation for
any essential difference which such acts may have subsequently made in their relative situation. If the interference of the French government in the general
affairs of Europe; if their interposition with respect to
Switzerland and Holland, whose independence was
guarantied by them at the time of the conclusion of
the treaty of peace; if the acquisitions which have
been made by France in various quarters, but particularly those in Italy, have extended the territory and increased the power of France, His Majesty would be

33

warranted, consistently with the spirit of the treaty of peace, in claiming equivalents for these acquisitions as a counterpoise to the augmentation of the power of France. Under these circumstances, His Majesty feels that he has no alternative, and that a just regard to his own honour, and to the interests of his people, makes it necessary for him to declare that he cannot consent that his troops should evacuate the island of Malta until substantial security has been provided for those objects which, under the present circumstances, may be materially endangered by their removal."

On both sides the object was by the plunder of a third party to restrain or punish a rival; but it is manifest that in this career of injustice, Bonaparte had, in Europe, at least, gone very much beyond the other power.

These important matters were discussed at the Tuileries, at one of those private conferences, in which the first consul, carried away by the abundance of his ideas, energetically stated the wrongs done by his adversaries, without admitting that he had committed any himself.

"The principles of a maritime supremacy," he said to his counsellors, "are subversive of one of the noblest rights that nature, science, and genius have secured to man: I mean the right of traversing every sea with as much liberty as the bird flies through the air; of making use of the waves, winds, climates, and productions of the globe; of bringing near to one another, by a bold navigation, nations that have been separated since the creation; of carrying civilization into regions that are a prey to ignorance and barbarism. This is what England would usurp over all other nations."

One of the ministers who were present enjoyed the privilege of speaking to him with freedom. He said: " Have not the English as many motives for dreading a continental supremacy and being alarmed at your great influence over all Europe?" He seemed to reflect; but, instead of replying to so direct an argument, he turned to the extracts, which were always made for him from the debates in the English house of commons, and read a passage, with which he appeared very much irritated. " France," said the speech referred to, " obliges us to recollect the injury which she did us twenty-five years since, by forming an alliance with our revolted colonies. Jealous of our commerce, navigation, and riches, she wishes to annihilate them. The proceedings of the first consul, at the end of a peace made with too much facility, compel us to appeal anew to arms. The enemy, by a dash of the pen, appropriates to himself territories more extensive than all the conquests of France for many centuries. He hastens his preparations; let us not wait till he attacks us, let us attack first."

" Now," continued the first consul, " propose your theories and your abstract propositions, and see if they can resist the efforts of these usurpers of the sovereignty of the sea. Leave commerce and navigation in the exclusive possession of a single people, and the globe will be subjected by their arms, and by the gold which occupies the place of armies." He then added these words, in which are found the first indication of his policy respecting the United States, and which a sort of inaccuracy renders still more energetic. " To emancipate nations from the commercial tyranny of England, it is necessary to balance her influence by a maritime power that may one day become her rival; that power is the United States. The English aspire to dispose of all the riches of the world. I shall be useful to the whole universe, if I can prevent their ruling America as they rule Asia."

Circumstances apparently less important than conferences with ambassadors or speeches in parliament, tended to redouble the habitual irritation of the first consul.

Out of the two houses the English expressed themselves with still more vehemence than in the parliamentary debates. It was to be seen from the newspapers, in which public opinion manifests itself, that the people would soon know how injurious to England had been the policy of those who had strengthened by a solemn treaty the establishment of a powerful republic in Europe, and that liberty, once acclimated in a country so happily situated as France, would make advances there, which England would sooner or later have reason to regret.

A French Journal, published in London, was particularly distinguished by the extreme violence with which it was written. The intention of exciting the nation to a war plainly appeared; and of this object, indeed, the abuse aimed at the Chief of the French government, did not permit a doubt to be entertained. It was known how easily he was irritated, and he was insulted even in the persons of the members of his family. The papers printed at Paris were not more moderate with respect to England and the reigning house, and they excited more attention, as it was well understood that the first consul was no stranger to their composition. The opinion of the English was not unanimous for the resumption of arms. Those who paid the most attention to the complaints raised against the treaty, easily remarked that commercial jealousy and maritime interests had the greatest share in them. Every permanent agreement seemed impossible between two nations, whose pretensions were so irreconcilable. The one wished a monopoly of the commerce of the world; the other desired to participate in it.

These discussions were to be terminated by war, and Bonaparte, who relied on himself alone to carry it on with success on the continent, well knew that colonies could not be defended without naval forces; but so great a revolution in the plan of his foreign policy was not suddenly made. It may even be perceived, from the correspondence of the minister of foreign affairs at this period, how gradually and in what manner the change was effected. M. Talleyrand renewed, after a long silence, his communications with Mr. Livingston.* Bonaparte had only a very reduced navy

* Appendix, No. 12.

to oppose to the most formidable power, that has ever had the dominion of the ocean. Louisiana was at the mercy of the English, who had a naval armament in the neighbouring seas, and good garrisons in Jamaica and the Windward Islands. It might be supposed that they would open the campaign by this easy conquest, which would have silenced those voices in parliament that were favourable to the continuance of peace. He concluded from this state of things that it was requisite to change without delay his policy in relation to St. Domingo, Louisiana, and the United States. He could not tolerate indecision; and before the rupture was decided on, he adopted the same course of measures, as if it had been certain.

He had no other plan to pursue when he abandoned his views respecting Louisiana than to prevent the loss, which France was about sustaining, being turned to the advantage of England. He, however, conceived that he ought, before parting with it, to inform himself respecting the value of an acquisition, which was the fruit of his own negotiations, and the only one that had not been obtained by the sword.

Though full of confidence in himself, and in his method of forming a prompt and bold decision on state affairs, he willingly consulted those who possessed practical experience, and he had too much reliance in his own powers to fear engaging in a discussion. He sometimes allowed it to be perceived to which side he inclined, and he was not above that paltry artifice, so common with many persons, who, though they ask advice, form beforehand an opinion which they desire to see triumph.

He wished to have the opinion of two ministers, who had been acquainted with those countries, and to one of whom the administration of the colonies was familiar. He was in the habit of explaining himself, without preparation or reserve, to those in whom he had confidence.

On Easter Sunday, the 10th of April, 1803, after having attended to the solemnities and ceremonies of the day, he called those two counsellors to him, and addressing them with that vehemence and passion which he particularly manifested in political affairs, said; " I know the full value of Louisiana, and I have been desirous of repairing the fault of the French negotiator who abandoned it in 1763. A few lines of a treaty have restored it to me, and I have scarcely recovered it when I must expect to lose it. But if it escapes from me, it shall one day cost dearer to those who oblige me to strip myself of it than to those to whom I wish to deliver it. The English have successively taken from France, Canada, Cape Breton, Newfoundland, Nova Scotia, and the richest portions of Asia. They are engaged in exciting troubles in St. Domingo. They shall not have the Mississippi which they covet. Louisiana is nothing in comparison with their conquests in all parts of the globe, and yet the jealousy they feel at the restoration of this colony to the sovereignty of France, acquaints me with their wish to take possession of it, and it is thus that they will begin the war.

They have twenty ships of war in the gulf of Mexico, they sail over those seas as sovereigns, whilst our affairs in St. Domingo have been growing worse every day since the death of Leclerc. The conquest of Louisiana would be easy, if they only took the trouble to make a descent there. I have not a moment to lose in putting it out of their reach. I know not whether they are not already there. It is their usual course, and if I had been in their place, I would not have waited. I wish, if there is still time, to take from them any idea that they may have of ever possessing that colony. I think of ceding it to the United States. I can scarcely say that I cede it to them, for it is not yet in our possession. If, however, I leave the least time to our enemies, I shall only transmit an empty title to those republicans whose friendship I seek. They only ask of me one town in Louisiana, but I already consider the colony as entirely lost, and it appears to me that in the hands of this growing power, it will be more useful to the policy and even to the commerce of France, than if I should attempt to keep it."

One of these ministers had served in the auxiliary army sent by France to the United States during their revolution. The other had, for ten years, been in the public employ, either as secretary of the French legation to the continental congress, or as the head of the administration of St. Domingo.

"We should not hesitate," said the last minister, "to make a sacrifice of that which is about slipping from us. War with England is inevitable; shall we be able with very inferior naval forces to defend Louisiana against that power? The United States, justly discontented with our proceedings, do not hold out to us a solitary haven, not even an asylum, in case of reverses. They have just become reconciled with us, it is true; but they have a dispute with the Spanish government, and threaten New Orleans, of which we shall only have momentary possession. At the time of the discovery of Louisiana the neighbouring provinces were as feeble as herself; they are now powerful, and Louisiana is still in her infancy. The country is scarcely at all inhabited; you have not fifty soldiers there. Where are your means of sending garrisons thither? Can we restore fortifications that are in ruins, and construct a long chain of forts upon a frontier of four hundred leagues? If England lets you undertake these things, it is because they will drain your resources, and she will feel a secret joy in seeing you exhaust yourself in efforts of which she alone will derive the profit. You will send out a squadron; but, while it is crossing the ocean, the colony will fall, and the squadron will in its turn be in danger. Louisiana is open to the English from the north by the great lakes, and if, to the south, they show themselves at the mouth of the Mississippi, New Orleans will immediately fall into their hands. What consequence is it to the inhabitants to whom they are subject, if their country is not to cease to be a colony? This conquest would be still easier to the Americans; they can reach the Mississippi by several navigable rivers, and to be masters of the country it will be

sufficient for them to enter it. The population and resources of one of these two neighbours every day increase; and the other has maritime means sufficient to
take possession of every thing that can advance her
commerce. The colony has existed for a century, and
in spite of efforts and sacrifices of every kind the last
accounts of its population and resources attest its
weakness. If it becomes a French colony and acquires
increased importance, there will be in its very prosperity a germ of independence, which will not be long in
developing itself. The more it flourishes, the less
chances we will have of preserving it. Nothing is more
uncertain than the future fate of the European colonies
in America. The exclusive right which the parent
states exercise over these remote settlements becomes
every day more and more precarious. The people feel
humbled at being dependent on a small country in Europe, and will liberate themselves, as soon as they have
a consciousness of their own strength.

"The French have attempted to form colonies in
several parts of the continent of America. Their
efforts have every where proved abortive. The English are patient and laborious, they do not fear the solitude and silence of newly settled countries. The
Frenchman, lively and active, requires society; he is fond
of conversing with his neighbours. He willingly enters
on the experiment, but at the first disappointment, quits
the spade or axe for the chase." The first consul, interrupting these observations, asked how it happened
that the French, who were incapable of succeeding in

a continental colony, had always made great progress in the West Indies. " Because," replied the minister, " the slaves perform all the labour. The whites, who would be soon exhausted by the heat of the climate, have, however, the vigour of body and mind necessary to direct their operations."—" I am again," said the first consul, " undecided as to maintaining or abolishing slavery. By whom is the land cultivated in Louisiana?" " Slavery," answered the minister, " has given to Louisiana half her population. An inexcusable imprudence was committed in suddenly granting to the slaves of St. Domingo, a liberty for which they had not been prepared. The blacks and whites have both been the victims of this great fault. But, without inquiring at this day how it would be proper to repair it, let us acknowledge that the colonies where slavery is preserved are rather burdensome than useful to France. At the same time, let us beware how we abandon them; they have not the means of governing themselves. The creoles are French, they have been encouraged in that mode of culture, and in that system which now causes their misfortunes. Let us preserve them from new calamitiés. It is our duty to provide for their defence, for the administration of justice and for the cares of government. But for what good purpose would you subject yourself to still greater embarrassments in Louisiana? You would there constantly have the colonial laws in collision with those at home. Of all the scourges that have afflicted the human race, slavery is the most detestable; but even humanity requires great precautions in the application of the remedy, and you cannot apply it if Louisiana should again become French. Governments still half resist emancipation: they tolerate in secret what they ostensibly condemn, and they are themselves embarrassed by their false position. The general sentiment of the world is favourable to emancipation; it is in vain that the colonists and planters wish to arrest a movement which public opinion approves. The occupation of Louisiana—a colony with slaves—will occasion us more expense than it will afford us profit.

"But there is another kind of slavery of which this colony has lost the habit: it is that of the exclusive system. Do you expect to re-establish it in a country contiguous to one where commerce enjoys the greatest liberty? The reign of prohibitory laws is over, when a numerous population has decided to throw off the yoke. Besides, the productions which were so long possessed exclusively by a few commercial people, are ceasing to be privileged articles. The sugar-cane and the coffee tree are every where cultivated, and at a very small expense. Every people expects to raise on its own account all the provisions adapted to its territory and climate. There are on the globe, between the tropics, lands a thousand times more extensive than our islands, and susceptible of the same kind of culture. Monopoly is rendered impossible when the productions are so multiplied, and the Louisianians will not permit it to enslave their commerce. Would you subdue resistance by force of arms? The malecontents will find support in the neighbourhood, and you will make the United States, with whom recipro- cal interests ought to connect us for centuries, enemies of France. Do not expect from the Louisianians any attachment for your person. They render homage to your fame and to your exploits; but the love of nations is reserved for those princes whom they regard as the authors of their happiness; and, whatever may be your solicitude with respect to theirs, it will be for a long time and perhaps for ever without effect. These co- lonists have lost the recollection of France; they are of three or four different nations, and hardly regard Louisiana as their country. Laws which are incessant- ly varying, chiefs who cannot know those whom they are sent to govern, and are not known by them, changes effected according to the unsettled interests of the ruling state or the inexperience of ministers, the con- tinual danger of becoming belligerents in quarrels to which they are really strangers; such are the causes which have for a hundred years extinguished in their hearts every sentiment of affection for masters who are two thousand leagues distant from them, and who would exchange them or convey them away like an ar- ticle of merchandise. In order that a country should exist and possess citizens, the certainty of stability must be united with the feeling of prosperity. The Louisianians, on learning that they had again become French, said to one another, ' *This change will not last longer than the others.*' If, citizen consul, you, who have by one of the first acts of your government made suf-

ficiently apparent your intention of giving this country
to France, now abandon the idea of keeping it, there
is no person that will not admit that you only yield to
necessity, and even our merchants will soon acknowledge that Louisiana free, offers to them more chances
of profit than Louisiana subjected to a monopoly.
Commercial establishments are at this day preferable
to colonies, and even without commercial establishments it is best to let trade take care of itself."

The other minister was of a totally opposite opinion.
" We are still at peace with England," said he, " the
colony has just been ceded to us, it depends on the
first consul to preserve it. It would not be wise in him
to abandon, for fear of a doubtful danger, the most important establishment that we can form out of France,
and despoil ourselves of it for no other reason than
the possibility of a war: it would be as well, if not better, that it should be taken from us by force of arms. If
peace is maintained the cession cannot be justified, and
this premature act of ill-founded apprehension would
occasion the most lively regrets. To retain it would,
on the other hand, be for our commerce and navigation an inestimable resource, and to our maritime provinces the subject of universal joy. The advantages
which we have derived from the colonies are still present to every mind. Ten flourishing cities have been
created by this trade; and the navigation, opulence,
and luxury which embellish Paris are the results of colonial industry. There can be no marine without colonies: no colonies without a powerful marine! The

political system of Europe is only preserved by a skilfully combined resistance of many against one. This
is as necessary with respect to the sea as to the land,
if it is not intended to submit to the tyranny of a universal sovereignty our commerce and the loss of the
immense advantages of a free navigation. To this you
will not submit; you will not acknowledge by your resignation that England is the sovereign mistress of the
seas, that she is there invulnerable, and that no one
can possess colonies except at her good pleasure. It
does not become you to fear the kings of England. If
they should seize on Louisiana, as some would have
you fear, Hanover would be immediately in your hands
as a certain pledge of its restoration. France, deprived of her navy and her colonies, is stripped of half
her splendour, and of a great part of her strength.
Louisiana can indemnify us for all our losses. There
does not exist on the globe a single port, a single city
susceptible of becoming as important as New Orleans,
and the neighbourhood of the American states already
makes it one of the most commercial in the world.
The Mississippi does not reach there till it has received twenty other rivers, most of which surpass in
size the finest rivers of Europe. The country is at last
known, the principal explorations have been made, and
expenses have not been spared, especially by Spain.
Forts exist: some fertile lands suitable to the richest
kinds of culture are already fully in use, and others
only await the necessary labour: this colony, open to

the activity of the French, will soon compensate them for the loss of India.

"The climate is the same as that of Hindostan, and the distance is only a quarter as great. The navigation to the Indies, by doubling the Cape of Good Hope, has changed the course of trade from Europe, and ruined Venice and Genoa. What will be its direction, if at the isthmus of Panama a simple canal should be opened to connect the one ocean with the other? The revolution which navigation will then experience will be still more considerable, and the circumnavigation of the globe will become easier than the long voyages that are now made in going to and returning from India. Louisiana will be on this new route, and it will then be acknowledged that this possession is of inestimable value.

"A boundless country belongs to us, to which the savages possess only an imaginary right. They overrun vast deserts, with the bow in their hand, in pursuit of wild beasts. But the social state requires that the land should be occupied, and these wandering hunters are not proprietors. The Indian has only a right to his subsistence, and this we will provide for him at a small expense.

"All the productions of the West Indies suit Louisiana. This variety of products has already introduced large capitals into countries that were so long an uninhabited wilderness. If we must abandon St. Domingo, Louisiana will take its place. Consider likewise the injury which it may do us if it becomes our rival in those productions, of which we have so long had the monopoly. Attempts have been made to introduce there the vine, the olive, and the mulberry tree; and these experiments, which Spain has not been able to prevent, have but too well succeeded. If the colony should become free, Provence and our vine-yards must prepare for a fearful competition with a country new and of boundless extent. If, on the other hand, it is subjected to our laws, every kind of culture injurious to our productions will be prohibited.

"It is even for the advantage of Europe that France should be rich. So long as she shared with England the commerce of America and Asia, the princes and cabinets that consented to be subsidized, profited by the competition in their offers. What a difference will it make to them all, if there is to be no more competition, and if England alone is to regulate this tariff of amity among princes! Alone rich, she alone would give the law.

"Finally, France, after her long troubles, requires such a colony for her internal pacification; it will be for our country what a century ago were for England, the settlements which the emigrants from the three kingdoms have raised to so high a degree of prosperity: it will be the asylum of our religious and political dissenters, it will cure a part of the maladies which the revolution has caused, and be the supreme conciliator of all the parties into which we are divided.

You will there find the remedies for which you search with so much solicitude."

The first consul terminated the conference without making his intentions known. The discussions were prolonged into the night. The ministers remained at St. Cloud; and at daybreak he summoned the one who had advised the cession of Louisiana, and made him read the despatches that had just arrived from London. His ambassador informed him that naval and military preparations of every kind were making with extraordinary rapidity.

" The English," said Napoleon, " ask of me Lampedousa, which does not belong to me, and at the same time wish to keep Malta for ten years. This island, where military genius has exhausted all the means of defensive fortification to an extent of which no one without seeing it can form an idea, would be to them another Gibraltar. To leave it to the English would be to give up to them the commerce of the Levant, and to rob my southern provinces of it. They wish to keep this possession, and have me immediately evacuate Holland.

" Irresolution and deliberation are no longer in season. I renounce Louisiana. It is not only New Orleans that I will cede, it is the whole colony without any reservation. I know the price of what I abandon, and I have sufficiently proved the importance that I attach to this province, since my first diplomatic act with Spain had for its object the recovery of it. I renounce it with the greatest regret. To attempt obstinately to retain it would be folly. I direct you to negotiate this affair with the envoys of the United States. Do not even await the arrival of Mr. Monroe: have an interview this very day with Mr. Livingston; but I require a great deal of money for this war, and I would not like to commence it with new contributions. For a hundred years France and Spain have been incurring expenses for improvements in Louisiana, for which its trade has never indemnified them. Large sums, which will never be returned to the treasury, have been lent to companies and to agriculturists. The price of all these things is justly due to us. If I should regulate my terms, according to the value of these vast regions to the United States, the indemnity would have no limits. I will be moderate, in consideration of the necessity in which I am of making a sale. But keep this to yourself. I want fifty millions, and for less than that sum I will not treat; I would rather make a desperate attempt to keep these fine countries. To-morrow you shall have your full powers." The new plenipotentiary then made some general observations on the cession of the rights of sovereignty, and upon the abandonment of what the Germans call the *souls*, as to whether they could be the subject of a contract of sale or exchange. Bonaparte replied; " You are giving me in all its perfection the ideology of the law of nature and nations. But I require money to make war on the richest nation of the world. Send your maxims to London; I am sure that they will be greatly admired

there, and yet no great attention is paid to them when
the question is, the occupation of the finest regions of
Asia.

" Perhaps it will also be objected to me, that the
Americans may be found too powerful for Europe in
two or three centuries: but my foresight does not embrace such remote fears.   Besides, we may hereafter
expect rivalries among the members of the Union.
The confederations, that are called perpetual, only last
till one of the contracting parties finds it to its interest
to break them, and it is to prevent the danger, to
which the colossal power of England exposes us, that
I would provide a remedy."

The minister made no reply. The first consul continued: " Mr. Monroe is on the point of arriving.   To
this minister, going two thousand leagues from his
constituents, the president must have given, after defining the object of his mission, secret instructions,
more extensive than the ostensible authorization of
congress, for the stipulation of the payments to be
made.   Neither this minister nor his colleague is prepared for a decision which goes infinitely beyond any
thing that they are about to ask of us.   Begin by
making them the overture, without any subterfuge.
You will acquaint me, day by day, hour by hour, of
your progress. The cabinet of London is informed of
the measures adopted at Washington, but it can have
no suspicion of those which I am now taking.   Observe the greatest secrecy, and recommend it to the
American ministers; they have not a less interest than

yourself in conforming to this counsel. You will correspond with M. de Talleyrand, who alone knows my intentions. If I attended to his advice, France would confine her ambition to the left bank of the Rhine, and would only make war to protect the weak states and to prevent any dismemberment of her possessions. But he also admits that the cession of Louisiana is not a dismemberment of France. Keep him informed of the progress of this affair."

The conferences began the same day between Mr. Livingston and M. Barbé Marbois, to whom the first consul confided this negotiation. But the American minister had not the necessary powers. He had resided at Paris about two years. The first object of his mission had been indemnities claimed by his countrymen for prizes made by the French during peace. The vague answers, and even the expectations that had been held out to him, had been attended with no result. The republican pride had been irritated, and Mr. Livingston, who had become distrustful, feared that the overtures relating to Louisiana were only an artifice to gain time. He received, without putting entire confidence in it, the overture which was made to him by Marbois of a cession of the whole province. However, after some discussion on a sum that was vaguely brought forward, he refused to go beyond thirty millions, saving an augmentation of this price by the amount of the indemnity to be given for the prizes taken from the Americans in time of peace. He was, indeed, unwilling to agree upon so high a price, unless

the stipulation was accompanied by a clause of not
making any payments till after the ratification by congress.

These preliminary discussions were scarcely entered
on, and their results could not have been anticipated,
when information was received of the landing of Mr.
Monroe at Havre.

Mr. Livingston, always inclined to feel distrust, in
which he seemed to be justified by the many decep-
tions that had been previously practised on him, wrote
to Mr. Monroe, on his arrival, that the true means of
succeeding in his negotiation was, " to give an assurance that the United States were already in possession
of New Orleans."*   Mr. Monroe arrived at Paris on
the 12th of April, and immediately had with his colleague a conference, little calculated to make him expect success from his mission.   " I wish," said Mr. Livingston to him, " that the resolution offered by Mr.
Ross in the senate had been adopted.   Only force can
give us New Orleans.   We must employ force.   Let us
first get possession of the country and negotiate afterwards."†

Mr. Monroe, anxious, though not discouraged, began
his conferences the next day with M. de Marbois.

Up to this period the controversy had its branches
on the Mississippi, at Washington, at Paris, and at Madrid.   The French and Spanish courts, having their attention drawn to other subjects, did not even corres-

* Appendix, No. 13.
† Journal of the mission by Colonel John Mercer.   Mr. Monroe's Memoir.

pond respecting it with their ministers at Washington; and these envoys, left to themselves, were under the necessity of acting at a venture. The arrival of Mr. Monroe changed this state of things. The powers of which he was the bearer were common to him and Mr. Livingston. The French and American ministers had an equal interest in not allowing the negotiation to linger; it had at last a central point, and made rapid progress.

The first difficulties were smoothed by a circumstance, which is rarely met with in congresses and diplomatic conferences. The plenipotentiaries having been long acquainted, were disposed to treat one another with mutual confidence.

Mr. Livingston, chancellor of the State of New York, had been a member of congress and minister of foreign affairs. He was the head of one of those patrician families, which in consequence of former services, honourable conduct, and a large fortune worthily employed, are the ornaments of the states to which they belong. Mr. Monroe, who had previously been governor of the state of Virginia, is the same individual, who has since been president of the United States for eight years, and justified in that high office the confidence of his fellow citizens. Marbois, who was employed to negotiate with them, had been engaged for thirty-five years in public affairs of great importance; for which his qualifications had been a correct judgment, and a character thoroughly independent. He had during the whole war of the American revolution resided near the congress. The affairs of this new power had long been familiar to him, and those of the southern continent had become equally so by a particular circumstance. The French directory, whose improper measures he had always opposed, had revenged themselves by banishing him to Sinnamari, and two years and a half of exile had made him still better acquainted with the wants, and general condition of the colonies.

The three negotiators had seen the origin of the American republic, and for a long time back their respective duties had established between them an intercourse on public affairs, and an intimacy, which does not always exist between foreign envoys, and the ministers of the power to which they are sent. They could not see one another again without recollecting that they had been previously associated in a design, conceived for the happiness of mankind, approved by reason and crowned after great vicissitudes by a glorious success. This good understanding of the plenipotentiaries did not prevent their considering it a duty to treat, on both sides, for the conditions most advantageous to their respective countries.

Mr. Monroe, still affected by the distrust of his colleague, did not hear without surprise the first overtures that were frankly made by M. de Marbois. Instead of the cession of a town and its inconsiderable territory, a vast portion of America was in some sort offered to the United States. They only asked for the mere right of navigating the Mississippi, and their sovereignty was about to be extended over the largest rivers of the world. They passed over an interior frontier to carry their limits to the great Pacific Ocean.

Deliberation succeeded to astonishment. The two joint plenipotentiaries, without asking an opportunity for concerting measures out of the presence of the French negotiator, immediately entered on explanations, and the conferences rapidly succeeded one another.

The negotiation had three objects. First, the cession, then the price, and, finally, the indemnity due for the prizes and their cargoes. After having communicated their respective views on these different points, it was agreed to discuss them separately, and even to make three distinct treaties. The subject of the cession was first considered. The full powers of the American plenipotentiaries only extended to an arrangement respecting the left bank of the Mississippi, including New Orleans. It was impossible for them to have recourse to their government for more ample instructions. Hostilities were on the eve of commencing. The American plenipotentiaries had not to reflect long to discover that the circumstances, in which France was placed, were the most fortunate for their country.

In the space of twenty-five years, the United States had, by treaties with the European powers and the Indians, gradually advanced to the Mississippi. By the proposed cession, vast regions to the west were about to belong to them without dispute. It relieved them from the necessity of erecting forts and maintaining

36

garrisons on a French frontier. Whilst ambition and passion for conquests expose the nations of Europe to continual wars, commerce, agriculture, equitable laws, and a wise liberty must guaranty to the United States all the benefits of the social state, without any of its dangers. A serious but pacific struggle might then take place between the enlightened and improved industry of the old nations, and the territorial riches of a new people; and this rivalship, useful to the world, was going to be exercised in the most extensive career that has ever been opened to the efforts of man.

At the same time, a consideration of another description was presented to the view of the negotiators. They were about once more to dispose of Louisiana, not only without consulting its inhabitants, but without its being possible that they should suspect, at the distance of two thousand leagues, that their dearest interests were then to be decided on. The three ministers expressed their sincere regrets at this state of things. But a preliminary of this nature was rendered impossible by circumstances, and to defer the cession would have been to make Louisiana a colony of England—to render that power predominant in America, and to weaken for centuries the state whose aggrandizement in that part of the globe the whole world must desire. This difficulty, which could not be solved, was at once set aside.

As soon as the negotiation was entered on, the American ministers declared that they were ready to treat on the footing of the cession of the entire colony, and they did not hesitate to take on themselves the responsibility of augmenting the sum that they had been authorized to offer. The draft of the principal treaty was communicated to them. They had prepared another one, but consented to adopt provisionally as the basis of their conferences that of the French negotiator, and they easily agreed on the declaration contained in the first article; "The colony or province of Louisiana is ceded by France to the United States, with all its rights and appurtenances, as fully and in the same manner as they have been acquired by the French republic, by virtue of the third article of the treaty concluded with His Catholic Majesty at St. Ildephonso, on the 1st of October, 1800." Terms so general seemed, however, to render necessary some explanations, relative to the true extent of Louisiana. The Americans at first insisted on this point. They connected the question of limits with a guarantee on the part of France, to put them in possession of the province, and give them the enjoyment of it.

In treaties of territorial cession, the guarantee of the grantor is a usual clause. Publicists even assert that where it is omitted in terms, it is not the less obligatory of right.

There were some historical and diplomatic researches on the first occupation and earliest acts of sovereignty. But they were only attended with the results usual in such cases. Travellers and historians had not left on this subject any but vague and general notions: they had only narrated some accidents of navigation, some acts of occupation, to which contradictory ones might be opposed. According to old documents, the bishopric of Louisiana extended to the Pacific Ocean, and the limits of the diocess thus defined were secure from all dispute. But this was at the most a matter in expectancy, and the Indians of these regions never had any suspicion of the spiritual jurisdiction, which it was designed to exercise over them. Besides, it had no connexion with the rights of sovereignty and property. One important point was, however, beyond all discussion; according to the then existing treaties, the course of the Mississippi, in descending this river to the thirty-first degree of north latitude, formed the boundary line, leaving to the United States the country on its left bank; to the right, on the other hand, there were vast regions without well defined boundaries, although France had formerly included a great part of them in what was called Upper Louisiana: this was particularly the case with the territories to the south of the Missouri.

The limits of Louisiana and Florida, to the south of the thirty-first degree, were not free from some disputes, which possessed importance on account of the neighbourhood of the sea, and the embouchure of the rivers. However, this country, disregarded by the European powers, that successively possessed it, was scarcely mentioned in the conferences. France had had only the smallest portion of it. The name of Florida could not have been inserted in the treaty without preparing great difficulties for the future.

The boundary to the north and north-west was still less easy to describe. Even the course of the Mississippi might give rise to some border disputes; for that great river receives beyond the forty-third degree several branches, then regarded as its sources. A geographical chart was before the plenipotentiaries. They negotiated with entire good faith; they frankly agreed that these matters were full of uncertainty, but they had no means of quieting the doubts. The French negotiator said; " Even this map informs us that many of these countries are not better known at this day than when Columbus landed at the Bahamas; no one is acquainted with them. The English themselves have never explored them. The circumstances are too pressing to permit us to concert matters on this subject with the court of Madrid. It would be too long before this discussion could be terminated, and perhaps that government would wish to consult the viceroy of Mexico. Is it not better for the United States to abide by a general stipulation, and, since these territories are still at this day for the most part in the possession of the Indians, await future arrangements, or leave the matter for the treaty stipulations that the United States may make with them and Spain? In granting Canada to the English, at the peace of 1763, we only extended the cession to the country that we possessed. It is, however, as a consequence of that treaty, that England has occupied territory to the west, as far as the great Northern Ocean." Whether the American plenipotentiaries had themselves desired what was proposed to them, or that these words afforded them a ray of light, they declared that they kept to the terms of the 3d article of the treaty of St. Ildephonso, which was inserted entire in the first article of the treaty of cession.*

M. Marbois, who offered the draft, said several times; " The first article may in time give rise to difficulties, they are at this day insurmountable; but if they do not stop you, I, at least, desire that your government should know that you have been warned of them.".

It is in fact important not to introduce ambiguous clauses into treaties: however, the American plenipotentiaries made no more objections, and if, in appearing to be resigned to these general terms through necessity, they considered them really preferable to more precise stipulations, it must be admitted that the event has justified their foresight. The shores of the Western Ocean were certainly not included in the cession; but the United States are already established there.

The French negotiator, in rendering an account of the conference to the first consul, pointed out to him the obscurity of this article and the inconveniencies of so uncertain a stipulation. He replied, " that if an obscurity did not already exist, it would perhaps be good policy to put one there."

We have reported this answer in order to have an opportunity of observing that the article finds a better justification in the circumstances of the time, and that sound policy disavows all obscure stipulations. If they

* Appendix, No. 14.

are sometimes advantageous at the moment of a difficult negotiation, they may afford matter in the sequel for the greatest embarrassments.

Before passing to the other articles of the treaty, we will conclude our remarks on the subject of the boundaries.

The negotiations which took place several years afterwards with Spain, relative to the limits of Louisiana, were long and difficult.* The government of the

---

* Louisiana was ceded by France to the United States, with all its rights and appurtenances, as fully and in the same manner as they had been acquired by the French republic. The treaty of St. Ildephonso retrocedes to France, "the province of Louisiana, with the same extent that it now has in the hands of Spain, and that it had when France possessed it; and such as it should be after the treaties subsequently entered into between Spain and other states."

To understand the question, long agitated between the United States and Spain, it is necessary to remember that Louisiana was dismembered by France in 1762–3; the portion east of the Mississippi, excepting the island of Orleans, being conveyed to England, and the remainder of the province to Spain. The section which was ceded to Great Britain includes what is now Illinois, Kentucky, Tennessee, Mississippi, and *West Florida.*

By the same treaty that France ceded the eastern part of Louisiana to England, Spain also yielded to her Florida and all that she possessed on the continent of North America to the east and south-east of the Mississippi. By the treaty of 1783 between Spain and Great Britain, the latter power granted to the former not only all of Florida that she had lost in the preceding war, but also a considerable portion of what had been held by France as Louisiana.

Under these circumstances, it was contended by the United States that they were entitled by the treaties of cession from Spain to France and from France to the United States, not only to the portion of Louisiana, which Spain had received direct from France in 1762–3, and to which it was attempted to restrict their claim, but to the whole of the province possessed by France before the dismemberment, so far as Spain was capable of ceding it at the date of the treaty of

United States, instead of frankly acknowledging that there was ground for reasonable doubts, attempted to establish their claims as incontestable. The ministers of the catholic king put forward maxims which apparently belong to the law of nations, but which are without any efficacy when they have only publicists for champions. The following passage is extracted from a note addressed by Don Louis de Onis to the secretary of state, on the 5th of January, 1813, ten years after the cession: " It is a principle of public law that the property of a lake, of a strait of the sea, or of a country, whatever may be its extent, is acquired by the occupation of its principal points, provided no other power has made a settlement in the interior." Thus spoke the minister. A few years afterwards, the vast possessions of Spain in America were withdrawn from her sovereignty.

The cession of the Floridas, by confounding the two territories, put an end to a discussion till that time inextricable respecting the eastern boundaries of Louisiana; the western were then the more easily settled, as Spain already found herself under the necessity of removing every obstacle that might tend to render her interests complicated in those countries; and the treaty concluded on the 22d of February, 1819, terminated one of the disputes in which this power was involved. It was then agreed that the Sabine should separate the dominions of the two states.

St. Ildephonso, and including, of course, a part of what was then called Florida. See Appendix. No. 19.—TRANSL.

This same treaty determines their boundary line, in going from the sources of the Arkansas to the Pacific Ocean. It follows the course of the Arkansas to its sources in the forty-second degree, and thence proceeds by that parallel of latitude to the South Sea.

An ukase of the Emperor Alexander of the $\frac{4}{16}$th of September, 1821, asserts that the claims of Russia to the north-west coast of America extend from the northern extremity of that continent to the fifty-first degree of north latitude.* It is likewise at the fifty-first degree that the United States, setting out from the forty-second degree, limit their pretensions. They have even shown a disposition to stop at the forty-ninth degree.

England and the United States have not been able to agree on the occupation of these regions. By a convention of the 20th of October, 1818, the territory respectively claimed by them was to be open for ten years to the subjects of both powers. This term has recently expired, and the arrangement has probably terminated.† In pursuance of the treaty of Ghent, the important post on the Columbia river was restored by the English to the United States.

* By the 3d article of the convention of St. Petersburg, of the $\frac{5}{17}$th of April, 1824, it was agreed that no Russian establishment should be formed on the north-west coast of America, south of 54° 40′ north latitude, and no American north of the same parallel.— TRANSL.

† This agreement was indefinitely renewed by the convention of the 6th of August, 1827, as will be seen in a note to Part III.— TRANSL.

The cession of Louisiana was a certain guarantee of the future greatness of the United States, and opposed an insurmountable obstacle to any design formed by the English of becoming predominant in America. They afterwards supposed that the negotiations for peace, opened at Ghent, offered them the means of recovering the advantages that they had lost. Their plenipotentiaries renewed their pretensions to a free navigation of the Mississippi. They demanded, as a *sine qua non*, that a neutral Indian district should be taken from the territory of the United States for the purpose of separating the contracting powers by limits, within which all acquisition of the lands of the Indians should be prohibited; and their declarations on this subject were announced as irrevocable. It was even reported that they would require that Louisiana should be restored to Spain.* But no mention of so strange a pretension was made at the conferences at Ghent.

The charter given by Louis XIV. to Crozat included all the countries watered by the rivers, which empty directly or indirectly into the Mississippi. Within this description comes the Missouri, a river that has its sources and many of its tributary streams at a little distance from the Rocky Mountains. The 1st article of the treaty of cession to the United States meant to convey nothing beyond them, but the settlement in the interior, which has resulted from it, and the one on the

* Letters of Mr. Monroe to the ministers plenipotentiary of the United States, of 25th June, 1814, and 19th August, 1814.

Pacific Ocean, at the west, have mutually strengthened each other.

The acquisition of Louisiana and of the Floridas, together with the extinction of some grants or Indian titles has cost the United States about 160,000,000 francs: the land that has been acquired contains more than 300,000,000 acres, of which only 18,000,000 have been sold.* What yet remains to be sold will, in less than a century, be worth to the United States many thousand millions of francs: the value that these lands will possess, in the hands of individuals, defies all calculation.

The cession was followed by judicious and bold explorations, made by order of congress, as well as by travellers and traders who arrived at the shores of the Western Ocean, after having crossed a country until then unknown to civilized nations. They found hospitable and pacific tribes, and were only opposed by natural obstacles. These regions are of greater extent than the whole original states of the Union. There is room there for numerous republics, and centuries may pass away before population and civilization are there carried to the highest point of which they are susceptible. It would be idle to inquire respecting the form of government that will be adopted by these communities, or the bonds that will connect them with one another or with a parent state. It is sufficient to foresee that those that shall be formed upon the model of the

* See Appendix, No. 20.—TRANSL.

United States will certainly be happy, and that the new world will witness what the old world has never seen;— communities founded for the benefit of all their members, and not for that of their founders, or to augment their riches, increase their power, or administer to their vain glory. Even if the new states separate from the confederacy, they will remain united by the protecting laws of peace, and by every thing that secures the public happiness.

By the 2d article, " all public lots and squares, vacant lands, and all public buildings, fortifications, barracks, and other edifices that were not private property were included in the cession. The archives, papers, and documents relative to the domain and sovereignty of Louisiana and its dependencies, were to be left in the possession of the commissioners of the United States, and copies were afterwards to be given in due form to the magistrates and municipal officers, of such of the said papers and documents as might be necessary to them."

The plenipotentiaries, being all three plebeians, easily agreed on the stipulations of the 3d article, founded on a perfect equality between all the inhabitants of the ceded territories.

It provided, "that they should be incorporated in the Union of the United States, and admitted as soon as possible, according to the principles of the federal constitution, to the enjoyment of all the rights, advantages, and immunities of citizens of the United States; and, that they should in the meantime, be maintained and protected in the free enjoyment of their liberty, property, and the religion which they profess."

These provisions prepared the way for a great change in the constitution of Louisiana, or rather guarantied to it the advantage of having at length a constitution, laws, and self-government. There was not a single family in the colony but must profit sooner or later by this revolution.

The first consul, left to his natural disposition, was always inclined to an elevated and generous justice. He himself prepared the article which has been just recited. The words which he employed on the occasion are recorded in the journal of the negotiation, and deserve to be preserved. "Let the Louisianians know that we separate ourselves from them with regret; that we stipulate in their favour every thing that they can desire, and let them hereafter, happy in their independence, recollect that they have been Frenchmen, and that France, in ceding them, has secured for them advantages which they could not have obtained from a European power, however paternal it might have been. Let them retain for us sentiments of affection; and may their common origin, descent, language, and customs perpetuate the friendship."

The character of the Indians was well known to the negotiators. The efforts that had been made, and the expenses that had been incurred for three centuries have not effected any change in the habits of these tribes; but they obstinately avoid civilization. Far from loving their country, as some writers have pretended, they abandon their native soil without much resistance, as soon as the white men settle in their neighbourhood. They prefer their own dispersion, and even annihilation to the meliorations which would impose restraints on them or subject them to labour; but they do not like to be despoiled by force.

These Indians whom we treat as barbarians and savages, when they defend their lakes, their rivers, and their forests, whom we reproach with perfidy, when they oppose stratagem and cunning to tactics and superior arms, have sometimes been our friends. But they treated us as enemies or usurpers when we came to disturb their peaceable possessions. When they were encouraged by better treatment, they called the king of France their father, and this title among them carries with it even more authority than that of king. These tribes, always children, require to be paternally governed. They preferred the French to other nations, and willingly adopted them into their tribes. Though ever ready to use freely whatever in our huts and houses suited their convenience, or to appropriate it to themselves, they were submissive to our orders. They were well inclined to render us services, and even as warriors to unite their arms with ours.

Many of the treaties concluded between the powers of Europe since the discovery of America dispose of the territories of the Indian nations without any reserve of their rights. More attention was this time paid to the interests of these tribes. The treaty of cession separated us from them for ever. The three negotiators regarded them as an innocent people, who, without having any participation in the cession, were to be included in it.

By the 6th article, " The United States promise to execute such treaties and articles as may have been agreed on between Spain and the tribes or nations of Indians." " This stipulation," Mr. Monroe observed, " becomes us, though these people must be for ever ignorant of the care that we take of their interests."

This article prepared the good understanding that now exists between the Indians and the United States. They are treated with humanity: it is wished, it is true, to remove them from the settled parts of the country, a plan which is resisted by some of the tribes. The Cherokees have even given themselves a constitution, which appears to have been dictated by some whites settled among them.* This phantom of a government has not seemed to deserve much attention. The intermixture with the whites has, however, introduced into the tribe the first elements of civilization.

The 7th article contained a reserve which was then deemed important for the commerce of France and Spain, namely; " the privilege of bringing in French or Spanish vessels from the ports of those two kingdoms or of their colonies, into the ports of Louisiana, the produce or manufactures of those countries or of their colonies, during the space of twelve years, without being subjected to any other or greater duties than those paid by the citizens of the United States."

* July 18, 1827.

The commerce of the colony had been to that time almost exclusively carried on by the French under the Spanish flag. The 7th article would have preserved this advantage to France, if the peace of Amiens had not been broken at the same time that the treaty of cession was signed. The war lasted nearly twelve years, during which period this trade passed into the hands of the English and Americans: and the loss of St. Domingo put the seal to the separation. It is not believed that a single French ship profited by the provisions of this article.

The 8th article, which secures to French ships the treatment of the most favoured nation, has given rise to discussions, the result of which we ought not to anticipate.*

* " Art. 8. In future, and for ever after the expiration of the twelve years, the ships of France shall be treated on the footing of the most favoured nations in the ports above-mentioned."

By an act of congress of March 3, 1815, the several acts imposing discriminating duties on the tonnage of foreign vessels, and on the goods, &c. imported therein, so far as they were the produce or manufacture of the nation to which such foreign vessel belonged, were repealed in favour of such nations as should not levy a discriminating or countervailing duty to the prejudice of the United States.

Conventions, in compliance with the overtures thus made, were early concluded with Great Britain and Sweden, and arrangements by mutual legislation were entered into with other states; several of which have been recently confirmed by treaty. France, however, did not immediately accede to these propositions of reciprocity; but began to maintain in 1817, and has ever since continued to assert, that she was entitled to enjoy gratuitously in the ports of Louisiana all the privileges which the vessels of England, whom she considered as *the most favoured nation*, possessed there under the treaty of commerce, and for which an equivalent was

Such are the principal stipulations of the treaty of cession.*

The contracting parties would have desired that Spain should join in this negotiation; and, as this power had reserved, by the treaty of the 1st of October, 1800, a right of preference, in case of cession, its previous assent was undoubtedly necessary. On the other hand, the least delay was attended with very many dangers; and the distance from Paris to Madrid, with the usual

paid. It was urged, in reply to the demands of France, that she claimed to enjoy a privilege without fulfilling the condition on which it was granted. She asked to be treated not as favourably, but more favourably than the nation she called most favoured. " The stipulation," said the American secretary of state, " to place a country on the footing of the most favoured nations, necessarily meant, that, if a privilege was granted to a third nation for an equivalent, that equivalent must be given by the country which claimed the same privilege by virtue of such stipulation."

The practical importance of this question has been greatly diminished by the treaty of 1822, by the operation of which all the discriminating duties upon the vessels of the United States and France, in either country, ceased on the 1st of October, 1827. By a separate article, also attached to that convention, the extra duties, levied exclusively on French vessels by the act of the 15th of May, 1820, as well as those imposed on American vessels by a French *ordonnance* of the same year, were directed to be refunded.

But, the general discriminating duties on foreign vessels, which were demanded from those of France in the ports of Louisiana, as in the rest of the Union, anterior to the treaty of commerce, are still brought forward as a barrier to the settlement of American claims for spoliations and seizures under the imperial government. These reclamations, besides the cases arising from condemnations under illegal decrees against neutral commerce and the burning of ships at sea, include large demands for property sequestered in the ports of France and provisionally sold, respecting which no adjudication has ever taken place.—TRANSL.

* Appendix, No. 1.

38

tardiness in the deliberations of that cabinet, would
have led to a total failure of the negotiation. The
treaty was therefore not communicated to the Spanish
ministry till after its conclusion. They complained bitterly of the little regard that had been paid to a right
that was incontestably reserved to Spain, and for nearly a year it was impossible to obtain from that court
an approbation of the treaty. Its complaints were well
grounded. It was only on the 10th of February, 1804,
that Don Pedro Cevallos wrote to Mr. Pinckney, minister of the United States, " that His Catholic Majesty had thought fit to renounce his opposition to the
alienation of Louisiana, made by France, notwithstanding the solid reasons on which it is founded:
thereby giving a new proof of his benevolence and
friendship to the United States."

The draft, which the American plenipotentiaries had
at first proposed, contained an article, according to
which the first consul was to interpose his good offices
with the king of Spain, in order to obtain the cession
of the country situated to the east of the Mississippi,
and in the neighbourhood of their southern frontier.
These stipulations of good offices are not rare in treaties, but their execution is almost always attended with
embarrassments; and the French negotiator induced
the Americans to be satisfied with the assurance, that,
should the occasion arise, the first consul would afford
them all the assistance in his power.

Spain had manifested, on several occasions, her
dread of having the United States in the immediate

neighbourhood of her continental or insular colonies. Marbois communicated to the American ministers the apprehensions of this power, and added that a great many politicians were also alarmed for the French West Indies, as they conceived that sooner or later the United States would aim at their possession, and, finally, conquer them. Livingston said, in reply;— "Mark well the answer that I am going to give you; I believe that I can assure you that it will be confirmed by the event. The French West Indies are far from aspiring to an independence which would soon put the European inhabitants, who are not numerous enough to sustain themselves, in the power of the slave population. The whites require to be governed, protected, and defended against this internal enemy; but it would be contrary to our institutions and even our interests to undertake this charge. The principal trade of these islands will sooner or later belong to us on account of our proximity, and all the prudence of the European governments will not retard this change half a century. Should these colonies hereafter wish to belong to us and to enter into the Union, we could not receive them; we could still less have them as dependent and subject possessions. I do not foresee what will happen if, in their emergencies, they should resort to our generosity and protection. But do not fear that we shall ever make the conquest of that which we would not wish to accept even as a gift."

Two important conventions, signed the same day, were annexed to the treaty as well as referred to in it, in order that they might have the same force and effect as if they had been inserted in terms.

The first related to the payment of the price of the cession. This instrument was made separately from the treaty, as some embarrassment was felt in mentioning, at the same time, the abandonment of the eminent right of sovereignty and the sale for money of the property of the territory.

The necessity of the cession being acknowledged, it was easy to justify the conditions. The motives which determined them had been pointed out by the first consul himself, and we will refer to them here.

For a century the settlement and government of Louisiana had required from France and Spain advances, for which they had never been indemnified by the commercial imposts. The churches, the forts upon both banks of the Mississippi, as well as many other public buildings, had been erected at the expense of the two powers. There were also there magazines and arsenals; funds had been advanced to commerce and agriculture; a great many other expenses, having in view the benefit of the colony, had likewise been incurred. The acts of cession, made to Spain in 1764, contained provisions respecting the moveable property. We find the following passages in a letter of the 21st of April, 1764, from Louis XV. to M. D'Abadie: "It is my particular desire that an inventory, in duplicate, should be signed by you and the commissioner of His Catholic Majesty of all the artillery and other military stores, magazines, hospitals, ships, &c. which belong to me in the said colony, in order that, after having put the said commissioner in possession of the ships and buildings, a statement may be prepared of the value of all the articles that shall remain there, the price of which shall be reimbursed by His Catholic Majesty, according to the said estimate." The same reimbursement is required in a letter written on the 15th of October, 1802, by the king of Spain to the captain general, to order him to deliver up the province of Louisiana to the commissioner of the French government. These reservations were, it must be admitted, of little consequence, and were moreover merely formal stipulations. But the first consul regarded in another point of view the condition of the price. Though this valuation in money of a right of sovereignty, formerly so familiar to the princes of Europe, was a necessary clause of the bargain, he wished at least that it should never be a charge on the country ceded. The price, whatever it might be, could not be stipulated for an advantage such as that of independence, the lustre of which it would have tarnished. The amount was paid by the United States not exclusively, as in the case of previous cessions and retrocessions, for moveable effects. but as the price of vast territories which they acquired, and of the great augmentation of power which would result from them to the Union in general. The cession made France lose nothing, and it possessed great advantages for the United States.

The first consul, supposing that he carried his valuation very high, had said that he calculated on fifty

millions. The French plenipotentiary, without entering into any explanation with him, considered this estimate a good deal too low, and, as soon as the price
became the subject of conference, stated that it was
fixed at eighty millions, and that it would be useless to
propose a reduction.*

The American plenipotentiaries could not have foreseen that the negotiation, which their government had
intrusted to them, would become so important, and
they were without special powers to consent to pay
the price that was demanded. " Our fellow-citizens,"
said Mr. Livingston, " have an extreme aversion to
public debts; how could we, without incurring their
displeasure, burden them with the enormous charge
of fifteen millions of dollars?"

M. de Marbois, on his part, insisted upon the first
demand of eighty millions, and said, that for the United
States, this was a sum very much below the true value
of these immense territories. The negotiators themselves were but very imperfectly acquainted with them;
but they knew that, on passing to the right bank of the
Mississippi, the Americans would find unknown tribes,
or a wilderness that had never yet tempted the ambition or cupidity of any European nation, which cultivation could not fail to enrich, and which would be
gradually annexed to the territory of the Union. These
adventitious domains would possess the peculiar advantage of acquiring every day greater importance and
a higher value, without any other attention on the part

* Appendix, No. 15.

of the sovereign power than that of directing their ex-
ploration and survey.

The two plenipotentiaries finally acquiesced,* on
condition that twenty millions out of the eighty should
be employed in a manner settled by a special convention. This became the third instrument of the negotiation, and we will here enter into some explanations
relative to the origin of the claim for which it provided.

The convention of the 30th of September, 1800, had
for its object the securing of reciprocal satisfaction to
the citizens of the two states, and the preventing as
far as possible of any thing that could for the future
affect their good understanding. We there find the
principle, the wisdom and legality of which only one nation in the world disputes: " that free ships make free
goods, although they are the property of an enemy."

A special promise had been given to pay the debts
arising from requisitions, seizures, and captures of ships
made in time of peace; but the execution of the agreement had not followed the treaty. For two years and
a half the minister of the United States had been re-
iterating his reclamation and demanding in vain the re-
paration of these losses.†

* Appendix, No. 2.

† Between 1793 and 1800 serious injuries had been inflicted on
our commerce by the capture and confiscation of our vessels by
France, in violation of the law of nations and existing treaties.
Losses had also been sustained by our merchants from embargoes,
and from the neglect of the different revolutionary governments to
comply with their contracts, many of which arose from forced requisitions for supplies.

These claims, the justice of some of which, abstractedly consi-

The cession of Louisiana afforded the means of realizing promises that had been so long illusory. The

dered, was not denied, were resisted on the ground of the failure
of the United States to comply with the guarantee of the French
possessions in America, contained in the treaty of 1778, and with
the provisions of the consular convention of 1788. The retaliatory
measures of the American government in authorizing the capture
of vessels of war, belonging to France, hovering on our coasts, and
in repealing the treaty of alliance had also, since 1798, interposed
additional obstacles to the payment of indemnities.

Of the means taken to procure redress, anterior to the mission
of Messrs. Ellsworth, Davie, and Murray, it is not necessary here
to speak. By a convention, which these gentlemen signed with
the French plenipotentiaries on the 30th of September, 1800, it
was declared,—

"Art. 2. The ministers plenipotentiary of the two parties not
being able to agree at present respecting the treaty of alliance of
the 6th of February, 1778, the treaty of amity and commerce of
the same date, and the convention of the 14th of November, 1788,
nor upon the indemnities mutually due or claimed; the parties will
negotiate farther on these subjects at a convenient time, and until
they may have agreed upon these points, the said treaties and convention shall have no operation, and the relations of the two countries shall be regulated as follows:"

By the 3d article, the public ships that had been captured were
to be mutually restored.

"Art. 4. Property captured and not yet definitely condemned,
or which may be captured before the exchange of ratifications (contraband goods destined to an enemy's port excepted,) shall be mutually restored on the following proofs of ownership, &c."

"Art. 5. The debts contracted by one of the two nations with
individuals of the other, or by the individuals of the one with the
individuals of the other, shall be paid, or the payment may be prosecuted in the same manner as if there had been no misunderstanding between the two states. But this clause shall not extend to indemnities claimed on account of captures or confiscations."

The senate of the United States, on the convention being submitted to them, expunged the second article, and the first consul,
on giving his ratification, assented to the retrenchment, on condition "that the two states should renounce the respective preten-

Americans consented to pay eighty millions of francs on condition that twenty millions of this sum should

sions which are the object of the said article." After these conditional ratifications and their exchange, President Jefferson submitted the convention anew to the senate, who resolved that they considered it as fully ratified.

The French government failed to comply with their engagements under the 4th and 5th articles, though repeatedly urged to do so by the United States, and a discussion took place between the American minister in Paris and the French minister of foreign affairs, which was not terminated when the Louisiana treaty was negotiated, as to the extent to which the 5th article applied.

Notwithstanding the mutual abandonment of the claims forming the object of the 2d article of the treaty of 1800, the third convention of the 30th of April, 1803, purports to be expressly founded on the 2d and 5th articles of that of the 30th of September, 1800; but the provision which it makes for the liquidation of claims does not embrace all the cases falling within the purview of either article. The specifications of the debts, included by it, are given in the following words:—

" Art. 2. The debts provided for, &c., are those whose result is comprised in the conjectural note annexed to the present convention, and which, with the interest, cannot exceed the sum of twenty millions of francs. The claims comprised in the said note, which fall within the exceptions of the following articles, shall not be admitted to the benefit of this provision."

" Art. 4. It is expressly agreed that the preceding articles shall comprehend no debts but such as are due to citizens of the United States, who have been and are yet creditors of France, for supplies, embargoes, and for prizes made at sea, in which the appeal has been properly lodged within the time mentioned in the said convention of the 8th Vendemiaire, tenth year, (30th September, 1800.)"

Art. 5, points out the cases to which the preceding articles apply, and the exceptions to them.

The terms of this convention, by which some classes of cases were totally excluded, while others having no greater merit were to be paid in full, with interest, met with a very unfavourable reception at Washington. The article also, which required every decision to be made within a year, excluded any *bona fide* demands,

be assigned to the payment of what was due by France
to the citizens of the United States.

The two ministers fixed this condition of an indemnity at twenty millions of francs, and they probably ex-

the presentation of which was at all delayed, and there was no
provision for an apportionment among the claimants, confessedly
within the meaning of the treaty, in the event of a deficiency of
the fund; but each debt, &c. due by France to American citizens
was to be satisfied as soon as it was certified by the commissioners, named under the authority of the convention.

Mr. Livingston, the then minister at Paris, was instructed to
propose the extension of the provisions of the convention of 1803
to all those who had claims under that of 1800, but were not included in the subsequent treaty. The French government declined
making a new convention, but stated that if the liquidation of
the claims in the conjectural note should not absorb the twenty
millions of francs, the residue of that sum might be employed to
satisfy other cases; though in any event the whole of the American
claims were to be placed to the account of the federal government.
The reclamations, comprised in the conjectural list, appears to
have been principally for supplies received by the French, and for
losses sustained by the detention of ships at Bourdeaux, in consequence of the embargo of 1793.

Immediately after the promulgation of the convention of 1800,
accompanied by the declaration of the first consul as to the effect
of expunging the 2d article, it was contended by those who had
had claims on France for captures and confiscations, that they were
entitled to look to their own country for indemnity, inasmuch as
their rights had been renounced for a release of the guarantee and
other valuable considerations, the benefit of which accrued to the
nation at large. These demands on the United States acquired
new force from the transactions connected with the Louisiana treaties. They have been repeatedly presented to congress, with various success in the committees to whom the subject was referred,
but without any final decision on them in either house.

It is hardly necessary to add that the claims, which are referred
to in this note, are wholly distinct from those which the American
government has been pressing for many years on the attention of
France, all of which are of a date subsequent to the convention of
1800.—TRANSL.

pected that they would be required to state the grounds
of this estimate, in order that they might be discussed
and a reduction effected. But no opposition was made,
and it was instantly agreed that this amount should be
deducted from that of the eighty millions. The intention of extinguishing all former claims was sincere on
both sides. The round sum of twenty millions was
evidently an estimate formed on reasonable conjectures, and could not be an absolute result established
by documents. But the American negotiators agreed
that if there was any difference, the amount rather
exceeded than fell short of the claims, and the French
plenipotentiary gave assurances that in no case should
this excess be claimed by France. Thus the respective demands were easily agreed to. A mutual frankness, which smooths all the difficulties from which the
most simple negotiations are not always exempt, was
the only address employed by the ministers of either
party.

The manner of making the payment at first presented some difficulties: it seemed natural that the French
treasury, which was the debtor, should, after having
acknowledged its debt, acquit it with the twenty millions. On the other hand, the American creditors being better known in their own country than they could
be in France, the disputes among the claimants might
be more easily settled before their own tribunals. We
must add that the liquidations or settlements of cre-
dits, made under the authority of the French government, did not then inspire entire confidence. It ap-

peared more convenient that the respective governments should name commissioners, who should examine each particular debt, and then leave the payment to be afterwards made, in America, by the treasury of the United States.

This third convention, just in its object, was, moreover, connected with the treaty of cession by a great political interest, which was to destroy every cause of discontent between the two nations and extinguish that animosity that always arises from the refusal to acquit a legitimate debt. The time sometimes arrives when a nation repents not having seasonably done an act of justice, which costs dearer when it is obliged to repair the omission. The relations of amity and good faith, which are not deferred till the moment of danger, lay the foundation of lasting confidence between nations. Those who were well aware of the importance of having a perfectly good understanding between the two countries, estimated at a much higher price the twenty millions thus employed than the sixty that were received by the treasury of France.*

The payment of this last sum was effected in a manner which deserves to be mentioned. The war between France and England could be no longer doubtful. No French banker was willing to become the medium of so considerable a pecuniary transaction. The bank of France, to which the proposal was made, refused it, under the pretext that such affairs were not within its province, and probably, also, because the re-

* Appendix, No. 3.

gents of the bank were afraid of rendering it dependent on an authority that was too ready to interfere in
matters of which a reciprocal confidence ought to constitute the basis.

On the other side, the American ministers were very
desirous that the payments should be made through the
intervention of the most stable house in Europe. The
partners of this house were established at Amsterdam
and London. Bankers from these two cities did not
fail to be at Paris at the appointed day. They were
eager to reap the profits that were disdained by the
French bankers, and the first consul perceived no inconvenience in their being abandoned to them. It is
believed that, on its part, the British ministry, notwithstanding the certainty of war, saw, without regret, an English house undertake so profitable a
negotiation. The terms agreed on, as well for the
payment of what was due to the treasury as for the indemnity to the American merchants, were punctually
observed. The United States, which still sustained
the weight of a part of the debts contracted during
the war of the revolution, were only incumbered by an
addition of eighty millions of francs to the public bur-
dens; and this people, whose riches are acquired by
industry and economy, kept their engagements with a
punctuality that would have done honour to the banking house in the highest credit. The payments were
to have been made at successive days; but the United
States had inspired an entire confidence in their good
faith, and the bankers made all the advances that were

asked of them without being solicited or requiring extraordinary profits, and they undoubtedly found their own advantage in this evidence of confidence.*

At the moment of signing them, the Americans asked that the three instruments should be drawn up in French and English. They admitted, however, that it was impossible to have two original texts in two languages; it was declared, adopting the form with which the treaties of 1778 concluded, "that the original had been agreed on and written in the French language." The translation required three days; and from this incident it happened that the treaties, which were concluded on the 30th of April, 1803, and are dated on that day, were only actually signed four days afterwards. Two months had not then elapsed since Mr. Monroe had set sail from New York to proceed to Paris.

The authors of those solémn instruments, that regulate the lot of nations, cannot be insensible to the honour of having done acts useful to their country. A sentiment superior even to glory seemed to animate the three ministers, and never perhaps did negotiators taste a purer joy. As soon as they had signed the treaties, they rose and shook hands, when Livingston, expressing the general satisfaction, said: "We have lived long, but this is the noblest work of our whole lives. The treaty which we have just signed has not been obtained by art or dictated by force; equally advantageous to the two contracting parties, it will change vast

* Messrs. Hope and Labouchere of Amsterdam, and Barings of London.

solitudes into flourishing districts. From this day the United States take their place among the powers of the first rank; the English lose all exclusive influence in the affairs of America. Thus one of the principal causes of European rivalries and animosities is about to cease. However, if wars are inevitable, France will hereafter have in the new world a natural friend, that must increase in strength from year to year, and one which cannot fail to become powerful and respected in every sea. The United States will re-establish the maritime rights of all the world, which are now usurped by a single nation. These treaties will thus be a guarantee of peace and concord among commercial states. The instruments which we have just signed will cause no tears to be shed: they prepare ages of happiness for innumerable generations of human creatures. The Mississippi and Missouri will see them succeed one another, and multiply, truly worthy of the regard and care of Providence, in the bosom of equality, under just laws, freed from the errors of superstition and the scourges of bad government."

The first consul had followed with a lively interest the progress of this negotiation. It will be recollected that he had mentioned fifty millions as the price which he would put on the cession; and it may well be believed that he did not expect to obtain so large a sum. He learned that eighty millions had been agreed on; but that they were reduced to sixty by the deduction stipulated to be previously made for the settlement of the debt due by France to the Americans. Then forgetting, or feigning to forget, the consent that he had given, he said with vivacity to the French minister: "I would that these twenty millions be paid into the treasury. Who has authorized you to dispose of the money of the state? The rights of the claimants cannot come before our own." This first excitement was calmed as soon as he was brought to recollect that he had previously consented to treat for a much smaller sum than the treasury would receive, without including the twenty millions of indemnity for the prizes. "It is true," he exclaimed, "the negotiation does not leave me any thing to desire: sixty millions for an occupation that will not perhaps last but a day! I would that France should enjoy this unexpected capital, and that it may be employed in works beneficial to her marine." At the very instant he dictated a decree for the construction of five canals, the projects of which had occupied him for some time. But other cares made him in a few days forget this decree. The negotiation, so happily terminated, had required so little skill, and had been attended with so little labour that the professions of Napoleon's satisfaction would be deemed exaggerated, if history stopped at these details.

The following words sufficiently acquaint us with the reflections that then influenced the first consul: "This accession of territory," said he, "strengthens for ever the power of the United States; and I have just given to England a maritime rival, that will sooner or later humble her pride."

Fifteen days after the signature of the treaties, Mr. Monroe set out for London; he remained there a considerable time unsuccessfully employed in endeavouring to settle articles of navigation and neutrality.

War was inevitable: the sixty millions were spent on the preparations for an invasion that was never to be carried into effect, and these demonstrations were sufficient to oblige the English government to make defensive arrangements which cost a much greater sum.

The arrival of Mr. Monroe at Paris had attracted the attention of the English ambassador. The object of this envoy's mission was not known at London, except from the purport of the resolutions of congress. The secret of the conferences was well kept, and Lord Whitworth did not even suspect that they had for their result a cession of all Louisiana. This affair being terminated, the French cabinet ceased to temporize. The British government, on its side, considered indecision out of season. However, the respective ambassadors, after having received their recall, had still some communications that seemed pacific. On the 4th of May, the day after the signature of the treaty of cession, and four days after its conclusion, the first consul caused a note to be sent to Lord Whitworth, in which he demanded that Malta should be delivered over provisionally to Austria, Russia, and Prussia, which powers should be the guarantees of the independence of the island. The note concluded with these words: " If this proposal is rejected, it will be manifest that England has never wished to execute the treaty of Amiens,—

that she has not even had good faith in any of her demands."

England only proposed to keep Malta during the time necessary to put the island of Lampedousa upon the footing of a naval station; but she wished that France should bind herself by a secret article not to require its evacuation before the end of ten years, and that Switzerland and Holland should be evacuated a month after the ratification of the convention. The knights, assisted by all the powers of Christendom, had employed two centuries and a half to fortify Malta, and the English had made themselves masters of it without effort and without expense. The first consul was heard to say on this subject: " They will never restore that island except by force, were it even reclaimed by the knights." From thenceforward, their perseverance in the decision to keep possession of this station, authorized the presumption that they aspired to the same dominion in the Mediterranean as in the other seas, and that they aimed at ruling there more absolutely than any of the states that occupy its shores. Perhaps readier and easier communications with India then likewise entered into the designs of England.

The king of Great Britain also demanded for the king of Sardinia an indemnity in Italy, and, on these conditions, he consented to acknowledge the Italian and Ligurian republics.

France, in rejecting these overtures, offered to accept the mediation proposed by Russia.. These communications, in appearance pacific, were insincere:

both sides knew that they would not be accepted. The negotiation was broken off, and the ambassadors quitted, the one France, the other England, on the same day, the 17th of May, 1803.

War was the result of the jealous policy and passion of aggrandizement, which actuated the two powers. It was rekindled, with an ardour inspired, on the one side, by the necessity of self-preservation and, on the other, by pride leading genius astray.

In France were to be seen military talents of the highest order, a boundless capacity, a bold character, a firm and persevering will, which presaged long and brilliant success. These qualities were, however, blended with an immoderate passion for glory, an unbridled ambition, and a disregard of the rights of others. Some men, whose foresight then seemed pusillanimous, from that time dreaded the most deplorable catastrophes.

In England, there were more able councils, a better regulated state of affairs, an administration friendly to national liberty, strong in the esteem and confidence of the people, and by their support superior to all the factions. At the same time, the statesmen, who were at the head of the British councils, badly dissembled their determination to retain the direction of the affairs of Europe, and to make constant acquisitions in Asia and America.

Hostilities commenced on the 22d of May by the capture of some French merchantmen. On the same day Bonaparte gave his ratification to the treaty of cession, without waiting for that of the United States.

It was important that the accomplishment of this formality, on the part of France, should not leave any ground for considering the colony as still French. The ratifications and their exchange could experience no delay at Washington, and after these proceedings and the delivery of possession, every attempt of the English on Louisiana would have been directed against a province of the American Union, and would have afforded room for just reclamations on the part of the whole confederacy.

THE

HISTORY OF LOUISIANA.

PART III.

EXECUTION OF THE TREATY OF CESSION.——EVENTS ARISING
FROM THE CESSION.

HISTORY OF LOUISIANA.

PART THE THIRD.

EXECUTION OF THE TREATY OF CESSION.—EVENTS ARISING FROM THE CESSION.

THE foresight of the first consul and his anxiety respecting the part which England would adopt under the then existing circumstances were fully justified. The English ministers, when informed of the object of Mr. Monroe's mission, conceived that there was no longer time to undertake the conquest of Louisiana, unless it was attempted with the concurrence of the United States. They made a proposition to that effect to Mr. Rufus King, the American envoy at London, giving him to understand that the province would be retroceded to his government at the peace. A few days after the signature of the treaty, the two American plenipotentiaries at Paris were made acquainted with this overture by Mr. King. It was easy for them to conjecture at what sacrifices the United States would have had to purchase the profferred retrocession, even if England, once in possession, had consented to carry it into effect: they were, therefore, far from regretting that they were no longer in a situation to accept the British proposal. On another account, it was important that the

British government should know the result of the negotiation, and it was accordingly communicated to it
without delay.

The war with France having commenced, the English were interested in preserving a good understanding with the United States. The proposition to take
possession of Louisiana being set aside, Mr. King received from Lord Hawkesbury a satisfactory answer
respecting the cession. He transmitted it without delay to his government. But, in the uncertainty in which
Bonaparte still was on this subject, he adopted the
course of having the ratifications exchanged at Washington instead of Paris. He wished above all, by thus
gaining time on England, to hasten the transmission
of the money that had been stipulated to be paid.

The treaties, forwarded to Washington with as much
despatch as possible, arrived there on the 14th of July,
1803. The original documents intended for Louisiana
were sent with them. M. Pichon, the chargé d'affaires
of France, had orders to transmit them to M. Laussat,
the prefect of the province, as soon as the ratifications
were exchanged.

The prohibition respecting the entrepôt at New Orleans was finally taken off, and the intendant had, by a
proclamation of the month of May, 1803, annulled
the one of the 16th of October preceding, which had
excited so much agitation.

This difficulty had scarcely ceased, when the Spanish minister at Washington stated, " that he had orders to warn the federal government to suspend the

ratification and execution of the treaties of cession of Louisiana, as the French government, in receiving the province, had contracted an engagement with Spain not to retrocede it to any other power: and, besides, one of the conditions, in reference to which the king his master had transferred it to France, was that the latter power should obtain from all the courts of Europe the acknowledgment of the king of Etruria. France not having executed that engagement, the treaty of cession was null."

The Marquis de la Casa Yrujo had given publicity to his protest, and this complication of embarrassments, arising from distrusts and contradictory interests, had nearly again thrown the business into the state of confusion from which the treaty of Paris had extricated it. Some pretended to see in the opposition of His Catholic Majesty's minister a concert between Spain and England to prevent the effect of the cession. Others, imputing to France the most disgraceful deception, asserted that Spain was only acting under her influence; and they insisted, especially, that the price agreed on should not be paid till after possession was taken.

M. Pichon had orders so to combine his proceedings and communications that the two cessions, namely, from Spain to France and from France to the United States, should be made without leaving such an interval of time as might justify an expedition on the part of the English. He was informed of the suspicions which it was attempted to throw on the good faith of the cabinet of the Tuileries; a few malecontents also raised clamours respecting the enormity of the price that had been agreed on. This excitement checked the good intentions of the American government, which would otherwise have been disposed to deliver without delay the money and stock that were impatiently expected at Paris. M. Pichon, in no way diverted from his purpose by the protest of M. Yrujo, sent by land to M. Laussat on the 14th of October the orders which he was instructed to transmit to him. Those who censured the treaty were obstinate in asserting that the apparent dissension between the two ministers was only an artifice contrived by the cabinets of Paris and Madrid.

Mr. Jefferson, on his part, rising superior to the alarms that had been circulated, and disdaining all want of confidence, convened congress, anticipating, on account of the crisis, the usual period. He opened the session on the 17th of October, 1803, and submitted the treaties to the examination and constitutional sanction of the senate. The magnitude of the sum, and even the nature of the contract, gave rise to discussions. The senators who opposed the ratification, men deserving of esteem, but advocates of rigorous theories, invoked in support of their argument those maxims of universal justice, which necessity and even expediency so often silence. " Congress," they said, " had not the power of annexing by treaty new territories to the confederacy. This right could only belong to the whole people of the United States." These senators likewise required the free acquiescence of the Louisianians. " This was their natural right; and the formal consent of the two people was," according to them, "indispensable; namely, the consent of the one party to belong to the Union, and that of the other to enlarge its territory. Neither the constitution nor any act that had emanated from them had authorized the president to conclude such a treaty."

These opponents brought forward, in the very bosom of a republican legislature, the example of the absolute sovereigns of Europe. " We have seen," they said, " these princes show more respect for the original and primitive rights of the people, and not dispose of a state and its inhabitants as if it was a question respecting the sale of a manufacture or a flock of sheep. Maria Theresa, in abandoning to the king of Prussia certain fiefs which depended on the kingdom of Bohemia, acknowledged that the abandonment could not be consummated till the states of that kingdom had made a solemn renunciation of them; and are we, the citizens of a free country, about to give an example of a violation of this natural right!"

Jefferson himself, a zealous republican, would have wished to diminish the powers of the government instead of extending them. The branch of the federal government, to which the general powers of the confederacy at home and abroad are confided, seemed to him to menace the republic with a consolidation prejudicial to the authority of the individual states. He considered his own authority too monarchical.

He would have desired to have had the assent of the people to the treaties previously to their ratification. But there was a real danger in the delay, and he, on this occasion, did violence to his own principles.

It was not difficult to demonstrate to him the great advantages which would result from the treaty as well to the United States as to the Louisianians. The confederacy had only aspired to the enjoyment of a free navigation of the Mississippi, and the treaty gave it almost another world.

The senate approved the treaties at the very moment that the Marquis de la Casa Yrujo was protesting with the most violence. The constitution requires the concurrence of two-thirds of the senators present, and there was a majority of twenty-four votes against seven. The president ratified them the next day, the 21st of October, 1803, without awaiting the return of the messenger, who was carrying to Laussat the orders of his government. There was no where any reserve, and the exchange of the two instruments was executed purely and simply in the ordinary form. Mr. Jefferson, in giving his ratification, declared that as soon as the United States should be in possession of the colony, by a legal transfer to them through the French commissioner, the treaty should be deemed to have had its entire execution.

All the documents relating to this affair were immediately afterwards communicated to the house of representatives. A few of the members raised objections, which were principally drawn from the exorbitant price that the plenipotentiaries had stipulated. They were replied to with force, and one of the delegates, who approved the treaties, pronounced on the occasion the following words, which this history ought to preserve: " In a few years," said he, " we shall rank with the most powerful states of the world. Even the acquisition that we are now making will promptly extinguish the debt that we are going to contract. The possession of Louisiana will enrich all the eastern states. Others will be formed from it that will contribute to our public revenue. Let us religiously observe the rules of justice, and let us fulfil our engagements with the utmost exactitude. We will soon be a power formidable to all the states that succumb under the weight of their debts."

The three powers* of the American government concurred in ratifying the treaties without any modification. The necessity of this concurrence to carry a treaty into full effect might embarrass the most simple negotiation, if one of them was against it; but the opposition were in a very small minority. The acts, which it was requisite that congress should pass, encountered no difficulty. They gave the president power to cause possession to be taken, and by other laws

---

* The president, with the advice and consent of the senate, concludes treaties which are declared by the constitution to be the supreme law of the land; but where an appropriation of money is required, it is necessary to pass an act of congress, in which the house of representatives must of course concur. In such cases, however, it has been supposed that the national faith is pledged to enact the laws proper to carry the treaties into effect.—TRANSL.

they created the public stock. The American ministers at Paris had previously authorized, under their
guarantee, an anticipation of the public credit for two
millions of dollars, and the advance of this payment
to the French treasury had been generally approved at
Washington. Some even regarded this partial execution of the contract as a means of rendering the cession irrevocable. This general eagerness, an authentic sign of the good faith of congress, was also an evidence of the opinion which it entertained of the great
advantages of the acquisition that had been made.
The laws and royal ordinances were provisionally
maintained in Louisiana, but for only a very short
time. The president and the two houses of congress
ordered that the laws of the American Union should
be proclaimed and executed there.

The orders sent to M. Laussat and the American
officers had anticipated the possible case of a resistance on the part of the Spanish authorities, and, as
the concurrence of the latter was indispensable, there
was some uneasiness respecting the final issue of the
affair. Spain abdicated the sovereignty of the country. The French dominion was only to last a few
days. The United States had not yet any authority
there. The articles of the treaty were not known.
The present was for many a motive for regretting the
past: the future offered to all only uncertain hopes.
The Spanish authorities and officers feared for their
old settlements the influence of the neighbourhood of
a free and independent colony. The French prefect

and other officers saw vanish, with regret, the hope that they had entertained of concurring in the foundation of a great colonial establishment, which was deemed necessary to the prosperity of the French commerce. St. Domingo seemed irreparably lost: refugee planters arrived every day bringing most melancholy news; and Louisiana, where they had hoped to find a new France, no longer appeared to them an asylum.

M. Laussat had resided for nine months at New Orleans, without assuming his public character. M. Landais, the French officer who was sent to him from Washington by land, traversed the countries inhabited by the Creeks and Cherokees. We would here remark that these tribes have not yet evacuated these territories, and would also add, that the federal city of Washington communicates at this day, (1828,) with New Orleans by an easy and safe road, frequented by numerous travellers who pass through the Indian country.

M. Landais arrived on the 23d of November, 1803. On the 26th the French prefect had a conference with Messrs. De Salcedo and Casa Calvo, the commissioners of the catholic king, and immediately afterwards, preparations of every kind announced to the public the cession that was about to be made to France.

On the 30th of November, Laussat, in his character of commissioner of the French government, announced, by the following proclamation, addressed to the Louisianians, the mission with which he was charged:

" This mission," said he, " less agreeable to me than

the one which I had come to fulfil, however, offers me the consolation that it will be more advantageous to you than the first could have been. The return of the French sovereignty will be only momentary. The approach of a war, which threatens the four quarters of the world, has given a new direction to the beneficent views of France towards Louisiana. She has ceded it to the United States of America.

" The treaty secures to you all the advantages and immunities of citizens of the United States. The particular government, which you will select, will be adapted to your customs, usages, climate, and opinions.

" Above all, you will not fail to experience the advantages of an upright, impartial, incorruptible justice, where the publicity and invariable forms of the procedure, as well as the limits carefully interposed to the arbitrary application of the laws, will concur with the moral and national character of the judges and juries in effectually guarantying to the citizens their property and personal security.

" The Mississippi, which washes not deserts of burning sand, but the most extensive, the most fertile, and the most favourably situated plains of the new world, will, at the quays of this new Alexandria, be forthwith crowded with thousands of vessels of all nations.

" I have great pleasure, Louisianians, in opposing this picture to the touching reproaches of having abandoned you, and to the tender regrets, to which this indelible attachment of very many of you to the country of your ancestors makes you give utterance on the present occasion. France and her government will hear the account of these regrets with affection and gratitude; but you will soon be convinced that they have marked their conduct towards you by the most eminent and most memorable of favours.

"By this proceeding the French republic gives the first example in modern times of the voluntary emancipation of a colony;—an example of one of those colonies of which we are delighted to find the prototype in the glorious ages of antiquity: may a Louisianian and a Frenchman never meet now or hereafter in any part of the world without feeling sentiments of affection, and without being mutually disposed to call one another brothers."

On the morning of the same day, the Spanish troops and militia were drawn up in front of the City Hall. The French and Spanish commissioners came there, followed by a procession of the merchants and other inhabitants of their respective nations. Three chairs were arranged in the council chamber, and Salcedo occupying the middle one, Laussat presented to him the decree of October 15th, 1802, by which the king of Spain ordered his representative to deliver the colony to the French plenipotentiary. This order was dated more than a year back. M. Laussat produced, at the same time, the authority of the first consul to take possession of the country in the name of the French people. After the public reading of these acts, the Spanish governor, leaving his seat, delivered him the keys of the city, and the Marquis de la Casa Calvo announced, " that the Louisianians, who should not declare that they wished to retire under the Spanish authority, were absolved from their oath of fidelity to the catholic king." At a signal, given by the firing of cannon, the Spanish colours were lowered and the French hoisted.

The French forces only consisted of a small number of officers of artillery and engineers. The charge of the forts and of the different posts on the Mississippi was confided to the local militia.

The French sovereignty lasted from the 30th of November to the 20th of December, 1803. M. Laussat, in his character of chief of the government during this interval, provided for the administration of justice in summary and urgent matters. In spite, however, of his anxious care, this short space of time was not exempt from troubles.

The districts of Attakapas and Opelousas, in the neighbourhood of New Orleans, but on the other side of the river, were composed of plantations, whose proprietors, imperfectly informed of the circumstances of the change, explained it in different ways according to their particular interests: these quarrels would have led to acts of violence, had they not been appeased by the proclamations of the prefect and some measures of the actual government, which, though transitory, were sufficient to show that the colony was not entirely given up to anarchy.

Messrs. De Salcedo and Casa Calvo had exercised an absolute authority: but, far from their being reproached with any abuse of power, it was admitted that they had administered the government with wisdom, moderation, and justice; the inhabitants, indeed, only waited till the cession was made to the United States, and their authority had entirely ceased, to render them a public proof of affection and gratitude. Thenceforth no favour was hoped for from them, and these testimonies of respect had a much more certain character of sincerity than those which are invariably addressed to rulers on their accession to power.

The United States had garrisons on the frontier posts. General Wilkinson, having taken command of them, advanced to the left bank of the Mississippi, and established his camp, on the 17th and 18th of December, 1803, at half a league from New Orleans. As soon as this division was in sight, the Spanish troops embarked and set sail for the Havannah.

The next day, discharges of artillery from the forts and vessels in the road announced the farewell which the French magistrates were then taking of the colony. They became for ever strangers to a province alternately Spanish and French, and which bore the name of one of our greatest kings; they once more addressed as countrymen those whom they were never again to see. This colony, which had been always exposed to inevitable vicissitudes under the laws of a state, from which it was separated two thousand leagues, was now undergoing its last crisis. This event put an end to uncertainties that had lasted for a century, and fixed for ever the fate of these fine regions. The spontaneous acknowledgment of the independence of Louisiana, its annexation to the confederacy of a prosperous people were the acts of the wisest policy; and those who shall hereafter be in a condition to observe their consequences, will admit that they ought to rank with the most important occurrences in the history of our times.

On the 20th of December, the day fixed for the delivery of the colony to the United States, Laussat, accompanied by a numerous retinue, went to the City Hall. At the same instant the American troops were, by his orders, introduced into the capital.

Claiborne and Wilkinson were received in form in the City Hall, and were placed on the two sides of the prefect. The treaty of cession, the respective powers of the commissioners, and the certificate of the exchange of ratifications were read. Laussat then pronounced these words: " In conformity with the treaty, I put the United States in possession of Louisiana and its dependencies. The citizens and inhabitants, who wish to remain here and obey the laws, are from this moment exonerated from the oath of fidelity to the French republic." Mr. Claiborne, the governor of the territory of Mississippi, exercising the powers of governor general and intendant of the province of Louisiana, delivered a congratulatory discourse, addressed to the Louisianians. " The cession," said he, "secures to you and your descendants the inheritance of liberty, perpetual laws, and magistrates, whom you will elect yourselves." These formalities being fulfilled, the commissioners of the two powers, on retiring, might have witnessed an incident produced by the last impressions which this transfer occasioned.

On the arrival of M. Laussat, nine months before his recall, the colony might have considered itself again French, and a little time had sufficed to revive in the hearts of some old inhabitants sentiments, which so long a separation had not been able entirely to extinguish. They manifested them on occasion of the change of the flag. During the twenty days that the French sovereignty lasted, the French colours had been displayed on the City Hall. Some French soldiers retired for many years to Louisiana, others, brought together from different places on the Mississippi by accident or their respective interests, had assembled at the sight of the national colours. To the number of fifty, they had, at their own suggestion, constituted themselves guardians of a flag rendered illustrious by so many victories, and they watched over it as if it had been specially intrusted to them. The change of the flags was effected by raising the one and lowering the other. When they met midway, they were kept stationary for a few instants, and the artillery and trumpets celebrated the union; when the flag of the United States rose to its full height and waved in the air, the Americans expressed their joy by the usual shouts; at the same time, the colours of the French republic were lowered and re-

ceived in the arms of the French who had guarded
them; their regrets were openly expressed, and to render a last homage to this token, which was no longer
that of the sovereignty of the country, the sergeant-
major wrapped it around him as a scarf, and, after traversing the city, proceeded towards the house of the
French commissioner. The little troop accompanied
him; they were saluted in passing before the lines of
the Americans, who presented arms to them. The
officers of the militia, for the most part of French origin, followed in a body. They said to Laussat, on his
receiving them; "We have wished to give to France a
last proof of the affection, which we will always retain
for her. It is into your hands that we deposite this
symbol of the tie which had again transiently connected us with her." Laussat replied: "May the prosperity of Louisiana be eternal."

This magistrate only quitted the colony, the 23d of
April of the ensuing year, leaving there an honourable
reputation. Mr. Claiborne, the commissioner who administered the government, declared that the authority
of the United States was established, and the public
officers installed in the exercise of their functions. His
proclamation guarantied to the inhabitants the preservation of their religious, civil, and private rights. The
promises which he made to them would have seemed
too magnificent, if they had not had a sort of guarantee in the prosperity of the other states of the confederacy.

The Spanish, French, and American chiefs had neglected nothing to maintain harmony between the three nations. On the first days, however, after the occupation, several accidents were occasioned by the diversity of language, usages, and habits, as well as by the regret which many felt at seeing broken for ever the ties that had united them to another people. Complaints were also made of the insolence of some American patrols to the inhabitants.* The discretion and firmness of the magistrates easily repressed these movements.

The revolution which had just taken place, was in fact very different from that which in 1763, had caused such violent commotions, and led to the shedding of the blood of the colonists, who were discontented with a new sovereignty. The Americans and Louisianians coalesced after having been near engaging in a war, and even after commercial hostilities had actually commenced. On the eve of the change, it was supposed that agriculture, commerce, and navigation, were ruined. A few reflections had sufficed to calm this agitation. All the white inhabitants of every class were about to participate in the advantages of liberty.

The treaty had only placed Louisiana in the situation most favourable for liberty, and if France had attempted to keep it and maintained the exclusive system there, no human effort could have prevented its incorporation into the American confederacy.

* General order of December 26th, 1803.

From that moment we were authorized to believe that the hopes entertained by the negotiators of the treaties were realized. Their correctness may at this day be still better appreciated. Has Louisiana, during the last twenty-six years, made any progress in agriculture and commerce? Have the laws meliorated the condition of the inhabitants? Is it now a matter beyond all doubt, that there exists a vast portion of the world, where agriculture, navigation, sciences so highly favourable to the happiness of mankind, are going to be freely developed? These questions naturally present themselves as a sequel to the history of the treaty. We will answer them by giving a statement of the situation of the colony under these different points of view.

On the 20th of March, 1804, congress divided Louisiana into two territories. The southern section was called Orleans, and the northern Louisiana, but they did not long retain these names, and we will hereafter mention the reasons for their being changed.

The Louisianians of the lower country, governed after the cession as inhabitants of a territory not yet admitted to the rank of a state of the confederacy, aspired to that privilege. It was not till eight years after that event, that congress authorized them to form a constitution, in order to their being received into the Union, on the footing of the original states.

This fundamental law was framed by a convention, assembled at New Orleans. It bears date January

22d, 1812.   It was subsequently submitted to congress, who approved it under the title of the constitution of Louisiana.   It will be sufficient to point out its principal provisions.

The three departments of the government are separate and distinct.

" The legislative power is composed of a senate and house of representatives.   To be a representative, it is necessary to be a free white citizen, of the age of twenty-one years or upwards, to possess landed property to the value of five hundred dollars, and to have resided within the state for two years.   Every free white citizen of the age of twenty-one years, paying a state tax, is an elector after one year's residence.

" To be a senator, it is necessary to have resided within the state for four years, to be twenty-seven years old, and to hold landed property of the value of one thousand dollars.

" No person, while he continues to exercise the functions of a clergyman, priest, or teacher of any religious persuasion, society, or sect, is eligible to the general assembly, or to any office of profit or trust under the state.

" No bill shall have the force of a law, until, on three several days, it be read over in each house of the general assembly, and free discussion allowed thereon; unless, in case of urgency, four-fifths of the house where the bill shall be depending, may deem it expedient to dispense with this rule.

" The governor is elected for four years: he must be at least thirty-five years of age, have been an inhabitant of the state at least six years preceding his election, and shall hold in his own right a landed estate of five thousand dollars value.

" No member of congress or person holding any office under the United States, nor a minister of any religious society, is eligible to the office of governor.

" Every bill that has passed both houses, is presented to the governor. If he approves it, he signs it; if not, he returns it with his objections, to the house in which it originated. After being thus returned, the bill can only become a law, if approved by two-thirds of all the members elected to each house."

Louisiana had, till the adoption of this constitution, been governed by the civil and criminal laws of the kingdom of France; and those, who, a century before, had prepared this first legislation, had thought so little of accommodating it to the climate and local circumstances, that to abridge their labour, they had subjected the province to the custom of Paris, (*coutume de Paris.*) This is, however, still the law of Lower Canada and of other colonies which either now are, or formerly were French.

Before the cession, an appeal from the judgments of the tribunals, was carried to the superior council of Havannah, and, in certain cases, to the council of Madrid. Justice was oftentimes not rendered till after a lapse of several years. Justice long delayed or which must be sought for at a distance, is not true justice.

The laws of Spain, France, and the United States, have ceased since 1825, to prevail in this country, where these three powers have successively ruled: competent and learned men have undertaken the great task of reconciling them. A civil code has been adopted, and the one which is now established in France has been of no little service in its compilation.*

The new constitution, granted to the Louisianians the important right of *habeas corpus;* a jury trial in civil cases at the request of either of the parties; the power of giving bail in all cases not capital, and, finally, the trial by jury in all criminal prosecutions. The French settlers thus found again on the borders of the Mississippi, the trial by their country and their peers, which was so dear to their ancestors, and which they might consequently receive as the restoration of a right.

Mr. Edward Livingston, a brother of the minister who signed the treaty of cession, has since prepared the plan of a criminal code, in which he proposes the abolition of capital punishment.

The convention that formed this constitution, was composed of forty representatives, of whom twenty-two were of French origin, and eighteen Americans from the United States.

The name of Louisiana was at first that of the whole ceded province. It was then applied only to the country washed by the Missouri, from its mouth to a defined boundary at the west. New Orleans gave its name to the territory situated below that of Louisiana and to the right of the Mississippi; but these denominations have since been changed. The territory of New Or-

---

* A digest of civil laws for Louisiana was prepared and adopted by the legislature of the then territory of Orleans in 1808.—TRANSL.

leans has become the state of Louisiana, and the district which bore this latter name, is now called the state of Missouri. It was not till the 10th of August, 1821, that Missouri was admitted into the Union.

The general assembly of Louisiana held its first session in 1812. Congress had authorized it to include in the limits of the state a territory situated to the east of the Mississippi, and which Spain persisted in claiming, as a part of West Florida. The Louisianians themselves agreed that it had been considered to belong to Florida, but, nevertheless, the assembly declared, by one of its first acts, that this district of country was a portion of Louisiana. It was certainly a very convenient possession for New Orleans, which drew from it a great part of its supplies; but this eagerness to strengthen doubtful pretensions by possession, does not accord with the spirit of justice that characterizes the other political acts of the United States.*

Ten years later the state would have obtained the same augmentation of territory by an incontestable title. But, at the period when the Louisianians seized on it, Spain was far from admitting their right. As early as the year 1803, whilst Mr. Monroe was negotiating at Paris the treaty of cession, Mr. Pinckney, the minister of the United States at Madrid, was asking of Don Pedro Cevallos that the Floridas should be ceded to them; and he proposed, as a sort of equivalent, to guaranty to the king and his successors certain dominions of Spain situated beyond the Mississip-

* See Part II. page 287, note.—TRANSL.

pi. This offer of guarantee was at that time disdained by the court of Madrid, and when, in 1818, it manifested an anxiety to accept it, and include within its operation Mexico and the northern colonies, circumstances had changed: the revolt had every where broken out. The United States were far from interfering in this quarrel, which in no way alarmed them, and which they did not desire to see terminate otherwise than in the establishment of those principles of liberty, to which they were so fondly attached. Mr. Erving, their envoy, declared that the offer, not accepted fifteen years before, was the same as if it had never been made. Reciprocal complaints, reclamations for indemnities on account of prizes illegally made at sea, had in this long interval rendered the negotiation complicated. Spain was engaged in difficulties which did not permit her to give any farther attention to the Floridas: she ceded them, and the United States thus accomplished, by the treaty of the 22d of February, 1819, the great design which they had formed many years before, of having only the sea for a boundary to the east and south.

As the price of this new cession, they took on themselves claims for indemnities of their own ship-owners and merchants, to the amount of five millions of dollars.

Thus, they were indemnified by Spain, as they had been by France, for spoliations, which privateers, furnished with the instructions of a doubtful authority, and disavowed by the law of nations, had been able to practise with impunity on their commerce; and these states, scarcely admitted to the rank of nations, proved to the world that they would never suffer any unjust aggression.

This acquisition added new value to that of Louisiana. Some navigable rivers, which traverse the Floridas to their embouchure in the sea, have their rise and a considerable part of their course in the old states. The United States became masters in the gulf of Mexico of naval stations suitable for the reception of vessels of the first class. Finally, by means of all these aggrandizements, they have formed one of the most powerful empires in the world.

The wretched and miserable races, who have inhabited for centuries these various and extensive countries, have not left a single one of those monuments of genius and the arts, which attest that human creatures have embellished their abodes and meliorated the land where Providence gave them birth. Some traces are, however, to be seen of an incipient civilization. In many places are to be found conical or pyramidical mounds of earth, of a height that could only have been raised by many thousand labourers, employed during a great number of years. Some of them are at their base more than twenty-five hundred feet in circumference, and nearly two hundred in height. The pyramid is terminated by a platform of several feet in diameter. There are also others of small dimensions, which are placed without any regularity, and so close together that the voice is without difficulty heard from one to another of them. These elevations could not have

been places of asylum or defence, and the Indians themselves, when interrogated as to their destination, do
not assign them any.

Some more extensive and less elevated platforms are
likewise to be noticed. They are formed on a regular
plan, and are either oval or square. The means employed to render the access to them difficult, seems to
indicate an intention of defence. In other parts of the
country these constructions are different, and some
have supposed that they distinguished in them courses
of stone. Near the junction of the Muskingum with
the Ohio, in the neighbourhood of the Miamis, and in
the vicinity of Zanesville, a great number of these
mounds are to be seen. Some are surrounded by ramparts, and are excavated within. The ramparts are
sometimes even two hundred feet in height, and enclose
areas of twenty-five or thirty acres. A great many human bones are scattered in them, which would induce
us to take them for tombs, if the enclosure was not
too large to have had only such a destination. It is
calculated that there are nearly three thousand of these
hillocks in the parts of the country that have been examined. Travellers have thought that they recognised
in them places consecrated to the worship of idols.

These monuments, as ancient perhaps as those of
Egypt, do not in any other respect resemble them.
But, though rude, they could not have been constructed without the co-operation of a great many men accustomed to obedience, habituated to discipline, and
directed by chiefs not wholly strangers to the practical

rules of geometry. The native inhabitants of the present day would be neither sufficiently docile, nor sufficiently numerous for their chiefs to undertake similar works. They consequently attest the presence of races less ignorant than those which we see there, though they might not have been much farther advanced in civilization. The first races to which we refer have not existed for several centuries, the others are about to disappear. Their imperfect traditions scarcely go back a thousand years, and we may conclude that they were arrested in their career by some political or natural catastrophe.

History makes us acquainted with man, as an inhabitant of the earth, for upwards of fifty or sixty centuries. But, during this great number of years, the two hemispheres have continued unknown to one another, and a circumstance so extraordinary can only be explained by the slight progress which navigation had made up to the period of the discovery of America.

Researches have been in vain made to ascertain whether the inhabitants of the old and new world were of the same origin, and whether the one race was more ancient than the other; nothing has led to the solution of the doubts on these questions.

A treaty of peace and friendship has been concluded between the Osages, on the one part. and the Delaware nation, its allies the Shawnees, the Kickapous, the Piankashaws, the Weas, the Peorias, and the Senecas on the other. These tribes reside in the countries ceded by France on the Missouri and Arkansas. This pacification took place in the town of St. Louis on the 7th of October, 1826. We cannot rely on its durability. An unfortunate circumstance occasions frequent hostilities among the Indian nations who occupy the countries situated between the Mississippi and the Rocky Mountains. The white hunters, settled on the frontiers, ruin these tribes by destroying their game. They, on their side, pressed by want, fall back on the other Indians of the north and west, and, although inferior in numbers, almost always attack them with success, because their neighbours, the whites, furnish them with arms, and sometimes join with them. The United States hold it as a principle that the eminent right of sovereignty over these territories belongs to them, but that they cannot have the proprietorship of the soil without giving to the aborigines an equivalent in money or merchandise. This is an abstract distinction.

A few years since some Trapists, who had emigrated from Europe, were found on one of the great prairies. Brackenridge, who visited them in 1812, says that their village contained an enclosure of a hundred acres, five little cabins, and all the other buildings necessary for agriculture. " They have," says this traveller, " renounced the use of speech, one of the noblest gifts of God to man; and they attempt to live in society, deprived of the principal agent of all society." These fathers, whose number was about thirty or forty, were almost all French or Germans. They seemed to seek in solitude and silence a place of re-

44

pose, which, however, soon ceased to satisfy them. The people, who are beginning to settle in this country, are not disposed to encourage such exaltations. The Trapists, weary perhaps at having so few witnesses of their silence, and tired of a kind of perfectibility which no one admired, have within a short time dispersed.

The Mississippi, one of the greatest rivers of the universe, and which had for so many centuries only served for the navigation of a few canoes, is already equal in importance to the finest water communications in the world. From its mouth to the first cataracts, it traverses, in a course of fourteen or fifteen hundred miles, lands of excellent quality. In some spots, where its banks approach near together, it flows with a rapidity of four or five miles an hour. It receives the Missouri and other rivers, which bring it a prodigious quantity of trees that are torn up by the inundations or by the ice. These waters deposite in the plains a rich slime, formed from vegetables that were decomposed centuries ago. The river carries off the greatest portion of it to the gulf of Mexico, where it is swallowed up and lost for reproduction. The accumulation of this slime sometimes obstructs the channel and alters its position. The bed of the river successively rises in different places. The western or right banks become higher than the plains which they are to defend against the inundations; and these immense volumes of water are, with an admiration mingled with dread, seen to move on, increase in bulk, overrun the banks, and inundate those superb valleys, the soil of which is lower than the level of the shore. Unfortunately these dykes, which are not capable of arresting the inundation, afterwards prevent the return of the water to the bed of the river. The evaporation which comes on in summer, without having any effect on the deep deposites, increases the calamity, and the ground being only half drained, stagnate pools are every where formed, which render the atmosphere unhealthy, and the country almost uninhabitable. Some elevations, the work of nature, or of these very inundations, exist beyond the strands which extend along the river. But the waters reach even these little islands, and if a few cultivators have dared to settle on them, they must with their families and cattle hasten to gain a height, from whence they see their houses and fields completely under water.

This calamity, too general on the lower Mississippi, will, for a long time, prevent improvements being made proportionate to the extent of the country. But these inundations will one day be changed into an artificial irrigation; breaches will be opened by the cultivator himself for the waters to run off after having deposited on the land a fertile slime. Thus another Egypt is gradually forming. The climate of lower Louisiana, the immense river which runs through it, the sources of which have been for so long a time unknown, its inundations, its falls, its embouchures, the neighbourhood of a gulf, will unite in rendering the resemblance with the Delta and the Nile complete.

However, these sub-marine alluvions at its mouth begin to obstruct it by a bar, which makes the entrance of the river every day more and more difficult. To obviate this inconvenience, it is proposed to open a canal from New Orleans to the gulf. Large ships will be able to navigate it, and the undertaking offers advantages very superior to the expense.

The course of the Mississippi is twelve hundred leagues, and the Missouri fifteen hundred, of the Arkansas a thousand, and of the Red River seven or eight hundred. These rivers and their tributaries water two hundred thousand square leagues, within the space of country called the basin of the Mississippi. This internal navigation, prepared by nature, has already been wonderfully extended and improved by canals, excavated by the labour of man; and steam-boats descend and ascend against wind and tide, brave the most rapid currents with more speed, and with more convenience than the finest roads in Europe can be travelled. Wood and coal, indispensable agents in this navigation, abound on the shores of the rivers, and the steam engine has put an end to the difficulty of communication, heretofore one of the greatest obstacles that were ever opposed to the improvement of colonies.

At the junction of the Mississippi and Missouri, the lands lying towards the north-west are of admirable fertility; emigration already inclines there, and these districts, though very remote from the sea, will one day be as well peopled as any other country of the world.

A vast plain and prairies extend beyond the Missouri and Red River, following the base of the great chain which separates the tributary waters of the Mississippi from those which flow into the Pacific Ocean. This valley is neither a perfect level nor mountainous, but is gently undulating; it is divided into spacious plains where only a few streams flow, the waters of which are remarkably clear. The most abundant pasture-grounds are there adorned with an infinite variety of flowers and flowering shrubs. Those who have traversed this country have admired the beauty of the situation, the mildness of the climate, the excellence and purity of the air. Very few Indian villages are to be seen; but there are numerous flocks of buffaloes and wild bisons. These animals keep together in order to defend themselves against the hunters, who only succeed in killing the stragglers. There are sometimes five or six hundred of them together.

This district is not subject to the sudden and violent rains which between the tropics fall in torrents and destroy the productions of the fields. The night and morning dews are sufficient to refresh the land and to supply with water a multitude of little trenches. But whether it be the consequence of several conflagrations, or arises from some other natural cause still unknown, large tracts of country are to be seen there, so entirely without wood, that a settler could not find on them the branches and bark necessary to construct and repair his cabin. For many days' journey not a tree is to be found, and if the winds bring seeds there, if some of them begin to shoot up, they only produce a feeble degenerate shrub. The excellence and depth of the soil make this singularity inexplicable. The country in question is scarcely inhabited. A pastoral population will settle there, an agricultural one will follow, and under the effects of industry, it will no longer have any occasion to envy the advantages of other lands.

A few Europeans have already built some huts there. They do not yet avail themselves of the plough; it is enough for them slightly to stir the mould, which has been at rest for many centuries. They confide the grain to it, which they then leave to nature, by whom they are liberally recompensed.

On the two sides of the river Plate, are vast plains of sand from a hundred to a hundred and fifty leagues in extent, where no indication of living creatures is to be found. These arid regions bear marks of the presence of the ocean at a very remote period. It is believed that its waters have washed the base of the Rocky Mountains, at the foot of which the desert terminates.

To the south of this district, vegetation has resumed all its vigour. The Red River and the Arkansas, in a part of their respective courses, intersect these fine countries so long uninhabited. The ridges from which they descend are covered with forests. Every year the inundations of the Red River tear up by the roots and carry away trees of an extraordinary size. They are heaped up on the rocks. which, in several places, obstruct or contract the current of the waters, and they have formed, even above the bed of the river, a natural vault, which is from twenty to twenty-five leagues in length, in the direction of the river: it is not, however unbroken, but the river reappears from time to time. This accidental formation must have commenced several centuries ago; for a new forest has already covered the rubbish, and one may cross the river on these bridges, and consider himself on the firm ground. The lower Mississippi presents the same singularities.

From time to time, subterraneous noises, like distant thunder, are heard in the valleys and extend under the bed of the rivers. Different reasons are given for this phenomenon, but every explanation would be premature, till a greater number of observations are collected.

The Rocky Mountains offer a still more extensive field for conjecture. These peaks touch one another at their bases, and form a chain which is more than three hundred miles in length. The summit of the largest is perceived at the distance of one hundred and forty miles. Their steepness and entire nakedness does not leave the least room for vegetation.

The clearing of the land frequently leads to the discovery of considerable heaps of bones. These remains have belonged to a species of animals, which, according to the accounts of them, must have been two or three times larger than the elephant: the species is un-

known at this day, and seems to have wholly disappeared from the globe.

Mineral salt, of an excellent quality, is found in abundance in a great many places at the surface of the
earth. In ascending the Arkansas, and at nearly two
hundred leagues from the great village of that name,
are the salt plains. A water strongly saturated with salt,
soaks thoroughly in the ground, and penetrates it during
the damp and rainy weather. During the droughts of
summer, it forms on the surface a solid and firm layer of
salt of from two to six inches in thickness. Its quality
is equal to that which is obtained by artificial crystalli-
zation and evaporation. This inexhaustible treasure
is possessed by the Osages, who were for a long
while one of the most savage of the Indian tribes.
They plundered the caravans, when they were not sufficiently numerous to defend themselves, and continually
alarmed the inhabitants of the frontier. In the middle of 1825, the United States concluded an important
treaty with them. By the terms of it, the nation of the
great and little Osages, cedes to the United States all
the country situated west of the territory of Arkansas,
and the state of Missouri, north and west of the Red
River, south of the Kanzas river, and east of a line
drawn from the sources of the river Kanzas through
the Rock Saline. This treaty, as well as several others
of the same nature, contain stipulations and grants of
land in favour of a mixed race, the descendants of
French and Indians.

A part of the salt bed has passed under the sovereignty of the confederacy. A day may come when its products will be more useful, and as much sought after as those of the silver and gold mines of Mexico.

The first phenomena observed in a country of which only the rivers are known, and in which the population is confined to their shores, do not present any great distinctions between the physical state of the new and old world. They have, however, seemed sufficient to render it doubtful, whether this other hemisphere has not emerged later than ours from the bosom of the waters. The disorders which follow a great natural revolution are so much the more evident on the surface of this new continent, as human industry has not as yet done any thing to cause them to disappear. But, however this may be, a new career in all branches of knowledge has been opened to mankind, and we may predict that very extraordinary discoveries await those who examine the interior of this country in search of the productions of our globe, and to study its revolutions.

Caravans of Americans crossing arid deserts, have gone with wagons from the village of the Arkansas to Santafe in Mexico, in twelve days. They have been hospitably received by the Mexican officers. The population of Santafé passed without the least disturbance from the royal government to a republican constitution.

In 1724, Charlevoix, the best historian of our discoveries in America, confidently asserted, that the metallic riches promised in 1721 to the partisans of Law's system, were not to be found in Louisiana. Charlevoix was probably mistaken. There are some indications of gold and silver mines, and if the prediction of another traveller should be verified, this country, before the lapse of a century, will have returned to the United States a hundred times the weight of gold which it has cost them. Other metals of every kind are found in abundance in all the old and new states. They already afford facilities for the developement of industry to a degree which Europe has only attained by efforts prolonged through many centuries. Agricultural riches, disdained a hundred years ago, are now estimated at their proper value, and they have in a few years raised the inhabited parts of this country to a high degree of prosperity. If the metallic treasures had been realized, they would never have equalled those which are acquired by agriculture, commerce, and manufactures. Twenty years of good government have effected what ages could not have accomplished under the prohibitory system. General and local interests have sprung up and made rapid advances. The population, which, under an absolute government, was stationary, has been tripled since the cession.

The lands are capable of producing every thing useful to man, from articles of primary necessity, to those of opulence and luxury. Louisiana has been enriched by the disasters of St. Domingo, and the industry that formerly gave so much value to that island, now fertilizes the valley of the Mississippi.

Since the end of the last century, the Louisianians have begun to understand better the riches of the soil that they possessed: the sugar cane was then cultivated in the gardens. The sugar now made in the ceded territories is adequate to the consumption of almost half the United States. The other productions of the territory have made proportionate advances.

The temperature of Louisiana is that of the countries most favoured by nature. The inconveniences inseparable from new settlements, the dangers from the neighbourhood of the Indians, diminish in proportion as the new population increases. The Indians have even taken an active interest in an important branch of commerce. It is through their means, that heaps of furs of every kind are now to be seen on the quays of New Orleans. The ermine, the martin, and the beaver, are brought there from the highlands on the north shores of the Mississippi, and the store houses in which they are deposited, likewise receive the sugar, the tobacco, and the cotton, that are grown on the southern borders of this river. New Orleans, which was founded in 1707, and which languished for nearly a century, is, after enjoying a free system for twenty-five years, one of the most flourishing cities of America. The increased facilities of its intercourse with Europe has diminished the price of all kinds of merchandise that the colony receives from thence, and it pays for them by its own crops of corn, cotton, and sugar. Some of its riches are obtained without effort, viz. horses, cattle,

&c., which only cost the trouble of bringing them to market.

The lands in the interior, which were sold at an insignificant price under the French and Spanish dominion, acquired immediately after the cession a considerable value. Ancient titles, forgotten for a century, were searched for, and it was in the archives of the French colony of the Illinois, that the descendants of Philip Renaud found the document containing the great grant made to their ancestor by the Mississippi Company. It includes the lead mines of St. Geneviève, which are so abundant, that veins and heaps of the metal are obtained by only digging a few feet in the ground.

Other grants were made, while the colony was subject to France and Spain. But the grantees, though at first very eager, had subsequently neglected their rights; as the lands soon acquired a high value under the republican government, this indifference ceased, and the number of claims was rapidly increased.

The small planters, for a long time humbled by their poverty, have since the cession been in the situation which accompanies an easy independence, and the rich ones have probably considered themselves lowered by the elevation of the other classes. Their opulence and a superior education had given them an importance, which has diminished since fortune and instruction have been within the reach of all. Mechanics, rich in consequence of their industry, capitalists and foreign merchants have assumed their place in a class previously exclusive, and to these causes is perhaps to be attributed the dissatisfaction of a few great proprietors, whose influence has vanished. The inhabitants of French origin have not as yet been able to amalgamate with the Americans. The two races retain their habits, and carry this spirit of jealousy even into the public affairs.

The population is likewise composed of Spaniards, English, and Germans: the difference of language and customs keeps them separate. But the public tranquillity is rarely disturbed, and liberty and equality will one day make one nation of these people of heterogeneous origin. The race of the Indians alone persists in keeping separate from all others. Families of them appear from time to time in the capital, but they retain their independence and their indolence; and though still deprived of the enjoyments of the social state, they have no longer as heretofore the advantage of being ignorant of their existence.

It is only requisite to pass from the left to the right bank of the Mississippi, in order to find other customs and inhabitants that may be almost considered as belonging to another species. The shepherds and planters of Opelousas and Attakapas are nearly all of French origin. They are in general without much instruction, and still speak the French of the time of the bucaniers; but the rudeness of their language does not extend to their deportment: they are of mild manners; hospitality is no where exercised with more cordiality, and the rusticity which is blended with it proves its sincerity still more fully. Here the luxury of the city has entirely disappeared, and the cloth-loom is oftentimes the only ornament of the drawing room.

Those who are acquainted with Europe, and the numberless enjoyments which it offers to all ages and ranks, know also with how much wretchedness this luxury is accompanied. At Attakapas there is no magnificence, and no poverty. All are happy at little expense, and on the same conditions. The dwellings in this settlement are very much scattered, churches are rare, and the number of priests is very small. It is, however, observed that the people are extremely religious. The head of the family is its spiritual pastor, and the divine morality of the gospel is transmitted to the future generation by the discourse and example of men who, for the most part, cannot read.

All the unsettled lands that had not been granted by France or Spain became, in consequence of the treaty, the property of the United States. They had scarcely taken possession of Louisiana when they sent out exploring parties in all directions to examine those western regions, which geographers still distinguish by the name of unknown countries or wild deserts. To explore them, to traverse them was in some sort to acquire the sovereignty of them.

Jefferson immediately perceived how important it was that the United States should extend by land to the shores of the Pacific Ocean. Some parts of its coasts were still undiscovered by European navigators.

or were not occupied by other powers: it is well known that they all considered themselves in possession of vast countries, when one of their officers erected, at the place of landing, a flag-staff, on which he wrote the name of the state he was serving.

Two persevering and courageous men, Messrs. Lewis and Clarke, were intrusted with the conduct of the first expedition, which was attended with truly useful results. As they followed the course of the rivers, their journey, including the return, extended to nearly four thousand leagues. A new world was in some sort discovered, and the United States learned the importance of their acquisition.

Another exploring party, under the direction of General Ashley, ascertained that it was possible to cross the Rocky Mountains towards the sources of the River Platte. The formidable barrier formed by this long chain becomes lower in this place, and opposes to the communication of the valley of the Missouri with the Pacific Ocean no more obstacles difficult to surmount.

Conquerors extend their states by war: they distinguish their reigns by the blood of the men and the desolation of the countries which they subject. They only leave after them the remembrance of disasters. The republic of the United States is enlarged by sending geometers and men of science to a distance of fifteen hundred leagues. It establishes, without any obstacle, the limits of its peaceable conquests, and secures by good laws the lasting happiness of the communities that may settle within them, as well as that of the innumerable generations that are to succeed.

The decrees of the kings of Spain were the only title of these monarchs to countries where their subjects had never yet penetrated, and which were five or six times more extensive than all their European dominions. These regions were only inhabited by tribes separated by great deserts. The mother country had intended to treat them with mildness. Its agents, however, too much disposed to believe that the trade of furs and other merchandise, sold or exchanged with the Indians, was their own patrimony, granted and farmed out the privilege of carrying on this trade, and those who obtained the contract abused it to the prejudice of the natives. The latter, instructed in this school, became in their turn deceitful. ·Acts of violence, robberies, and assassinations were the consequences of this bad faith.

The independence of Louisiana has re-established the intercourse, which so bad a system of government had interrupted. Rich cargoes of furs annually arrive at St. Louis, which are brought from the countries to the east of the Rocky Mountains by a river navigation of twelve hundred leagues, and good faith has restored confidence to these same savages whom fraud had frightened away.

France, in forming this colony, had imposed on it all the shackles which the jealousy of commerce is capable of forging. She had even forbidden the rais-

ing of corn. The Louisiana planters can now cultivate their lands according to their own interest or ca-
price. They have themselves proclaimed the happiness which they enjoy: it was after an experience of
more than twenty years that the house of representatives expressed by a unanimous resolution, " its veneration for Mr. Monroe, and its gratitude for the part
which he had taken in the proceedings that united Louisiana to the American confederacy."*

Mr. Jefferson, during his lifetime, received the same
marks of respect. This illustrious citizen having died
in want, the senate and house of representatives of
Louisiana, animated by a just sense of gratitude, came
to the succour of his family.†

Should any one suppose that he sees in the account
of so many meliorations a picture of the losses which
the cession has occasioned to France, we would merely observe that our commerce with Louisiana has increased tenfold since that colony has become independent.

It was not, however, till it had passed through many
trials, even after the cession, that the country attained
this high degree of prosperity.

The peace of the Union, and more particularly that
of Louisiana was, for a moment, endangered by the
bold enterprise of one of those men, whom great qualities seem to destine to the honourable service of their
country, but who, to satisfy the ambition by which they

* February, 1825.   † Appendix, No. 16.

are led astray, disregard the happiness of their native land. Aaron Burr had aspired to the place of president of the United States, and this active, enterprising, and energetic man had balanced the party that supported Jefferson. The votes had been at first equally divided between them. His wise competitor was, however, preferred.

Burr was one of the most ardent leaders of the republican party. Hamilton, a distinguished man on the opposite side, knew the disorder of his affairs. He happened one day to say publicly that Burr was a man without principle; and, as he declined either retracting or explaining his words, the latter challenged him to a duel. Hamilton detested this practice, which has descended to us from barbarous times; he went, however, to the appointed place, saying to the witnesses, "I will receive his fire, but intend to fire in the air." He fell by the ball of his adversary.

Burr, the murderer of one of the best citizens of America, returned to preside over the senate. But this unfortunate event had destroyed his influence even in the republican party, and, after the first four years had expired, he was not re-elected. His affairs becoming worse every day, he gave another direction to his efforts for re-establishing them. He announced, in 1805, a great plan for a settlement at Wachitta on the shores of the Mississippi. He concealed under this pretended undertaking a project which he had confided to a few adventurers as indiscreet as himself. The United States were at peace with all their neighbours, and Colonel Burr attempted to involve them in war with Mexico, where the Spanish forces were very superior to those which the United States then had in that part of the continent. The rumour had been spread that the Spaniards had crossed the Sabine, and carried their arms into the territory of the United States. Under this pretext, those who engaged in the plot said that the honour of the country required that reprisals should be made on Mexico, and this design was but too generally approved in Kentucky and Tennessee. It was there that Burr made his preparations to descend the Mississippi to New Orleans, to pass the Sabine, and to march against the capital of Mexico. He had found partisans even in New Orleans, among whom was named Mr. Daniel Clarke, the same Louisianian who had appeared at Paris at the period when the cession was made to France. It was, indeed, asserted that there were conspirators in the two houses of congress. The interests of the western states seemed, in fact, to have assumed a new direction in consequence of the treaty. One party had formed the plan of a division of the United States, and asserted that the line of separation was marked by the Alleghany Mountains.

This plot, which had been for some time prepared, assumed a grave character at the end of 1806, and too many important persons were engaged in it for it to remain a secret. As early as the month of November, Jefferson apprized the citizens of the Union that a criminal expedition was prepared, that arms and ships

were collected, and officers commissioned.   This vigilant magistrate found in congress and the several states
all the support of which he stood in need; and, in spite
of the efforts of the factious, the plan of dissolving the
sacred compact of the Union was repelled by an almost
unanimous sentiment.   It may, however, be conceived
that the danger had been imminent, since even the chief
justice, when Burr was indicted before the federal court
of Kentucky, dared not proceed with the prosecution.*

Far from being intimidated, Burr continued his preparations, and embarked at Nashville on the 22d of
December, 1806, but he was arrested and brought to
Richmond in Virginia.   Accused a second time, he
ultimately escaped a capital sentence by giving bail.
He did not appear to answer the indictment, and fell
into a sort of general neglect, from which his talents
might have raised him, had it been possible to forget
that he had once jeoparded the public peace.   A few
years afterwards Louisiana was the theatre of events
of greater importance, which are connected with this
history.

The United States had just made the world aware
that England had new rivals, and that the commerce
of the globe did not belong to her without competition.
Her apprehensions were increased after the cession of
Louisiana.

The influence of the violent crisis, which Europe experienced soon after that period, became so extended
about the year 1808 that it was impossible that the

* November 11th, 1806.

United States should not feel its effects. England had in her orders in council proclaimed, without disguise, her isolated and absolute maxims.* On all sides, she had been answered by acts equally hostile, under the denominations of ukases, cedules, and decrees; and France invoked, in the name of all Europe, the principles established at Utrecht, as the rules of the law of nations in relation to these matters. The United States found themselves involved in the general excitement, and published their embargo and non-intercourse acts. The ports of the old and new world were closed to English vessels, as much on the principle of reprisals as in obedience to Bonaparte. England had to suffer from three bad harvests, which completed her embarrassments. The price of all articles of the first necessity was very much augmented. Manufactures and navigation were suspended, and internal discontents carried to their height. The coalition of the maritime powers then appeared to her truly formidable: but two unexpected circumstances changed the aspect of affairs— the revolt of the Spanish colonies and the transfer of the throne of Portugal to the Brazils. A new career was thus opened to the policy, navigation, and industry of the English, and they entered on it with ardour.

On recovering their liberty of action, their attention was directed to the conduct, far from generous, of the American government. The profits obtained by this new people, in the trade which they carried on with all parts of the globe which were then accessible to

* Orders in council of 1807.

their seamen, made the English anticipate and dread the period when their marine would no longer be able to sustain an unequal struggle, and commercial jealousy was revived more actively than ever. Their efforts were not ineffectual, and two years sufficed, if not to restore to England all her preponderance, at least to enable her to reassume a high rank among the powers of the world.

The French forces had evacuated Portugal; the British arms had obtained signal advantages in the Peninsula. Russia had emancipated herself from a yoke too hard to be endured: Sweden had not incurred the disgrace of it. Other powers, it is true, still appeared to bend under the triumphant arm of Napoleon: but they assisted him with reluctance, fully determined to turn their forces against him on the first favourable opportunity; and he alone seemed to be ignorant of their secret understanding with his declared enemies. It was then that the English ministry, tranquil on the side of Europe, supposed that the moment had arrived for recovering the ascendency that they had possessed in America.

Canada, conquered by England fifty years before, for the advantage of her thirteen continental colonies, was useless in that respect since their independence. Closed to navigation by the ice during a part of the year, and too remote from the English colonies in the gulf of Mexico, it was far from occupying the place of those thirteen provinces which were accessible to vessels at all seasons, and which were rich in grain, in cattle, and in timber for ship building. New Brunswick was slowly peopled, Nova Scotia, our ancient Acadia, was without doubt of great importance on account of the port of Halifax. But these countries, a feeble counterpoise to the United States, showed no small disposition to render themselves independent. The means best calculated to connect them in interest with the mother country, was to detach Louisiana from the confederacy, to limit the United States to the Mississippi, and perhaps to realize the great project formed by Louis XIV., of uniting Canada to Louisiana.

The conduct of the French government had not a little contributed to strengthen the English party in the United States. The right of capturing and confiscating property, which Napoleon attempted to exercise, a right till that time unknown, was not directed solely against his enemies: it reached the mercantile marine of all the powers that did not effectually resist the arbitrary rules of the English maritime code. According to this code, merchandise belonging to neutrals, found in an enemy's ship, was not acquired by the captors of the vessel. But if merchandise, the property of an enemy, was found on board of a neutral vessel, it was good prize. This jurisprudence, which the simple notions of justice do not recognise, was in every way conformable to the interest of a people that arrogated to themselves the empire of the sea. In this competition of injustice and hatred, the most extraordinary acts on the part of the two governments succeeded one another. They ordered embargoes, and declared contraband all merchandise that was not protected by formalities difficult and sometimes even impossible to be executed. A remedy was in vain sought in modifications; the first measures were changed or revoked, but the revocation was accompanied by conditions that only made the situation of the navigators worse.

To the peaceable and useful intercourse by sea, which should be open to all nations, universal piracies were substituted. The most innocent navigators were victims of these excesses. The exceptions aggravated the evil and augmented the general loss to the profit of a few. Licenses, certificates of origin and permissions to trade fraudulently with the enemy, on condition of exporting certain domestic productions were granted. The enemy, in its turn, prohibited the introduction of these articles; but the cargo was then composed of merchandise of no value, and thrown into the sea during the passage, so that both the order to export and the prohibition to import were obeyed. New laws, in contempt of the rights of neutrality, subjected to confiscation every neutral vessel that had any intercourse with the enemy, and at the same time the ships of the belligerants constantly went, under false colours, from the one country to the other.

During ten years of war, more than twenty thousand licenses were annually granted.* But cupidity soon drew greater advantages from these inventions, and it has been stated, that the officers in London and Paris,

* The Report of the Duke of Bassano of the 10th of March, 1812.

had at last such a perfect mutual understanding, that this commerce, which had become in a manner regular,. even in the midst of hostilities, only afforded profits, which were faithfully divided among the subordinate officers employed in the transaction.

The imperial government, indeed, conceived the idea of benefiting the treasury by those fraudulent transactions; but England denied herself this source of revenue, and prohibited these deceitful practices. What had never before occurred, she forbade the trade in her own productions, and the licenses, instead of being a protection, afforded sufficient grounds for pronouncing the confiscation, when a cruiser found them on board of its prize.

At the same period, the Americans professed and practised rules whose justice and moderation are admitted by all who have meditated on the laws of nations. But, after having enjoyed as neutrals the profits of a commercial navigation, that was almost universal in its extent, they became the principal victims of those violent proceedings. The number of vessels which they lost in less than eight years is estimated at two thousand five hundred, of which five hundred and thirteen arose from prizes made by the French, and nine hundred and seventeen from captures by the English. The others were the prey of the allies of the two belligerant states.

Such was the deplorable condition of the commerce of the Americans at a time that they desired to be at peace with all nations.

The English had roused the Americans by putting forward pretensions, with an arrogance, that was founded on the false opinion that so feeble and timid an adversary would not dare to make resistance. They attempted to subject American ships to an examination on the high seas, and even in neutral ports. They had invented the new principle of an imaginary blockade, which all the navies in the world could not have realized. This rule, unknown even in the times of extreme barbarism, was no longer limited to places really blockaded, or to the carrying of munitions of war to an enemy; it embraced, by an absurd fiction, immense countries,* and extended to the most innocent communications with neutrals. France attempted to repel it by a blockade equally chimerical, but accompanied by measures more effectual for excluding all English merchandise from the continent. Napoleon declared that he would not permit any flag going from the ports of England to enter those of France, and, according to the British orders in council, no intercourse could take place with France except through the ports of England.† These two powers competed

* In May, 1806, the continent from the Elbe to Brest was declared in a state of blockade.

† "Such," said the British minister, Mr. Percival, "will be our law of reprisals as long as the continental system is maintained." The principal secretary of state of His Britannic Majesty was at Paris in the month of May, 1814. This plenipotentiary, speaking of the crisis which England had just experienced, said: "Bonaparte brought us within two inches of our destruction." He probably made the same remark to others, as well as to the author of this history.

with one another in inflicting injuries on the Americans, in order to force them to depart from their neutrality. The French envoy at Washington wished again to unite the two nations by treaty. The English minister made similar efforts to effect an alliance with his country, and, at the same time, increased the irritation of the public mind by the haughtiness of his language and his insulting proceedings.

The Americans, however, foresaw that England, once relieved from her European war, would fall on the United States with all her strength. They knew that if the English principles should prevail, their maritime commerce, the most flourishing in the world, after that of Great Britain, would be entirely ruined. Information was daily received of new affronts; they even went so far as to press sailors from on board of American ships of war and force them to spill their blood for a cause which was foreign to them. The public indignation increased. So many violent acts excited the strongest suspicions, and the best citizens were accused of treason. The truth is, that the government, calculating on the duration of peace, had neither land nor naval forces; a few ruined forts did not present even the phantom of a defence. To declare war suddenly against the English seemed a desperate resolution, and yet the government was induced to it by circumstances that became every day more serious.

The English in Canada, taking improper advantage of their proximity, had by means of presents and solicitations excited the savage tribes to lay waste the frontier. For several years a silent discontent had been remarked in the northern states, and the separation of the confederacy, which had been so long a source of only distant apprehension, became every day more to be dreaded.

Powerful states have no more solid foundation for their greatness and prosperity than justice and moderation. These rules, at the same time so useful and of such easy application, and which in consequence of their very wisdom have become common-place, were particularly adapted to England, where so many public men invoked with good faith the laws of equity and respect for treaties and the rights of others.

The practices of the governor of Canada will then be learned with astonishment. Under the pretence of good neighbourhood, Sir James Craig attempted to kindle civil war in the United States.* An able and bold intriguer, by the name of Henry, succeeded in gaining the confidence of this governor. Craig sent him to Boston and the northern states, in order to engage in a plot some persons of consideration among the federalists.

He instructed him to observe the parties, so as to form as correct an opinion as possible respecting the result of an open struggle between them. He was to neglect nothing to effect a schism, and to ascertain whether the federalists would, if it took place, apply to England and be disposed to unite their interests with

* January 26th. 1809.

that power. He had been provided with a cipher, and precautions were taken to secure the secrecy of the correspondence. Craig even signed instructions, and delivered to him a sort of letter of credence, which he was authorized to show to those who were sufficiently open in their communications to merit such a mark of confidence. It was couched in the following terms:—

" (SEAL.) The bearer Mr. John Henry is employed by me, and full confidence may be placed in him for any communication which any person may wish to make to me, *in the business committed to him.* In faith of which, I have given him this under my hand and seal, at Quebec, this 6th day of February, 1809.

"J. H. CRAIG."

Henry, thus empowered to act, commenced his important mission. In less than a month, he conceived that he had made sufficient progress to give the governor assurances that, in the event of a war, the inhabitants of that part of the state of Vermont, which borders on Canada, would refuse obedience to congress; and that they might be considered allies of Great Britain. On his arrival at Boston, his hopes having increased with the information that he had collected on the journey, he wrote to him that Massachusetts would declare against the general government, and that open resistance would be made by the establishment of a congress of the eastern states.

The agent pursued his design with some address. Persuaded that as the northern states were devoted to commerce, and those of the south were agricultural, such discordant interests could not fail to separate them, he concluded that whether they were enemies of England, or on good terms with her, a dissolution of the confederacy could not but be favourable to the policy of the British cabinet. He saw in it the guarantee of the preservation of Canada and Nova Scotia; and concluded that the jealousy of the two parties would ultimately render the influence of England so powerful that the states, though free in name, would in fact be dependent on her. "Another revolution," said he, "must be brought about in this country, in order to overturn the only republic whose existence would prove that a government founded on political equality could secure, in the midst of tumults and dissensions, the happiness of a nation, and be in a condition to repel foreign attacks. It should then be the particular object of Great Britain to foster divisions between the north and the south, and extinguish any remaining attachment for France. By succeeding in this, she may carry into effect her own projects in Europe, with a total disregard of the resentments of the American democrats. Her superiority at sea will enable her to dictate to the ship-owners of the north, and even to the agriculturists of the south, whose productions would be of no value if our naval forces prevented their exportation."

A part of the predictions of this emissary were subsequently verified, and, when war was declared, Massachusetts refused to put her militia at the disposal of the United States.   However, patriotic sentiments in the end prevailed, even among the federalists, and Henry at last discovered that the menaces of separation could never be realized.

After having resided five months in the United States, he returned to Quebec, only bringing back from his journey the information, little favourable to the English system, that the love of country and of liberty was the governing principle of the whole population.   His mission was without result: he had compromitted the governor of Canada, and as his promises were not accomplished, his employer seemed little disposed to fulfil those that had been made to him.

Henry valued his services at 32,000 pounds sterling. Craig heard his reclamations, but, obliged to fail in his promises, he induced him to apply to the British government.   At London, he was told that the affair concerned the governor of Canada, and that he should be recommended to the successor of Sir James Craig.

But good offices of this sort are almost always badly requited by a successor.   Henry understood that the British government wished to get rid of his importunities, and wearied with ineffectual solicitations, and irritated at the contempt with which he was treated, he conceived the project of taking vengeance of those who had deceived him.   He came to Washington in 1812, and discovered to the American government the whole secret of his mission, placing in its hands the original documents, which the English ministers had in vain attempted to withdraw from him.

By bringing forward the charge himself, he became protected from all judicial prosecutions; but it was of such great importance to the United States, that President Madison did not hesitate to communicate it to the senate. He had, at the same time, the prudence to avoid all investigations and proceedings which could compromise the Americans who had engaged in criminal communications with Henry; and he confined himself to establishing, " that Great Britain had, in the midst of peace, and of amicable professions for the United States, attempted to bring about a dissolution of the Union, and to involve their citizens in the horrors of a civil war." These facts, thus discovered, were made public through the journals. To divide the states into two factions, and to excite a civil war was the greatest offence which it was possible to commit against them.

The English minister at Washington solemnly disclaimed having had the least knowledge of the mission of Henry, and expressed his conviction that from what he knew *of those branches of his government*, with which he was in the habit of having intercourse, no countenance whatever was given by them to any schemes hostile to the internal tranquillity of the United States. But the very form of this justification badly disguised hostile projects, and the hand of the English always appeared in every circumstance, where they could have any hope of detaching from the Union countries, the acquisition of which would for ever strengthen their power. This discovery gave extraordinary strength to the republican party, and the partisans of the parent state, relieved from apprehension by the prudent resolution which the government adopted of making no inquiry respecting those who had taken part in Henry's intrigues, united with the true friends of their country. The official communications ceased on the 6th of June.

War was declared a few days afterwards, (18th of June, 1812,*) and this resolution was less the work of congress than the consequence of the resentment of the people.

From this moment the Union made incredible efforts to obviate the inconveniences occasioned by long neglect. Congress, to all the dispositions of vigour and prudence required by the circumstances in which they were placed, united means which European governments do not always employ. They concealed nothing from the people with regard to the dangers of their situation, and proved to them by a multitude of facts that England, considering the United States as her commercial rivals, also regarded their happiness, their aggrandizement, and their independence as incompatible with her prosperity; in a word, they informed them of the causes and justice of the war, with the circumstances of which the most inconsiderable citizens might have acquainted themselves as fully as the ministers at

* Appendix, No. 17.

48

the head of affairs. Public speeches, pamphlets, and
newspapers exposed, with perfect sincerity, the motives
for having recourse to arms, and the necessity of a vigorous defence. Even the instructions that had been
given to the envoys and ministers were made public.
From the simple labourer to the first magistrate, from
the admiral to the most insignificant sailor, all knew
that the dearest interests of their commerce and navigation were in question, and this appeal to the honour
of the flag was for them neither vain nor deceptive: it
expressed a sentiment truly national.

The English government at first directed its attention to Canada, and made arrangements for assuming
the offensive. It also turned its views to the eastern
coasts of the Union. The Americans, on their side,
had been fully aware that it would be impossible for
them to resist the efforts of so formidable a power
without a great change in their naval tactics, and they
had entirely reformed their system of ship building.
They had increased the size and force of their frigates,
the calibre of their guns, and strengthened their crews
in proportion.

It is well known with what violence this war was
conducted on the part of the English. Slaves were
armed against their masters or carried off and sold to
the West India colonists; the Indians massacred all the
inhabitants of the frontiers who had delayed making
their escape; cities and defenceless places were given
up to pillage or as a prey to the flames. The results
of this struggle are also known. Europe, which had

at first seen in the resistance of the Americans only an excess of audacity and imprudence, learned with astonishment that they had appeared as equals in the naval engagements, in which they were, indeed, more frequently the victors than the vanquished party. The case was not the same on the American continent. The war was not carried on with ability by either the federal or English armies. Canada remained in a defenceless state.

Among a great number of faults, for which even inexperience could not afford an apology, the following has been cited. The entire frames of two large frigates were sent from England to Quebec on board of several vessels. They were forwarded by the river St. Lawrence to Lake Ontario, where they were to be put together and completed. It was expected that this superior force would easily destroy the American flotillas. But the other party, on their side, built a vessel of still greater strength. They employed for the purpose the wood of the fine forests in the neighbourhood of the lake. Only three months were required for its construction, and their vessel was sailing when the English ships were still in the yard without deck or side planks.* England would have inevitably lost Upper Canada, if the Americans had not likewise committed great faults.

The English themselves were astonished at not ob-

---

* It was stated in parliament, in July, 1828, that the transportation of the materials of one of the two frigates from Montreal to Kingston had cost 30,000 pounds sterling.

taining any advantage over their former colonies, when the aspect of affairs in Europe entirely changed. They had subdued Napoleon, their implacable enemy. The numerous armies which Wellington had commanded were now unemployed. Considerable forces could at last be directed against the United States, and brilliant successes were to efface unexpected humiliations. Until that time Louisiana had been at peace. Admitted into the great confederacy a long time after the war of independence, the Louisianians wanted that glorious, though melancholy consanguinity, which results from victories obtained by common efforts. They unexpectedly learned that their country was about to have its turn in the perils of the war.

The precautions required for defence had been still more neglected there, than in any other part of the United States. It was easily believed, that a peace which had endured for a century would not be disturbed, and New Orleans had, to defend it, only a few men barely adequate to the purposes of police.

The English were aware of this situation of things, but foreseeing that other states of the Union, that were more populous and better trained to war might hasten to the defence of the place, they formed the plan of keeping them back by combining an attack on the side of Canada with the one which they directed by sea against New Orleans.

England assigned fourteen thousand regular troops to the expedition by the gulf of Mexico. Such a force is considered very great in that country, and the pillage of New Orleans was announced to the army as a magnificent recompense for its dangers and toils. In fact, the crops of cotton and other rich productions of these vast countries were stored in this city, it being the limit and entrepôt of the navigation of the Mississippi and Missouri. The English, however, in aiming at the conquest of Louisiana, did not announce the intention of keeping it. They even pretended that they only wished to take it from the United States, in order to restore it to Spain at the price of a few advantageous stipulations for their islands. It appears more certain that they likewise calculated on the inaction, and perhaps on the concurrence of the northern states of the Union, where they still had partisans.

One would wish, that the history of a great and illustrious nation should never recall any events unworthy of its glory. But culpable, not less than glorious actions, fall within the province of true history.

One circumstance, in particular, shows to what a degree England conceived herself interested in wresting from the confederacy, the countries which it had recently acquired, and in preventing its dominions extending to the right bank of the Mississippi.

After the conclusion of treaties with the Indians to arm them against the United States, the English officers sought one of those alliances which the law of nations, the law of all civilized people, condemns. British commanders had no hesitation in treating with a community of pirates then well known, who, they believed, would oppose an additional obstacle to the navigation and commerce of the Americans.

Till that time, the government of Louisiana had neglected to take possession of some islands near the Lake of Barataria and the mouths of the Mississippi. After having been for a long time inhabited by mere fishermen, pirates seized on them, and established their quarters there. These sea robbers had as their chief a man of the name of Lafitte: his bravery, his activity, and his piracies, but too well recalled the exploits of the bucaniers who, a century before, had exercised their infamous trade with impunity in the gulf sea. They respected no flag, not even that of the United States. In the course of two years, more than one hundred merchant ships became their prey. After having pillaged their cargoes and murdered their crews, they burnt the vessels and kept the commerce of those seas in continued dread.

William H. Percy, commanding the English forces in the gulf, gave orders to one of the officers on his station to hasten to Barataria, in order to enter on negotiations with Lafitte.* If this chief refused to commit hostilities against the United States, the officer was, while he stipulated at all events for neutrality, to request him to join the English. Percy even wrote to Lafitte to urge him, "to enter with his naval and military forces, into the service of the king of England."

---

* August 30th, 1814.

The skill of these pirates in the use of cannon rendered them valuable auxiliaries.

Edward Nichols, one of the principal English officers, in a proclamation to the inhabitants of the left bank of the Mississippi, promised them the free navigation of the river. Then, addressing the natives of Louisiana, he said to them: "Put an end to the American usurpation over this country, that it may be restored to its legitimate proprietor. I am at the head of a numerous body of Indians; we will make the Americans return to the limits prescribed by my sovereign." This was the same thing as saying in sufficiently clear terms: "The dominion of England over the seas of America is at an end, if the United States maintain themselves on the right bank of the Mississippi."

Lafitte and his band, in which there were some Louisianians, rejected these overtures of the English with indignation. These men saw no dishonour in enriching themselves by plunder, but they had a horror of treason.

The government of the state was informed of these proceedings, and, having no knowledge of the dispositions of the Baratarians, considered it to be its duty to reduce them by arms. A flotilla, collected with great despatch, sailed from New Orleans, and was soon in sight of Barataria. The pirates prepared for resistance; but vigorous demonstrations inspired them with so much fear that they abandoned the nine ships which composed their marine. They dispersed, and their store-houses, vessels, and a considerable booty fell into the power of the Americans.*

Lafitte, who had escaped, wrote from his place of retreat to Governor Claiborne, and sent him the originals of the correspondence with the British officers. He proposed, at the same time, to surrender himself. This confidence appeared to require that indulgence should be shown to this man and his party, and a pardon, grounded on the services which he had rendered, was announced to him, and a few months after granted in the name of the United States.

Congress, informed of the danger of Louisiana, directed all its attention to that quarter. It had learned to appreciate the importance of this province, and no one would then have dared to repeat what some had said at the period of the cession, that the territories beyond the river were only a troublesome burden. All admitted that the object of England, when she undertook to make this conquest, was to limit the extent of the states, to balance their influence in the general affairs of America, and to prevent their becoming a preponderating power.

In the summer of 1814, the English landed a few troops upon the Spanish territory of the Floridas, and all their movements announced an early attack on Louisiana. There were in this state neither troops nor a general; the local bank had suspended its payments. Love of country seemed frozen at the ap-

* September 20th, 1814.

proach of an army still inflated with the successes which it had met with in Europe. To reanimate it required one of those men whose appearance creates resources and raises courage. Such a man was found. He was Andrew Jackson, a major-general in the American army. On his arrival at New Orleans, he was neither alarmed at finding great consternation there, nor in learning that some English emissaries were carrying on their intrigues in the very bosom of the legislative assembly. At the sound of his voice, committees were formed, a city peopled with merchants and planters changed in a day the habits of a century. An extraordinary activity took the place of an inexcusable negligence. Expresses, arriving in succession from the upper country of the Mississippi, announced that a population of two millions of inhabitants would not allow themselves to be subdued, and that imposing forces were about to descend the river. The decisive moment approached. By the first day of December, the English had on the coasts of Louisiana one hundred and forty vessels of all sizes, among which were several ships of the line. They brought a numerous flotilla, through difficult passes and the lakes in its neighbourhood, to within a very short distance of the capital.

In the mean time, the succour which had been promised and was expected at New Orleans, did not arrive. The English, informed that this city had scarcely more than two thousand men in arms to oppose to them, advanced towards it, and were, on the 23d of December, at only four leagues distance. Calculating on fears

which no longer existed, and on their numbers, which
could be at a moment's warning increased, they had
taken none of the precautions that prudence requires
in an enemy's country.   Jackson profited by this security.   His little army was formed of Louisianians, re-
solutely determined to defend themselves with courage,
though uninitiated in war, of Tennesseans, excellent rifle-
men, and a battalion of free coloured people, emigrants
from St. Domingo.   This militia, of various origin, no
longer formed but one people. A battalion that wished,
however, to retain the name of Orleans was composed
of men of the two nations. No rivalry disturbed their
good understanding. A detachment, marching out of
the city at night, fell suddenly on the enemy's camp,
killed four hundred men, and retired with little loss.

This bloody lesson warned the English of the necessity of awaiting the reunion of their forces.   The delay afforded time to the Kentucky militia to arrive, and
on the 4th of January, 1815, they entered the city to
the number of two thousand two hundred and fifty
men, but scarcely one-third of them had brought arms.
They were not, however, useless. An old canal, seventeen hundred yards in length commencing at a cypress
marsh, terminated on the left bank of the Mississippi,
in a direction perpendicular to the river. These men
raised a rampart behind this canal, and called it Jackson's lines.

An express, sent from Quebec to the commander of
the English army, informed him that the severity of the
season, and the danger of too much weakening the

Canadian army, would prevent the garrisons in that country from making the promised diversion.

On the 8th of January, 1815, the English, having re-assembled all their forces with the exception of two thousand men, who had crossed to the right bank of the river, advanced in columns against the lines. A few of the bravest reached them, after having made for themselves a road by filling the ditch with fascines of sugar cane. They were all killed. This day was to decide the fate of Louisiana. Ten or eleven thousand combatants began the general attack, at daylight, with intrepidity, but with a rashness and improvidence for which their chiefs were inexcusable. The fire of the Americans made terrible carnage in their columns. They fell back a moment, but were twice brought up to the assault, though without success, and the gene-ral-in-chief, Packenham, remained on the field of bat-tle the victim of his imprudent valour. The affair only lasted an hour. In this short space of time the Eng-lish lost nearly three thousand men. The Americans experienced scarcely any loss. The defeat of an army of fourteen thousand brave men, well disciplined, and exercised in a long European war, was the work of four thousand militia, hastily levied, and armed with fowling pieces, which to that day had never been used for the purposes of war. Their enemies, made ac-quainted at their own expense with the energy and re-sources of a free people, that defend their own fire-sides, and, informed that the city was about receiving new succours, feared that they would soon have to resist the population of the west, which from all quarters was flocking to the common defence. The diversion made on the right bank experienced scarcely any resistance on the part of the Americans, and yet it could not second the principal attack on the left of the river. The English seriously contemplated a retreat, and, on the 19th of January, Lambert, who had become general-in-chief, declared that they abandoned the expedition against New Orleans. The campaign only lasted a month, but it settled for ever the fate of Louisiana.

The legislature of the state solemnly thanked the troops of Tennessee, Kentucky, and Mississippi. The name of General Jackson was not included among those to whom the approbation of the assembly extended. This ingratitude arose from the resentment of a few delegates. At the moment of peril, Jackson had made use of violence against several citizens; but this disregard for the laws had preserved the province, and we cannot consider that as a crime which ensured its safety. Perhaps he was even excusable, while the public mind was still very much agitated, to prolong after victory the dictatorship that he had assumed. He had likewise suspended the power of the legislature; and this violation of the public rights is the one which most keenly wounds and irritates a free people. Honourable marks of approbation, emanating from congress, repaired the injustice; thanks were voted to him, as well as to his army. The government acknowledged, in express terms, that the difficulties had been unprecedented, and that it would be unjust to use severity against one who had secured, even by illegal acts, the triumph of liberty.* Congress likewise expressed their high esteem for the patriotism, fidelity, and valour with which the people of Louisiana had defended all their political and social rights. They praised the benevolence and humanity manifested not only by the succours given to the wounded of the American army, but also by the generous care bestowed on the prisoners taken from the enemy.

Thirteen years afterwards, Jackson returned to New Orleans, invited by the legislature of the state, and was received there with joy and gratitude. The period of the election of a president of the United States having arrived, some Louisianians endeavoured to secure him the votes of the state. But one of his best friends thus combated the proposition: " Services in a particular department, however eminent, do not afford a title to universal confidence. If we were again obliged to defend our country, sword in hand, we would with one voice call Jackson to the chief command. But, as we enjoy a profound peace, the suffrages of Louisiana for the supreme presidency should be given to a citizen endowed with the virtues of peace."

During this important election, each party puts forward the pretensions of its candidate, and severely

---

* Letter from Mr. Dallas, acting secretary of war to General Jackson. Mr. John Quincy Adams, now at the end of his presidential term, has likewise borne the same testimony to his services.

scrutinizes the life of his competitor. Looking to the violence of the animosities, some are alarmed, and consider them the precursors of an approaching separation between the northern and southern states. But each party exists in the interior of all the states, and the clamours are appeased as soon as the new president is named. Up to the day that we are writing, the votes are pretty equally divided between Mr. John Quincy Adams, now president, whose re-election is powerfully supported, and Andrew Jackson, eminent by his great services. We shall know in a very short time whether the qualities of the warrior, and a courage superior to all obstacles, will be preferred to the modest virtues which, with less *éclat*, have secured the happiness of the nation. But whatever may be the result of this domestic contest, the wisdom of the constitution is a guarantee as well for the moderation of the general as for the firmness of the magistrate.*

The English ministers were still ignorant of the result of the expedition against Louisiana, when they opened at Ghent negotiations for peace: they were terminated by a treaty which contains an implied renunciation of that conquest even in case it had been made. It was signed on the 24th of December, 1814, fifteen days before the deliverance of New Orleans. The precipitation with which it was concluded left many important points undecided, and it was only in the month

---

* General Jackson was elected president, and inaugurated in that office on the 4th of March, 1829.—TRANSL.

of September, 1827, that several new articles were settled by plenipotentiaries of the two nations.*

* Mr. Gallatin during his mission to England in 1826-7, concluded four conventions with the plenipotentiaries, specially appointed to negotiate with the United States, namely, Mr. Huskisson, to whom, on his resignation in the summer of 1827, Mr. Grant was substituted, and Mr. Addington.

1. A convention, signed the 13th of November, 1826, by which $1,240,960 were paid to the United States in lieu of their demands, under the 1st article of the treaty of Ghent.

The claims for slaves, &c. taken away at the peace of 1815, had been referred to the Emperor of Russia, who gave in 1822 an award conformable to the American construction of the treaty of Ghent; but new difficulties having arisen in carrying this decision into effect, it was agreed by the United States to accept a gross sum, to be by them distributed to their citizens.

2. A convention, signed the 6th of August, 1827, to continue in force the commercial convention of 1815, originally made for four years, and extended in 1818 to ten years from that time.

It regulates the trade between the United States and Great Britain, including her possessions in the East Indies. By its provisions, as mentioned in a previous note, equality of duties is established on American and British vessels in the respective ports of the two countries. We are also allowed to trade with the principal settlements in the East Indies, our vessels paying in the permitted ports no higher or other duties than the most favoured European nation. By the 2d article of the commercial convention of 1827, it is competent for either party to annul it, on giving twelve months' notice.

3. A convention, signed on the same day with the one last mentioned, to continue in force the third article of the convention of 1818.

By the article referred to, it had been agreed that the country claimed by either party, westward of the Stony Mountains, should be free to both powers, without prejudice to their respective claims, for ten years. The new convention, concluded by Mr. Gallatin, extends indefinitely the term of joint occupancy, but contains the same provision as the commercial convention, permitting either party to put an end to it, on giving to the other twelve months' notice.

The war had cost many lives to the two countries. It added three hundred millions of dollars to the debt

An attempt was made, but without success, to settle a permanent boundary between the United States and Great Britain on the
Pacific Ocean. The discussion, however, induced the plenipotentiaries of the two powers to place on record statements of their respective claims, which were attached to the protocols of their 6th
and 7th conferences, and laid before congress at the session of
1827–8. As one of the principal points, on which the right of the
United States is maintained, grows out of the Louisiana treaty, the
subject naturally connects itself with the present history.

It is remarked, at the commencement of the British paper, that
"from the 42d to the 49th degree north latitude, the United States
claim full and exclusive sovereignty. *Great Britain claims no exclusive sovereignty over any portion of that territory.* Her present claim, not in respect to any part, but to the whole, is limited
to a right of joint occupancy in common with other states, leaving
the right of exclusive dominion in abeyance."

The 49th degree of north latitude was proposed by the American government as a boundary in the spirit of compromise, it being conceived that the pretensions of the United States extend
much farther. They are, however, prevented by the convention
with Russia from forming settlements north of 54° 40'.

The claims of the United States, as examined by the British
plenipotentiaries, result, 1st, from their own *proper* right: 2d. from
Spain, which power ceded to them by the treaty of Florida, all its
rights north of the 42d degree: 3d. from France, to whom the
United States succeeded as possessors of Louisiana.

Great stress is laid by Great Britain on the binding effect of the
Nootka Sound convention, concluded by her with Spain in 1790,
and which allows access to the subjects of both powers to places on
the Pacific Ocean not then occupied. This argument is brought
forward as applicable as well to our title derived through Louisiana, which province belonged to Spain in 1790, as to that de-
duced from the Florida treaty of 1819. The Nootka Sound convention, however, expressly left the sovereignty in abeyance, and
is considered by us to have been only intended to regulate the con-
flicting pretensions to the trade with the natives.

Our claims, as founded on the prior discovery and first occupancy of the country, are also contested, with what justice may be

of England. The losses and expenses of the United States are estimated at one hundred and twenty mil-

seen by a reference to the statements of the respective plenipotentiaries. The American title is farther sustained by the old charters of the Atlantic colonies which extended westward to the Pacific Ocean—by the settlement of the northern boundary of Louisiana by the commissioners under the treaty of Utrecht at the 49th degree of latitude, and by the contiguity of the inhabited territory of the United States.

It is to be observed, though the fact is overlooked by the author, when speaking, at page 290, of the extension of the American sovereignty to the country on the Pacific Ocean, that Crozat's grant did not include the whole of Louisiana, even as it was held by France herself before the cession to Spain. The sources of the Mississippi were supposed in 1712 not to extend beyond the forty-second degree. Louisiana was bounded on the north by the Illinois, then a part of Canada, and on the west by Mexico, whose limits were at that time understood to be north of the forty-second degree. Consequently, no territory west of the Rocky Mountains was then granted. But, by an *ordonnance* of 1717, the Illinois was annexed to Louisiana, and, after the acquisition of Canada by the British, the line of demarcation between their possessions and those of France, west of Lake Superior, was fixed at the forty-ninth degree of north latitude. By the convention of 1818 between the United States and Great Britain, this boundary was recognised as far as the Rocky Mountains.

4. Convention, signed 29th of September, 1827, to regulate the reference to a friendly sovereign or state, in conformity to the 5th article of the treaty of Ghent, of the dispute relative to the northeastern boundary.

The treaty of Ghent provides several commissions for fixing the boundary line between the United States and Great Britain, as defined in the treaty of 1783, and stipulates, in the event of the disagreement of the commissioners of the two powers, that their reports should be submitted to a friendly sovereign or state, whose decision should be final. The case contemplated having occurred, with respect to the part of the boundary embraced in the 5th article, the object of the convention of London was to settle the time for appointing the arbiter, and to simplify the duties to be relions of dollars, but the peace left them tranquil possessors and exclusive sovereigns of the Mississippi.

quired of him, by substituting to the voluminous papers in the controversy, statements on which a decision might be founded.

The ratifications of this last convention, as well as of the two concluded on the 6th of August, 1827, were exchanged at London on the 2d of April, 1828, and, in pursuance of its provisions, negotiations were immediately thereafter commenced between the British secretary of state and Mr. Lawrence, the American chargé d'affaires, which resulted in the selection of the king of the Netherlands as sovereign arbitrator, before whom the question of our northeastern boundary line is therefore now pending.

The right of the United States to navigate the St. Lawrence was also discussed between Mr. Gallatin and the British plenipotentiaries, but without the negotiations leading to any result.

The trade with the British colonies formed the subject of a long correspondence between Mr. Gallatin and Mr. Canning, which was continued with his successor, the Earl of Dudley. At the negotiation of the commercial treaty in 1815, it was the wish of the United States to make the same arrangements for the colonies as for the mother country. This was then refused by England, though the proposition was subsequently brought forward, particularly at the conferences of 1818 and 1824, with well-grounded expectations of the two parties coming to a satisfactory understanding. In consequence of the British act of 1822, the trade, which had been for some time closed by the operation of the previous regulations of the two powers, was opened to a modified extent. After the suspension, however, of the negotiations of 1824, and before they could be resumed, the British government passed the act of 1825, regulating the trade of foreign states with the West India possessions. Not supposing that it was intended that this law should apply to us, and having no intimation that we were to consider the suspended negotiations as terminated, congress failed to comply with the requirements necessary to entitle us to the provisions of the act of parliament. Taking advantage of this omission, an order in council was issued by England in July, 1826, a few days before Mr. Gallatin's arrival in London, closing the West India ports against our vessels from and after the 1st of December following—a measure that was met by putting in force our countervailing prohibitions, which had been suspended in 1822.

They were thenceforth authorized to calculate that nothing could prevent the extension of their sovereignty to the Western Ocean. A settlement has been formed on its shores at the mouth of the Columbia River. The founder is Mr. Astor, who called the post Astoria.

It is especially in the neighbourhood of the Mississippi that indications of former French colonization are to be found. Ruins of forts and bastions which they erected are still to be seen even on the Missouri. Indian families, who allied themselves, a century ago, with a Norman or a Briton, boast of their origin, and bear with pride the names of their ancestors. Those of Iberville, Pontchartrain, Maurepas, and Jumonville are

It may be here remarked that the course pursued by the British government, in relation to the colonial trade, ought not to be ascribed to any proceedings on the part of the United States. The treaties of reciprocity, concluded in 1824 with several of the powers of Europe, had made the ministry very unpopular with the ship owners, and to gratify that important interest it was deemed expedient to exclude the Americans from the West Indies. In corroboration of this assertion, it may be added, that though the act of parliament of 1825, with the exposition intended to be given to it in England, was in no way brought to the attention of our government, (with whom a negotiation on the subject was then pending,) it is within the knowledge of the writer of this note that it was not only communicated to, at least one European state, but that the power referred to was strenuously, though ineffectually urged, through its minister in London, by Mr. Huskisson as well as Mr. Canning, to comply with the conditions of the British statute.

It is not improbable that, owing to the changes in the English administration, since the date of the discussions with Mr. Gallatin, particularly the retirement of Mr. Huskisson, an arrangement may soon be made that will secure to the United States a participation in the trade in question.—TRANSL.

preserved with a kind of gratitude. It is a similar feeling which in the old states of the Union has given to counties and towns the names of Bourbon, Luzerne, Lafayette, Steuben, Louisville, and Fulton. The city where congress sits, and a great number of districts bear the name of Washington.

To the south of the regions watered by the Red River, runs the Trinity, which traverses the province of Texas. This country, for a long time considered a part of Louisiana, remained by treaty in possession of Spain: and the United States, as ambitious as old monarchies, regret having too easily abandoned it.

It was there, a few years ago, that some Frenchmen, exiled from their country, attempted to form a settlement. The narrative of their misfortunes will conclude my account of the cession of Louisiana.

The sudden and unexpected return of Bonaparte to France from the island of Elba, had brought around him half of that youth who, under this great captain, had known no other glory than that of arms, and no other happiness than that of triumphs and victories. His party, hastily formed, incautiously brought together, was soon crushed. Several chiefs, menaced by the tribunals, preferred exile to the dangers of a trial, and retired to the United States. They were there hospitably received. In March, 1817, congress granted them lands* on the borders of the Alabama, at the

* By the act of congress of the 3d of March, 1817, 92,160 acres were granted, on condition of introducing there the vine and olive.

confines of Florida, and the country of the Creek Indians. They fixed a very moderate price, payable in fourteen years, and the grant of congress was a liberal present disguised under the form of a sale. The lands were well selected; the gift was worthy of being offered by a free people to courageous, though misled, men. But the grantees, habituated to military activity or to the leisure of a camp, novices in agriculture and in the art of clearing new land, soon abandoned their undertaking. Several of them retroceded their portions, and dispersed. Others, while they removed from Alabama, persisted in the design of forming an agricultural settlement.

It was towards Texas that their expectations were turned. Generals Lallemand and Rigaud conducted thither a small body of soldiers and labourers. The hope of finding in this country another France offered to them an attraction which those who never have been banished cannot appreciate. They had advanced ten miles within the territory, and acknowledged Lallemand for their commander. He supposed that he could subject to agricultural labour men who knew no other activity than that of war. There were in the country a great many wild bulls, cows, and horses. Game and fish abounded, but the clearing of the ground is laborious, and requires so long a time that it can never be followed by a harvest within the year. Even on the best soil one must expect to be opposed by the climate, and an extraordinary drought interrupted their labour and suspended all vegetation. They were not, howe-

ver, discouraged, and, while they waited for the season
to become more favourable, they lived on the provisions they had brought with them, and on what they
obtained from hunting and fishing. The natives had
received them kindly, and a petty traffic had been established with them. Lallemand had given the name
of *Champ d'Asile* to the post that he had chosen. He
was beginning to fortify it, to prescribe regulations, and
to invite other emigrants, when his feeble progress was
arrested by obstacles which he had not foreseen.

The Spaniards directed him to discontinue the clearing of the land and his other labours, or acknowledge
the sovereignty of the catholic king. They even
marched in arms against *Champ d'Asile*. The little
colony was in no state of defence, and did not undertake to make a useless resistance. These unfortunate
men, fugitives from their own country, were expelled
from a territory where the aborigines had received
them with hospitality, and which ought to have belonged only to those who were the first to occupy it
beneficially. This little community no longer exists;
its chiefs have perished, or their fate is unknown.

Texas is one of the finest countries in the world;
and yet the Europeans, eager as they have been to
make conquests in America, have seemed almost to the
present day ignorant of its existence. The new inhabitants, notwithstanding their weakness, supposed that
they might take advantage of the troubles which agitated Mexico, and in 1826 declared their independence.

The emigrants who fly from the old world in search

of happiness in the new, expect to obtain it without effort. They will not be disappointed in finding liberty there, and they will become proprietors at little expense. But unless they are laborious, persevering, and economical they will be deceived in their hopes of fortune. Those who have preceded them have smoothed for them a great many difficulties. The country is now known, the Indians are either dispersed or little to be feared. Lands of an excellent quality are sold there at the most moderate price. Congress would not be averse to give them gratuitously to any one in a condition to cultivate them, and this liberality would more certainly contribute to render the state powerful and rich than the price at which they are ceded. Property gives diligence to the most idle, and perhaps this is the characteristic which most distinguishes American from European communities. In the latter, families emerged from servitude, six centuries ago, form at this day the class of day labourers, justly so called, because they only labour and exist, as it were, by the day's work. As they have no other property than the hoe and spade, they make no meliorations: they experience frequent privations, and are yet so improvident of the future that they give themselves up to repose and sloth whenever the provisions of primary necessity are at a low price. In America, on the contrary, the new-comers can want neither work nor wages. They have the example of an active, enterprising people, instructed in all the useful arts. The emigrant is always kindly received, and has nothing to fear but his own faults. A good carpenter, an industrious mason, a clever mechanic see only the laws above them.   No where else do we find so much ease and contentment, the fruits of industry, of discreet conduct, and good morals.   In all the countries, whose occupation followed the treaty of cession, settlements are formed, and are rapidly extending. The federal government watches over them till the time comes for constituting them states of the Union. The protection which they receive renders them safe from every aggression, and they will, in their turn, add to the strength of the confederacy.   Thus it has need neither of war nor conquests to become powerful and formidable.   By religiously maintaining their wise institutions, constantly observing the laws of their adoption, never losing sight of the rules of justice, but making all their interests subordinate to them, the United States will more effectually secure their prosperity and promote their glory than by battles or victories.   Respected abroad, happy at home, fearing nothing as a nation, having little to desire as a people, they will then enjoy all the blessings that were the object of the revolution.

APPENDIX.

APPENDIX.

No. 1.

TREATY AND CONVENTIONS BETWEEN THE UNITED STATES
AND THE FRENCH REPUBLIC.*

Treaty between the French Republic and the United States, concerning the Cession of Louisiana, signed at Paris the 30th of April, 1803.

THE president of the United States of America, and the first consul of the French republic, in the name of the French people, desiring to remove all source of misunderstanding relative to objects of discussion, mentioned in the second and fifth articles of the convention of the 8th Vendemiaire, an 9, (30th of September, 1800,) relative to the rights claimed by the United States, in virtue of the treaty concluded at Madrid the 27th of October, 1795, between His Catholic Majesty and the said United States, and willing to strengthen the union and friendship which at the time of the said convention was happily re-established between the two nations, have respectively named their plenipotentiaries; to wit, the president of the United States of America, by and with the advice and consent of the senate of the said states, Robert R. Livingston, minister plenipotentiary of the United States, and James Monroe, minister plenipotentiary and envoy extraordinary of the said states, near the government of the French republic; and the first consul, in the name of the French people, the French citizen Barbé Marbois, minister of the public treasury, who, after having respectively exchanged their full powers, have agreed to the following articles:—

ART. 1st. Whereas, by the article the third of the treaty concluded at St. Ildephonso, the 9th Vendemiaire, an 9, (1st October, 1800,) between the first consul of the French republic and His Catholic

* The treaty and convention are given from the American copies, and the United States are consequently named first in them.—TRANS.

Majesty, it was agreed as follows: "His Catholic Majesty promises and engages, on his part, to retrocede to the French republic, six months after the full and entire execution of the conditions and stipulations herein relative to his Royal Highness the Duke of Parma, the colony or province of Louisiana, with the same extent that it now has in the hands of Spain, and that it had when France possessed it; and such as it should be after the treaties subsequently entered into between Spain and other states." And, whereas, in pursuance of the treaty, and particularly of the third article, the French republic has an incontestable title to the domain, and to the possession of the said territory: The first consul of the French republic, desiring to give to the United States a strong proof of his friendship, doth hereby cede to the said United States, in the name of the French republic, for ever and in full sovereignty, the said territory, with all its rights and appurtenances, as fully and in the same manner as they had been acquired by the French republic in virtue of the above-mentioned treaty concluded with His Catholic Majesty.

Art. 2d. In the cession made by the preceding article are included the adjacent islands belonging to Louisiana, all public lots and squares, vacant lands, and all public buildings, fortifications, barracks, and other edifices which are not private property. The archives, papers, and documents, relative to the domain and sovereignty of Louisiana and its dependencies, will be left in the possession of the commissaries of the United States, and copies will be afterwards given in due form to the magistrates and municipal officers of such of the said papers and documents as may be necessary to them.

Art. 3. The inhabitants of the ceded territory shall be incorporated in the Union of the United States, and admitted as soon as possible, according to the principles of the federal constitution, to the enjoyment of all the rights, advantages, and immunities of citizens of the United States; and in the mean time they shall be maintained and protected in the free enjoyment of their liberty, property, and the religion which they profess.

Art. 4th. There shall be sent by the government of France a commissary to Louisiana, to the end that he do every act necessary, as well to receive from the officers of His Catholic Majesty the said country and its dependencies, in the name of the French republic, if it has not been already done, as to transmit it in the name of the French republic to the commissary or agent of the United States.

ART. 5th. Immediately after the ratification of the present treaty by the president of the United States, and in case that of the first consul shall have been previously obtained, the commissary of the French republic shall remit all the military posts of New Orleans, and other parts of the ceded territory, to the commissary or commissaries named by the president to take possession; the troops, whether of France or Spain, who may be there, shall cease to occupy any military post from the time of taking possession, and shall be embarked as soon as possible, in the course of three months after the ratification of this treaty.

ART. 6th. The United States promise to execute such treaties and articles as may have been agreed between Spain and the tribes and nations of Indians, until, by mutual consent of the United States and the said tribes or nations, other suitable articles shall have been agreed upon.

ART. 7th. As it is reciprocally advantageous to the commerce of France and the United States to encourage the communication of both nations for a limited time in the country ceded by the present treaty, until general arrangements relative to the commerce of both nations may be agreed on, it has been agreed between the contracting parties, that the French ships coming directly from France or any of her colonies, loaded only with the produce or manufactures of France or her said colonies; and the ships of Spain coming directly from Spain or any of her colonies, loaded only with the produce or manufactures of Spain or her colonies, shall be admitted during the space of twelve years in the ports of New Orleans, and in all other legal ports of entry within the ceded territory, in the same manner as the ships of the United States coming directly from France or Spain or any of their colonies, without being subject to any other or greater duty on merchandise, or other or greater tonnage than those paid by the citizens of the United States.

During the space of time above-mentioned, no other nation shall have a right to the same privileges in the ports of the ceded territory: the twelve years shall commence three months after the exchange of ratifications, if it shall take place in France, or three months after it shall have been notified at Paris to the French government, if it shall take place in the United States: it is, however, well understood that the object of the above article is to favour the manufactures, commerce, freight, and navigation of France and of Spain, so far as relates to the importations that the French and Spanish shall make into the said ports of the United States, without in any sort affecting the regulations that the United States may make concerning the exportation of the produce and merchandise of the United States, or any right they may have to make such regulations.

ART. 8th. In future, and for ever after the expiration of the twelve years, the ships of France shall be treated upon the footing of the most favoured nations in the ports above-mentioned.

ART. 9th. The particular convention, signed this day by the respective ministers, having for its object to provide for the payment of debts due to the citizens of the United States by the French republic, prior to the 30th of September, 1800, (8th Vendemiaire, an 9,) is approved, and to have its execution in the same manner as if it had been inserted in the present treaty; and it shall be ratified in the same form, and in the same time, so that the one shall not be ratified distinct from the other.

Another particular convention, signed at the same date as the present treaty, relative to the definitive rule between the contracting parties, is in the like manner approved, and will be ratified in the same form, and in the same time, and jointly.

ART. 10th. The present treaty shall be ratified in good and due form, and the ratifications shall be exchanged in the space of six months after the date of the signature by the ministers plenipotentiary, or sooner if possible.

In faith whereof, the respective plenipotentiaries have signed these articles in the French and English languages; declaring, nevertheless, that the present treaty was originally agreed to in the French language; and have thereunto put their seals.

Done at Paris, the tenth day of Floreal, in the eleventh year of the French republic, and the 30th of April, 1803.

ROBERT R. LIVINGSTON,
JAMES MONROE,
BARBÉ MARBOIS.

No. 2.

Convention between the United States of America and the French Republic, of the same date with the preceding Treaty.

THE president of the United States of America and the first consul of the French republic, in the name of the French people, in consequence of the treaty of cession of Louisiana, which has been signed this day, wishing to regulate definitively every thing which has relation to the said cession, have authorized to this effect the plenipotentiaries, that is to say: the president of the United States has, by and with the advice and consent of the senate of the said states, nominated for their plenipotentiaries, Robert R. Livingston, minister plenipotentiary of the United States, and James Monroe, minister plenipotentiary and envoy extraordinary of the said United States, near the government of the French republic; and the first consul of the French republic, in the name of the French people, has named as plenipotentiary of the said republic, the French citizen Barbé Marbois, who, in virtue of their full powers, which have been exchanged this day, have agreed to the following articles:—

ART. 1st. The government of the United States engages to pay to the French government, in the manner specified in the following articles, the sum of sixty millions of francs, independent of the sum which shall be fixed by another convention for the payment of debts due by France to citizens of the United States.

ART. 2d. For the payment of the sum of sixty millions of francs, mentioned in the preceding article, the United States shall create a stock of eleven millions two hundred and fifty thousand dollars, bearing an interest of six per cent. per annum, payable half yearly in London, Amsterdam, or Paris, amounting by the half year to three hundred and thirty-seven thousand five hundred dollars, according to the proportions which shall be determined by the French government, to be paid at either place: the principal of the said stock to be reimbursed at the treasury of the United States, in annual payments of not less than three millions of dollars each; of which the first payment shall commence fifteen years after the date of the exchange of ratifications: this stock shall be transferred to the government of France, or to such person or persons as shall be authorized to receive it, in three months at most after the exchange of the ratifications of this treaty, and after Louisiana shall be taken possession of in the name of the government of the United States.

It is farther agreed, that if the French government should be desirous of disposing of the said stock to receive the capital in Europe, at shorter terms, that its measures for that purpose shall be taken so as to favour, in the greatest degree possible, the credit of the United States, and to raise to the highest price the said stock.

ART. 3d. It is agreed that the dollar of the United States, specified in the present convention, shall be fixed at five francs $\frac{3333}{10000}$, or five livres eight sous tournois. The present convention shall be ratified in good and due form, and the ratifications shall be exchanged in the space of six months, to date from this day, or sooner if possible.

In faith of which, the respective plenipotentiaries have signed the above articles both in the French and English languages; declaring, nevertheless, that the present treaty has been originally agreed on and written in the French language; to which they have hereunto affixed their seals.

Done at Paris, the tenth of Floreal, eleventh year of the French republic, (30th April, 1803.)

> ROBERT R. LIVINGSTON, (L. S.)
> JAMES MONROE, (L. S.)
> BARBÉ MARBOIS, (L. S.)

No. 3.

Convention between the United States of America and the French Republic, also of the same date with the Louisiana Treaty.

THE president of the United States of America and the first consul of the French republic, in the name of the French people, having by a treaty of this date terminated all difficulties relative to Louisiana, and established on a solid foundation the friendship which unites the two nations, and being desirous, in compliance with the second and fifth articles of the convention of the 8th Vendemiaire, ninth year of the French republic, (30th September,

1800,) to secure the payment of the sum due by France to the citizens of the United States, have respectively nominated as plenipotentiaries, that is to say: the president of the United States of America, by and with the advice and consent of the senate, Robert R. Livingston, minister plenipotentiary, and James Monroe, minister plenipotentiary and envoy extraordinary of the said states, near the government of the French republic, and the first consul, in the name of the French people, the French citizen Barbé Marbois, minister of the public treasury; who, after having exchanged their full powers, have agreed to the following articles:—

Art. 1st. The debts due by France to the citizens of the United States, contracted before the 8th Vendemiaire, ninth year of the French republic, (30th September, 1800,) shall be paid according to the following regulations, with interest at six per cent., to commence from the period when the accounts and vouchers were presented to the French government.

Art. 2d. The debts provided for by the preceding article are those whose result is comprised in the conjectural note annexed to the present convention, and which, with the interest, cannot exceed the sum of twenty millions of francs. The claims comprised in the said note, which fall within the exceptions of the following articles, shall not be admitted to the benefit of this provision.

Art. 3d. The principal and interest of the said debts shall be discharged by the United States by orders drawn by their minister plenipotentiary on their treasury; these orders shall be payable sixty days after the exchange of the ratifications of the treaty and the conventions signed this day, and after possession shall be given of Louisiana by the commissioners of France to those of the United States.

Art. 4th. It is expressly agreed, that the preceding articles shall comprehend no debts but such as are due to citizens of the United States, who have been and are yet creditors of France for supplies, embargoes, and for prizes made at sea, in which the appeal has been properly lodged within the time mentioned in the said convention of the 8th Vendemiaire, ninth year, (30th September, 1800.)

Art. 5th. The preceding articles shall apply only, 1st, to captures of which the council of prizes shall have ordered restitution; it being well understood that the claimant cannot have recourse to the United States otherwise than he might have had to the government of the French republic, and only in case of the insufficiency of the captors: 2d. the debts mentioned in the said fifth article of the convention, contracted before the 8th Vendemiaire, an 9, (30th September, 1800,) the payment of which has been heretofore claimed of the actual government of France, and for which the creditors have a right to the protection of the United States; the said fifth article does not comprehend prizes whose condemnation has been or shall be confirmed: it is the express intention of the contracting parties not to extend the benefit of the present convention to reclamations of American citizens, who shall have established houses of commerce in France, England, or other countries than the United States, in partnership with foreigners, and who by that reason and the nature of their commerce ought to be regarded as domiciliated in the places where such houses exist. All agreements and bargains concerning merchandise, which shall not be the property of American citizens, are equally excepted from the benefit of the said convention, saving, however, to such persons their claims in like manner as if this treaty had not been made.

Art. 6th. And that the different questions which may arise under the preceding article may be fairly investigated, the ministers plenipotentiary of the United States shall name three persons, who shall act from the present and provisionally, and who shall have full power to examine, without removing the documents, all the accounts of the different claims already liquidated by the bureau established for this purpose by the French republic; and to ascertain whether they belong to the classes designated by the present convention and the principles established in it, or if they are not in one of its exceptions, and on their certificate, declaring that the debt is due to an American citizen or his representative, and that it existed before the 8th Vendemiaire, ninth year, (30th September, 1800,) the creditor shall be entitled to an order on the treasury of the United States, in the manner prescribed by the third article.

Art. 7th. The same agents shall likewise have power, without removing the documents, to examine the claims which are prepared for verification, and to certify those which ought to be admitted by uniting the necessary qualifications, and not being comprised in the exceptions contained in the present convention.

Art. 8th. The same agents shall likewise examine the claims which are not prepared for liquidation, and certify in writing those which in their judgments ought to be admitted to liquidation.

ART. 9th. In proportion as the debts mentioned in these articles shall be admitted, they shall be discharged with interest at six per cent. by the treasury of the United States.

ART. 10th. And that no debt which shall not have the qualifications above-mentioned, and that no unjust or exorbitant demand may be admitted, the commercial agent of the United States at Paris, or such other agent as the minister plenipotentiary of the United States shall think proper to nominate, shall assist at the operations of the bureau, and co-operate in the examination of the claims; and if this agent shall be of opinion that any debt is not completely proved, or if he shall judge that it is not comprised in the principles of the fifth article above-mentioned; and if, notwithstanding his opinion, the bureau established by the French government should think that it ought to be liquidated, he shall transmit his observations to the board established by the United States, who, without removing the documents, shall make a complete examination of the debt and vouchers which support it, and report the result to the minister of the United States. The minister of the United States shall transmit his observations, in all such cases, to the minister of the treasury of the French republic, on whose report the French government shall decide definitively in every case.

The rejection of any claim shall have no other effect than to exempt the United States from the payment of it, the French government reserving to itself the right to decide.definitively on such claim so far as it concerns itself.

ART. 11th. Every necessary decision shall be made in the course of a year, to commence from the exchange of ratifications, and no reclamation shall be admitted afterwards.

ART. 12th. In case of claims for debts contracted by the government of France with citizens of the United States, since the 8th Vendemiaire, ninth year, (30th September, 1800,) not being comprised in this convention, they may be pursued, and the payment demanded in the same manner as if it had not been made.

ART. 13th. The present convention shall be ratified in good and due form, and the ratifications shall be exchanged in six months from the date of the signature of the ministers plenipotentiary, or sooner if possible.

In faith of which, the respective ministers plenipotentiary have signed the above articles, both in the French and English languages; declaring, nevertheless, that the present treaty has been originally agreed on and written in the French language; to which they have hereunto affixed their seals.

Done at Paris, the tenth day of Floreal, eleventh year of the French republic, (30th April, 1803.)

> ROBERT R. LIVINGSTON, (L. S.)
> JAMES MONROE, (L. S.)
> BARBÉ MARBOIS, (L. S.)

No. 4.

COMPANY OF THE INDIES.

Order to the agent of the Company at Cape François, respecting the two Chiefs of the Natchez Indians, who had been removed there with their Families from Louisiana.

April, 23d, 1732.

It having been stated that among the Natchez Indians, taken in war, in the month of January, 1731, were two chiefs with their families, making eight persons in number, and that, although the *Sun,* one of the two chiefs, died on the 28th of September last, the company had incurred on their account expenses to the amount of eighteen hundred livres and seven sous; and it having been farther stated, that on an application made to M. de Maurepas to relieve the company from this charge, M. de Maurepas had replied that he was not aware of any other course to adopt than to order the sale of the survivors of these two Indian families, or to send them back to Louisiana, it was thereupon resolved to order forthwith the sale of the survivors of the aforesaid two families of Natchez Indians.

No. 5.

Extract from the Public Law of Europe.

"I beg leave to compare the evil consequences which result to France from the enormous expenses that her wars have occasioned, with those that she has sustained from the loss of several provinces that she formerly possessed on the continent of North America. Undoubtedly this kingdom may be happy and very powerful without colonies; but it is certain that its strength is impaired by the debts with which it is burdened."—*Droit Public de l'Europe par Mably, tom. 3.* Peace of 1763.

No. 6.

Note relative to the Succession of Bavaria.

THE Elector of Bavaria was attacked by the small-pox, a year after the inquiry was made respecting his health, and he died of the disease. The Austrians suddenly entered Bavaria, but France was too far committed to the Americans to recede. It was, indeed, at this period that the treaty of alliance between France and the United States was signed, and it was supposed in England that France would not be able to avoid a continental war. It was kept out of it principally by the prudence of the ministry. It must also be admitted that it was greatly owing to the firmness and decision of the king of Prussia that the palatine branch of the house of Bavaria preserved the ancient patrimony of the common stock of Wittelspach. This monarch extricated France from the untoward position in which she had been placed by so unexpected an event, and for this time Austria was not brought into the neighbourhood of the two landgraviates of Alsace, the ancient inheritance of that powerful house. Perhaps, in 1815, she allowed it to be too clearly seen that one hundred and sixty-seven years had not sufficed to take away from her every hope of accomplishing her object.

No. 7.

A Letter written from New Orleans, 14th of October, 1803, a few days after the Treaty had been signed at Paris.

THE French prefect has arrived. His declarations respecting the Americans are as yet very friendly. But I suppose that.

on the establishment of the French government, his tone will change. He expects General Victor and the French troops before entering on his administration. Every expedient will be exhausted in order to lull us into a false security. All the inhabitants of this country, except the creoles, ardently desire to see the people of the west adopt energetic measures.

We are still refused a place of deposite, and have therefore the best possible occasion to procure ourselves satisfaction for the past and security for the future. If we let it go by, I fear that we shall never regain it. A handful of men would take this place: they would experience little or no resistance. You would be surprised to see the lively interest that the people of the country take in the future prosperity of our nation, and with what enthusiasm they read and repeat the speeches of those senators who are in favour of an immediate occupation of this place.

I earnestly pray that our western militia may be immediately equipped and armed, so that we may not lose a moment in putting ourselves in a situation to provide for our safety. Our enemies accuse us of a want of public spirit. The Spaniards, who are settled here, see their government on the edge of a precipice, towards which it is driven by the intrigues of French policy; and, like people in despair, they no longer dare anticipate the future. They are impatient at our delay, and often express their surprise at our moderation and pusillanimity.

I fear that our plan of negotiations will only be productive of delays. If it does not succeed, I shall lament the unfortunate destinies of our degraded country.

No. 8.

Extract of a Letter from the Minister Plenipotentiary of the United States to the French Minister of Foreign Affairs.

Paris, December 11th, 1802.

SIR,

I HAVE just learned that the government of New Orleans has refused the Americans the right of deposite in that port, under pretence that the term stipulated in the treaty had expired.

You are not ignorant, sir, of the value which the inhabitants of the western states attach to this right, nor of the energy with which they would defend it. Were the government, indeed, even indifferent on this point, it would be obliged to yield to their views.

It is, sir, particularly unfortunate that this difficulty should arise at the precise moment when France is about entering on the possession of the country. I very much fear that this circumstance, connected with the silence that the French government observes respecting its intentions, may induce suspicious persons to suppose that the court of Spain has acted in this matter altogether in concert with France. Although I too justly appreciate the uprightness of her government, to believe that it would approve the infraction of a treaty, and thus mark, by an act of hostility, the period of our becoming neighbours, the subject is, nevertheless, of a nature to require, on the part of France, the most prompt attention to all those subjects, the disregard of which has excited the warmest sensations in the United States. I avail myself of this occasion to present to you the sketch of a treaty which, I hope, will procure for France the greatest advantages, and bind closer those ties which all enlightened Americans desire to see exist between her and the United States.

In taking possession of Louisiana, France can only have three objects in view: 1st, the command of the gulf; 2d. the supply of her islands; 3d. a place of settlement for her surplus inhabitants, in case of an excess of population in her European possessions.

She will effectually secure the first object by the possession of East Florida. There is no port of the least importance to the west of the Mississippi.

The second object will be better answered by confining the settlement within reasonable limits, on the borders or at a moderate distance from the sea, than by dispersing men and capital over an immense territory—a course of proceeding that would lead the inhabitants to a migratory life and to independence, and would compel France to multiply very expensive military establishments to protect them against the incursions of the Indians.

This country must be peopled by foreigners or French emigrants. In the first case, there is no nation in Europe that can keep them in a state of dependence; for as soon as the settlements extend a few hundred miles from the borders of the sea, they will be out of reach of its power. In the second case, such a quantity of men and money will leave France as to inflict a terrible blow on her agriculture and commerce. And, after all, they will be independent of the mother country from the day that they are sufficiently rich and sufficiently strong to do without her assistance.

I am going to propose what I believe to be the true policy of France to adopt, and what will fulfil all her views, at the same time that it will be a means of conciliating the affection of the United States and securing the permanency of the settlement.

France should first cede to the United States the part of Louisiana which is above the mouth of the river Arkansas; there will thus be between the French part and Canada a barrier, without which the province might be easily attacked and lost to France before the arrival of assistance. She should retain the part which is west of the Mississippi and below the river of the Arkansas; this territory can maintain a population of fifteen millions, and will form a barrier between the United States and Mexico in case the Americans should entertain the extravagant design of carrying war into that country, which I hope will never happen. France should cede to the United States West Florida, New Orleans, and the territory upon the left bank of the Mississippi. This cession is only valuable to the Americans, inasmuch as it gives them the embouchure of the Mobile and other small rivers which pass through their territory, and would calm their anxiety respecting the Mississippi. If we except a narrow strip of land on the borders of the river, all this portion of territory consists of sand barrens and marshes, while that which France will retain to the west of the Mississippi embraces a rich and fertile country. It may be supposed that New Orleans is a place of some importance; it is so without doubt for the United States, but not for France. And as the greater part of the settlements are on the other bank of the river, it will be requisite to remove the capital there, even though France should remain in possession of New Orleans, a city built of wood, and for which France will have incurred useless expenditures in public buildings, when the capital shall be removed.

The right of deposite claimed by the United States, a right which they will never yield, will be between the two nations a perpetual source of disputes and animosities, that will at some time or other force the United States to aid a foreign power to expel the French from the colony. Independently of all this, the capital at New Orleans being almost entirely in the hands of the Americans, will be sent immediately to Natchez, a post to which the United States can give such advantages that New Orleans will be of little importance.

If any other course is adopted, *the whole settlement will fall into the hands of the English,* who, at the same time that they command the sea, have within reach a warlike colony possessing all the means of attack; and while their fleet blockades the harbours, they may, without the least difficulty, cause New Orleans to be attacked, through Canada, by fifteen or twenty thousand men, aided by hordes of Indians.

France, by seizing on a wilderness and an insignificant city, and thus throwing the United States *into the scale on the side of England, is going to make this power the mistress of the new world:* the possession of Louisiana and of the Trinity will put the Spanish colonies at her mercy, and by taking away the Floridas from Spain and getting possession of the gulf of Mexico, she will command the West Indies; the two Indies will pour their riches into her ports; the precious metals of Mexico, united with the treasures of Hindostan, will furnish the means of buying nations, whose forces she will employ to secure her power.

Congress is now in session: if, before it adjourns, there is no treaty concluded, or if a minister is sent with only powers to treat, without being the bearer of any thing decisive, he will have to make his way through a thousand suspicions, and a thousand jealousies; and the negotiation once commenced, he will have to contend against all the intrigues of the court of London, which has the greatest interest in arresting the success of an affair so opposed to its views.

Accept the assurances, &c.

(Signed)   R. R. LIVINGSTON.

No. 9.

Memorial of the Legislative Council and House of Representatives of the Mississippi Territory to the President, Senate, and House of Representatives of the United States.

Your memorialists beg leave to express their feelings and sentiments relative to an event by which the interests of western America in general, and of this territory in particular, are materially affected:

While the treaty of San Lorenzo el Real secured the free navigation of the Mississippi, and a convenient place of deposite for the merchandise and effects of American traders, it politically incorporated this country as a part of the United States. Under this auspicious change, we saw our trade flourishing, our property rising rapidly in value, and we felicitated ourselves in being the free and happy citizens of an independent republic.

Reposing in national faith for a continued observance of *stipulated* privileges, we had indulged the sanguine expectation that this state of prosperity would not have been soon interrupted.

The motives which may have influenced the Spanish government to withhold from us a place of deposite are a subject of conjecture; but no doubt can exist as to the act itself being a direct infraction of our treaty with that nation.

A recent order by the government of Louisiana, prohibiting all intercourse between the citizens of the United States and the subjects of Spain, has considerably increased the embarrassment upon our trade, and breathes a spirit of still greater enmity to the United States.

Your memorialists, conscious of the wisdom, justice, and energy of the general government, rest assured that no succour will be withholden which existing circumstances may require; and so far as may depend on ourselves, we tender to our country our lives and fortunes in support of such measures as congress may deem necessary to vindicate the honour and protect the interest of the United States.

WM. GORD. FORMAN,
Speaker of the House of Representatives.

JOHN ELLIS,
President of the Council.

Council Chamber,
January 5, 1803.

No. 10.

Memorial to the President, Senate, and House of Representatives of the United States.

January, 1803.

Your memorialists, inhabitants of the states west of the Alleghany Mountains, humbly state that the port of New Orleans is closed to them by a decree of the Spanish intendant; that they owe the United States taxes which have just accrued, as well as large arrearages, and that they have no other means to pay them but the produce of their farms. That, excluded as they are from a market in the east for their produce, it must rot in their granaries, unless the government consents to receive it from them at a reasonable price, or protects them in the enjoyment of a lawful trade; that they humbly conceive that prompt and decisive measures are necessary, the maxim that protection and allegiance are reciprocal being particularly applicable to their situation. In announcing their confidence in the government of the Union, and in giving assurances of their co-operation in all the measures that may be adopted to cause the just rights of every portion of the United States to be respected, they declare that they have a right to require, and do require that the government shall either take measures to guaranty the exercise of a legitimate right or release them from every contribution whatever. Without interfering in the measures that have been adopted to bring about the amicable arrangement of a difference, which has grown out of the gratuitous violation of a solemn treaty, they desire that the United States may explicitly understand that their situation is critical; that the delay of only a single season would be ruinous to their country, and that an imperious necessity may consequently oblige them, if they receive no aid, to adopt themselves the measures that may appear to them calculated to protect their commerce, even though those measures should produce consequences unfavourable to the harmony of the confederacy.

No. 11.

Extract of a Letter, dated Natchez, 13th April, 1803.

PUBLIC opinion is here in a state of the greatest excitement. The Spaniards have insulted and injured us, and we have borne with them: we might, without striking a blow, have seized on New Orleans, the palladium of the west. They have provoked our pride; they have seen that neither interest nor national honour can determine the American cabinet to act with energy. We have, in truth, shown to the universe that we are well disposed to place our existence at the mercy of foreign nations.

The French are in possession of New Orleans. I have seen the proclamation, or rather manifesto of the prefect. It is like all the other French manifestoes. There is not a well-informed man in this territory who does not perceive that our country is ruined. Moreover, it is the president alone who is to blame. It is he who by his pusillanimity has allowed the blood of the west to stagnate, and in order better to secure our destruction, he has, without the least opposition, allowed our most cruel enemy to put his inexorable hand on the mouth of the artery through which alone the blood can circulate.

In a word, my dear sir, we are convinced that we must familiarize ourselves to the colonial and military despotism of Bonaparte. The inhabitants residing near the western waters will necessarily be ruled by those who dispose of their productions. Those who can do so are preparing to put themselves under the prudent and stable governments of New England.

No. 12.

Copy of a Letter from M. Talleyrand to Mr. Livingston, dated Paris, 24th March, 1803.

                    Paris, 1 Germinal, 11th year, (24th March, 1803.)
SIR,
    I see with pleasure by the last letters of the French legation to the United States, that the species of fermentation raised there on account of Louisiana, has been brought down by the wisdom of

your government, and the just confidence which it inspires, to that state of tranquillity which is alone suited to discussions, and which, in the relations of sentiment and interest existing between the two people, cannot but lead them to understand one another respecting mere accidental difficulties, and to bind more closely the bonds of their union. I ought to own to you, sir, that, in the éclat which has been so lately given in your country to matters connected with Louisiana, it has been difficult to discover the ancient sentiments of attachment and of confidence with which France has ever endeavoured to inspire the people of the United States, who, from the first moment of their existence as an independent and sovereign nation, have always held their relations with France above all other political connexions.

How could the neighbourhood of France affect unfavourably the American people, either in their commercial or political relations ? Has the French republic ever shown a desire to impede the prosperity of the United States, to lessen their influence, to weaken the means of their security, or oppose any obstacle to the progress of their commerce ? Your government, sir, ought to be well persuaded that the first consul bears to the American nation the same affection with which France has been at all times animated, and that he considers the new means which the possession of Louisiana afford him of convincing the government and people of the United States of his friendly disposition towards them, in the number of the advantages which must result from that acquisition.

I shall, for the present, confine myself to this declaration, which ought to remove the distrust that appears in your last letters. The information that has been received is not sufficient to authorize a detailed explanation. In announcing to me, moreover, the approaching departure of Mr. Monroe, appointed minister extraordinary to discuss this subject, you give me to conclude that your government desires that this minister be waited for and heard, in order that every matter, susceptible of contradiction, be completely and definitively discussed ? In the mean time, sir, the first consul charges me to assure your government, that, far from thinking that our new position in Louisiana could be an object of solicitude, or cause the least injury to the United States, he will receive the minister extraordinary whom the president sends to him with the greatest pleasure, and that he hopes that his mission will terminate to the satisfaction of both nations.

CH. M. TALLEYRAND.

No. 13.

Copy of a Letter from Robert R. Livingston to Mr. Monroe, dated Paris, 10th April, 1803.

DEAR SIR,

I congratulate you on your safe arrival. We have long and anxiously wished for you. God grant that your mission may answer yours and the public expectation. War may do something for us, nothing else would. I have paved the way for you, and if you could add to my memoirs an assurance that we were now in possession of New Orleans, we should do well: but I detain Mr. Bentalou, who is impatient to fly to the arms of his wife. I have apprized the minister of your arrival, and told him you would be here on Tuesday or Wednesday. Present my compliments and Mrs. L's. to Mrs. Monroe, and believe me, dear sir,

Your friend, and humble servant,

ROBT. R. LIVINGSTON.

To his Excellency JAMES MONROE.

No. 14.

Article 3d of the Treaty concluded at St. Ildephonso on the 1st of October, 1800.

" His Catholic Majesty promises and engages, on his part, to retrocede to the French republic, six months after the full and entire execution of the conditions and stipulations, herein relative to His Royal Highness the Duke of Parma, the colony or province of Louisiana, with the same extent that it now has in the hands of Spain, and that it had when France possessed it; and such as it should be after the treaties subsequently entered into between Spain and other states."

No. 15.

Extract from a Memoir of Mr. James Monroe, published after his retirement from the Presidency.

Virginia, 1828.

My reception by the French government, in my second mission, on my return in 1803, was as kind and friendly as could have been expected from what had before occurred. That the mission contributed to the result contemplated—to prevent war, and secure to us, by the treaties which were then concluded with the French government, not only the free navigation of the Mississippi, but all Louisiana, M. Talleyrand's letter to Mr. Livingston, which was written after my appointment was known in France, while I was at séa, Mr. Livingston's letter to me in reply to mine, announcing my arrival at Havre, and the extract from Colonel Mercer's journal of what passed between Mr. Livingston and me on the evening of my arrival in Paris, will distinctly show. M. Talleyrand states, in explicit terms, that the first consul thought it improper to commence a negotiation, on the ground of Mr. Livingston's complaints, until Mr. Monroe, the minister extraordinary, whom the president had appointed to discuss the subject, should arrive, and be heard, that every matter susceptible of contradiction might be completely and definitively discussed. He states, also, that the first consul had charged him to assure our government, that, far from thinking that their new position in Louisiana could be an object of solicitude, or cause the least injury to the United States, he would receive the minister extraordinary whom the president had sent·to him, with the greatest pleasure, and that he hoped that this mission would terminate to the satisfaction of both states. Mr. Livingston congratulates me on my arrival, and expresses an ardent desire that my mission may answer mine and the public expectation. War, he says, may do something for us; nothing else would: that he had paved the way for me by his memoirs; and, if I could add to them an assurance that we were in possession of New Orleans, we might do well. With the sentiments contained in this letter, those which were declared by Mr. Livingston, after my arrival in Paris, were in strict accord, as appears by the extract from Colonel Mercer's journal of what passed in our first interview. On being informed that the motion which had been made in the senate, for taking possession of New Orleans by force had failed, he expressed his regret at it, under a belief that force only could give it to us. It is just to observe, that, in expressing this opinion, Mr. Livingston showed no excitement whatever, but appeared to speak under a thorough conviction of what he believed to be the fixed policy of the French government, founded on his communications with the ministers, and what he knew of the character and policy of the first consul in other respects. It affords me pleasure to add, that, in the negotiation which was commenced immediately afterwards, and in the result procured by the treaties in which it terminated, great harmony prevailed between Mr. Livingston and myself.

The representation then made to me, and by authority entitled to confidence, was that the first consul having his cabinet assembled at St. Cloud, and walking in the garden with the members who composed it, having heard of the arrival of the minister extraordinary at Havre, communicated to them the fact, and then observed that the negotiation should be immediately commenced, and, addressing himself to M. Marbois, added, that "being an affair of the treasury, I will commit it to you." His motive for committing the negotiation to M. Marbois, and in a manner not to wound the feelings of M. Talleyrand, may be readily conceived. It was added, by the same authority, that, until that moment, so decided was believed to be the purpose of the first consul, to cede no portion of the territory in question, and unchangeable his views, after making a decision, that none of his ministers would have ventured to propose it to him. The sum suggested in the first interview with M. Marbois, as that which his government had a right to claim for this territory, was one hundred and twenty millions of francs, the estimated value of Tuscany, which had been given for it; but this was not insisted on, nor explicitly proposed. It was the subject only of free communication. The first proposition which he made, was that we should give for it eighty millions, of which sixty should be paid to France in cash, in one year, in Paris—the other twenty to our own citizens; and that the vessels and goods of France should be perpetually exempted, in the ports of the ceded territory, from foreign duties. The change which was made, by the payment in stock, instead of cash, with the limitation of the exemption of French vessels and goods from foreign duties, to twelve years, with every other change, from this project, was the effect of negotiation and accommodation. I add with pleasure that the conduct of M. Marbois, in every stage of the negotiation, was liberal, candid, and fair, indicating a very friendly feeling for the United States, and a strong desire to preserve the most amicable relations between the two countries.

It is just to state, that the frank, candid, and friendly conduct of the two great houses of Hope, of Amsterdam, and of Baring, of London, by offering to us loans to any amount we might require, at the usual interest, rendered to the United States essential service in the negotiation. We had reason to believe, that the knowledge of those offers, and the confidence with which it inspired the French government, that our stock might be converted through them into cash, at a fair price, aided us in prevailing on that government to accept the payment in stock, and to lessen the amount demanded for the territory ceded.

Some time afterwards, Mr. Monroe, correcting this first memoir, thus expressed himself in a letter to M. Marbois.

"*Oakhill, Virginia, April 4th,* 1828.

" I have said, in my memoir, that at our first interview one hundred and twenty millions of francs were asked for the cession of the territory of Louisiana. I have since reviewed the authentic documents, and admit that I was mistaken; and that although you may have mentioned this sum as the estimated value of the territory, you never asked it. You only asked the eighty millions that are stipulated in the treaty. I have had sincere pleasure, on discovering this error, to correct it without any observation on your part, for never was a transaction of such importance conducted with more candour and honour.

"I have given an account of these events, so important for France and the world. I am one of the witnesses who have taken the deepest interest in them.

(Signed) JAMES MONROE."

No. 16.

Grant to the Family of the late Mr. Jefferson, by the State of Louisiana, as a mark of its gratitude.

WHEN Thomas Jefferson died, assurances of public affection were transmitted to his family from all parts of the Union, accompanied by grants from the legislative assemblies, and from committees that were formed in the principal cities. Those proceedings gave a new contradiction to the maxim, so frequently repeated, that republics are ungrateful.

Mr. Johnson, governor of Louisiana, addressed a message on this subject to the house of representatives. The committee, to whom it was referred, state in their report, that—

" Thomas Jefferson, one of the principal founders of those liberal institutions, which are the envy of so many other nations, has died in poverty; he who has contributed to consolidate our social edifice has claims on the gratitude of all the states of the Union. But Louisiana owes him even more than the rest: it is he who, from a dependent colony, has made her a free state, &c."

In conformity with this report, the legislature, on the 16th of March, 1827, passed the following act:—

" Thomas Jefferson, after a life devoted to the service of his country and of human nature, has died, leaving to his children as their only inheritance the example of his virtues and the gratitude of the people whose independence he has proclaimed to the universe. The legislature of Louisiana, a state acquired for the Union by his wisdom and foresight, owes to him her political and civil liberty; and, to perpetuate the remembrance of her profound respect for the talents and virtues of this illustrious benefactor, it is enacted by the senate and house of representatives of Louisiana, in general assembly convened, that ten thousand dollars be transmitted to Thomas Jefferson Randolph, for the benefit of the family of Thomas Jefferson."

No. 17.

Extract from the Declaration of War, made by Congress on the 18th of June, 1812.

The statement of grievances which congress published did not, like the manifestoes traced by the docile hand of a secretary under the dictation of a minister, contain motives for war which reason and justice disavowed.

" By the blockade of the whole coast of the continent from the Elbe to Brest inclusive," says this document, " the well-established principles of the law of nations, principles which have served for ages as guides and fixed the boundaries between the rights of belligerents and neutrals, were violated. By the law of nations, as recognised by Great Britain herself, no blockade is lawful, unless it be sustained by the application of an adequate force, and that an adequate force was applied to this blockade in its full extent, ought not to be pretended.   *   *   *   *   *   *

" Under the pretext of impressing British seamen, our fellow-citizens are seized in British ports, on the high seas, and in every quarter to which the British power extends, are taken on board British men-of-war, and compelled to serve there as British subjects. In this mode our citizens are wantonly snatched from their country and their families, deprived of their liberty, and doomed to an ignominious and slavish bondage, compelled to fight the battles of a foreign country, and often to perish in them. Our flag has given them no protection, it has been unceasingly violated, and our vessels exposed to danger by the loss of the men taken from them. *   *   *   *   *   *   *   *   *

" Whether the British government has contributed by active measures to excite against us the hostility of the savage tribes on our frontiers, your committee are not disposed to occupy much time in investigating. Certain indications of general notoriety may supply the place of authentic documents; though these have not been wanting to establish the fact in some instances. It is known that symptoms of British hostility have never failed to produce corresponding symptoms among those tribes. It is also well known that on all such occasions, abundant supplies of the ordinary munitions of war have been afforded by the agents of British commer-

cial companies, and even from British garrisons, wherewith they
were enabled to commence that system of savage warfare on our
frontier, which has been at all times indiscriminate in its effects on
all ages, sexes, and conditions, and so revolting to humanity.

" Your committee would be much gratified if they could close
here the detail of British wrongs; but it is their duty to recite another act of still greater malignity than any of those which have been
already brought to view.   The attempt to dismember our Union
and overthrow our excellent constitution, by a secret mission, the
object of which was to foment discontent and excite insurrection
against the constituted authorities of the nation, as lately disclosed
by the agent employed in it, affords full proof that there is no
bound to the hostility of the British government towards the United
States—no act, however unjustifiable, which it would not commit
to accomplish their ruin.   This attempt excites the greater horror
from the consideration that it was made while the United States
and Great Britain were at peace, and an amicable negotiation was
pending between them for the accommodation of their differences
through ministers regularly authorized for the purpose."

No. 18.

(The following instructions from Mr. Madison, secretary of state,
to Messrs. Livingston and Monroe, with their despatch accompanying the Louisiana treaty, are taken from a message of the president of the United States to the senate, dated 20th of May, 1826.
Though not inserted in the original work, they are deemed a proper
supplement to the French plenipotentiary's history of that important diplomatic transaction.—Transl.)

*Mr. Madison, Secretary of State of the United States, to Messrs.
Robert R. Livingston and James Monroe, Ministers Plenipoten-
tiary of the United States to France, dated Department of State,
March, 2d, 1803.*

Gentlemen:—You will herewith receive a commission and letters
of credence, one of you as minister plenipotentiary, the other as
minister extraordinary and plenipotentiary, to treat with the go-

vernment of the French republic on the subject of the Mississippi and the territories eastward thereof, and without the limits of the United States. The object in view, is to procure, by just and satisfactory arrangements, a cession to the United States of New Orleans, and of West and East Florida, or as much thereof as the actual proprietor can be prevailed on to part with.

The French republic is understood to have become the proprietor, by a cession from Spain, in the year ——, of New Orleans, as part of Louisiana, if not of the Floridas also. If the Floridas should not have been then included in the cession, it is not improbable that they will have been since added to it.

It is foreseen that you may have a considerable difficulty in overcoming the repugnance and the prejudices of the French government, against a transfer to the United States of so important a part of the acquisition. The apparent solicitude and exertions, amidst many embarrassing circumstances, to carry into effect the cession made to the French republic, the reserve so long used on this subject by the French government, in its communications with the minister of the United States at Paris, and the declaration finally made by the French minister of foreign relations, that it was meant to take possession before any overtures from the United States would be discussed, show the importance which is attached to the territories in question. On the other hand, as the United States have the strongest motives of interest and of a pacific policy, to seek by just means the establishment of the Mississippi, down to its mouth, as their boundary, so there are considerations which urge on France a concurrence in so natural and so convenient an arrangement.

Notwithstanding the circumstances which have been thought to indicate in the French government designs of unjust encroachment, and even direct hostility on the United States, it is scarcely possible to reconcile a policy of that sort, with any motives which can be presumed to sway either the government or the nation. To say nothing of the assurances given, both by the French minister at Paris, and by the Spanish minister at Madrid, that the cession by Spain to France was understood to carry with it all the conditions stipulated by the former to the United States, the manifest tendency of hostile measures against the United States, to connect their councils and their colossal growth with the great and formidable rival of France, can neither escape her discernment, nor be disregarded by her prudence, and might alone be expected to produce very different views in her government.

On the supposition that the French government does not mean to force or to court war with the United States; but, on the contrary, that it sees the interest which France has in cultivating their neutrality and amity, the dangers to so desirable a relation between the two countries, which lurk under a neighbourhood, modified as is that of Spain at present, must have great weight in recommending the change which you will have to propose. These dangers have been always sufficiently evident; and have, moreover, been repeatedly suggested by collisions between the stipulated rights or reasonable expectations of the United States and the Spanish jurisdiction at New Orleans. But they have been brought more strikingly into view by the late proceeding of the intendant at that place. The sensibility and unanimity in our nation, which have appeared on this occasion, must convince France that friendship and peace with us must be precarious until the Mississippi shall be made the boundary between the United States and Louisiana; and, consequently, render the present moment favourable to the object with which you are charged.

The time chosen for the experiment, is pointed out also by other important considerations. The instability of the peace of Europe, the attitude taken by Great Britain, the languishing state of the French finances, and the absolute necessity of either abandoning the West India Islands, or of sending thither large armaments at great expense, all contribute, at the present crisis, to prepare in the French government a disposition to listen to an arrangement which will at once dry up one source of foreign controversy, and furnish some aid in struggling with internal embarrassments. It is to be added, that the overtures committed to you, coincide in a great measure with the ideas of the person through whom the letter of the president, of April 30th, 1802, was conveyed to Mr. Livingston, and who is presumed to have gained some insight into the present sentiments of the French cabinet.

Among the considerations which have led the French government into the project of regaining from Spain the province of Louisiana, and which you may find it necessary to meet in your discussions, the following suggest themselves as highly probable.

1st, A jealousy of the Atlantic states as leaning to a coalition with Great Britain, not consistent with neutrality and amity towards France, and a belief that, by holding the key to the commerce of the Mississippi, she will be able to command the interests and attachments of the western portion of the United States; and thereby either control the Atlantic portion also; or, if that cannot be done, to seduce the former into a separate government, and a close alliance with herself. In each of these particulars the calculation is founded in error.

It is not true that the Atlantic states lean towards any connexion with Great Britain, inconsistent with their amicable relations to France. Their dispositions and their interests equally prescribe to them amity and impartiality to both of those nations. If a departure from this simple and salutary line of policy should take place, the causes of it will be found in the unjust or unfriendly conduct experienced from one or other of them. In general it may be remarked, that there are as many points on which the interests and views of the United States and of Great Britain may not be thought to coincide, as can be discovered in relation to France. If less harmony and confidence should therefore prevail between France and the United States than may be maintained between Great Britain and the United States, the difference will lie, not in the want of motives drawn from the mutual advantage of the two nations; but in the want of favourable dispositions in the governments of one or other of them. That the blame in this respect will not justly fall on the government of the United States, is sufficiently demonstrated by the mission and the objects with which you are now charged.

The French government is not less mistaken if it supposes that the western part of the United States can be withdrawn from their present union with the Atlantic part, into a separate government, closely allied with France.

Our western fellow-citizens are bound to the Union, not only by the ties of kindred and affection, which for a long time will derive strength from the stream of emigration peopling that region; but by two considerations which flow from clear and essential interests.

One of these considerations is, the passage through the Atlantic ports of the foreign merchandise consumed by the western inhabitants, and the payments thence made to a treasury in which they would lose their participation by erecting a separate government. The bulky productions of the western country may continue to pass down the Mississippi; but the difficulties of the ascending navigation of that river, however free it may be made, will cause the imports for consumption to pass through the Atlantic states. This is the course through which they are now received, nor will the impost to which they will be subject, change the course even if the passage up the Mississippi should be duty free. It will not equal the difference in the freight through the latter channel. It is true that mechanical and other improvements in the navigation of the Mississippi may lessen the labour and expense of ascending the stream: but it is not the least probable, that savings of this sort will keep pace with the improvements in canals and roads, by which the present course of imports will be favoured. Let it be added, that the loss of the contributions thus made to a foreign treasury, would be accompanied with the necessity of providing by less convenient revenues for the expense of a separate government, and of the defensive precautions required by the change of situation.

The other of these considerations results from the insecurity to which the trade from the Mississippi would be exposed by such a revolution in the western part of the United States. A connexion of the western people as a separate state with France, implies a connexion between the Atlantic states and Great Britain. It is found, from long experience, that France and Great Britain are nearly half the time at war. The case would be the same with their allies. During nearly one half the time, therefore, the trade of the western country from the Mississippi, would have no protection but that of France, and would suffer all the interruptions which nations, having the command of the sea, could inflict on it.

It will be the more impossible for France to draw the western country under her influence, by conciliatory regulations of the trade through the Mississippi; because the regulations which would be regarded by her as liberal, and claiming returns of gratitude, would be viewed on the other side as falling short of justice. If this should not be at first the case, it soon would be so. The western people believe, as do their Atlantic brethren, that they have a natural and indefeasible right to trade freely through the Mississippi. They are conscious of their power to enforce their right against any nation whatever. With these ideas in their minds, it is evident that France will not be able to excite either a sense of favour, or of fear, that would establish an ascendancy over them. On the contrary, it is more than probable that the different views of their respective rights would quickly lead to disappointments and disgusts on both sides, and thence to collisions and controversies fatal to the harmony of the two nations. To guard against these consequences is a primary motive with the United States in wishing the arrangement proposed. As France has equal reasons to guard against them, she·ought to feel an equal motive to concur in the arrangement.

2d. The advancement of the commerce of France, by an establishment on the Mississippi, has doubtless great weight with the government in espousing this project.

The commerce through the Mississippi will consist, 1st, of that of the United States; 2d. of that of the adjacent territories to be acquired by France.

The 1st is now, and must for ages continue the principal commerce. As far as the faculties of France will enable her to share in it, the article to be proposed to her on the part of the United States on that subject promises every advantage she can desire. It is a fair calculation, that, under the proposed arrangement, her commercial opportunities would be extended rather than diminished; inasmuch as our present right of deposite gives her the same competitors as she would then have, and the effect of the more rapid settlement of the western country consequent on that arrangement would proportionably augment the mass of commerce to be shared by her.

The other portion of commerce, with the exception of the island of New Orleans, and the contiguous ports of West Florida, depends on the territory westward of the Mississippi. With respect to this portion it will be little affected by the cession desired by the United States. The footing proposed for her commerce on the shore to be ceded, gives it every advantage she could reasonably wish, during a period within which she will be able to provide every requisite establishment on the right shore; which, according to the best information, possesses the same facilities for such establishments as are found on the island of New Orleans itself. These circumstances essentially distinguish the situation of the French commerce in the Mississippi after a cession of New Orleans to the United States, from the situation of the commerce of the United States, without such a cession; their right of deposite being so much more circumscribed, and their territory on the Mississippi not reaching low enough for a commercial establishment on the shore within their present limits.

There remains to be considered the commerce of the ports in the Floridas. With respect to this branch, the advantages which will be secured to France by the proposed arrangement ought to be sa-

tisfactory.   She will here also derive a greater share from the increase which will be given by a more rapid settlement of a fertile
territory to the exports and imports through those ports, than she
would obtain from any restrictive use she could make of those ports
as her own property.   But this is not all.   The United States have
a just claim to the use of the rivers which pass from their territories through the Floridas.   They found their claim on like principles with those which supported their claim to the use of the Mississippi.   If the length of these rivers be not in the same proportion
with that of the Mississippi, the difference is balanced by the circumstance that both banks in the former case belong to the United
States.

With a view to permanent harmony between the two nations, a
cession of the Floridas is particularly to be desired, as obviating
serious controversies that might otherwise grow even out of the regulations, however liberal in the opinion of France, which she may
establish at the mouths of those rivers.   One of the rivers, the Mobile, is said to be at present navigable for four hundred miles above
the 31° of latitude, and the navigation may no doubt be opened
still farther.   On all of them, the country within the boundary of the
United States, though otherwise between that and the sea, is fertile.
Settlements on it are beginning, and the people have already called
on the government to procure the proper outlets to foreign markets.
The president accordingly gave, some time ago, the proper instructions to the minister of the United States at Madrid.   In fact, our
free communication with the sea through these channels is so natural, so reasonable, and so essential, that eventually it must take
place, and in prudence, therefore, ought to be amicably and effectually adjusted without delay.

3d.   A farther object with France may be to form a colonial establishment, having a convenient relation to her West India Islands,
and forming an independent source of supplies for them.

This object ought to weigh but little against the cession we wish
to obtain, for two reasons: 1st, Because the country which the cession will leave in her hands on the right side of the Mississippi, is
capable of employing more than all the faculties she can spare for
such an object, and of yielding all the supplies which she could expect or wish from such an establishment.   2d. Because, in times of
general peace, she will be sure of receiving whatever supplies her
islands may want from the United States, and even through the
Mississippi, if more convenient to her; because in time of peace

with the United States, though of war with Great Britain, the same sources will be open to her, whilst her own would be interrupted; and because, in case of war with the United States, which is not likely to happen without a concurrent war with Great Britain, (the only case in which she could need a distinct fund of supplies,) the entire commerce of the sea, and of the trade through the Mississippi, would be against her, and would cut off the source in question. She would consequently never need the aid of her new colony but when she could make little or no use of it.

There may be other objects with France in the projected acquisition, but they are probably such as would be either satisfied by a reservation to herself of the country on the right side of the Mississippi, or are of too subordinate a character to prevail against the plan of adjustment we have in view, in case other difficulties in the way of it can be overcome. The principles and outlines of this plan are as follows, viz:

1. France cedes to the United States, for ever, the territory east of the river Mississippi; comprehending the two Floridas, the island of New Orleans, and the islands lying to the north and east of that channel of the said river which is commonly called the South Pass, together with all such other islands as appertain to either West or East Florida: France reserving to herself all her territory on the west side of the Mississippi.

II. The boundary between the territory ceded and reserved by France, shall be a continuation of that already defined above the 31st degree of north latitude, namely, the middle of the channel or bed of the river, through the said South Pass to the sea. The navigation of the river Mississippi, in its whole breadth from its source to the ocean, and in all its passages to and from the same, shall be equally free and common to citizens of the United States and of the French republic.

III. The vessels and citizens of the French republic may exercise commerce to and at such places on their respective shores below the said thirty-first degree of north latitude as may be allowed for that use by the parties to their respective citizens and vessels. And it is agreed that no other nation shall be allowed to exercise commerce to or at the same or any other place on either shore, below the said thirty-first degree of latitude, for the term of ten years, to be computed from the exchange of the ratifications hereof. The citizens, vessels, and merchandises of the United States and of France, shall be subject to no other duties on their respective shores below the said thirty-first degree of latitude than are imposed on their own citizens, vessels, and merchandises. No duty whatever shall, after the expiration of ten years, be laid on articles the growth or manufacture of the United States, or of the ceded territories, exported through the Mississippi in French vessels; so long as such articles so exported in vessels of the United States shall be exempt from duty: nor shall French vessels, exporting such articles, ever afterwards be subject to pay a higher duty than vessels of the United States.

IV. The citizens of France may, for the term of ten years, deposite their effects at New Orleans, and at such other places on the ceded shore of the Mississippi as are allowed for the commerce of the United States, without paying any other duty than a fair price for the hire of stores.

V. In the ports and commerce of West and East Florida, France shall never be on a worse footing than the most favoured nation; and for the term of ten years her vessels and merchandise shall be subject therein to no higher duties than are paid by those of the United States. Articles of the growth and manufacture of the United States, and of the ceded territory, exported in French vessels from any port in West or East Florida, shall be exempt from duty as long as vessels of the United States shall enjoy this exemption.

VI. The United States, in consideration of the cession of territory made by this treaty, shall pay to France ——— millions of livres tournois, in the manner following; namely, They shall pay ——— millions of livres tournois immediately on the exchange of the ratifications hereof; they shall assume, in such order of priority as the government of the United States may approve, the payment of claims which have been, or may be, acknowledged by the French republic to be due to American citizens, or so much thereof as, with the payment to be made on the exchange of ratifications, will not exceed the sum of ———: and, in case a balance should remain due, after such payment and assumption, the same shall be paid at the end of one year from the final liquidation of the claims hereby assumed, which shall be payable in three equal annual payments—the first of which is to take place one year after the exchange of ratifications, or they shall bear interest at the rate of six per cent. per annum, from the date of such intended payments, until they shall be discharged. All the above-mentioned payments shall be made at the treasury of the United States, and at the rate of one dollar and ten cents for every six livres tournois.

VII. To incorporate the inhabitants of the hereby ceded territory with the citizens of the United States, on an equal footing, being a provision which cannot now be made, it is to be expected, from the character and policy of the United States, that such incorporation will take place without unnecessary delay. In the mean time they shall be secure in their persons and property, and in the free enjoyment of their religion.

Observations on the Plan.

1st. As the cession to be made by France, in this case, must rest on the cession made to her by Spain, it might be proper that Spain should be a party to the transaction. The objections, however, to delay, require that nothing more be asked, on our part, than either an exhibition and recital of the treaty between France and Spain, or an engagement, on the part of France, that the accession of Spain will be given. Nor will it be advisable to insist, even on this much, if attended with difficulty or delay, unless there be ground to suppose that Spain will contest the validity of the transaction.

2d. The plan takes for granted, also, that the treaty of 1795, between the United States and Spain, is to lose none of its force, in behalf of the former, by any transactions whatever between the latter and France. No change, it is evident, will be, or can be, admitted to be produced in that treaty, or in the arrangements carried into effect under it, farther than it may be superseded by stipulations between the United States and France, who will stand in the place of Spain. It will not be amiss to insist on an express recognition of this by France, as an effectual bar against pretexts, of any sort, not compatible with the stipulations with Spain.

3d. The first of the articles proposed in defining the cession, refers to the South Pass of the Mississippi, and to the islands north and east of that channel. As this is the most navigable of the several channels, as well as the most direct course to the sea, it is expected that it will not be objected to. It is of the greater importance to make it the boundary, because several islands will be thereby acquired—one of which is said to command this channel, and to be already fortified. The article expressly includes, also, the islands appertaining to the Floridas. To this there can be no objection. The islands within six leagues of the shore are the subject of a British proclamation in the year 1763, subsequent to the cession of the Floridas to Great Britain by France, which is not known to have been ever called in question by either France or Spain.

The second article requires no particular observations.

Article third is one whose import may be expected to undergo the severest scrutiny. The modification to be desired is that which, whilst it provides for the interest of the United States, will be acceptable to France, and will give no just ground of complaint, and the least of discontent to Great Britain.

The present form of the article ought, and probably will, be satisfactory to France: First, because it secures to her all the commercial advantages in the river which she can well desire: Secondly, because it leaves her free to contest the mere navigation of the river, by Great Britain, without the consent of France.

The article, also, in its present form, violates no right of Great Britain, nor can she reasonably expect of the United States that they will contend, beyond their obligation, for her interest, at the expense of their own. As far as Great Britain can claim the use of the river, under her treaties with us, or by virtue of contiguous territory, the silence of the article, on that subject, leaves the claim unaffected. As far, again, as she is entitled, under the treaty of 1794, to the use of our bank of the Mississippi, above the 31st degree of north latitude, her title will be equally entire. The article stipulates against her only in its exclusion of her commerce from the bank, to be ceded, below our present limits. To this she cannot, of right, object—1st, because the territory, not belonging to the United States at the date of our treaty with her, is not included in its stipulations; 2dly, because the privileges to be enjoyed by France are for a consideration which Great Britain has not given, and cannot give; 3dly, because the conclusion, in this case, being a condition on which the territory will be ceded and accepted, the right to communicate the privilege to Great Britain will never have been vested in the United States.

But, although these reasons fully justify the article, in its relation to Great Britain, it will be advisable, before it be proposed, to feel the pulse of the French government with respect to a stipulation, that each of the parties may, without the consent of the other, admit whomsoever it pleases to navigate the river, and trade with their respective shores, on the same terms as in the other ports of France and the United States, and as far as the disposition of that government will concur to vary the proposition accordingly. It is not probable that this concurrence will be given; but the trial to obtain it will not only manifest a friendly regard to the wishes of Great Britain, and, if successful, furnish a future price for privileges within her grant, but is a just attention to the interests of our western fellow-citizens, whose commerce will not otherwise be on an equal footing with that of the Atlantic states.

Should France not only refuse any such change in the article, but insist on a recognition of the right to exclude all nations, other than the United States, from navigating the Mississippi, it may be observed to her, that a positive stipulation to that effect might subject us to the charge of intermeddling with, and prejudging, questions existing merely between her and Great Britain; that the silence of the article is sufficient; that, as Great Britain never asserted a claim on this subject against Spain, it is not to be presumed that she will assert it against France on her taking the place of Spain; that, if the claim should be asserted, the treaties between the United States and Great Britain will have no connexion with it, the United States having, in these treaties, given their separate consent only to the use of the river by Great Britain, leaving her to seek whatever other consent may be necessary.

If, notwithstanding such expostulations as these, France shall inflexibly insist on an express recognition to the above effect, it will be better to acquiesce in it, than to lose the opportunity of fixing an arrangement, in other respects satisfactory; taking care to put the recognition into a form not inconsistent with our treaties with Great Britain, or with an explanatory article that may not, improbably, be desired by her.

In truth, it must be admitted that France, as holding one bank, may exclude from the use of the river any nation not more connected with it, by treaty, than Great Britain is understood to be. As a river, where both its banks are owned by one nation, belongs exclusively to that nation, it is clear that, when the territory, on one side, is owned by one nation, and on the other side by another nation, the river belongs equally to both, in exclusion of all others. There are two modes by which an equal right may be exercised;

the one, by a negative in each on the use of the river by any other nation, except the joint proprietor; the other, by allowing each to grant the use of the river to other nations without the consent of the joint proprietor.   The latter mode would be preferable to the United States: but, if it be found absolutely inadmissible to France, the former must, in point of expediency, since it may in point of right, be admitted by the United States.   Great Britain will have the less reason to be dissatisfied on this account, as she has never asserted, against Spain, a right of entering and navigating the Mississippi: nor has she, or the United States, ever founded, on the treaties between them, a claim to the interposition of the other party, in any respect, although the river has been constantly shut against Great Britain, from the year 1783 to the present moment, and was not opened to the United States until 1795, the year of their treaty with Spain.

It is possible, also, that France may refuse to the United States the same commercial use of her shores, as she will require for herself on those ceded to the United States.   In this case it will be better to relinquish a reciprocity than to frustrate the negotiation. If the United States held, in their own right, the shore to be ceded to them, the commercial use of it allowed to France would render a reciprocal use of her shore, by the United States, an indispensable condition.   But as France may, if she chooses, reserve to herself the commercial use of the ceded shore, as a condition of the cession, the claim of the United States, to the like use of her shore, would not be supported by the principle of reciprocity, and may, therefore, without violating that principle, be waved in the transaction.

The article limits to ten years the equality of French citizens, vessels, and merchandises, with those of the United States.   Should a longer period be insisted on, it may be yielded.   The limitation may even be struck out, if made essential by France; but a limitation, in this case, is so desirable, that it is to be particularly pressed, and the shorter the period the better.

Art. 4.   The right of deposite, provided for in this article, will accommodate the commerce of France, to and from her own side of the river, until an emporium shall be established on that side; which it is well known will admit of a convenient one.   The right is limited to ten years, because such an establishment may, within that period, be formed by her.   Should a longer period be required, it may be allowed: especially, as the use of such a deposite, would probably fall within the general regulations of our commerce there. At the same time, as it will be better that it should rest on our own regulations, than on a stipulation, it will be proper to insert a limitation of time, if France can be induced to acquiesce in it.

Art. 5. This article makes a reasonable provision for the commerce of France, in the ports of West and East Florida. If the limitation to ten years, of its being on the same footing with that of the United States, should form an insuperable objection, the term may be enlarged; but it is much to be wished that the privilege may not, in this case, be made perpetual.

Art. 6. The pecuniary consideration to be offered for the territories in question, is stated in article 6. You will, of course, favour the United States as much as possible, both in the amount, and the modifications of the payments. There is some reason to believe that the gross sum expressed in the article has occurred to the French government, and is as much as will be finally insisted on. It is possible that less may be accepted, and the negotiation ought to be adapted to that supposition. Should a greater sum be made an ultimatum, on the part of France, the president has made up his mind to go as far as fifty millions of livres tournois, rather than lose the main object. Every struggle, however, is to be made against such an augmentation of the price, that will consist with an ultimate acquiescence in it.

The payment to be made immediately on the exchange of ratification, is left blank; because it cannot be foreseen either what the gross sum or the assumed debts will be, or how far a reduction of the gross sum may be influenced by the anticipated payments, provided for by the act of congress, herewith communicated, and by the authorization of the president and secretary of the treasury, endorsed thereon. This provision has been made with a view to enable you to take advantage of the urgency of the French government, for money, which may be such as to overcome the repugnance to part with what we want, and induce them to part with it on lower terms, in case a payment can be made before the exchange of ratifications. The letter from the secretary of the treasury to the secretary of state, of which a copy is herewith enclosed, will explain the manner in which this advance of the ten millions of livres, or so much thereof as may be necessary, will be raised most conveniently for the United States. It only remains here to point out the condition or event on which the advance may be made. It will be essential that the convention be ratified by the French government, before any such advance be made; and it may be farther required, in addition to the stipulation to transfer possession of the ceded territory as soon as possible, that the orders for the purpose, from the competent source, be actually and immediately put into your hands. It will be proper also to provide for the repayment of the advance, in the event of a refusal of the United States to ratify the convention.

It is apprehended that the French government will feel no repugnance to our designating the classes of claims and debts, which, embracing more equitable considerations than the rest, we may believe entitled to a priority of payment. It is probable, therefore, that the clause of the 6th article, referring it to our discretion, may be safely insisted upon. We think the following classification such as ought to be adopted by ourselves:—

1st, Claims under the 4th article of the convention of September, 1800.

2d. Forced contracts, or sales imposed upon our citizens by French authorities; and,

3d. Voluntary contracts, which have been suffered to remain unfulfilled by them.

Where our citizens have become creditors of the French government, in consequence of agencies or appointments derived from it, the United States are under no particular obligations to patronize their claims, and therefore no sacrifice of any sort, in their behalf, ought to be made in the arrangement. As far as this class of claimants can be embraced, without embarrassing the negotiation, or influencing, in any respect, the demands or expectations of the French government, it will not be improper to admit them into the provision. It is not probable, however, that such a deduction from the sum ultimately to be received by the French government, will be permitted without some equivalent accommodation to its interests, at the expense of the United States.

The claims of M. Beaumarchais, and several other French individuals, on our government, founded upon antiquated or irrelevant grounds, although they may be attempted to be included in this negotiation, have no connexion with it. The American government is distinguished for its just regard to the rights of foreigners, and does not require those of individuals to become subjects of treaty, in order to be admitted. Besides, their discussion involves a variety of minute topics, with which you may fairly declare yourselves to be unacquainted. Should it appear, however, in the course of the negotiation, that so much stress is laid on this point, that without some accommodation, your success will be endangered; it will be allowable to bind the United States for the payment of one million of livres tournois, to the representatives of Beaumarchais, heretofore deducted from his account against them; the French government declaring the same never to have been advanced to him on account of the United States.

Article 7th is suggested by the respect due to the rights of the people inhabiting the ceded territory, and by the delay which may be found in constituting them a regular and integral portion of the Union. A full respect for their rights might require their consent to the act of cession; and if the French government should be disposed to concur in any proper mode of obtaining it, the provision would be honourable to both nations. There is no doubt that the inhabitants would readily agree to the proposed transfer of their allegiance.

It is hoped that the idea of a guarantee of the country reserved to France, may not be brought into the negotiation. Should France propose such a stipulation, it will be expedient to evade it, if possible, as more likely to be a source of disagreeable questions between the parties concerning the actual casus fœderis than of real advantage to France. It is not in the least probable that Louisiana, in the hands of that nation, will be attacked by any other, whilst it is in the relations to the United States, on which the guarantee would be founded; whereas nothing is more probable than some difference of opinion as to the circumstances and the degree of danger necessary to put the stipulations in force. There will be less reason in the demand of such an article, as the United States would set little value on a guarantee of any part of their territory, and, consequently, there would be no just reciprocity in it. Should France, notwithstanding these considerations, make a guarantee an essential point, it will be better to accede to it than to abandon the object of the negotiation; mitigating the evil as much as possible, by requiring for the casus fœderis a great and manifest danger threatened to the territory guarantied, and by substituting for an indefinite succour, or even a definite succour, in military force, a fixed sum of money payable at the treasury of the United States. It is difficult to name the proper sum, which is in no posture of the business to be exceeded, but it can scarcely be presumed that more than about —— dollars, to be paid annually, during the existence of the danger, will be insisted on.

Should it be unavoidable to stipulate troops in place of money, it will be prudent to settle the details with as much precision as possible, that there be no room for controversy, either with France or with her enemy, on the fulfilment of the stipulation.

The instructions thus far given, suppose that France may be willing to cede to the United States the whole of the island of New Orleans, and both the Floridas. As she may be inclined to dispose of a part or parts, and of such only, it is proper for you to know that the Floridas, together, are estimated at one-fourth the value of the whole island of New Orleans, and East Florida at half that of West Florida. In case of a partial cession, it is expected that the regulations of every other kind, so far as they are onerous to the United States, will be more favourably modified.

Should France refuse to cede the whole of the island, as large a portion as she can be prevailed on to part with may be accepted; should no considerable portion of it be attainable, it will still be of vast importance to get a jurisdiction over space enough for a large commercial town and its appurtenances, on the bank of the river, and as little remote from the mouth of the river as may be. A right to choose the place would be better than a designation of it in the treaty. Should it be impossible to procure a complete jurisdiction over any convenient spot whatever, it will only remain to explain and improve the present right of deposite, by adding thereto the express privilege of holding real estate for commercial purposes, of providing hospitals, of having consuls residing there, and other agents, who may be authorized to authenticate and deliver all documents requisite for vessels, belonging to and engaged in the trade of the United States, to and from the place of deposite. The United States cannot remain satisfied, nor the western people be kept patient under the restrictions which the existing treaty with Spain authorizes.

Should a cession of the Floridas not be attainable, your attention will also be due to the establishment of suitable deposites at the mouths of the rivers, passing from the United States through the Floridas, as well as of the free navigation of those rivers by citizens of the United States. What has been above suggested in relation to the Mississippi, and the deposite on its banks, is applicable to the other rivers; and additional hints relative to them all may be derived from the letter, of which a copy is enclosed from the consul at New Orleans.

It has been long manifest, that, whilst the injuries to the United

States, so frequently occurring from the colonial officers, scattered over our hemisphere, and in our neighbourhood, can only be repaired by a resort to their respective governments in Europe, that it will be impossible to guard against the most serious inconveniences. The late events at New Orleans strongly manifest the necessity of placing a power somewhere nearer to us, capable of correcting and controlling the mischievous proceedings of such officers towards our citizens, without which a few individuals, not always among the wisest or best of men, may at any time threaten the good understanding of the two nations. The distance between the United States and the old continent, and the mortifying delays of explanations and negotiations across the Atlantic, on emergencies in our neighbourhood, render such a provision indispensable, and it cannot be long before all the governments of Europe, having American colonies, must see the necessity of making it. This object, therefore, will likewise claim your special attention.

It only remains to suggest, that, considering the possibility of some intermediate violences between citizens of the United States and the French or Spaniards in consequence of the interruption of our right of deposite, and the probability that considerable damages will have been occasioned by that measure to citizens of the United States, it will be proper that indemnification in the latter case be provided for, and that in the former it shall not be taken on either side as a ground or pretext for hostilities.

These instructions, though as full as they could be conveniently made, will necessarily leave much to your discretion. For the proper exercise of it, the president relies on your information, your judgment, and your fidelity to the interests of your country.

JAMES MADISON.

Mr. Madison, Secretary of State of the United States, to Messrs. Livingston and Monroe, dated April, 18, 1803.

[EXTRACT.]

A month having elapsed since the departure of Mr. Monroe, it may be presumed that by the time this reaches you, communications will have passed with the French government sufficiently explaining its views towards the United States and preparing the way for the ulterior instructions which the president thinks proper should now be given.

In case a conventional arrangement with France should have resulted from the negotiations with which you are charged: or in case such should not have been the result; but no doubt should be left that the French government means to respect duly our rights, and to cultivate, sincerely, peace and friendship with the United States, it will be expedient for you to make such communications to the British government as will assure it that nothing has been done inconsistent with our good faith, and as will prevent a diminution of the good understanding which subsists between the two countries.

If the French government, instead of friendly arrangements or views, should be found to meditate hostilities, or to have formed projects which will constrain the United States to resort to hostilities, such communications are then to be held with the British government as will sound its dispositions and invite its concurrence in the war. Your own prudence will suggest that the communications be so made, as, on one hand, not to precipitate France into hostile operations, and, on the other, not to lead Great Britain from the supposition that war depends on the choice of the United States, and that their choice of war will depend on her participation in it. If war is to be the result, it is manifestly desirable that it be delayed until the certainty of this result can be known, and the legislative and other provisions can be made here; and also of great importance that the certainty should not be known to Great Britain, who might take advantage of the posture of things to press on the United States disagreeable conditions of her entering into the war.

It will probably be most convenient in exchanging ideas with the British government, to make use of its public minister at Paris; as less likely to alarm and stimulate the French government, and to raise the pretensions of the British government, than the repairing of either of you to London, which might be viewed by both as a signal of rupture. The latter course, however, may possibly be rendered most eligible by the pressure of the crisis.

Notwithstanding the just repugnance of this country to a coalition of any sort with the belligerent policies of Europe, the advantages to be derived from the co-operation of Great Britain in a war of the United States, at this period, against France and her allies, are too obvious and too important to be renounced. And notwithstanding the apparent disinclination of the British councils to a renewal of hostilities with France, it will probably yield to the various motives which will be felt to have the United States in the scale of Britain against France, and particularly for the immediate purpose of defeating a project of the latter, which has evidently created much solicitude in the British government.

The price which she may attach to her co-operation cannot be foreseen, and therefore cannot be the subject of full and precise instructions. It may be expected that she will insist at least on a stipulation, that neither of the parties shall make a peace or truce without the consent of the other; and as such an article cannot be deemed unreasonable, and will secure us against the possibility of her being detached in the course of the war, by seducing overtures from France, it will not be proper to raise difficulties on that account. It may be useful, however, to draw from her a definition, as far as the case will admit, of the objects contemplated by her, that whenever with ours they may be attainable, by peace, she may be duly pressed to listen to it. Such an explanation will be the more reasonable, as the objects of the United States will be so fair and so well known.

It is equally probable that a stipulation of commercial advantages in the Mississippi, beyond those secured by existing treaties, will be required. On this point it may be answered at once, that Great Britain shall enjoy a free trade with all the ports to be acquired by the United States on the terms allowed to the most favoured nation in the ports generally of the United States. If made an essential condition, you may admit that in the ports to be acquired within the Mississippi, the trade of her subjects shall be on the same footing for a term of about ten years with that of our own citizens. But the United States are not to be bound to the exclusion of the trade of any particular nation or nations.

Should a mutual guarantee of the existing possessions or of the conquests to be made by the parties be proposed, it must be explicitly rejected, as of no value to the United States, and as entangling them in the frequent wars of that nation with other powers, and very possibly in disputes with that nation itself.

The anxiety which Great Britain has shown to extend her domain to the Mississippi, the uncertain extent of her claims, from north to south, beyond the western limits of the United States, and the attention she had paid to the north-west coast of America, make it probable that she will connect with a war on this occasion a pretension to the acquisition of the country on the west side of the Mississippi, understood to be ceded by Spain to France, or at least of that portion of it lying between that river and the Missouri. The evils involved in such an extension of her possessions in our neighbourhood, and in such a hold on the Mississippi, are obvious. The acquisition is the more objectionable, as it would be extremely displeasing to our western citizens: and as its evident bearing on South America might be expected to arouse all the jealousies of France and Spain, and to prolong the war on which the event would depend. Should this pretension, therefore, be pressed, it must be resisted as altogether repugnant to the sentiments and the sound policy of the United States. But it may be agreed, in alleviation of any disappointment of Great Britain, that France shall not be allowed to retain or acquire any part of the territory from which she herself would be precluded.

The moment the prospect of war shall require the precaution, you will not omit to give confidential notice to our ministers and consuls, and to our naval commanders in the Mediterranean, that our commerce and public ships may be as little exposed to the danger as possible. It may, under certain circumstances, be proper to notify the danger immediately to the collectors in the principal ports of the United States.

Herewith enclosed, are two blank plenipotentiary commissions and letters of credence to the French and British governments. Those for the British government are to be filled with the name of Mr. Monroe, unless his mission · to France should have an issue likely to be disagreeable to Great Britain; in which case the president would wish Mr. Livingston's inserted, if the translation be not disagreeable to him, and the name of Mr. Monroe inserted in the commission for the French republic. To provide for the event of Mr. Livingston's translation, a letter of leave is enclosed.

A separate letter to you is also enclosed, authorizing you to enter into such communications and conferences with British ministers as may possibly be required by the conduct of France. The letter is made a separate one, that it may be used with the effect, but without the formality of a commission. It is hoped that sound calculations of interest, as well as a sense of right, in the French government will prevent the necessity of using the authority expressed in this letter. In a contrary state of things the president relies on your own information to be gained on the spot, and on your best discretion, to open with advantage the communications with the British government, and to proportion the degree of an understanding with it, to the indications of an approaching war with France. Of these indications also, you will be best able to judge. It will only be observed to you, that if France should avow or evince a determination to deny to the United States the free navigation of the Mississippi, your consultations with Great Britain may be held, on the ground that war is inevitable. Should the navigation not be disputed, and the deposite alone be denied, it will be prudent to adopt your consultations to the possibility that congress may distinguish between the two cases, and make a question how far the latter right may call for an instant resort to arms, or how far a procrastination of that remedy may be suggested and justified by the prospect of a more favourable conjuncture.

These instructions have thus far supposed that Great Britain and France are at peace, and that neither of them at present intend to interrupt it. Should war have actually commenced, or its approach be certain, France will no doubt be the more apt to concur in friendly accommodations with us, and Great Britain the more desirous of engaging us on her side. You will of course avail yourselves of this posture of things for avoiding the necessity of recurring to Great Britain, or if the necessity cannot be avoided for fashioning her disposition to arrangements which may be the least inconvenient to the United States: whatever connexion, indeed, may be eventually formed with Great Britain, in reference to war, the policy of the United States requires that it be as little entangling as the nature of the case will permit.

Messrs. Livingston and Monroe, to Mr. Madison, Secretary of State of the United States, dated May 13, 1803.

[EXTRACT.]

We have the pleasure to transmit to you by M. D'Erieux, a treaty which we have concluded with the French republic for the purchase and cession of Louisiana. The negotiation of this important object was committed, on the part of France, to M. Marbois, minister of the treasury, whose conduct therein has already received the sanction of his government, as appears by the ratification of the first consul, which we have also the pleasure to forward to you.

Our acquisition of so great an extent was, we well know, not contemplated by our appointment; but we are persuaded that the circumstances and considerations which induced us to make it, will justify us in the measure to our government and country.

Before the negotiation commenced, we were apprized that the
first consul had decided to offer to the United States, by sale, the
whole of Louisiana, and not a part of it. We found in the outset
that this information was correct; so that we had to decide as a
previous question whether we would treat for the whole, or jeopar-
dize, if not abandon the hope of acquiring any part. On that point,
we did not long hesitate, but proceeded to treat for the whole.
We were persuaded that, by so doing, it might be possible, if more
desirable, to conclude eventually a treaty for a part, since being
thus possessed of the subject, it might be easy, in discussion, at
least, to lead from a view of the whole to that of a part, and with
some advantages peculiar to a negotiation on so great a scale. By
treating for the whole, whereby we should be enabled to ascertain
the idea which was entertained by this government of its value; we
should also be able to form some estimate of that which was affixed
to the value of its parts. It was, too, probable that a less sum
would be asked for the whole, if sold entire to a single purchaser,
a friendly power who was able to pay for it, and whom it might be
disposed to accommodate at the present juncture, than if it should
be sold in parcels, either to several powers or companies of individuals: it was equally so, if this government should be finally prevailed on to sell us a part, that some regard would be paid in the
price asked for it, to that which was demanded for the whole; last-
ly, by treating for the whole, whereby the attention of this government would be drawn to the United States as the sole purchasers,
we might prevent the interference of other powers, as also that of
individuals, which might prove equally injurious in regard to the
price asked for it, whether we acquired the whole or any part of
the territory. We found, however, as we advanced in the negotiation, that M. Marbois was absolutely restricted to the disposition of
the whole; that he would treat for no less portion, and of course
that it was useless to urge it. On mature consideration, therefore,
we finally concluded a treaty on the best terms we could obtain for
the whole.

By this measure, we have sought to carry into effect to the ut-
termost of our power, the wise and benevolent policy of our government, on the principles laid down in our instructions. The
possession of the left bank of the river, had it been attainable alone,
would, it is true, have accomplished much in that respect; but it
is equally true that it would have left much still to accomplish.
By it our people would have had an outlet to the ocean, in which
no power would have a right to disturb them; but while the other

bank remained in the possession of a foreign power, circumstances might occur to make the neighbourhood of such power highly injurious to us in many of our most important concerns. A divided jurisdiction over the river might beget jealousies, discontents, and dissensions, which the wisest policy on our part could not prevent or control. With a train of colonial governments established along the western bank, from the entrance of the river, far into the interior, under the command of military men, it would be difficult to preserve that state of things which would be necessary to the peace and tranquillity of our country. A single act of a capricious, unfriendly, or unprincipled subaltern might wound our best interests, violate our most unquestionable rights, and involve us in war. But, by this acquisition, which comprises within our limits this great river and all the streams that empty into it, from their sources to the ocean, the apprehensions of these disasters is banished for ages from the United States. We adjust by it the only remaining known cause of variance with this very powerful nation: we anticipate the discontent of the great rival of France, who would probably have been wounded at any stipulation of a permanent nature which favoured the latter, and which it would have been difficult to avoid, had she retained the right bank. We cease to have a motive of urgency, at least for inclining to one power, to avert the unjust pressure of another. We separate ourselves in a great measure from the European world and its concerns, especially its wars and intrigues; we make, in fine, a great stride to real and substantial independence, the good effect whereof will, we trust, be felt essentially and extensively in all our foreign and domestic relations. Without exciting the apprehensions of any power, we take a more imposing attitude with respect to all. The bond of our union will be strengthened, and its movements become more harmonious by the increased parity of interest which it will communicate to the several parts which compose it.

In deliberating on this subject in a financial view, we were strongly impressed with the idea, that while we had only a right of deposite, or, indeed, while the right bank remained in the possession of a foreign power, it was always to be expected that we should, at some time or other, be involved in war on questions resulting from that cause. We were well satisfied that any war would cost us more than hereby is stipulated to be given for this territory; that none could produce a more favourable result, while it might, especially in the present disturbed state of the world, prove the ruin of our affairs.

There were other considerations which, though of minor importance, had, nevertheless, their due weight in our decision on this great question. If France, or any other power holding the right bank of the river, imposed lighter duties than comport with the revenue system of the United States, supposing even that we had acquired the left bank, all the supplies destined for our extensive and populous settlements, on the other side, would be smuggled in through that channel, and our revenue thereby considerably diminished. Should such power open offices for the sale of lands on the western bank, our population might be drained to the advantage of that power, the price of our lands be diminished, and their sale prevented. But by the possession of both banks, these evils are averted.

The terms on which we have made this acquisition, when compared with the objects obtained by it, will, we flatter ourselves, be deemed advantageous to our country. We have stipulated, as you will see by the treaty and conventions, that the United States shall pay to the French government sixty millions of francs, in stock, bearing an interest of six per cent. and a sum not exceeding twenty millions more to our citizens in discharge of the debts due to them by France, under the convention of 1800; and also to exempt the manufactures, productions, and vessels of France and Spain, in the direct trade from those countries, respectively in the ports of the ceded territory, from foreign duties for the term of twelve years. The stock is to be created irredeemable for fifteen years, and discharged afterwards in equal annual instalments: the interest on it is to be paid in Europe, and the principal, in case this government thinks proper to sell it, disposed of in such manner as will be most conducive to the credit of the American funds. The debts due to our citizens are to be discharged by drafts on our treasury. We omit a more minute view of the stipulations of these instruments, since, as you will possess them, it is unnecessary.

Louisiana was acquired of Spain by France in exchange for Tuscany, which latter is settled by treaty on the son-in-law of the king of Spain, with the title of king of Etruria, and was estimated in the exchange, in consideration of its revenue, at 100,000,000 francs. The first consul thought he had made an advantageous bargain in that exchange, as appears by the high idea which he entertained of its value, as shown on many occasions. Louisiana was the territory which he promised in his proclamation at the peace as an asylum to those who had become unfortunate by the revolution, and which he spoke of as vast and fertile. When he made up his mind to offer the cession of it to the United States, it was contemplated to ask for it 100,000,000, exclusive of the debts they owed to our citizens, which they proposed we should also pay, with a perpetual exemption from foreign duties on the manufactures, productions, and vessels of France and Spain, in the ports of the ceded territory. From that demand, however, in respect to the sum, he receded, under the deliberation of his own cabinet, for the first proposition which M. Marbois made to us, was, that we should pay eighty millions, sixty of which in cash, the balance to our citizens, the whole in one year in Paris, with a perpetual exemption from foreign duties, as above. The modification in the mode of payment, that is by stock, for from the quantum he never would depart, and the limitation of the term of the duties to twelve years, with the proviso annexed to it, which was introduced into the treaty with every other change from his project, was the effect of negotiation and accommodation, in which we experienced on his part and that of his government, a promptitude and candour which were highly grateful to us.

In estimating the real value of this country to the United States, a variety of considerations occur, all of which merit due attention. Of these we have already noticed many of a general nature, to which, however, it may be difficult to fix a precise value. Others present themselves of a nature more definite, to which it will be more practicable to fix some standard. By possessing both banks, the whole revenue or duty on imports will accrue to the United States, which must be considerable. The value of the exports, we have understood, was last year four millions of dollars. If a portion only of the imports pass through that channel, as under our government we presume they will, the amount of the revenue will be considerable. This will annually increase in proportion as the population and productions in that quarter do. The value of the lands, in the province of Louisiana, amounting to some hundred millions of acres of the best quality, and in the best climate, is, perhaps, incalculable. From either of these sources, it is not doubted that the sum stipulated may be raised in time to discharge the debt.

No. 19.

THE following letter is taken from the same congressional document as the papers in No. 18.—TRANSL.

Mr. Livingston to Mr. Madison, Secretary of State of the United States, dated Paris, 20th May, 1803.

[EXTRACT.]

I called this morning upon M. Marbois for a farther explanation on this subject, (the cession of Louisiana,) and to remind him of his having told me that Mobile made a part of the cession. He told me that he had no precise idea on the subject, but that he knew it to be an historical fact, and on that only he had formed his opinion. I asked him what orders had been given to the prefect that was to take possession, or what orders had been given by Spain as to the boundary in ceding it. He assured me that he did not know, but that he would make the inquiry and let me know. At four o'clock I called for Mr. Monroe to take him to the minister for foreign affairs, but he was prevented from accompanying me. I asked the minister what were the last bounds of the territory ceded to us; he said he did not know; we must take it as they had received it. I asked him how Spain meant to give them possession; he said according to the words of the treaty. But where did you mean to take? I do not know. Then you mean that we shall construe it our own way? I can give you no direction; you have made a noble bargain for yourselves, and I suppose you will make the most of it.

No. 20.

Table of the Purchase and Sales of the Public Lands, from the 4th of July, 1776, to the 31st of December, 1825, extracted from Watterston and Van Zandt's "Tabular Statistical Tables."—TRANSL.

	Expenses of Indian treaties from July 4, 1776, to January 1, 1827.	Quantity of land purchased by the United States. Acres.	Expenses of surveying public lands, and salaries of surveyors, &c. Salaries.	Expenses of surveying.	Expenses of selling public lands. Dollars.	Nett amount of sales, deducting lands relinquished. Acres.	Dollars.	Quantity of land remaining unsold 1st January, 1826. Acres.	Lands appropriated for colleges and schools. Acres.
Ohio		24,388,745,80			498,434,48	8,778,715,35	16,235,123,75	6,191,927,53	746,585,16
Indiana		16,060,036,70			169,070,17	3,068,868,42	5,611,197,22	12,131,461,90	492,192,13
Illinois		29,517,262,62			103,848,75	1,222,442,25	1,729,145,58	24,161,662,93	866,003,96
Michigan		17,561,470,00			19,990,29	291,839,28	416,096,07	16,600,554,26	510,858,61
Missouri		39,119,018,89			66,475,11	980,372,41	1,971,217,84	35,522,350,69	1,132,719,41
Arkansas		33,661,120,00			7,499,60	39,177,61	49,115,90	31,441,309,31	958,071,11
Louisiana		31,463,040,00			20,451,62	150,375,67	265,907,22	25,392,602,67	920,061,66
Mississippi		14,188,454,00			80,176,37	1,155,562,28	2,220,132,81	11,643,275,05	440,203,72
Alabama		24,482,159,83			186,776,91	3,496,369,68	11,763,351,88	20,268,863,58	726,139,99
Florida		31,254,120,00			2,228,54	55,689,08	90,591,92	30,237,952,17	914,250,00
	$3,868,379,52	261,695,427,84	$251,852,45	$1,912,515,97	1,154,951,84	19,239,412,03	40,351,880,19	213,591,960,09	7,707,085,75

Quantity of land appropriated as military bounty lands, for private claims and special donations.	Purchase of Louisiana.	Paid state of Georgia and Yazoo scrip.	Florida Treaty.	Quantity of uncided land north and west of states and territories.
Acres.	Dollars.	Dollars.	Dollars.	Acres.
21,593,749,84	15,000,000	6,200,000	50,000,000	750,000,000

ERRATA.

Owing to the absence of the Translator from the place of publication, a number of typographical inaccuracies will be found in this work; most of which, it is believed, are pointed out in the following list:—

Page 19, line 7, for *It was* read *It is.*
" 24, line 4, for *catastrophies* read *catastrophes.*
" 26, line 23, for *Adams* read *Adamses.*
" 29, line 1, for *permit* read *cause.*
" 29, line 17, for *efforts* read *exertions.*
" 30, line 10, for *in* read *from.*
" 47, line 14, for *deaths* read *death.*
" 48, line 28, for *citizens* read *citizen.*
" 60, line 9, for *would find* read *should find.*
" 61, line 20, for *Jumonville* read *Jumonvilles.*
" 73, note, for *Columbus* read *Columbia.*
" 79, line 29, for *Jesuit's* read *Jesuits'.*
" 89, line 9, for *this* read *that.*
" 105, line 1, for *the* read *any.*
" 106, line 6, for *Purd'homme* read *Prud-'homme.*
" 114, transpose marks of quotation (") from line 15 to 28.
" 116, line 6, add *of* after *foundation.*
" 131, line 17, for *as numerous* read *so numerous.*
" 131, line 17, for *or as* read *nor so.*
" 142, line 9, for *by* read *for.*
" 146, line 10, for *1778* read *1788.*

Page 150, line 27, add comma (,) after *perpetual.*
" 161, line 18, for *it* read *she.*
" 165, last line, dele *they.*
" 166, line 16, for *disarmed* read *unarmed.*
" 182, line 12, for *of* read *to.*
" 184, line 18, add *on* after *drawn.*
" 196, line 11, dele *for.*
" 207, line 16, for *forsee* read *foresee.*
" 216, last line, for *establishing* read *establish.*
" 232, line 4, for *depends* read *depend.*
" 265, line 12, for *chances we will* read *chance we shall.*
" 271, line 5, for *our* read *over,* and add *to* before *the.*
" 287, line 15 of note, for *that* read *in which.*
" 306, line 16 of note, for *appears* read *appear.*
" 309, line 20, for *which* read *who.*
" 322, line 2, for *enormity* read *enormousness.*
" 347, line 8, for *stagnate* read *stagnant.*
" 348, line 9, for *and* read *of.*
" 349, line 25, for *arises* read *arise.*
" 355, line 3, for *that they possessed* read *which they possess.*
" 369, line 29, for *that* read *when.*
" 375, line 26, for *vengeance of* read *vengeance on.*

INDEX

Abbadie, Jean Jacques d', Governor of Louisiana (D'Abadie in text), 136, 300
Acadians, 125–28
Adams, John: and quasiwar with France under the Directory, 173, 235–37; mentioned, 26
Adams, Samuel, 26
Amiens, Peace of: preliminaries signed, 174, final terms of, 176; and issues in Great Britain leading to a rupture, 179–84, 246–49; and British protests against French military forces in Holland and Northern France, 251–52; and Bonaparte's views on inevitability of war, 253; and increasing hostility, 254–61; and resumption of war, 313–15
Ashley exploring party, 359

Barbé-Marbois, François: advises Bonaparte to cede Louisiana to the United States, 264–70; entrusted with the negotiation, 274–76; conference of, with Livingston, 277–78; career of, summarized, 279–80; negotiating the sale of Louisiana, 279–312; on significance of the cession, 290
Bernadotte, Charles, 204
Blount, William: and scheme to transfer Florida and Louisiana to Great Britain, 163–65
Bonaparte, Napoleon: secures the retrocession of Louisiana from Spain to France, 168–71; concludes Peace of Amiens with Great Britain, 174–77; voted first consul for life, 178; plan of, for occupation of St. Domingue, 184–200; plan of, for the government of Louisiana, 204–209; and the reorganization of France, 248; and rupture of the Peace of Amiens, 252–54; and the British ambassador, 254–56; desire to strengthen maritime power of United

States, 260; changes policy on St. Domingue and Louisiana, 262; consults with two ministers on Louisiana, 262–74; decision of, to sell Louisiana to the United States, 274–75; on the significance of the cession to the United States, 312; ratifies treaty of cession, 315
British colonies in North America: westward expansion of, 108; and territories acquired in 1763, p. 134; mentioned, 17–22
Burr, Aaron: plots and adventures of, in the West, 361–64

Carondelet, Francisco Luis Hector, Baron de, 138
Casa Yrujo, Marquis de: protests the sale of Louisiana, 321; mentioned, 245
Cevallos, Don Pedro: and Spain's acquiescence in the cession of Louisiana, 298
Charlevoix, Father, 113–15
Claiborne, William Charles Cole, 334
Company of the Indies, 115–17
Connecticut, 19
Convention of 1800, pp. 173, 237–39
Crozat, Antoine, 109–10

Declaration of Independence, 20
Directory: and quasiwar with the United States, 166–67, 235–37; mentioned, 161

Europe: the role of monarchy in, 98–100

Floridas, 232, 284, 288, 340, 341–42
France: and French Revolution, 23–25, 68; interest in Louisiana after 1748, pp. 122–24; and Seven Years War, 130–32; Family Compact of, with Spain, 133; supports American Revolution, 139–43; treaty of alliance with